watchOS

by Tutorials

Third Edition

By the raywenderlich.com Tutorial Team

Ehab Amer, Scott Atkinson, Soheil Azarpour, Matthew Morey, Ben Morrow, Audrey Tam & Jack Wu

watchOS by Tutorials Third Edition

Ehab Amer, Scott Atkinson, Soheil Azarpour, Matthew Morey, Ben Morrow, Audrey Tam & Jack Wu

Copyright ©2017 Razeware LLC.

Notice of Rights

Notice of Liability

Trademarks

ISBN: 978-1-942878-45-2

Dedications

"To my supporting parents. And to my love, thank you for always being there for me."

— *Ehab Amer*

"To my amazing wife and family, who encourage me to never stop."

— *Jack Wu*

"To Kerri, my beautiful and supportive wife, who gave me my Mac and encouraged me to do something different."

— *Scott Atkinson*

"To my lovely, always supportive wife Elnaz, our son Kian and my parents."

— *Soheil Azarpour*

"To my amazing wife Tricia and my parents - Thanks for always supporting me."

— *Matthew Morey*

"For Dad, who has my back, through times think and thin."

— *Ben Morrow*

"To my parents and teachers, who set me on the path that led me to the here and now."

— *Audrey Tam*

About the authors

Ehab Amer is a software developer in Cairo, Egypt. In the day, he leads mobile development teams create cool apps, In his spare time he spends dozens of hours improving his imagination and finger reflexes playing computer games... or at the gym!

Scott Atkinson lives in Alexandria, VA with his wife, Kerri, and daughter, Evelyn. In his day job, he is a software developer at Capital One. When not writing software, he spends time rowing on the Potomac river or exploring new restaurants and cooking great food.

Soheil Azarpour is an engineer, developer, author, creator, husband and father. He enjoys bicycling, boating and playing the piano. He lives in Merrimack, NH, and creates iOS apps both professionally and independently.

Matthew Morey is an engineer, author, hacker, creator and tinkerer. As an active member of the iOS community and CTO at MJD Interactive he has led numerous successful mobile projects worldwide. When not developing apps he enjoys traveling, snowboarding, and surfing. He blogs about technology and business at matthewmorey.com. matthewmorey.com.

Ben Morrow delights in discovering the unspoken nature of the world. He'll tell you the surprising bits while on a walk. He produces beauty by drawing out the raw wisdom that exists within each of us.

Audrey Tam retired in 2012 from a 25yr career as a computer science academic. Her teaching included many programming languages, as well as UI design and evaluation. Before moving to Australia, she worked on Fortran and PL/1 simulation software at IBM. Audrey now teaches iOS app development to non-programmers.

Jack Wu has built dozens of iOS apps and enjoys it very much. Outside of work, Jack enjoys coding on the beach, coding by the pool, and sometimes just having a quick code in the park.

About the editors

Antonio Bello is a tech editor of this book. Antonio is a veteran code writer who started tapping on keyboards when memory was measured in bytes instead of gigabytes, storage was an optional add-on, and the most used language was BASIC. Today he loves developing iOS apps, writing node.js backends, and he never misses a chance to learn something new. He finds Swift a very expressive language, and still thinks Objective-C is great and unconventional.

Chris Belanger is the editor of this book. Chris is the Book Team Lead and Lead Editor for raywenderlich.com. He was a developer for nearly 20 years in various fields from e-health to aerial surveillance to industrial controls. If there are words to wrangle or a paragraph to ponder, he's on the case. When he kicks back, you can usually find Chris with guitar in hand, looking for the nearest beach. Twitter: @crispytwit.

Soheil Azarpour is the final pass editor of this book. Soheil is an engineer, developer, author, creator, husband and father. He enjoys bicycling, boating and playing the piano. He lives in Merrimack, NH, and creates iOS apps both professionally and independently.

Table of Contents:

Introduction

In the old days, you always had to install iTunes on your PC to update or sync your iPhone. There were neither over-the-air updates nor iCloud backup or synchronizations. Just as you thought those days were gone, Apple came out with Apple Watch — the tiniest member of the personal devices family. Despite its coolness and elegance, Apple Watch was clumsy. Except for telling time, you needed a paired iPhone to do literally anything. You were always presented with a loading spinner that would sometime go on for seconds, and the navigation was awkward and you had to drill down few pages on a tiny screen to get to your info.

In watchOS 2 we saw a leap forward and Watch apps started running on the Watch itself rather than the phone. In watchOS 3, overall performance of the system was optimized and apps became faster and more responsive. watchOS 4 continues the theme of performance and new and improved features, including a unified runtime process between the Watch and the iPhone, a frontmost app state, Core Bluetooth support for BLE devices, and inline audio recording.

About this book

Writing a book to teach development on a brand new platform is no easy task. In order to create the most helpful and approachable book possible, this book follows these principles:

- **Real world use cases:** There are enough API's available for watchOS to fill a whole shelf of books! We've focused on the API's and real world problems you're most likely to run in to. No matter what your app idea is, you'll gain valuable insight from these pages.

- **Minimum experience required, meaningful value for all:** This book assumes little about your experience prior to reading. We've made sections easy to follow for beginners, and easy to skim for advanced programmers. But even if you're an experienced engineer, we've added tons of content to help you on your journey of watchOS app development.

- **High-quality tutorials:** Our site is known for its high-quality programming tutorials, and we've put a lot of time and care into the tutorials in this book to make them equally valuable, if not more so. Each chapter has been put through a rigorous multi-stage editing process – resulting in some chapters being rewritten several times! We've worked hard to ensure that each chapter contains great technical content while also being fun and easy to follow.

Introducing the third edition

It's been about two years since we released the first edition of *watchOS By Tutorials*, but we're happy you're reading the new third edition, updated for watchOS 4 and Swift 4! Every single chapter in this book has been updated to Swift 4 to ensure it works flawlessly with Xcode 9 and watchOS 4.

We've added a few new chapters in this edition:

- **Chapter 17, Recording Audio:** Now that you can perform inline audio recording in watchOS 4, we've created a dedicated chapter to showing you how to interact with this functionality in your own apps. This replaces the "Playing Audio and Video" chapter from the previous edition.

- **Chapter 21, Handoff Video Playback:** We've expanded the original "Handoff" chapter and migrated some of the video portion from the previous edition's "Playing Audio and Video" chapter.

- **Chapter 25, Core Bluetooth:** In watchOS 4, you can pair and interact directly with Bluetooth LE devices. Learn how to send data and control instructions directly from the Watch to a BLE device! This chapter replaces the Haptic Feedback" chapter from the previous edition.

What you need

To follow along with the tutorials in this book, you need the following:

- **A Mac running macOS Sierra 10.12.4 or later**: This is so you can install the latest version of the required development tool: Xcode.

- **Xcode 9 or later**: Xcode is the main development tool for iOS, watchOS, tvOS and macOS; you'll need Xcode 9 or later to follow along with this book.

- **To run the samples on physical hardware, you'll need an iPhone running iOS 11 or later and an Apple Watch running watchOS 4.0 or later**. Almost all of the chapters in the book let you run your code on the iOS and Apple Watch simulators that come bundled with Xcode. However, a few chapters later in the book do require one or more physical devices for testing.

Once you have these items in place, you'll be able to follow along with every chapter in this book.

Who this book is for

This book is for intermediate or advanced iOS developers who already know the basics of iOS and Swift development and want to broaden their horizons by exploring Apple's smart watch platform.

If you are a complete beginner to iOS development, we recommend you read through *The iOS Apprentice* first. Otherwise this book may be a bit too advanced for you.

- https://store.raywenderlich.com/products/ios-apprentice

This book does require some basic knowledge of Swift. If you do not know Swift, you can still follow along with the book because all of the instructions are in step-by-step format. However, there will likely be parts that are confusing due to gaps in your knowledge.

Before beginning this book, you might want to go through our *Swift Apprentice* series, which covers the basics of Swift development:

- https://store.raywenderlich.com/products/swift-apprentice

As with raywenderlich.com, all the tutorials in this book are in Swift.

How to use this book

This book can be read from cover to cover, but we don't recommend using it this way unless you have a lot of time and are the type of person who just "needs to know everything". (It's okay; a lot of our tutorial team is like that, too!)

Instead, we suggest a more pragmatic approach — pick and choose the chapters that interest you the most, or the chapters you need immediately for your current projects. The chapters are self-contained, so you can go through the book in any order you wish.

Looking for some recommendations of important chapters to start with? Here's our suggested Core Reading List:

• Chapter 1, "Hello, Apple Watch!"

• Chapter 2, "Designing Great Watch Apps"

• Chapter 3, "Architecture"

• Chapter 6, "Layout"

• Chapter 7, "Tables"

• Chapter 15, "Complications"

• Chapter 16, "Watch Connectivity"

That covers the "Big 7" topics of watchOS 4; from there you can dig into other topics of particular interest to you.

Book overview

The Apple Watch is still a relatively new platform, and watchOS 4 is the latest iteration of the OS powering the amazing hardware, built on a unique architecture, with lots of new and unusual concepts and paradigms. Here's what you'll be learning about in this book:

Chapter 1, Hello, Apple Watch!: Dive straight in and build your first watchOS 4 app — a very modern twist on the age-old "Hello, world!" app.

Chapter 2, Designing Great Watch Apps: Talks about the best practices based on Apple recommendations in WWDC this year, and how to design a Watch app that meets these criteria.

Chapter 3, Architecture: watchOS 4 might support native apps, but they still have an unusual architecture. This chapter will teach you everything you need to know about this unique aspect of watch apps.

Chapter 4, UI Controls: There's not a `UIView` to be found! In this chapter you'll dig into the suite of interface objects that ship with WatchKit–watchOS' user interface framework.

Chapter 5, Pickers: `WKInterfacePicker` is one of the programmatic ways to work with the Digital Crown. You'll learn how to set one up, what the different visual modes are, and how to respond to the user interacting with the Digital Crown via the picker.

Chapter 6, Layout: Auto Layout? Nope. Springs and Struts then? Nope. Guess again. Get an overview of the layout system you'll use to build the interfaces for your watchOS apps.

Chapter 7, Tables: Tables are the staple ingredient of almost any watchOS app. Learn how to set them up, how to populate them with data, and just how much they differ from `UITableView`.

Chapter 8, Navigation: You'll learn about the different modes of navigation available on watchOS, as well as how to combine them.

Chapter 9, Digital Crown and Gesture Recognizers: You'll learn about accessing Digital Crown raw data, and adding various gesture recognizers to your watchOS app interface.

Chapter 10, Snapshot API: Glances are out, and the Dock is in! You'll learn about the Snapshot API to make sure that the content displayed is always up-to-date.

Chapter 11, Networking: `NSURLSession`, meet Apple Watch. That's right, you can now make network calls directly from the watch, and this chapter will show you the ins and outs of doing just that.

Chapter 12, Animation: The way you animate your interfaces has changed with watchOS 3, with the introduction of a single, `UIView`-like animation method. You'll learn everything you need to know about both animated image sequences and the new API in this chapter.

Chapter 13, CloudKit: You'll learn how to keep the watch and phone data in sync even when the phone isn't around, as long as user is on a known WiFi network.

Chapter 14, Notifications: watchOS offers support for several different types of notifications, and allows you to customize them to the individual needs of your watch app. In this chapter, you'll get the complete overview.

Chapter 15, Complications: Complications are small elements that appear on the user's selected watch face and provide quick access to frequently used data from within your app. This chapter will walk you through the process of setting up your first complication, along with introducing each of the complication families and their corresponding layout templates.

Chapter 16, Watch Connectivity: With the introduction of native apps, the way the watch app and companion iOS app share data has fundamentally changed. Out are App Groups, and in is the Watch Connectivity framework. In this chapter you'll learn the basics of setting up device-to-device communication between the Apple Watch and the paired iPhone.

Chapter 17, Audio Recording: As a developer, you can now record audio directly on the Apple Watch inline in your apps, without relying on the old-style system form sheets. In this chapter, you'll gain a solid understanding of how to implement this, as well as learn about some of the idiosyncrasies of the APIs, which are related to the unique architecture of a watch app.

Chapter 18, Interactive Animations with SpriteKit and SceneKit: You'll learn how to apply SpriteKit and SceneKit in your Watch apps, and how to create interactive animations of your own.

Chapter 19, Advanced Watch Connectivity: In Chapter 15, you learned how to set up a Watch Connectivity session and update the application context. In this chapter, you'll take a look at some of the other features of the framework, such as background transfers and real-time messaging.

Chapter 20, Advanced Complications: Now that you know how to create a basic complication, this chapter will walk you through adding Time Travel support, as well giving you the lowdown on how to efficiently update the data presented by your complication.

Chapter 21, Handoff Video Playback: Want to allow your watch app users to begin a task on their watch and then continue it on their iPhone? Sure you do, and this chapter will show exactly how to do that through the use of Handoff.

Chapter 22, Core Motion: The Apple Watch doesn't have every sensor the iPhone does, but you can access what is available via the Core Motion framework. In this chapter, you'll learn how to set up Core Motion, how to request authorization, and how to use the framework to track the user's steps.

Chapter 23, HealthKit: The HealthKit framework allows you to access much of the data stored in user's health store, including their heart rate! This chapter will walk you through incorporating HealthKit into your watch app, from managing authorization to recording a workout session.

Chapter 24, Core Location: A lot of apps are now location aware, but in order to provide this functionality you need access to the user's location. Developers now have exactly that via the Core Location framework. Learn everything you need to know about using the framework on the watch in this chapter.

Chapter 25, Core Bluetooth: In watchOS 4, you can pair and interact with BLE devices directly. Learn how to send control instructions and other data directly over Bluetooth.

Chapter 26, Localization: Learn how to expand your reach and grow a truly international audience by localizing your watch app using the tools and APIs provided by Apple.

Chapter 27, Accessibility: You want as many people as possible to enjoy your watch app, right? Learn all about the assistive technologies available in watchOS, such as VoiceOver and Dynamic Type, so you can make your app just as enjoyable for those with disabilities as it is for those without.

Book source code and forums

You can get the source code for the book here:

https://www.raywenderlich.com/store/watchos-by-tutorials/source-code

Some of the chapters have starter projects or other required resources that are also included, and you'll definitely want to have these on hand as you go through the book.

We've set up an official forum for the book:

https://forums.raywenderlich.com/c/books/watchos-by-tutorials

This is a great place to ask any questions you have about the book or about making apps with watchOS, or to submit any errata you may find.

Digital editions

We also have PDF and ePub digital editions of this book available, which can be handy if you want a soft copy to take with you, or you want to quickly search for a specific term within the book.

Buying the digital edition of the book also has a few extra benefits: free updates each time we update the book, access to older versions of the book, and you can download the digital editions from anywhere, at anytime.

Visit the book store page here:

• https://store.raywenderlich.com/products/watchos-by-tutorials

And since you purchased the print version of this book, you're eligible to upgrade to the digital edition at a significant discount!

Simply email support@razeware.com with your receipt for the physical copy and we'll get you set up with the discounted digital edition of the book.

License

By purchasing *watchOS by Tutorials*, you have the following license:

• You are allowed to use and/or modify the source code in *watchOS by Tutorials* in as many apps as you want, with no attribution required.

- You are allowed to use and/or modify all art, images, or designs that are included in *watchOS by Tutorials* in as many apps as you want, but must include this attribution line somewhere inside your app: "Artwork/images/designs: from the *watchOS by Tutorials* book, available at raywenderlich.com".

- The source code included in *watchOS by Tutorials* is for your own personal use only. You are NOT allowed to distribute or sell the source code in *watchOS by Tutorials* without prior authorization.

- This book is for your own personal use only. You are NOT allowed to sell this book without prior authorization, or distribute it to friends, co-workers, or students; they must to purchase their own copy instead.

All materials provided with this book are provided on an "as is" basis, without warranty of any kind, express or implied, including but not limited to the warranties of merchantability, fitness for a particular purpose and non-infringement. In no event shall the authors or copyright holders be liable for any claim, damages or other liability, whether in an action of contract, tort or otherwise, arising from, out of or in connection with the software or the use or other dealings in the software.

All trademarks and registered trademarks appearing in this guide are the property of their respective owners.

Acknowledgments

We would like to thank many people for their assistance in making this possible:

- **Our families:** For bearing with us in this crazy time as we worked all hours of the night to get this book ready for publication!

- **Everyone at Apple:** For developing several amazing operating systems and sets of APIs, for constantly inspiring us to improve our apps and skills, and for making it possible for many developers to have their dream jobs!

- **And most importantly, the readers of raywenderlich.com — especially you!** Thank you so much for reading our site and purchasing this book. Your continued readership and support is what makes all of this possible!

About the cover

Seahorses have a prehensile tail and wrap it firmly around the stalks of plants — or even around the tails of other seahorses as they *band* together. And although the *crown* they sport isn't digital, we still think seahorses are a pretty neat species to *watch*!

Chapter 1: Hello, Apple Watch!

Audrey Tam

The Apple Watch: coolest device ever to come out of Cupertino? I'm sure I'm not alone in answering with an unreserved, "Yes!" I got my Watch as soon as possible and seized the opportunity to upgrade my faithful old iPhone 4S to a 6 to interface with the Watch.

If you are reading this book, then you're likely just as excited as I am about developing Watch apps. This chapter will get you comfortable with the basics of creating a Watch app and running it in the simulator. This is where it all begins!

You'll start by running the empty Watch app template. Next, you'll add a label to display the traditional "Hello, World!" text. Then, to put a fun spin on things, you'll change the label to the following:

Finally, you'll take your app a step further by making it display randomized emoji fortunes.

This fortune suggests you're in for a chapter that is fun, successful, rewarding, thrilling and cool. Time to get started!

Getting started

Open the **HelloAppleWatch** starter project, and build and run:

This simple iPhone app displays **Hello, Apple Watch!** in emoji and then shows an emoji fortune. Tap the button to see a new fortune. You're about to create an Apple Watch app that does the same thing.

Note: If you're not in Apple's paid developer program and you want to run this app on your iPhone and watch, follow KMT's instructions in the Apple Developer Forums, at this link: http://apple.co/2vHzPmX. You must also change the app's bundle identifier so it's not using **com.razeware**. You can find more information in Apple's instructions for **Launching Your App on Devices**, available here: apple.co/1y6rvZD.

There's some parallelism in the way iPhone apps and Watch apps display and control their UI elements: iPhone apps use storyboards and view controllers, while Watch apps use storyboards and interface controllers. To create these, you'll add a Watch app target to your project.

Note: In the future, if you're starting without an existing iPhone app, use the **New Project** template **watchOS\Application\iOS App with WatchKit App**. It already has the Watch app target added for you.

Select **File\New\Target...** from the Xcode menu.

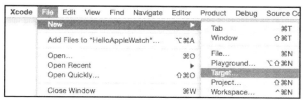

Select **watchOS\Application\WatchKit App** in the target template window.

Click **Next**. In the target options window, type **HelloAppleWatch WatchKit App** in the **Product Name** field, personalize the **Organization Name**, **uncheck** the **Include Notification Scene** option and click **Finish**.

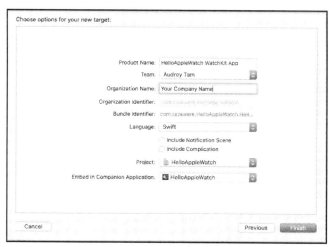

Click the **Activate** button in the pop-up window that appears. This creates an option on the Scheme menu to run the Watch app. To try it out, select **HelloAppleWatch WatchKit App\iPhone 7 Plus + Apple Watch Series 2 - 42mm** from the **Scheme** menu.

Build and run. You'll see not one, but two simulators: one for iPhone 7 Plus and another for the 42mm Apple Watch. It might take a while for the simulation to appear the first time you run your Watch app, as Apple has gone to great lengths to make the simulator reflect the performance of the real device as closely as possible.

Allow or disallow Faces to use your location, and eventually, the simulator will show a watch face, then the app's default launch screen and finally, a black screen with the time in the upper-right corner.

Note: If the simulator shows the watch face after flashing the app's launch screen, just run the app again.

The Series 2 42mm Watch is one of the devices you can select from the Simulator app's **Hardware\Devices** menu. The **Hardware** menu also lets you switch touch pressure, or press the side button. You can open multiple devices in the Simulator app, so you can run the iPhone app at the same time as the Watch app.

Two new groups now appear in the project navigator:

- **HelloAppleWatch WatchKit App** contains **Interface.storyboard**, which you'll use to lay out your app.

- **HelloAppleWatch WatchKit App Extension** contains **InterfaceController.swift**, which is similar to `UIViewController` on iOS.

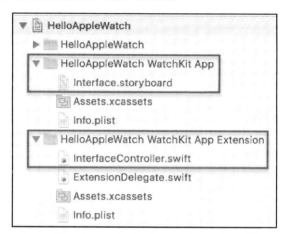

The workflow for creating a Watch app is similar to that of an iPhone app; you set up the UI in the storyboard and then connect the UI objects to outlets and actions in the controller.

Hello, World!

No introductory chapter would be complete without the traditional "Hello, World!" inaugural app, and this one is no exception. :]

You'll simply show a label on the screen, the text of which you set in the Attributes Inspector, but this will give you a taste of the capabilities — and limitations — of the Apple Watch interface. You'll learn more about creating interfaces for Apple Watch in Chapter 4, "UI Controls".

Open **Interface.storyboard**. In this chapter, you don't need the document outline, which covers the left side of the canvas. Click the square button in the lower-left corner of the canvas to close it. Then show the **Utilities** and the **Object Library**.

Enter **label** in the search field, and then drag a label from the Object Library onto the single interface controller. Show the Attributes Inspector to see options for customizing the label.

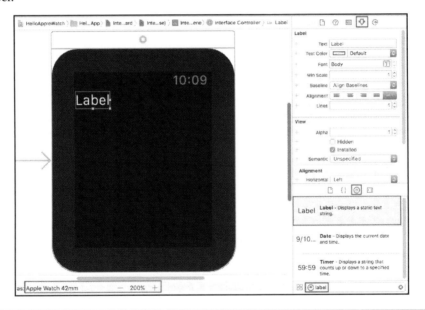

Note: The bottom toolbar has options to **View as:** Apple Watch 38mm or 42mm, and to change the zoom level using the - and + buttons.

By default, the label sits at the top-left of the interface. Unlike designing for iOS, you can't move the label by simply dragging it around in the interface. If you try, it just reverts back to the top-left position. Make the following changes in the Attributes Inspector to adjust its appearance:

- Set **Text** to **Hello, World!**.

- Set **Alignment\Horizontal** to **Center**.

- Set **Alignment\Vertical** to **Center**.

Notice that **Size\Width** and **Size\Height** are both **Size to Fit Content**, so the label resizes itself to fit its text.

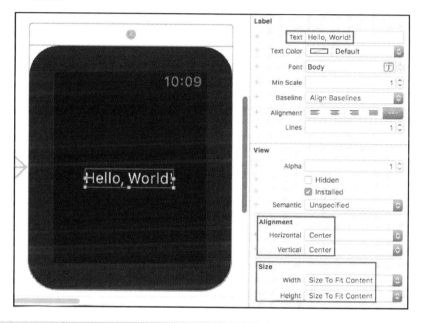

> **Note:** When you edit the text field in the Attributes Inspector, the change doesn't take effect until you press the Return key. You can also double-click on the label itself to select the text and change it in-place.

Build and run your Watch app; you should see the following:

Congratulations on creating your first Watch app!

Setting label text in code

You'd probably like your Watch app to be a little more dynamic. At the least, you'd want to set the label's text in the controller code. To do that, you need to create an outlet for the label in **InterfaceController.swift**.

Open the assistant editor and check that it's set to **Automatic** so that it displays **InterfaceController.swift**.

Select the **label** and, holding down the **Control** key, drag from the **label** to the space just below the class title in **InterfaceController.swift** . Xcode will prompt you to **Insert Outlet**. Release your mouse button and a pop-up window will appear.

Check that **Type** is set to WKInterfaceLabel, then set **Name** to label and click **Connect**.

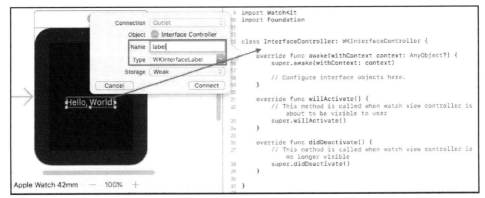

The following @IBOutlet declaration will appear in **InterfaceController.swift**:

```
@IBOutlet var label: WKInterfaceLabel!
```

Your code now has a reference to the label in your Watch app interface, so you can use this to set its text.

Add the following line to `willActivate()`, below `super.willActivate()`:

```
label.setText("Hello, Apple Watch!")
```

Build and run your app:

You've added a label to the Watch interface and set its text from code. Don't be deceived — this is a pretty cool moment. The code you wrote is actually *running on the Watch!*

> **Note:** Feel free to delete `awake(withContext:)` and `didDeactivate()`, as well as the comment in `willActivate()` in **InterfaceController.swift**.

Emoji!

A watch face isn't ideal for displaying a lot of text, but it's brilliant for emoji!

First, increase the font size: select the label in the storyboard, then click on the **T** icon in the **Font** attribute in the Attributes Inspector to invoke the font pop-up. Change **Font** to **System** and increase **Size** to 24, then click **Done**.

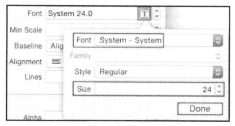

Next, you'll edit the `Hello, Apple Watch!` string directly in **InterfaceController.swift**. Select `Hello` and press **Control-Command-Space** to pop up the **emoji character viewer**

beneath the selected text. Next, click in the **Search** field and type **waving**, and the **waving hand** emoji will appear. Click this emoji to replace the `Hello` text.

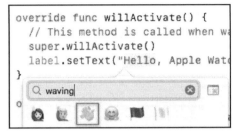

Repeat these steps to replace `Apple`, `Watch`, and the exclamation mark with suitable emoji. Delete the comma and spaces so your string looks like the following:

Build and run your app:

An ultra-cool greeting for an über-cool gadget! Next, you're going to take this emoji idea and run with it.

Casting emoji fortunes

On April 9th, 2014, @nrrdcore tweeted "Free idea: Emoji Fortune Cookies", and on May 14th, Luke Karrys launched emojifortun.es:

TENNIS WATER BUFFALO SHOWER

Wouldn't that look cool on an Apple Watch, without the words?

Apple Watch Series 2 - 42mm - watchOS 4.0

Sharing code between iPhone and Watch apps

Open **EmojiData.swift**; it contains an `Int` extension with a simple `random()` method and five arrays of emoji: `people`, `nature`, `objects`, `places` and `symbols`. You can either use the emojis below, or go wild and select your own. Feel free to add as many emojis as you wish to each array:

```swift
let people = ["😄", "😶", "😔", "😣", "😐", "👯", "💂"]
let nature = ["🍄", "🌸", "🍀", "🌳", "☁️", "🌿", "🐿"]
let objects = ["📱", "🍷", "🍎", "🎵", "💰", "⌚️"]
let places = ["🎿", "♨️", "🛷", "🚲", "🎢"]
let symbols = ["🔁", "🔀", "⏩", "◀️", "🆒"]
```

It's easy to share this file between the iPhone app and the Watch app. **Right-click EmojiData.swift** in the project navigator and select **New Group from Selection**. Name this group **Shared** and move it out of the HelloAppleWatch folder, so it sits between the **HelloAppleWatch** and **HelloAppleWatch** WatchKit App folders.

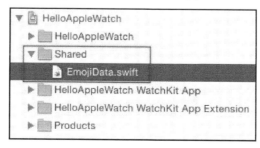

Open the **Shared** folder, select **EmojiData.swift** and show the File Inspector. In the **Target Membership** section, check **HelloAppleWatch WatchKit App Extension**.

That's it! Now **InterfaceController.swift** can use **EmojiData.swift**.

Creating a random emoji fortune

Open **InterfaceController.swift**, and create the following `EmojiData` object below the `@IBOutlet` statement, just above `awake(withContext_:)`:

```
let emoji = EmojiData()
```

Still in the same file, replace `label.setText()` in `willActivate()` with the following lines:

```
// 1
let people = emoji.people[emoji.people.count.random()]
let nature = emoji.nature[emoji.nature.count.random()]
let objects = emoji.objects[emoji.objects.count.random()]
let places = emoji.places[emoji.places.count.random()]
let symbols = emoji.symbols[emoji.symbols.count.random()]
// 2
label.setText(people + nature + objects + places + symbols)
```

`random()` calls a pseudo-random number generator `arc4random_uniform(_:)`. Here's what it does in detail:

1. For each array, generate a random number between `0` and the array's `count`, to index into the array.

2. Combines the emoji to create the label text.

Build and run your Watch app. Have fun trying to figure out whether your fortune is good, bad, indifferent or just unfathomable!

Refreshing the fortune

If you're running your app on the simulator, it's easy to run it again to get a new fortune. But to run it again on your Watch, you must return to the Home screen. You need a button you can press to get a new fortune! This isn't hard to implement, and the task will give you a chance to refactor your code.

Replacing the label with a button

Open **Interface.storyboard** and delete the label. Drag a **button** onto the interface controller. The button will snap to the top, but you'll make it cover most of the screen. That way, the user can tap almost anywhere on the watch face to get a new fortune.

In the Attributes Inspector, set the button's **Font** to **System 22.0**, **Alignment\Horizontal** to **Center** and **Alignment\Vertical** to **Bottom**. Set the button's **Size\Height** to **Relative to Container** with value **0.9**. This sets the button's height to 90% of the screen height.

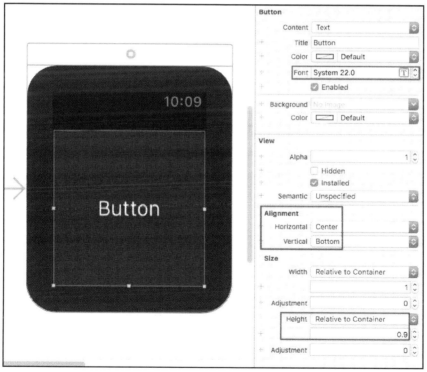

When you tap the button, the code that you put into `willActivate()` should run. Instead of writing it again, you'll pull it out into its own method so that both `willActivate()` and the button tap can call it.

Open **InterfaceController.swift**, and select all the lines you added to `willActivate()`, below `super.willActivate()`. Next, right-click on the highlighted code, and select **Refactor\Extract Method**:

```
// 1
let people = emoji.people[emoji.people.count.random()]
let nature = e            random()]
let objects =       Cut                           t.random()]
let places = e      Copy Symbol Name              andom()]
let symbols =       Paste                         t.random()]
// 2
label.setText(      Refactor              ►    Rename...
                                                Extract Function
                    Find Selected Text in Workspace   Extract Method
                    Find Selected Symbol in Workspace
```

Rename the new method `extractedFunc()` to `showFortune()`, and replace the call to `extractedFunc` in `willActivate()`, so your code looks like this:

```swift
fileprivate func showFortune() {
  // 1
  let people = emoji.people[emoji.people.count.random()]
  let nature = emoji.nature[emoji.nature.count.random()]
  let objects = emoji.objects[emoji.objects.count.random()]
  let places = emoji.places[emoji.places.count.random()]
  let symbols = emoji.symbols[emoji.symbols.count.random()]
  // 2
  label.setText(people + nature + objects + places + symbols)
}

override func willActivate() {
  super.willActivate()
  showFortune()
}
```

`label.setText()` is obsolete now, since you deleted the label from the interface controller. You'll connect the button in the same way that you connected the label.

Open **Interface.storyboard**. With the **assistant editor** showing **InterfaceController.swift**, **Control-drag** from the button to just above the `label` IBOutlet. In the pop-up window, check that **Type** is `WKInterfaceButton`, then name the outlet **button** and click **Connect**.

Now replace `label.setText` with `button.setTitle`, in the last line of `showFortune()`. The emoji fortune will replace the button's title you see in **Interface.storyboard**. Delete the `label` IBOutlet, as you don't need it anymore.

Next, you'll connect the button to an *action* that happens when the user taps it. **Control-drag** from the button to an open line below `showFortune()`. This time, in the pop-up window, be sure to change **Connection** from **Outlet** to **Action**. Name the action `newFortune` and press **Connect**.

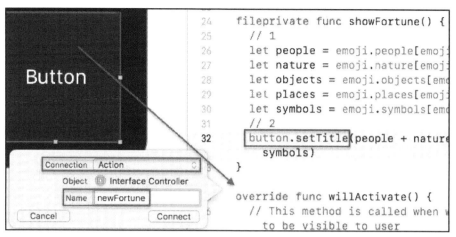

You'll see this empty method:

```
@IBAction func newFortune() {
}
```

> **Note:** If you create another IBOutlet by accident, get rid of the Xcode error by deleting the IBOutlet from code. Next, right-click on the button and delete its newFortune Referencing Outlet. Finally, perform the Control-drag action again, making sure to change **Connection** to **Action**.

The only thing newFortune() needs to do is call showFortune(), so add the following line in newFortune():

```
showFortune()
```

Dressing up your app

To make this a *real* fortune app, there's something you can add: a fortune cookie background image! Open **HelloAppleWatch WatchKit App\Assets.xcassets**. Click the + button and select **New Image Set**.

In the Attributes Inspector, change the **Name** to **Cookie**, check **Devices\watchOS\Apple Watch**, uncheck any other devices and change **Screen Width** to **38mm and 42mm**.

Finally, drag **38mm.png** and **42mm.png** one at a time from this chapter's folder into the corresponding spots:

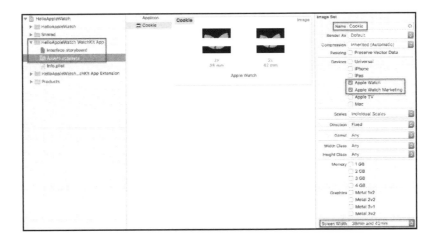

Note: If you uncheck **Apple Watch Marketing**, Xcode will just check its box again!

Open **Interface.storyboard**, select the **Interface Controller**, and use the Attributes Inspector to set **Background** to **Cookie**.

Build and run, and let your Watch tell your fortune over and over until you get *exactly* the one you want!

Where to go from here?

At this point, you have hands-on experience making a simple WatchKit-based app.

If you're new to iOS, you've also learned how to set up and use storyboard outlets, which work exactly the same way in plain old iOS apps that don't use WatchKit. On top of all that, you've learned a few tricks while making your way around Xcode.

I hope this chapter has whetted your appetite to try out all the cool stuff in the rest of this book, as well as boosted your confidence that *you can do this*!

In the next few chapters, you'll learn about design, architecture, basic UI controls and layout. Chapter 2, "Designing Great Watch Apps", is especially important, as it explains the Apple Watch design mantra of **Glanceable, Actionable, Responsive** and shows you how to create apps that follow Apple's best practices. All this will get you started using the watchOS 4 SDK to build more complex interfaces and apps.

Chapter 2: Designing Great Watch Apps

By Ben Morrow

The content of this book has changed quite a bit since the first edition. Apple, watchOS developers, and users have all changed the way they think about the Apple Watch with each iteration of the software and hardware.

Developers learned about WatchKit even before the Apple Watch launched, which meant we could create apps for the watch right away. The thought of a new app market was exciting; in the ten years of the iOS App Store, developers have earned over $70 billion USD from their apps.

Initially, Watch apps were so tightly coupled to the iPhone app that the iPhone actually performed all processing tasks, which led to unresponsive user interfaces. In the two years since then, Watch apps have gained more and more autonomy and better-performing interfaces.

watchOS 4 adds many SDK additions that you'll love, and Apple has new Watch hardware on the way. New hardware, coupled with a powerful new release of watchOS, means that users will expect a lot from the next generation of apps — and it's up to you to provide that experience to them!

The bar for well-designed apps on the watch is higher than ever, and this chapter will show you how to make apps that are both highly beautiful and highly usable. You'll learn what it takes to create a Watch app that users love to interact with on a daily basis. You'll learn about the new advancements in watchOS 4, and you'll learn best practices for designing a Watch app. I'll also show you some examples of existing Watch apps that embody these tips.

Glanceable, Actionable, Responsive

Apple's Watch design paradigm states a Watch app needs to be *immediately* available. It should be glanceable, actionable and responsive within two seconds. To enable those types of interaction, watchOS 4 has improvements that affect how you design your Watch apps.

Simplified Navigation

WKExtension properties

In watchOS 4, Apple provides a couple of optional system-level features for your apps. For workout apps, you can enable Water Lock. The feature will prevent accidental button presses on the touchscreen. For apps that are meant to be shared with other people, you can enable Autorotate. Consider using autorotate if your app displays text or visuals that a user would want to show to another person by flipping her wrist over. The interface will flip accordingly.

The Dock

The Dock continues its evolution in watchOS 4. App cards now scroll vertically. You can choose whether the Dock shows Favorites or Recents. The Dock provides a consistent interface to:

1. Glean quick details from apps

2. Have access to your most recently used app

3. Launch your favorite apps

You press the side button to bring up the Dock from anywhere in the interface – even inside another app.

Vertical page-based navigation

In watchOS 3, Apple introduced vertical navigation for hierarchical table-based apps. When you're on a table view interface, you tap on a cell to segue into a detail interface. You no longer have to tap the back button and then the next cell in the table to see the next detail interface from the table. Instead, you can navigate table detail interfaces with vertical page-based navigation. Swipe up and down or use the digital crown to scroll between detail interfaces.

> **Note:** Vertical page-based navigation only works with detail interfaces that fit on the screen without scrolling.

In watchOS 4, page-based apps get the vertical treatment. You can use `reloadRootPageControllers(withNames:contexts:orientation:pageIndex:)` and set orientation to `.vertical`. Your pages will show one at a time as you scroll vertically with the Digital Crown.

You can also set the `pageIndex` parameter to display a particular page when the user first launches the app. These new ways of thinking about pages will surely lead to some different interfaces in Watch apps.

Single page apps

Many of the built-in apps have moved from multi-page layouts to single screens. A good example of this is the Activity app. You don't have to swipe between pages to check out the details of your move, workout, and stand goals. Instead, all three goals have consolidated detailed information on one screen, so that you can get to the information much more quickly.

Scroll position

The Workout app has always used scrolling as a way of animating the interface. In watchOS 4, now you can use the set the scroll position in your interfaces. With `scroll(to:at:animated:)` you can scroll to the top, center, or bottom of any interface object.

You can elect to receive callbacks for user scrolling by overriding methods like, `interfaceDidScrollToTop()` and `interfaceOffsetDidScrollToBottom()`. Imagine using these to run an animation when the user scrolls to a certain position.

Full screen

In watchOS 4, SpriteKit and SceneKit can load full screen, with no status bar. Instead of a black status bar, you'll see is a black-to-transparent gradient and the current time on the right side of the screen.

Overlap layout

In previous iterations of watchOS, interface objects could not overlap each other because they stacked horizontally or vertically inside of groups. In watchOS 4, groups now have an `Overlap` setting which allows you to position objects on top of each other.

Quick-swap for clock faces

The new Siri clock face is an indication that clock faces are getting more and more powerful. Users edge-swipe from either left or right of the device to quickly change clock faces. That empowers the user to configure different clock faces for different activities or times of day.

Some ideas for useful clock faces:

- Health monitoring: heart rate, start a workout, activity rings

- Morning routine: sunrise time, a calendar showing your first meeting, weather, and traffic

- Bedtime: start sleep tracking, activate HomeKit devices, and play music

Think about how your app can offer contextually relevant content in your app's complication.

Discoverability

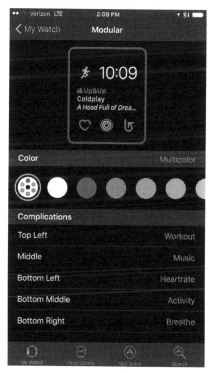

Users can configure clock faces in the Apple Watch app for iPhone; you can build your specific time-of-day clock faces with all the available complications. As a developer, this means your app has a better chance of being discovered as users fill up their clock faces.

For that reason, Apple now recommends that every app provide a complication. Yours can be as simple as an icon that launches your app when pressed. The Workout app is a good example of this; its complication is merely a static *running human* icon.

Session-based use

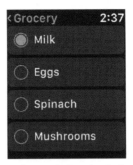

Previously, the Apple Watch always showed the clock face when you raised your wrist unless you were in the middle of a workout activity. Now apps stay alive for two minutes, by default, after you drop your wrist. A developer can request more time, up to eight minutes, with `isFrontmostTimeoutExtended`. If you bring your wrist back up inside that time limit, then the app will reappear. The timer resets each time you drop your wrist, so you can raise and lower your wrist several times during a session and have the Watch app immediately available.

A perfect example of a session is grocery shopping. As a user, you expect to look at your list each time you walk down a different aisle. When you're finished shopping, you make your way back home, and you no longer want to see the to-do list app when you raise your wrist; you expect to see the clock face instead. The frontmost timer allows for these kinds of sessions.

You no longer have to think of your app as being suspended as soon as the user drops her wrist. You can even intercept notifications and play haptics when your app is in the frontmost state and your user has her wrist down.

Quick launch for apps

Apps launch immediately when they're currently in the Dock or on the current clock face as a complication, as the operating system now keeps these apps in memory. These apps have effectively no loading time. Apps that launch from the honeycomb Home screen still experience a delay, but you do get a nice activity indicator with the app icon and a swirl around it:

As a developer, you need to give the user every reason to keep your app close at hand as a complication or in the Dock. Not only will the user see your app more often, but this gives them a more satisfying experience by launching and interacting immediately.

Inputs

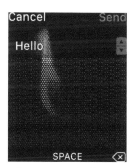

Entering text on the Watch was tricky, as you had to speak and let Siri interpret your message — not always the best experience. Now there's a new way to compose text by hand: Scribble. You use your finger to write each character on the screen, similar to Asian language support on iOS or Graffiti from the Palm PDA days. Now you can silently compose and send messages letter by letter.

API Overview

Background Refresh and Snapshot

There are several APIs that help you configure the view of your app in the Dock. The Snapshot API and the Background Refresh API help you make sure that the content displayed is always up-to-date, while the Background Refresh API will also let you keep code running after the user drops her wrist.

In-line Audio Recording and Background Mode

In watchOS 4, you can present custom audio controls during live recordings. You could build an interface for real-time language translation. Your app can also keep an audio recording session running in the background. A user could walk into a classroom, launch an app from a complication, and record an entire lecture.

Core Bluetooth

Apple Watches can communicate directly with Bluetooth peripheral devices like a glucose monitor. The Watch acts in *cental mode* and cannot be used as a peripheral itself. The Watch will receive speedy updates every 30ms while your app is in the foreground. The peripherals disconnect when your app gets suspended, but background-running apps can still connect to devices. Backgrounded apps receive updates every 120ms, but cannot scan for new devices. Also, keep in mind that the Watch is limited to two peripherals.

Location

Apps can request location updates in the background and watchOS 4 will continuously track the user's location. The user will know that their location is being tracked whenever they see the location icon in the status bar. This feature is especially useful for tracking routes during a workout.

Games

SpriteKit and SceneKit have made their way to the Watch, ushering in a new era for games on the Watch. Developers had made surprisingly good use of the limited functionality of layout animations in watchOS 2 for games. My favorite app was **Mini Watch Games 15-in-1** by AlhoGames:

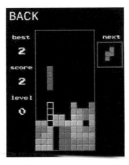

The fact these games were created with the old layout techniques was quite amazing. Now with SpriteKit and SceneKit, you can take it to *a whole 'nother level* with real physics engines and collision detection.

Gyroscope and Digital Crown

As games go high-fidelity, so does the sensor data. watchOS provides access to the accelerometer and the gyroscope for precise tracking of movement gestures. Fitness apps can sense which exercise you're doing by measuring your arm movement. For instance, the built-in Workout app automatically counts swim laps.

You can also read data from the Digital Crown anywhere in your app. Raw Digital Crown data is useful in games and in visual displays where you're drawing with the data. You're not limited to pre-rendered images or text pickers.

Interaction considerations

We have a good idea of what real-world use of the Watch looks like from the last few years of usage data. No one waits for apps to launch anymore; if you make the user wait, you've lost her.

That's where background refresh and quick launch from Dock and complications come in handy. But once the user opens your app, you can't stop there. Imagine the user only has two seconds to interact with your app. That's two seconds in total — not two seconds per screen.

Users don't have the patience to trudge through multiple levels of navigation hierarchy. A glance and a button press is basically all the time you can expect to have. Design your app around the two-second rule and you'll have a much higher daily return rate.

Anatomy of a Watch app

Unlike a Phone app, an Apple Watch app cannot stand on its own. If you want users to engage your app every day, you should think of the user experience as:

Complication + Notification + App

You need to implement all three in order to provide a good user experience. The app alone is not enough.

Use rich animations to communicate complex concepts

The Apple Watch screen is so small that you can pretty much only support one picture and one bit of text as the focus at any given time. You can work around this by condensing your information into images.

I have to brag on the Activity app again:

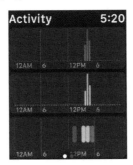

A graph condenses numerical data, but there are lots of other ways to present graphical information. When someone posts an album cover in a photo sharing app, you could animate the background of the notification, instead of simply showing one thumbnail or an obscure stack of images. In just a few seconds, the user can preview several of the photos:

Imagine three columns of images scrolling vertically in opposing directions, and you'll see how to show a massive amount of information in a very tiny space. Another good place for animation is icons in notifications. An airplane flight takeoff and landing would be so much cooler if the accompanying graphic actually showed a plane in motion on the runway. These kinds of things we've seen in banner advertisements on the web, but not as much in user interface design.

The time has come to bring your interface to life with animation, and to pack more information into a small space.

Planning versus implementing

Meditate on the simplicity of a single screen. Single screen apps help you keep interactions inside two seconds. To achieve a truly great Apple Watch experience, your planning process should take more time than implementing the code. If you find yourself spending too much time coding many different screens, you should probably rethink what you're trying to achieve.

Visual design considerations

You'll receive guidance on visual affordances throughout the book, but this section is the one place where you can review these best practices together.

Layout

Group interface objects to help users find the information they want.

If everything in your app looks the same, the user will get lost. Table cells are great containers for content. Separator objects can also help delineate boundaries and can orient both horizontally and vertically.

Make use of the full width of the screen.

Although you might be tempted to create a square button to fit around an icon, it's often better to let the button expand the width of the screen so it's easier to interact with. Consider that people might be walking while they use your app; you can't ask them to be super-precise with fiddly little components while in motion.

Avoid displaying too much information at once.

It is impossible to read a full paragraph of text or to discern all the tiny buttons from a professional workstation app on the Watch inside the two-second window. Keep your information brief and your interface objects few in number.

Color

This palette shows the current theme colors for Watch apps:

You don't have to use these colors. For instance, you might have certain colors that match your brand identity. But using the colors from this palette will help your app feel like it fits on the platform. The palette shows the RGB values for tint colors as well as opacity values for button backgrounds.

Customization

All apps look similar: a black background with a bit of text. The splashes of color you add will distinguish your app from all the others. Configuring the global tint color will change the way interface titles and notifications look. Your unique brand color will set your app apart. Remember to echo your global tint color in the design of your app icon.

Typography

In Interface Builder, the default font for apps on the Watch is "System". Behind the scenes, watchOS will select the most appropriate variant of the San Francisco font to maximize legibility. Mockups should use a resolution of 144 pixels per inch. As you design your app in a graphics tool like Photoshop or Sketch, consider which font variant watchOS will choose for your particular interface. For small text, 19 points or less, watchOS will choose **SF Compact Text**. For labels whose text is 20 points or larger, watchOS will choose **SF Compact Display**.

> **Note:** Users need to read text with a quick glance on the tiny Watch screen. Consider making text larger and even try extremely large font sizes for labels. Test your app on a real device. The simulator gives you a false sense of security with legibility because it shows your app larger and more stable than it will feel on a real device.

Use bold font weight, differing size, and color to emphasize your most important information. These highlights will make your interface glanceable. You want the user to immediately recognize what is being displayed; without even having to read the words, they should be able to tell what's shown based on the visual layout of the screen.

Icons

Watch icons are circular in shape and will display minuscule sizes on the Home screen. Therefore, you'll want to embrace simplicity. Strive for a single, easily recognizable shape that uniquely captures the essence of your app. Avoid clutter by eliminating details.

The icon's background should not be black. Instead, use a lighter color or add a border so that the icon doesn't blend into the Home screen background. Black essentially communicates empty space on the watch's OLED screen. You want your icon to fill the full circular bounds.

Images

As an iOS developer, you're probably accustomed to using PNG images rather than JPGs. However PNGs present the temptation to make the background transparent. Don't do it! If you have empty space around an image, provide a black matte background.

When you use a transparent image, the layout engine has to run extra compute cycles to calculate what should display for those pixels. By keeping your backgrounds opaque, you'll speed up your app load time and interaction.

Another iconographic PNG tip is to use the 8-bit color palette rather than full 24-bit color. That will reduce file size without reducing image quality. For photos, you'll want to use JPG images. You should optimize your JPG files to find a balance between size and quality. Try compressing down until you notice degradation. Compression can save significant disk space. You'll be surprised how much you can compress before visual quality degrades for a photo the size of the screen on the Watch.

For flat artwork and static cartoons, use the SVG format. Images created using SVG will scale to different sizes while maintaining sharp edges.

Apps in the App Store

I mentioned real-world apps throughout this chapter, and I've got some a few more examples to share. These companies are not sponsors, and I don't have any relationship with the developers.

That said, I believe observing what's in the App Store is a crucial step in the design process. Remember, watchOS is still new as a platform. We're all trying to figure out what works and what doesn't. As you think about capabilities for your app, you'll want to explore what's out there in the App Store.

Here's a rundown of my take on the top four apps available for the Watch today. Each one uses the current capabilities in pretty remarkable ways. With watchOS 4 and the next generation Apple Watch devices, things will only get more impressive from here.

4. AutoSleep by Tantsissa

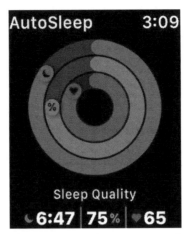

A dedicated Watch app can offer way more than just extending iOS features. AutoSleep lets you track your sleep quality by wearing the Watch overnight. It uses the accelerometer to gain insight into how you toss, turn, and get up throughout the night. Because the Watch is attached to your wrist, it can even account for times when you get up and walk around.

To have enough battery life to wear your Watch overnight, I recommend charging your Watch in your car during your commute or while you're taking a shower. That way, you will have enough charge to last overnight and you can track your sleep.

3. Letter Zap by Fanatee

The addictive word game incorporates haptic feedback. You tap on the letters to arrange a word. The app offers a Heartbeat mode where the faster your heart beats, the less time you have to play. This app makes use of SpriteKit to achieve smooth animations.

2. Remote S by Rego Apps

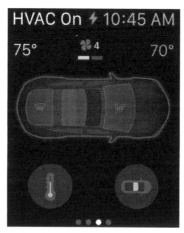

If you're lucky enough to own a Tesla, you can become Batman and summon your car from your Watch. The car will open the garage door, pull out into the driveway, and start heating up or cooling down depending on the type of weather. You can also unlock the doors and check the car's battery level. This app is less about innovation in the interface itself — after all, it is just buttons — but more about the experience those buttons dispatch.

1. Gymaholic by Devenyi Gabor

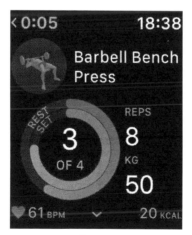

Going to the gym can be daunting since there are a thousand machines and weights to choose from. Gymaholic is a personal trainer app that selects the combination of weight lifting exercises you should do each day. You can choose from beginner, intermediate, and advanced levels. You mark the completion of every set by tapping on the screen.

After each set, the app shows a rest timer countdown before your next set. You'll no longer need to bring your phone inside the gym. You can keep track of your workout with Gymaholic and listen to synced playlists from Music app all from your watch.

Those are some of the fun apps built with watchOS. With new capabilities becoming available all the time, there will be even more amazing apps this year — perhaps even yours! Use these apps as an inspiration and build something even better.

Where to go from here?

As you dip your toes into designing watchOS 4 apps, here are a couple of good design resources:

- WWDC videos on watchOS 4: http://apple.co/2xIr6RI

- Sketch and Photoshop design templates: http://apple.co/2ckFVyX

You've now got a good grasp on what works well in Watch apps. In the coming chapters, you will learn all different capabilities you can add to your apps.

Chapter 3: Architecture

By Ehab Amer

The Apple Watch when it was first introduced was something completely new, and completely *different* from anything Apple has ever created before. A completely different user experience, a brand new User Interface, and above all ... A new developer framework to build on.

Just like any new thing, it goes through a set of improvements and enhancements or, in other words, it **matures**. It's also worth noting that the starting point for the Apple Watch and watchOS is miles ahead of what the iPhone had, in terms of hardware, software and the developer tools. Even then, it's not perfect and still has quite a bit of room to grow.

WatchKit for watchOS is in a situation similar to the early days of iOS. There are new tools, frameworks and methods for building Apple Watch apps. To build quality Watch apps now, and over the years and updates to come, you'll need a solid foundation in the architecture of both the Watch and the WatchKit framework. That's what this chapter aims to provide you.

Exploring the Watch

Before jumping into WatchKit, take a few minutes to familiarize yourself with what the Apple Watch is, and — more importantly — what it isn't.

Operating system

Here's a niggling question: What is the power behind the face of the Apple Watch? Is it iOS? Is it another flavor of iOS?

Apple calls this new software *watchOS*, which turns out to be built on top of iOS! While outside the scope of this book, a quick Google search for "PepperUICore" will return several articles detailing what's running under the hood of the Watch and the differences between the more elaborate, bundled Apple Watch apps and those you're able to build using WatchKit.

Interaction

Among the coolest features of the Apple Watch are the ways users can interact with it. Taken from the Apple Watch Human Interface Guidelines (apple.co/1IIMtDZ), there are four ways users can interact with your apps:

- **Action-based events**: These are what you're likely already familiar with: things like table row selection and tap-based UI controls.

- **Gestures**: The gesture system for the Apple Watch is more limited than the bountiful gesture options developers have in iOS, supporting only vertical and horizontal swipes and taps. Currently, the Watch *does not* support multi-touch gestures like pinches.

- **Force touch**: This is an interesting new gesture. The Apple Watch has special tiny electrodes around the display to determine if a tap is light or has more pressure and force behind it. This is a nice trade-off for losing multi-finger gestures.

- **The digital crown**: The excellently designed crown on the Apple Watch lets users navigate without obstructing the screen. For example, as with the pinch gesture, scrolling on the Watch screen is impractical because your fingers would likely hide the visual input you need to determine how far to scroll. You also have the option of using the crown to zoom and even input some forms of data.

Digital Crown

The Watch display

Right out of the gate, you'll need to support multiple screen sizes for the Apple Watch.

- The **38 mm** Watch screen is 272 pixels wide by 340 pixels tall.

- The **42 mm** Watch screen is 312 pixels wide by 390 pixels tall.

Luckily for developers, both Watches share an aspect ratio of 4:5, so, at least for the time being, you won't have to do a ton of extra work to support both screen sizes.

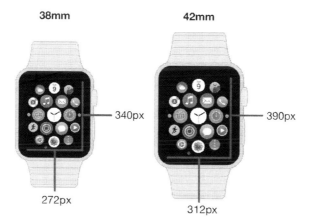

> **Note:** That doesn't mean you should hardcode your interfaces for this aspect ratio. Apple is notorious for adding additional screen sizes to their products, like how they added screen rotation to watchOS 4. Always design and build your interfaces to be screen-size agnostic!

Introducing WatchKit

A couple of months after announcing the Apple Watch, Apple provided eager developers the tools to start building Watch apps. Apple bundled the primary framework, called WatchKit, with Xcode 6.2.

Even though Apple released Swift only a few months before it released WatchKit, the framework had both Swift and Objective-C support.

What it is

Viewed from a high level, WatchKit is nothing more than a group of classes and Interface Builder additions that you can wire together to get an Apple Watch app working. Some of the important classes are:

> **Note: WK** in class names Stands for **WatchKit**, as you might expect. Also, an *Interface* in WatchKit is similar to a *View* in iOS.

- **WKInterfaceController**: This is the WatchKit version of UIViewController. Later in this chapter, you'll learn more about this class and how to use it.

- **WKInterfaceObject**: Instead of shipping with a Watch version of UIKit, WatchKit provides what could best be described as proxy objects for dealing with the user interface. This class is the base from which all of the Watch interface elements, like buttons and labels, inherit.

- **WKInterfaceDevice**: This class provides all of the information about the Watch, like screen size and locale.

You'll be building all of your user interfaces in storyboards — you **love** storyboards right...? Everyone does!

What it isn't

You'll build watch apps for watchOS as extensions, just as you might build a share extension. These are dependent apps — the Apple Watch can't install them without a paired iPhone.

That may sound weird, but carry on reading to learn more about how to compose Watch apps.

> **Note:** If you're interested in reading about how to build regular app extensions, check out this tutorial on building a Today extension: bit.ly/1wOP4Vd

WatchKit apps

There are three main parts to a Watch app:

- **iOS app:** This is the *host* or *parent* application that runs on an iPhone or iPad. You can never run an app on the Apple Watch without a host app.

- **Watch app:** This is the bundle of files and resources that is included with the host app but then installed on the Apple Watch. The bundle includes the app's storyboard and any images or localization files used *in the storyboard*.

- **Watch extension:** The last piece of the puzzle is the actual code that you write. This gets compiled and transferred to the Watch for execution. Any images or localizations accessed *in code* should be bundled with the extension.

In Xcode, these are all different targets. Creating a watchOS app or adding the target will create all of the Watch targets for you.

As you can see below, the app and menu icons require several sizes because the 38 mm and 42 mm Watches have different widths and heights.

Image	Apple Watch 38mm	Apple Watch 42mm
Notification center icon	29 pixels	36 pixels
Long Look notification icon	80 pixels	88 pixels
Home screen icon and Short Look icon	172 pixels	196 pixels
Menu icon canvas size	70 pixels	46 pixels
Menu icon content size	80 pixels	54 pixels

WatchKit classes

WatchKit consists of a set of entirely new classes. `WKInterfaceController` acts as the controller in the familiar model-view-controller pattern, and instances of `WKInterfaceObject` are used to update the UI.

WKInterfaceController

`WKInterfaceController` is essentially WatchKit's `UIViewController` — only this time, Apple engineers have taken notice of all the `UIViewController` pain points developers have struggled with, like passing data between controllers, handling notifications, and managing context menus, and improved the lot!

Lifecycle

`WKInterfaceController` has a lifecycle, just like `UIViewController`. It's much simpler, though — there are four main methods you need to know:

- **awake(withContext:)** is called on `WKInterfaceController` immediately after the controller is loaded from a storyboard. This method has a parameter for an optional context object that can be whatever you want it to be, like a model object, an ID or a string. Also, when this method is called, WatchKit has already connected any `IBOutlets` you might have set up.

- When **willActivate()** is called, WatchKit is letting you know the controller is about to be displayed onscreen. Just as with `viewWillAppear(_:)` on iOS, you only need to use this method to run any last-minute tasks, or anything that needs to run each time you display the controller. This method can be called repeatedly while a user is interacting with your Watch app.

- If there is anything you need to do once the system has finished initializing and displaying the controller, you can override the method **didActivate()**. This is analogous to `viewDidAppear(_:)` on iOS.

- Finally, there's **didDeactivate()**, which is called when the controller's interface goes offscreen, such as when the user navigates away from the interface controller or when the Watch terminates the app. This is where you should perform any cleanup or save any state.

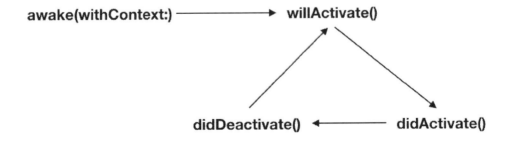

Segues

Since you're using storyboards to build your interfaces and connect your controllers, you're probably not surprised to hear that segues play a big part in managing the transition between two instances of `WKInterfaceController`.

Segues work in WatchKit very similarly to the way they work in iOS: They are still *stringly* typed, meaning they each need their own identifier string, and you create them by Control-dragging between controllers in Interface Builder. Instead of `performSegue(withIdentifier:sender:)`, WatchKit provides several amazingly convenient new methods you can override to pass context data in between controllers.

- **`contextForSegue(withIdentifier:)`** returns a context object of type `Any`. Use this to pass custom objects or values between controllers.

- **`awake(withContext:)`** is called when your `WKInterfaceController`'s UI is set up. Controllers can receive context objects from methods like `contextForSegue(withIdentifier:)`.

With these methods, you can simply check the identifier of the segue that's being performed and then return a relevant context object, which could be a model object, a string or just about anything else you might want!

Here's an example of using a segue to pass a context object to the next controller:

```
override func contextForSegue(withIdentifier
  segueIdentifier: String) -> Any? {
  if segueIdentifier == "RecipeIngredients" {
    return recipe?.ingredients
  }
  return nil
}
```

Interface objects

For dealing with user interfaces in iOS, UIKit provides an assortment of controls and objects that all seem to inherit from classes like `UIView`, `UIControl` and eventually `UIResponder`. This provides each view with basic functionality like touch handling, while allowing classes to add their own advanced features and overrides.

WatchKit is somewhat of a different story. There are only 19 interface-related classes available, and they all inherit from `WKInterfaceObject`, which then inherits from... `NSObject`!

This is because you're not dealing with real objects in the usual sense, but rather with *proxy objects*.

Proxy objects

Instead of having some sort of `WKView`, you'll be working with instances of `WKInterfaceObject` that act as proxy objects for the view state on the Watch. These objects are *write-only*, which means you can only set state, like background color or text.

Each class that inherits from `WKInterfaceObject` gets a handful of helpful methods:

- **setHidden(_:)** hides and shows the object. This method works by collapsing the space the object was taking up in the Watch layout system. More on this later.

- **setAlpha(_:)** changes the alpha of the object.

- **setWidth(_:)** and **setHeight(_:)** manually set the width and height of the object, respectively.

- **setAccessibilityLabel(_:)**, **setAccessibilityHint(_:)** and **setAccessibilityValue(_:)** configure the accessibility options for each object.

WatchKit views and controls

You will never add a `WKInterfaceObject` directly to any of your interfaces. Instead, you'll use these 19 subclasses:

- **WKInterfaceButton**: Your standard button. These come stocked with a background and a label, but through the use of groups and layouts, you can make really complex button styles.

- **WKInterfaceDate**: This class, unique to WatchKit, is a label built to display dates and times. That means no more fussing with `DateFormatter`!

- **WKInterfaceGroup**: This is another special WatchKit class that handles all of the interface layout and grouping. You can add other objects to a group to lay them out horizontally or vertically and adjust their spacing and padding, and how they can overlap on top of each other.

- **WKInterfaceImage**: This subclass is almost exactly the same as UIImageView. The one special quality of WKInterfaceImage is that it lets you set multiple images and animate them. The GIF is dead, *long live the GIF!*

- **WKInterfaceLabel**: This is your run-of-the-mill label, just like UILabel. You'll use this class anywhere you need to display text.

- **WKInterfaceMap**: This is a peculiar object. Maps on WatchKit are not interactive. In your controllers, you'll set an MKCoordinateRegion, which is simply a latitude, longitude and zoom level, and the map will configure a static view of that location. You can still add things like pins and custom annotations, but they won't be interactive.

- **WKInterfaceSeparator**: If you've been making iOS apps for a while, you've probably run into the scenario where you add a `UIView` or `CALayer` just to change the appearance of a table's separators. Now you have a fully-configurable `WKInterfaceSeparator` that you can use in tables and views, and that even works for vertical separation!

- **WKInterfaceSlider**: This is a slimmed-down version of `UISlider` in that it offers more limited functionality and shouldn't be subclassed. You can still customize the slider with min and max values, min and max icons and the number of steps. There is a new `continuous` property that you can set in Interface Builder to make the bar solid. With this property turned off, the bar is etched in the number of steps.

- **WKInterfaceTable**: Tables in WatchKit are quite useful, and it's likely you'll use them all over the place. An instance of `WKInterfaceTable` is automatically paired with it's owning `WKInterfaceController` for interaction events and segues. Tables are row-based and have no notion of sections. You'll make a relatively complex table later in this book and get a feel for how to use multiple row styles.

- **WKInterfaceTimer**: This is another special WatchKit interface object. Since watches traditionally handle time, Apple created a class that is basically a label that counts up or down to a specific date. You can configure what units to display: seconds, minutes, hours, days, weeks, months and even years.

- **WKInterfaceSwitch**: This object is also similar to its iOS counterpart, UISwitch, except now you get a handy built-in label.

- **WKInterfaceMovie**: Introduced in watchOS 2, it gives the ability to play videos. You'll have to include a video file, or download one, in order to play it. You can, at least, provide a placeholder cover photo.

- **WKInterfaceInlineVideo**: Introduced in watchOS 3, it lets you build custom video players instead of using the built-in playback and controls from WKInterfaceMovie. This control can be used to play videos inline, such as in a message thread or news feed.

- **WKInterfacePicker**: This object is a counterpart to the iOS `UIPickerView`. You have to add items to the picker in code, but you can configure it as a scrolling picker or as a sequence of images in the storyboard.

- **WKInterfaceSKScene**: Use this control to add SpriteKit scenes to your watch apps to use custom graphics and animations. This can be useful for games, displaying data, or advanced animated transitions.

- **WKInterfaceSCNScene**: This control brings the SceneKit to watchOS which provides a Swift/Objective-C API for building 3D games or apps.

- **WKGestureRecognizer**: Introduced in watchOS 3, those are custom gesture recognizers: WKLongPressGestureRecognizer, WKPanGestureRecognizer, WKSwipeGestureRecognizer, and WKTapGestureRecognizer. Previously, you only had access to button taps and control value changes, but now you can build custom gestures just like you do on iOS.

- **WKInterfacePaymentButton**: Apple brought even more SDK support for Apple Pay in iOS 10 and watchOS 3. Now you can add secure payments directly into your app with this simple button.

- **WKInterfaceHMCamera**: By providing a HomeKit camera source, you can display real time video data from a HomeKit enabled device. Imagine checking security cameras right from your wrist!

Layout

Looking at the methods on WKInterfaceObject, you will see that there isn't any reference to frame or Auto Layout. So how do you change the position of the objects? Auto Layout be gone! WatchKit provides its very own layout system that abstracts away most of the pain of layout and sizing and lets you focus on building your app. The WatchKit layout system defaults to sizing objects based on their content size and puts every object into either a horizontal or a vertical layout group. This works in much the same way as HTML and CSS layout. Content is king, and interface elements are spaced and laid out relative to the content that comes before them.

The number of lines in a label, the font size and the image size are all automatically calculated to lay out surrounding objects and even to size table row heights!

No more calculating text height for table views! Take a look at this more complex interface for a WKInterfaceTable with multiple row types. You're going to build this exact interface later in the book.

In this interface, all of the work is done in the storyboard, and the WKInterfaceController code only has to worry about wiring the data to the interface objects.

> **Note:** It's important to know that the user interface can only be created by the storyboard and *not* through code.

The dock

The dock keeps recently-used apps alive in a suspended state, in the background, so they launch more quickly. On top of that, users can also select apps to *keep* in their dock. watchOS then always keeps those apps in a suspended state when backgrounded.

While in the dock, apps can update their snapshots via the `WKSnapshotRefreshBackgroundTask` API so its content is up-to-date when users are viewing their dock. The snapshot doesn't even have to be a view in your app, it can be a more *glanceable* interface.

> **Note:** The dock is accessed via the hardware button next to the digital crown, replacing quick access to contacts.

Notifications

Notifications have been around since iOS 3. On Apple Watch, notifications work in almost exactly the same way they do in iOS. If the Watch receives a local or remote notification, it displays an alert, along with a vibration and an optional noise, and lights up the screen.

WatchKit introduces two new types of notifications: the **short look** and the **long look**.

While both notification types are triggered by a remote or local notification, the source of the notification can determine which, or both, of the notification types you'll want to use.

The short look

A short look is a very simple notification. The user sees only your app's icon, some text and the title of your app. If the user taps on the short look notification, then the Watch, like the iPhone, launches the full app.

The long look

A long look notification has a more complex interface that is completely customizable. The top part of the notification is called the **sash** and contains the name of your app and the icon, on top of a translucent, blurred bar.

Beneath the sash, you can add any content you want. Text content is driven by the notification and is either dynamic or static. With static notifications, you must bundle any image resources as part of the WatchKit extension. With dynamic notifications, you can customize the interface a bit more, but if you take too long, the system will fall back to the static notification.

You can also add any action items to the notification, so the user can jump into your app immediately and have it carry out the corresponding action. The user can dismiss your notification or simply tap anywhere in the content area to open your app.

One interesting feature of short and long look notifications is that if you've made both types available for your app, users can toggle between them using a wrist-based gesture. After receiving a notification, the Watch will first display the short look, and if the user brings her wrist up to look at the notification, the Watch will switch to the long look.

This feature can provide more context and flexibility to your users, so they don't have to fumble around navigating the tiny screen.

Note: You'll have the opportunity to build your own custom notifications in Chapter 14, Notifications.

Complications

Complications let you add third-party customizations to Watch faces. These are like the battery life, current temperature and next appointment widgets you're probably used to seeing, as below:

The `ClockKit` framework includes the functionality required to create custom complications, including the `CLKComplicationDataSource` protocol. An object that conforms to this protocol determines what the complication displays, and which features it supports. You can provide a basic complication, or you can take advantage of advanced features like timeline data and use the shared `CLKComplicationServer` object.

Note: You will learn more about `ClockKit` in Chapter 15, Complications.

New in watchOS 4

watchOS 4 introduces several architecture-related features that can improve the usability and performance of apps. You don't need to do anything to take advantage of many of these — except running your app on watchOS 4!

Unified process runtime

In a typical watchOS app, you have your application UI and your code. Prior to watchOS 4, the UI lived in the app process, and your code lived in WatchKit extension, which was executed by the system. In other words, your UI and the code ran on two different processes.

Starting from watchOS 4 this is no longer the case. They both run on the same process.

You must be thinking "How does this help me? ¯_(ツ)_/¯"

This means that your app is now much more responsive, with reduced touch-latency, improved FPS for gestures and even improved launch times. And the best thing about it: you don't need to do anything at all, even for you legacy Watch apps, as long as they are not a watchOS 1 app!

Increased memory limits

To further improve performance, your app is now allowed more memory. This means that if you have memory-intensive operations your app is now much less likely to run out of memory.

Frontmost app state

There is a new application state in watchOS 4 that improves the overall user experience. If the user does something in your app and expects that it might take a while to finish, they might lower their wrist (without pressing the crown button), and then after a while raise their wrist to check the progress.

Normally the user expects to see your app again with an update on the screen to mark the progress. However, when the wrist lowers the screen will dim and the app used to be taken to the background. Now, watchOS 4 allows your app to request permission to be in a new & unique state called **Frontmost State**!

It gives the app special background capabilities and a higher execution priority since the OS knows that the user is still interacting with your app, and just wants to rest their wrist a bit.

Haptic feedback for frontmost app

With the addition of the Frontmost state, your app can now provide feedback to the user through its taptic engine. This is only allowed for the app with the Frontmost state, and not for any app in the background.

WatchKit limitations

Even though Apple Watch is a powerful device and WatchKit Extension has a rich API, there are a few considerations that you should always keep in mind:

Intended for lightweight apps

From the Apple Watch Human Interface Guidelines:

"Apps designed for Apple Watch should respect the context in which the wearer experiences them: briefly, frequently, and on a small display."

You should look at building an Apple Watch app as literally extending an iPhone app to the user's wrist. The Watch is meant for quick and ephemeral interactions.

Small in size

Developers are used to having at least 320 points in width, amazingly sharp Retina displays and a screen big enough for four-finger gestures. But the Apple Watch is small — *really* small.

Remember that the Apple Watch takes extremely limited input and is strapped to the user's wrist. Your interfaces should be big and simple. Make your fonts and buttons large and use very few of them.

Where to go from here?

This has been an overview of the design and features of WatchKit — what it can and cannot do. There are many exciting, new and unique tools for building Apple Watch apps, and the best way to get familiar with them is to try them for yourself.

In the following chapters, you will indeed get to try out many of the different interface controls and objects in WatchKit, as well as begin construction of a larger Apple Watch app that will take you through building custom layouts, navigation, tables and much more!

Chapter 4: UI Controls

By Ehab Amer

watchOS delivers 19 interface controls with WatchKit, all of which inherit from `WKInterfaceObject`, which itself inherits from `NSObject`. Many of the interface controls have UIKit counterparts, but some are unique to WatchKit.

In this chapter, you'll get your hands on two new interface controls provided by WatchKit and see how to begin building a functional Watch app: **Carnivore**, a cooking companion that will do all the timing and calculating to help you prepare the perfect steak!

> **Note:** For a detailed review of each of the new controls, please refer to Chapter 3, "Architecture".

Getting started

To jump right into building and using the new interface objects, grab the **Carnivore** starter project. This is mostly empty, but we've provided it so you don't have to waste any time on setup and configuration.

Open **Carnivore.xcodeproj** and poke around the targets and the project files. You'll see that we've already created the WatchKit App **scheme** for you, as well as **groups** for the Carnivore WatchKit Extension and the Carnivore WatchKit App.

There's also **CarnivoreKit** that simply contains an `enum` that both the iPhone app and the Watch app you're about to build will use.

Select the **Carnivore WatchKit App** scheme and build and run to launch the Watch app in the Apple Watch simulator. You'll see a lot of empty space for you to work with.

> **Note:** If you want to know how to create a Watch app from scratch, see Chapter 1, "Hello, Apple Watch!"

Next, take a look at the **Carnivore WatchKit Extension** and **Carnivore WatchKit App** groups in the project navigator. You'll see the following files and groups in each:

Each group of files corresponds to an individual app target with the same respective name. This helps organize your files, while also keeping them accessible. It's a much cleaner setup than having a bunch of different Xcode projects crammed into a single workspace.

Make sure you understand the purpose of each group or target:

- **Carnivore WatchKit Extension**: This target houses all of the code that you write and gets bundled with the Watch app. Refer back to Chapter 3, "Architecture", for more.

- **Carnivore WatchKit App**: This target is for all of the resources that are physically stored on the Watch, including images, files and the interface storyboard.

Open **Interface.storyboard** from the **Carnivore WatchKit App** group and take a look at the default, blank interface controller:

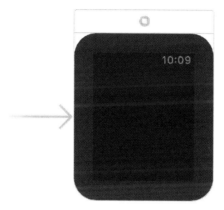

If you've worked with iOS storyboards, this should look pretty familiar. There is a main entry point arrow designating that this is the controller that the OS will load when the app launches.

Enough poking around — it's time to get into the *meat* of this chapter!

The timer object

In this chapter, you're going to create all of the interface elements for the app, one at a time. While you won't use all 19 UI controls provided by WatchKit, pay attention while you're working and you'll learn just how powerful WatchKit storyboards can be.

To cook the perfect steak, you need to know a couple of things about your meat and the preferences of you dinner guests, so that you can determine just the right amount of time to leave the meat in the oven — and for the sake of simplicity, we are assuming you are cooking with an oven!

All in all, you need your app to support the following actions:

- Start and stop a timer

- Increase and decrease the weight of the meat
- Select the diner's cooking preference, from rare to well done
- Toggle between metric and imperial units

With **Interface.storyboard** open, find **group** in the Object library and drag one onto the interface controller.

You'll see a dashed border with the word "Group" in the middle. This is just a placeholder. If you were to run the app now, you wouldn't actually see anything new on the screen.

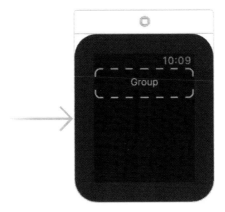

> **Note:** Groups are unique interface objects in that they occupy the space of their contents. You can specify a width and height for a group, but the real magic is in how they automatically lay themselves out. You can read more in Chapter 6, "Layout".

Next, drag a **timer** into the group. Timers also have placeholder text to give an idea of how their contents will be formatted.

With your new timer selected, open the Attributes Inspector and change the following attributes:

- In **Units**, select only **Second** and **Minute**.
- Change **Font** to **Text Styles – Headline**.
- Set **Alignment** to **Center** (the middle of the five buttons).

- Change the **Horizontal** position to **Center**.

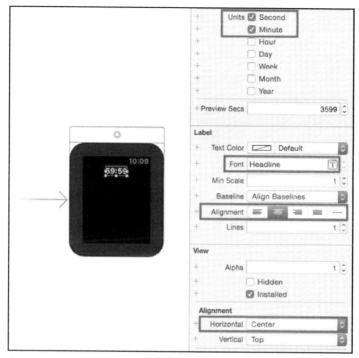

Wow, that's a lot of setup for such a tiny interface element! What exactly did you do?

The **Units** attribute configures what time units the timer will display. If you were to select Day, Month, Year and set a date of two months, three days and one year into the future, then the timer would read "1y 2m 3d". The timer is *really* smart in how it displays the time, which means no more fussing around with DateFormatter.

Position is a new type of attribute that's unique to WatchKit and is extremely powerful. It lets you lay out objects to the left, center or right of their container.

It might seem like a lot of setup, but think of all the steps you'd follow to build a similar interface object under iOS:

- Use DateFormatter to get a string representation of a Date.

- Subclass UILabel.

- Set up the necessary Auto Layout constraints on the label.

- Finally, use a Timer to update the label every second.

Using WKInterfaceTimer saved you from writing a whole lot of code and from running a bunch of tests!

With the Carnivore WatchKit App scheme selected, build and run the app to see your new timer:

Hmm. That looks kind of... *lame*. Why isn't it doing anything? Well, in your storyboard you've given the timer a placeholder number of seconds, but this doesn't carry over when you run the app; it's purely for design purposes. For the timer to work, you need to wire it up and trigger it in code.

First, you need something to trigger the timer. Find **button** in the Object Library and drag it next to the timer, or just below it if you're dragging it into the document outline. Make sure you add the button to the same group that contains your timer. You can confirm this by checking the document outline.

But wait! Where did your timer go?

The problem is, all groups have a horizontal layout by default. You need to change your group to make it vertical.

Select the **group** in the document outline. Then in the Attributes Inspector, change the **Layout** to **Vertical**.

Double-click on the text in the button and change it to **Start Timer**. You can also do this by selecting the button and changing the text in the **Title** field of the Attributes Inspector.

Build and run your Watch app to see the new button:

You'll be able to tap on the button and see the app both highlight it and depress it in 3D space. Now you're going to make that button do something!

Wiring the timer

Option-click on **Carnivore WatchKit Extension\InterfaceController.swift** to open the controller in the assistant editor. You should see the storyboard's and controller's Swift code side by side.

Control-drag from the timer in **Interface.storyboard** into **InterfaceController.swift** to create a new IBOutlet. In the pop-up, name the outlet timer, make it of type WKInterfaceTimer and give it a **weak** connection.

Now **Control-click** the **button**. Click on the **selector** option under **Sent Actions** and drag over to **InterfaceController.swift**. In the pop-up, name the new action onTimerButton.

Inside onTimerButton(), add a print statement to test that this method is wired up and working. Your method should look like this:

```
@IBAction func onTimerButton() {
  print("onTimerButton")
}
```

Build and run your app. Tap on the **Start Timer** button a couple of times and make sure you see some output in your console log:

```
onTimerButton
onTimerButton
onTimerButton
```

Now that you're confident you've wired up the button properly, how about using it to make the timer work?

Replace the contents of onTimerButton() with the following code:

```
// 1
let countdown: TimeInterval = 20
let date = Date(timeIntervalSinceNow: countdown)
// 2
timer.setDate(date)
timer.start()
```

Here's what you're doing with the above code:

1. You set a 20-second countdown variable and use it to instantiate a Date object. WKInterfaceTimer always uses date objects, not primitives, to count time.

2. You set the date for the timer and then start the timer. A timer won't do anything until you call start() on it. Any time that passes between setting the date and calling start() will be subtracted from the timer.

Build and run the app and then tap on the button. Now, instead of some boring console output, you'll see the timer start and count down all the way to zero!

Using a label and buttons to control weight

You've seen how to add interface objects to your storyboard as well as how to wire them into your controller. It looks like it's time to build out this app!

Open **Interface.storyboard** and drag a **label** from the Object Library to just below the first group that contains the timer and button. That's *below* the group — not inside it! Change the **Text** to **Weight: 16 oz** and the **Horizontal** position to **Center**.

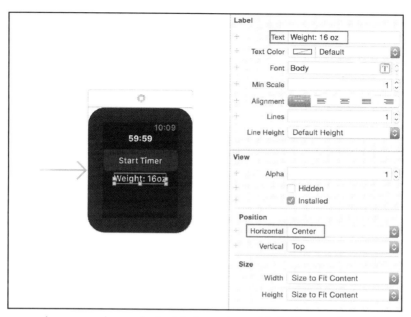

Next, drag another **group** beneath the label you just added. You can leave the Layout setting of this group as Horizontal.

Now drag a **button** into the group. With this new button selected, change the following attributes in the Attributes Inspector:

- Clear the **Title** field;

- Set the **Background** image to **minus**;

- Change the **Horizontal** position to **Center**;

- Set the **Width** size to **Size to Fit Content**.

You'll end up with a button that looks just like the following:

Next, click on your new button, **copy** and then immediately **paste**. This will paste a new button with the same configuration directly after the selected button, and within the same group.

Select this new button and change the **Background** image to **plus**.

If you're a fan of Apple design and documentation, you've probably run across the Human Interface Guidelines at least a couple of times. Apple puts a lot of emphasis on interactive element sizes and spacing. You can probably tell that those two blue buttons are way too close for comfort.

Groups have powerful attributes that make layout extremely easy. In the case of items being too crowded, there's an attribute called **Spacing** that fixes just this.

Select the **group** that contains your two blue buttons. You might have to use the document outline to select it. Change the **Spacing** attribute from Default to **20**. Press the Return key to commit the change and watch Interface Builder update automatically.

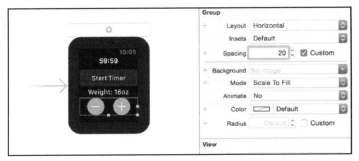

While you're at it, all of the items are getting a little tight vertically. Well, it turns out that the contents of `WKInterfaceController` are already in one big layout group! You know this because `WKInterfaceController` can contain other interface objects, are aligned vertically, and even have spacing and inset options.

Select the interface controller by clicking on the white header above all of your interface objects. In the Attributes Inspector, change **Spacing** to **10** and press Return. This will add a little vertical padding so your interface doesn't feel too crammed.

Open **InterfaceController.swift** in the assistant editor so you can see both it and **Interface.storyboard** at the same time. You're going to add a couple of outlets and actions.

Control-click on the **weight label** and drag to create an IBOutlet. Name it weightLabel, give it a type of WKInterfaceLabel and make it a **weak** connection.

Next, just as you did for the Start Timer button, add an IBAction for both the **plus** and **minus** buttons. Name them onMinusButton and onPlusButton, respectively.

If you did this correctly, you'll have added the following code to InterfaceController:

```
@IBOutlet weak var weightLabel: WKInterfaceLabel!

@IBAction func onMinusButton() {

}

@IBAction func onPlusButton() {

}
```

Now it's time to make the buttons functional. Close the assistant editor and open **InterfaceController.swift** in the main editor. Add a new variable to the top of the class:

```
var ounces = 16
```

This will keep track of the selected weight for your meat. A default of 16 ounces, or one pound, is a good starting point.

Add a new method just below awake(withContext:):

```
    func updateConfiguration() {
      weightLabel.setText("Weight: \(ounces) oz")
    }
```

This simple function updates your label with the current weight. You'll be adding a lot to this function in due course to update the interface to reflect the app's current state.

In onMinusButton(), add the following code:

```
ounces -= 1
updateConfiguration()
```

And in onPlusButton(), add the following code to increase the current weight:

```
ounces += 1
updateConfiguration()
```

Thanks to Swift, this code is short, clean and very readable!

Lastly, to make sure the app updates the interface with the proper state from the beginning, add a call to updateConfiguration() to the end of awake(withContext:):

```
override func awake(withContext context: Any?) {
  super.awake(withContext: context)
  updateConfiguration()
}
```

Build and run the Watch app. Click on the plus and minus buttons to see your label update accordingly:

> **Note:** If you want, you can add minimum and maximum values to the weight. As it stands, you can choose a steak that's the weight of an entire cow! Except it won't fit in your oven...

Using a slider object to control doneness

People have their own preferences when it comes to cooking meat, from rare to well done to cremated. To please your diners, you need to be able to regulate the cooking temperature.

Open **Interface.storyboard** and drag another **group** from the Object Library to just below the group containing the two blue buttons. Make sure it's in the same hierarchy level as the buttons, weight label and timer groups.

Drag a **label** and a **slider** into your new group. Since the group is horizontal by default, select the group, open the Attributes Inspector and change **Layout** to **Vertical**.

> **Note:** There is a new group layout that introduced in watchOS 4: **Overlap**. This is covered in Chapter 6, "Layout".

You'll have four cooking temperatures: rare, medium rare, medium and well done. For the user to select one of these options, you'll have to configure the slider appropriately.

Select your new slider and, in the Attributes Inspector, make the following changes:

• Change the **Slider Value** to **2** to select medium by default.

• Change the **Slider Minimum** to **0** for rare.

• Change the **Slider Maximum** to **3** for well done.

• Set the number of **Slider Steps** to **3**. There is also an empty state, which actually makes four steps, but you need to set the number of values in *addition* to the value zero.

Make sure that **Continuous** is **unchecked**. This will give you step dividers on the slider to make the available options and means of selection more obvious to the user.

Open **InterfaceController.swift** using the assistant editor. **Control-drag** from the new label to create an `IBOutlet`. Name the outlet `cookLabel`, make the type `WKInterfaceLabel` and make it a weak connection.

Control-click on the **slider** and drag the **selector** option into InterfaceController.swift to create an `IBAction`. Name the new action `onTempChange`.

To represent the cooking temperature, you could simply remember that rare is the integer 0, medium rare is 1 and so on, but Swift makes creating an `enum` to represent data structures like this too easy to pass up!

Open the file **MeatTemperature.swift** and take a look around. You should see possible enum values, like `.rare` and `.medium`, and helper methods to turn a value into a string or associate a cook time modifier.

Great! Not only do you have a way to represent cooking temperatures, but now you're supplying a readable string and a time modifier. Let's plug this into the app.

Go back to **InterfaceController.swift** and add another variable just under the `ounces` variable you added earlier.

```
var cookTemp = MeatTemperature.medium
```

This sets your default cooking temperature to .medium, which, in my experience, is a popular choice.

Find the onTempChange(_:) method that you connected to the slider earlier and add the following code:

```
if let temp = MeatTemperature(rawValue: Int(value)) {
    cookTemp = temp
    updateConfiguration()
}
```

This code does two things:

- It creates a MeatTemperature variable. WKInterfaceSlider changed values are always of the type Float, so you have to cast it to an Int before initializing.

- The code also sets the current cooking temperature and updates the interface if a MeatTemperature variable was created.

To update the interface, add the following line to updateConfiguration():

```
cookLabel.setText(cookTemp.stringValue)
```

Build and run, swipe down to the slider and tap around to change its value. Watch the label update every time you tap the plus or minus button on the slider.

Integrating the timer

What good are these interface objects if they don't tell you how long to cook your meat? Looks like it's time to make the timer functional.

Near the top of **InterfaceController.swift**, where your other properties are declared, add another to track the status of the timer.

```
var timerRunning = false
```

Your timer is not running when the controller is initialized, so it's safe to set its default value to `false`.

The timer counting down isn't enough to reflect the state of your app. It's a good idea to update the Start Timer button when the user taps it.

Open **Interface.storyboard** in the main editor and **InterfaceController.swift** in the assistant editor. **Control-click** and drag from the **Start Timer** button to create an outlet named `timerButton`.

Replace everything inside `onTimerButton()` so that it looks like this:

```
@IBAction func onTimerButton() {
  // 1
  if timerRunning {
    timer.stop()
    timerButton.setTitle("Start Timer")
  } else {
    // 2
    let time = cookTemp.cookTimeForOunces(ounces)
    timer.setDate(Date(timeIntervalSinceNow: time))
    timer.start()
    timerButton.setTitle("Stop Timer")
  }
  // 3
  timerRunning = !timerRunning
}
```

Taking each numbered comment in turn:

1. Upon a user tap, if the timer is already running, you stop it and update the button title. This causes the timer to stop updating its UI.

2. If the timer isn't running, you create a cooking time interval using `cookTimeForOunces(_:)`, found in the `MeatTemperature` enum, and use it to create a `Date`. Then you start the timer and update the button title.

3. As the timer state has changed with the user tapping the button, you reflect that in your variable.

Build and run your Watch app. Change your cooking configuration, then tap the Start Timer button and watch the title change and the timer begin to count down. You can stop and restart the timer as many times as you like.

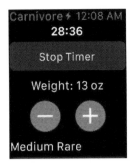

Interacting with scrolling

watchOS 4 introduces a few capabilities that allow you to query and control the scoll position of the screen. The user can move across the screen by either swiping, using the crown or by tapping on the status bar to go to the top of the screen, just like on the iPhone.

In some situations you will want to move to a specific area/element on the screen to show the user that something specific has changed. In our case, if the screen's scroll position isn't showing the timer we may want to move to its location to make sure the user can see that it has started or stopped.

Add the following code to the end of `onTimerButton`:

```
scroll(to: timer, at: .top, animated: true)
```

`scroll(to:at:animated:)` its first parameter is the Interface element you want to have visible on the screen, the second is where this element should appear on the screen which uses an enum with possible values of `top`, `bottom`, or `centeredVertically`

In other situations you may want to know when the user scrolls to the bottom top. watchOS 4 enables that with three new methods in `WKInterfaceController`: `interfaceDidScrollToTop()`, `interfaceOffsetDidScrollToTop()` and `interfaceOffsetDidScrollToBottom()`.

Add the following code to the end of the class:

```
override func interfaceOffsetDidScrollToTop() {
    print("User scrolled to top")
}

override func interfaceDidScrollToTop() {
    print("User went to top by tapping status bar")
}
```

```
override func interfaceOffsetDidScrollToBottom() {
    print("User scrolled to bottom")
}
```

Build and run your project and pan from top to bottom, tap the status bar a few of times for fun too and then go to the log in the debugger, it should look something like this:

```
user scrolled to top
user scrolled to bottom
user went to top by tapping status bar
user scrolled to bottom
user went to top by tapping status bar
user scrolled to bottom
user scrolled to top
```

Using the switch to change units

Since only three countries in the world use imperial units, it would be best to be able to toggle between imperial and metric. This is a perfect use-case for a `WKInterfaceSwitch`!

> **Note:** The three countries are Liberia, Myanmar and the United States, if you were curious, although in the US, they are called United States customary units.

Open **Interface.storyboard** and drag in one last **group** beneath the slider you added earlier. Make sure you add the group to the same hierarchy as your other groups.

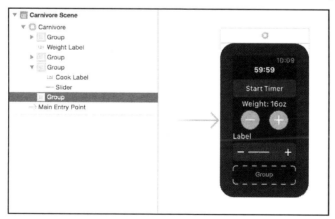

Drag a **switch** object into the new group. Open the Attributes Inspector and change the **Title** attribute to **Metric**. Also change the **State** to **Off**. Remember, you're using imperial units by default.

Open **InterfaceController.swift** in the assistant editor, and just as you've been doing, **Control-click** the new switch and **drag** from the **selector** option to create a new IBAction. Name this action onMetricChanged.

Near the top of **InterfaceController.swift**, where your other variables are in InterfaceController, add another variable:

```
var usingMetric = false
```

This variable will keep track of which unit system, imperial or metric, your user prefers.

Go back to the onMetricChanged(_:) method you just added and make it look like the following:

```
@IBAction func onMetricChanged(_ value: Bool) {
    usingMetric = value
    updateConfiguration()
}
```

In the code above, you simply change your new variable whenever the user taps the switch and then instruct the app to update the interface accordingly.

Find updateConfiguration() and change it to look like the following:

```
func updateConfiguration() {
    // 1
    cookLabel.setText(cookTemp.stringValue)

    var weight = ounces
    var unit = "oz"

    if usingMetric {
        // 2
        let grams = Double(ounces) * 28.3495
        weight = Int(grams)
        unit = "gm"
    }
    // 3
    weightLabel.setText("Weight: \(weight) \(unit)")
}
```

This code is pretty straightforward:

1. The measurement system doesn't affect the cooking temperature, so you don't alter this line.

2. There are approximately 28.3495 grams per ounce, so if you're in metric mode, you need to convert your units. Notice that the ounces variable is *always* in ounces; you only use the metric state when it comes to configuring the interface objects.

3. You set the text of the WKInterfaceLabel with the converted weight and the proper unit abbreviation.

Build and run the Watch app. Play around with the different settings. You should see your cooking weight change whenever you tap the switch:

Where to go from here?

You've learned a ton about new and familiar interface controls in this chapter: groups, labels, buttons, images, switches, sliders and timers. There are still several other controls you can explore, like WKInterfaceMap and WKInterfaceSeparator.

You could also extend the app by adding interface objects to change the oven temperature, which will affect the cooking time, or even to select between different meats and vegetables. Make the app work to accommodate just how you like to cook!

In the next few chapters, you're going to take a look at some of the more interesting aspects of Watch app interface design, including pickers, layout and navigation.

Chapter 5: Pickers

By Ehab Amer

The first version of WatchKit came with a decent starter kit of UI controls. There were buttons, switches, and tables, but this toolbox fell short when it came to interactions with some of the Apple Watch's physical interfaces. Most notable was the lack of controls that used the digital crown: one of the physical features most touted by Apple.

In watchOS 2 Apple introduced `WKInterfacePicker`. If you're familiar with iOS development, this control is functionally similar to `UIPickerView`, which is a sort of spinner control used to select an item from a long list.

One of the most common pickers is the `UIDatePicker` subclass which lets you easily select date components like days, months and years.

`WKInterfacePicker` provides the same functionality and usability for the Apple Watch. It lets you give your users a large list of items to pick from — without eating up the entire interface with buttons and options.

Using `WKInterfacePicker` is super simple:

1. Provide the picker a list of data, which can include both text and images.

2. Setup an `IBAction` and handle changes to the selected picker value.

That's it!

Another amazing feature of `WKInterfacePicker` is that it gives you access to the Digital Crown. The crown frees the user from covering up the Watch's screen while they select options so they can view more interface elements.

Since you use pickers to select from large lists of options, using the crown to see more of the screen is perfect! You can save your users from extra scrolling or add other features that are easy to get to.

In this chapter, you'll retool and enhance the previous chapter's Carnivore app to incorporate two styles of pickers, one simple and one advanced. Along the way, you'll acquaint yourself with the basics of `WKInterfacePicker` and get a taste of what this new control can do for your apps.

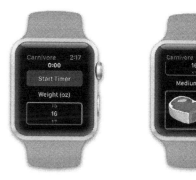

Getting started

If you completed the previous chapter on UI Controls, simply open that same project, **Carnivore.xcodeproj**, to pick up right where that chapter left off. If you got stuck or skipped the previous chapter, then open the **Carnivore.xcodeproj** starter project from this chapter's resources.

Build and run the **Carnivore WatchKit App** target and make sure you see something like the screenshot below. The Watch app should be fully functional: You should be able to start the timer, change the weight and cycle through cooking times.

> **Note:** If you haven't read Chapter 4, "UI Controls", we suggest you skim through it first to familiarize yourself with the Carnivore app.

Code slayer

Before you begin building pickers, you first need to rip out the old ways of selecting weights and temperatures for cooking your meats.

Instead of using buttons, `WKInterfacePicker` can make your app even more user-friendly.

Using buttons to make a selection from a range of data is much more cumbersome than quickly swiping through a list.

Every change requires a tap, and that can get annoying! Plus, being able to use the digital crown makes selection even easier.

Open **Carnivore WatchKit App/Interface.storyboard** and select the following interface elements:

- The **weight label**
- The **group** housing both the **increase and decrease buttons**
- The **group** with the **temperature label and slider**
- The **group** containing the **metric switch**

Once you have all of these elements selected, **delete** them! You can also remove the elements one at a time, if you prefer.

Your storyboard should now look like this:

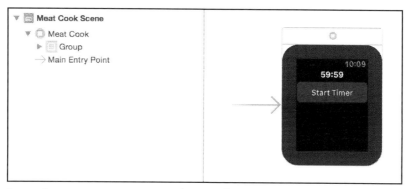

You're going to have to remove some code as well. Open **Carnivore WatchKit Extension/ InterfaceController.swift** and find your IBOutlets.

Delete `weightLabel` and `cookLabel`, since you just removed those elements from the storyboard.

Remove `usingMetric` and the entire `updateConfiguration()` method as well. From now on, you're going to be updating your state based on picker events!

While you're in the mode for culling code, remove a few more methods:

- `onTempChange(_:)`
- `onPlusButton()`
- `onMinusButton()`
- `onMetricChanged(_:)`

You removed all of these elements from the storyboard, so none of this code is going to do any good!

Lastly, to make the compiler happy, delete the call to `updateConfiguration()` in `awake(withContext:)`.

Build the app — you don't need to run it. Everything should compile just fine.

If you've slain your code with thoroughness and precision, your implementation of `InterfaceController` will still have the following `IBOutlets` and variables:

- **timer**, as an outlet to the `WKInterfaceTimer`
- **timerButton**, your start and stop button
- **ounces** to keep track of the selected ounces for your steak
- **cookTemp**, your desired cook temperature

- **timerRunning**, a flag that determines whether or not the timer is running

Also, you'll have only the following functions:

- **awake(withContext:)**, which simply has a call to `super`.

- **onTimerButton()**, which contains logic about what to do when the user taps the timer button.

You've made space for a few pickers, but you have more than one style of picker to choose from. Let's learn about them now.

Picker display styles

The `WKInterfacePicker` API comes with three different display styles for data, each with its own purpose. You can use your finger or the digital crown to navigate through all of the different picker styles.

The list style

The **list** style is the most common of the three. You'll use it when you want to display a series of vertically stacked elements consisting of titles and/or images.

You can mix and match to display just text, just images, or both! This style is the most similar to that of `UIPickerView`.

You would want to use this style to pick from things like dates, times, or small icons.

The stacked style

The second available style, called **stacked**, requires that all of the items you give to the `WKInterfacePicker` have an image; otherwise, nothing appears. The images are displayed in full screen, and when you scroll through the options, you'll notice a cool 3D fade-and-scale animation.

The following screenshot shows a stacked picker in the middle of a transition:

You use the stacked style to select from a set of larger images. A good rule of thumb for using the stacked style would be for any data that could be displayed on a card.

The sequence style

The last available picker style, called **sequence**, is similar to the stacked style in that both display full-screen images. But the sequence style doesn't use an animated transition. Instead, the images simply replace each other as you scroll through the items.

At first this might sound super boring, but sequence-style pickers exist so you can design a control that involves more than merely swiping through a list. This is where the digital crown comes into play. Imagine something like the circular progress control in the Activity app that you can scroll to fullness with the crown.

Start   End

To achieve this effect, all you have to do is provide a series of progressive images. Once assigned to your `WKInterfacePicker`, the picker will automatically scroll through the images you gave it.

But don't limit your image sequence imagination to just filling circles. You can combine all sorts of images in a series and scroll through them almost as if they were stills from an animation: weather effects, facial expressions, you name it!

If you put time and effort into designing your image sequences, you can achieve some really amazing controls.

But for your first picker, you'll start with the simplest and most familiar display style: the list.

Your first picker

Since you already removed the buttons to select a cook temperature, you're going to add a picker so that selecting the weight of your steak is much faster.

Open **Carnivore WatchKit App/Interface.storyboard** and in the Object Library, find the **picker** element. Drag and drop it beneath the **Start Timer** button.

With the new picker still selected, open the Attributes Inspector. Notice that there isn't a way to add any items, text or images to the picker. Configuration of items in WKInterfacePicker has to happen entirely in code, much the same way that tables and collections views with dynamic data must be set up in code.

Note: Oddly, while all data configuration **must** be done in code, a `WKInterfacePicker` must be initialized via the storyboard. Likewise, the style of the picker must be determined in the storyboard; it cannot be changed at runtime.

To configure your picker's items, you first need to create an `IBOutlet` for it. Open **Carnivore WatchKit Extension/InterfaceController.swift** in the assistant editor and Control-drag from the **picker** to `InterfaceController` to create an outlet. Name this outlet **weightPicker**.

Next, you will add a series of `WKPickerItems` to `weightPicker` to configure it. Unlike using a delegate for `UIPickerView`, instances of `WKInterfacePicker` are configured with a first-class object. Picker items hold the strings and images that are displayed by the picker. Find `awake(withContext:)`. It will be empty aside from a call to `super`. Add the following code:

```
// 1
var weightItems: [WKPickerItem] = []
for i in 1...32 {
  // 2
  let item = WKPickerItem()
  item.title = String(i)
  weightItems.append(item)
}
// 3
weightPicker.setItems(weightItems)
// 4
weightPicker.setSelectedItemIndex(ounces - 1)
```

Here's what happening:

1. This code first creates a mutable array that can only accept instances of `WKPickerItem`.

2. To cover a wide array of steak sizes, you iterate 32 times and create an item for each step. You simply use a string format of the integer as the title of the `WKPickerItem`.

3. The last step to populate the `WKInterfacePicker` is to call `setItems(_:)` with an array of `WKPickerItem`. If you were to run the app at this step, you would see a functional picker.

4. To make sure your picker is in sync with the current state of your controller, you use the `ounces` variable to set the index of the selected item.

Build and run the Watch app, and you'll see something like this:

> **Note:** If you're using the simulator, clicking and dragging will replicate scrolling the entire view. To scroll through a picker, use your laptop's trackpad or the scroll-wheel of a mouse. If you're running the app on your watch you can scroll with your fingers or the digital crown.

There it is: your first working `WKInterfacePicker`! However, it's not very usable yet. For starters, what's it for?

Go back to **Carnivore WatchKit App/Interface.storyboard** and drag a **label** element directly above the picker. Change the label's text to **Weight (oz)** and change its **Horizontal Position** to **Center**.

Notice that you can't scroll through the items unless you first tap on the picker. Wouldn't it be great to be able to tell when the picker is selected?

Apple's engineers have you covered! Still in **Interface.storyboard**, select the **picker** you just added and open the **Attributes Inspector**. Change the **Focus Style** to **Outline**.

While you're at it, make the picker a little shorter by changing the **Height (Fixed)** to 55.

Build and run the Watch app again, and try to use the picker. Now, selecting your picker surrounds it with a bright green indicator. Much more intuitive!

While your new picker is now easy to use, if you play around with the picker selection and the timer button, you'll notice that the cook time never deviates. That's because whenever `onTimerButton()` is triggered, `ounces` is always going to be the value to which it was initialized!

To fix this, you need to wire up an `IBAction` from your picker to the controller. Open **Carnivore WatchKit App/Interface.storyboard** in the main editor and **InterfaceController.swift** in the assistant editor.

Right-click the picker and drag from **selector** in the pop-up dialog to `InterfaceController`. Name your action `onWeightChanged`. Add the following code to your new method:

```
@IBAction func onWeightChanged(_ value: Int) {
  ounces = value + 1
}
```

The `value` parameter is the *index* of the item that is currently selected in your picker. Remember that when you set up your items, you used the range `1...32`, so your indices will actually be `0...31`.

Build and run. Your timer will now adjust based on the weight of the steak you're going to cook.

A sequence-style picker

Weight isn't the only factor when it comes to cooking the perfect steak. People prefer their food cooked in a variety of ways, from a light sear all the way to charred. To determine how long to cook a steak, you also need to know how done the diner wants it.

Recall from the previous chapter that the original Carnivore app let users select a doneness level ranging from rare to well done. WKInterfacePicker provides another convenient means of selecting an item from a set: a set of doneness levels based on the internal temperature of the meat while it's cooking or the cook temperature.

Knowing what "medium rare" means when actually cooking is much clearer if you can see an image that explains the concept! To accomplish this, you will add a **sequence** picker to make selecting a doneness level a more visual experience.

Open **Carnivore App/Interface.storyboard** and drag a **label** beneath the picker you previously added. Change your new label to have a **Horizontal Position** of **Center**, just like the weight label. This label will display the currently selected cook temperature.

Next, add another picker beneath that label. Change its **Style** to **Sequence**. Also, set its **Focus Style** to **Outline** so you can clearly tell when the picker is active. You'll use this picker to display a sequence of images representing the various cook temperatures or doneness levels.

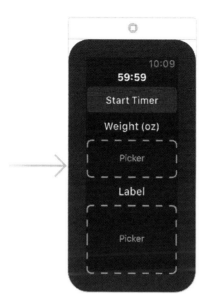

Open **InterfaceController.swift** in the assistant editor and add an IBOutlet for both the label and the picker you just added. Name them temperatureLabel and temperaturePicker, respectively.

While you're adding outlets, **right-click** the **new picker**, drag from the **selector** option to InterfaceController and add a new IBAction named onTemperatureChanged.

Change the code in onTemperatureChanged(_:) to the following:

```
@IBAction func onTemperatureChanged(_ value: Int) {
    let temp = MeatTemperature(rawValue: value)!
    cookTemp = temp
    temperatureLabel.setText(temp.stringValue)
}
```

This function takes the selected index in the picker and creates a MeatTemperature enum from it. It then sets the current cookTemp state variable and updates the temperatureLabel outlet you just created with the text that represents the cook temperature or doneness level.

> **Note:** If you don't remember which temperatures and strings are available, check out **CarnivoreKit/MeatTemperature.swift**.

The last step to set up your picker is to assign an image to each `WKPickerItem` to create a sequence. Before wiring it all up, open **Carnivore WatchKit App/Images.xcassets** and take a look at the numbered **temp** images.

These four images represent the cross section of a steak when cooked to various temperatures. As long as all of your images have the same dimensions, `WKInterfacePicker` will be able to cycle through them as you scroll with the digital crown.

> **Note:** All of the images have a black background because removing the transparency channel conserves image size. Apple recommends in the Apple Watch Human Interface Guidelines that you optimize your images as much as possible for the Watch's limited graphics processing power.

Go back to **InterfaceController.swift** and at the end of `awake(withContext:)`, add the following code:

```
// 1
var tempItems: [WKPickerItem] = []
for i in 1...4 {
  // 2
  let item = WKPickerItem()
  item.contentImage = WKImage(imageName: "temp-\(i)")
  tempItems.append(item)
}
// 3
temperaturePicker.setItems(tempItems)
// 4
onTemperatureChanged(0)
```

This should look familiar:

1. You create a mutable array to hold your instances of `WKPickerItem`, and iterate the range `1...4`.

2. You initialize a new `WKPickerItem` and assign a `WKImage` using the current step's value.

3. You set up the picker's items, just like you did with the previous picker.

4. Finally, you call `onTemperatureChanged(_:)` to initialize your controller and your label's state as if the first item had been selected.

Build and run the Watch app. Scroll through the meat selections, and your timer calculations will update according to the temperature and weight you select. Now that's well done!

Where to go from here?

In this chapter, you worked with two styles of `WKInterfacePicker`, each of which used the digital crown which lets you scroll through different picker items. You also got a glimpse of the creative possibilities of using pickers with image sequences.

Remember, there's also the stacked picker style. That style is best used for animating through a series of images that don't necessarily need to be in sequence but deserve their own images, such as cards or a photo album.

Pickers aren't the answer to fix every user experience, but whenever you need to select from any amount of data, `WKInterfacePicker` will make it incredibly easy to do so!

Chapter 6: Layout

By Ehab Amer

In 2008, when Apple first released the iOS SDK, layout was driven by *springs and struts*, a primitive layout system that automatically resized views based on their parents' edges. With the release of the iOS 6 SDK in 2012, Apple delivered a powerful new system called Auto Layout that's continued to improve over the years. Auto Layout is driven by *constraints* — relationships between views' sizes, positions and edges.

Fast forward to today, and WatchKit brings with it an entirely new layout system. Instead of deriving layout from constraints, WatchKit relies heavily on content size and spacing to position interface elements.

In this chapter, you'll learn the reasoning behind this new layout system and start to build an interface that's far more complex than the one in the previous chapter.

The app you'll make will display a photo along with some details, such as the time it was taken and the name of the photographer. You will focus only on the layout portion during this chapter — the remaining functionality is left as an exercise for the reader. :]

Getting started

Before jumping into building your first complex layout, you should take a look at the starter project's iPhone app to get a feel for what the Watch version will be like.

Open **Layout.xcodeproj** and build and run the scheme for the iOS app. You'll see something like the following screenshots:

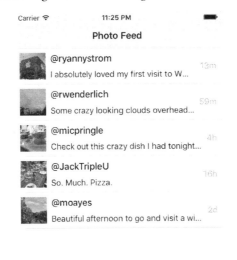 

Full-screen images look great when viewed on the iPhone. The larger screens on the 6 and 6s (and their upsized Plus versions) give you very detailed, super high resolution photos, with lots of screen real estate to add other metadata, such as the name of the person who posted the photo and any comments he or she might have about it.

But what happens when you only have 272x340 pixels on the 38 mm Apple Watch? Read on to find out how to use WatchKit layouts to transform a complex design into something simple and responsive.

> **Note:** Remember that both the 38 mm and 42 mm Apple Watches have Retina screens, so the 38 mm is really 136x170 *points* and the 42mm is 156x195.

Understanding layout in WatchKit

Before you start dragging, dropping and clicking in Interface Builder, you'll need a quick tour of the features of this new layout system.

There are only three new concepts you need to understand to get started building sophisticated interfaces: **groups**, **content sizing** and **relative spacing**.

Layout groups

You'll remember using several interface elements called **groups** in the previous chapter. Groups are instances of `WKInterfaceGroup`, which inherits from `WKInterfaceObject`, just like `WKInterfaceLabel` or `WKInterfaceTimer`.

If you've ever used an empty view in iOS as nothing more than a container to group and lay out other views, then groups in watchOS will feel instantly familiar. And just like `UIView`, `WKInterfaceGroup` is much more than a simple container for other interface elements. You can configure the appearance and behavior of a group in many different ways!

Open the header file **WKInterfaceGroup.h** and get a feel for all the things you can do with a group.

> **Note:** To open **WKInterfaceGroup.h** in Xcode, open the **Open Quickly** dialog (**Command-⇧-O**) and type "**WKInterfaceGroup**". When the autocomplete shows **WKInterfaceGroup.h**, press Return to view the file. Notice that the class is in Objective-C!

In addition to the functionality that they inherit from `WKInterfaceObject`, the appearance of groups can be highly customized:

- **`setBackgroundColor(_:)`** changes the background color.

- **`setCornerRadius(_:)`** changes the corner radius. No more fumbling with the `CALayer` property of a `UIView`!

- **`setBackgroundImage(_:)`** sets the background image using an image from the extensions asset catalog. It's nice to not have to add a `UIImageView`.

- **`setBackgroundImageData(_:)`** sets the background image data, usually when adding a series of images to animate.

- **`setBackgroundImageNamed(_:)`** sets the background image using an image from the Watch app's asset catalog.

- **`startAnimating()`** begins animating through the background images, if there's more than one.

- **`startAnimatingWithImagesInRange(_:duration:repeatCount:)`** is like `startAnimating()` but gives you a lot more control.

- **`stopAnimating()`** stops any image animations.

Look at the group-specific attributes in the Attributes Inspector in Interface Builder, and you'll see even more options you can use to create compelling layouts.

Layout is one of the most important attributes of a group, controlling the axis along which the interface elements inside the group are laid out. You can use either **Horizontal** or **Vertical**.

> **Note:** If you use a horizontal layout, make sure to pay attention to the sizes of any dynamic interface elements like labels. If they grow too big, they'll push any sibling elements offscreen.

Insets let you create a margin between the group and its contents. If you've ever worked with UIEdgeInset in classes such as UIScrollView, this will feel familiar. You can change the top, bottom, left and right insets independently for groups.

The Apple Watch Human Interface Guidelines recommend that interface elements in your interface controllers hug the side of the screen, because there's a black bezel around the physical screen that affords a natural margin. However, content towards the middle of the screen can sometimes benefit from a little extra padding, to prevent your interfaces becoming too cramped.

Spacing adjusts the distance *between* the elements within a group. Horizontal and vertical spacing add space to the x- and y-axes, respectively.

The attributes in the next section of the inspector are more self-explanatory. You can change the **Background** image, the drawing **Mode**, decide whether to **Animate** the background image, or simply select a background **Color**.

The last attribute in the section is **Radius**, which changes the corner radius of the group. The default radius value is 6 points, but this is only applied when you set either a background color or a background image; otherwise the group doesn't use rounded corners at all.

Note: When changing the radius attribute, pay attention to the layout and size of your content. Groups will automatically clip anything that falls outside the bounds of clipped corners. This is a great example of when it would be useful to adjust the insets.

Content size

Another interesting feature of this new layout system is that it's driven by **content size**: the combined size of all the content within each group in the interface.

In WatchKit, the space taken up by text is determined by an `NSAttributedString`, which contains attributes like the font, line spacing and color. WatchKit renders the text offscreen, determines the height and width based on the string's bounding box and then applies that to the layout.

Unlike in iOS, WatchKit automatically handles all of the layout for you.

Take a look at the example below. Instead of fussing with text bounding sizes, the groups are simply set to **Size To Fit Contents** and WatchKit takes care of the rest! To achieve the same effect in iOS, you'd have to create a number of constraints between your views and an outer scroll view.

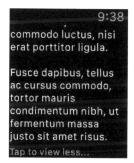

The **Lines** attribute is important when configuring any interface element that contains text, such as a label. This attribute informs the element to truncate any text where the number of lines exceeds the value you set here. Setting this property to 0 will allow as many lines as needed to lay out the text without truncating.

Relative spacing

The last important feature of the layout system provided by WatchKit is the ability to resize and position an interface element based on its parent's size and position. In WatchKit, the parent will always be a group.

Even when you're in Interface Builder, the root interface element of `WKInterfaceController` is a group.

Below, you can see the available attributes when editing any type of
`WKInterfaceObject` in Interface Builder:

You can change both the Horizontal and Vertical position attributes. You can align the
Horizontal position to the left, right or center and the Vertical position to the top, center
or bottom.

The layout system updates the position of any interface elements at three major points:

• When the interface is first loaded

• Any time the content, such as label text and background images, changes

• Any time sibling elements are hidden or unhidden

You can change the **Height** and **Width** attributes of an interface element to fit their
content, be relative to their container or be fixed to a certain value.

If you change either height or width to **Size To Fit Content**, the layout system decides
how tall and wide the interface element needs to be to fit its content. With a label, if you
set the width to fit its content, the label won't grow beyond the size of its containing
group.

For images, you should almost exclusively use **Size To Fit Content** along with
appropriately sized images. This results in pixel-perfect layout of your interfaces.

The setting **Relative to Container** allows you to specify a multiplier between 0 and 1, which represents the size of the interface element as a proportion of its parent's size. You can also change the adjustment value, which offsets the final size.

```
Parent[width|height] * multiplier + adjustment = [width|height]
```

For example, if you had a parent group with a width of 250 points and you wanted equally-sized images side by side, you would set their multipliers to 0.5 (or 50%), making each image 125 points wide. If you then realized the images needed to shrink a bit to account for padding, you could set each image view's adjustment to -10, making each image 115 points wide.

The last size setting, **Fixed**, allows you to manually set a width or height value to which the interface element will adhere, no matter its content size.

The below image demonstrates a label nested in a group with a fixed width and height. Notice the label is truncated because the group is too small to fit the text on a single line.

Fixed size is a good option to have in your tool belt, but use it with caution. Remember the Watch comes in two different sizes, with two different pixel dimensions. A fixed size on one screen may not look right on another.

Laying it all out

It's time to grab the starter project, crack your knuckles and get down to business.

For this chapter, you're going to build the layout block for a single post. There won't be much code. Most of what you'll learn is how to compose groups and other `WKInterfaceObject` elements to create a more complex layout in Interface Builder.

Open **Layout WatchKit App/Interface.storyboard** and find the default controller; it will have the default Xcode project class of `InterfaceController`. The controller will look something like this:

That's not very exciting is it? To spice it up, add your first **group** by finding it in the Object Library and dragging it into the controller. Inside this group, add an **image** element, once again dragging it from the Object Library.

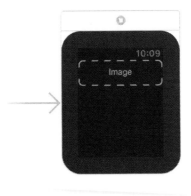

Select the image element you just added and open the Attributes Inspector; you'll see that the height and width are set to **Size to Fit Content**.

However, the image has the gray, dashed border because there isn't any content! Likewise, if you were to build and run the app now, you'd still have a black screen.

With the **image** still selected, change the **Image** property to **wwdc**.

Collecting metadata

Now that you've added the main attraction — the photo — it's time to add some of the other information included in a post. Remember, for now you're only adding user interface elements!

You need to add the username and time so that they appear right on top of the image, just like in the iPhone app, which is a new type of layout introduced in watchOS 4.

Go back to **Interface.storyboard** and add a new group inside the first group, above the image. You're going to add two labels: one for the username and one for the time the image was taken. Therefore you'll need something to contain them.

But wait a minute, where did your image go?

Look at the document outline, and you'll clearly see that the WWDC image element hasn't gone anywhere.

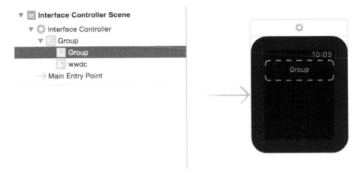

WKInterfaceGroup elements default to a *horizontal* layout. To add a header group, you're going to have to change that!

Select the group you added first, which contains both the group you just added and the WWDC image. Open the Attributes Inspector and change the **Layout** to **Overlap**, and change the horizontal alignment to **Left** or **Right**.

> **Note:** Make sure that the image is the first item in the document outline list, otherwise the image will block the content of the group behind it.

> **Note:** As of writing this chapter there's a bug in Xcode 9. Setting the horizontal alignment of an item to **Center** inside an overlap group with a height greater than the group, also aligns the item vertically. To avoid this behavior, you set the horizontal alignment to **Left** or **Right**.

That looks *much* better!

Drag two **labels** into this new group, and change the text to something more representative of the label, **@gruber** for the left and **13m** for the right.

Select the **rightmost label** that you just added and change its **Horizontal Alignment** to **Right**. This will make the label stick to the right edge of its container.

> **Note:** Any instance of `WKInterfaceObject`, including any descendants, default to having left horizontal alignment and top vertical alignment.

The nicely clipped corners are now gone from the image. This is because the new group has pushed the image down from the top of its parent, which was doing the clipping. However that was a nice visual touch, and `WKInterfaceGroup` makes rounded corners very simple!

Select the **parent group** that contains the header and image, and change its **Background Color** to **Black** with **50%** opacity.

It's starting to look good! But the header looks a little... *tight*, doesn't it? It would be nice to have room for longer usernames.

Select **both** of the **labels** in the header and change the font to **Text Styles - Subhead**. This will shrink the text a bit but still respect the user's font scaling preferences.

While you're at it, select the **rightmost label** and change its **Text Color** to **Light Gray**.

Finally, the labels are still sitting too close to the edge of their container group. The text lined up to the left and right edges is a little hard on the eyes. Let's cinch that in!

Select the **group** containing both of the labels and change the **Insets** to **Custom**, then enter the value 4 for both the **Left** and **right** insets.

Build and run. Behold your progress on the Watch!

Laying out buttons

Images and text are all well and good, but what use is an app that you can't interact with? Using buttons is an easy way to add interactive features to your app.

> **Note:** Check out Chapter 4, "UI Controls" to learn about other awesome interactive elements in WatchKit: maps, sliders and more!

Still in **Interface.storyboard**, drag a new **group** into the controller, just under the group that contains the image and labels, and then drag two **buttons** inside your new group.

You can only see one button. Remember how the WWDC image disappeared when you added the header group? That was because the group was set to a *horizontal* layout and the image was pushed offscreen. But this time, instead of switching to a vertical layout, change the **Width** of each **button** to **Relative to Container** with a value of **0.5**.

Using relative layouts is an easy way to squeeze all of your content into its container. It's like Auto Layout — without the pain!

> **Note:** Just because it's simple to cram all your elements into their containers doesn't mean you should. Interactions on the Apple Watch are *extremely* brief, and you want to make it as easy as possible for your users to do things like tap buttons. It's OK to make them big!

You're not going to wire up the buttons in this chapter, but for aesthetic purposes, change the **Text** of the buttons to **Like** and **Share**, respectively.

Dynamic layouts

Although you're restricted to using `WKInterfaceObject` elements and you have to use storyboards, that doesn't mean you can't get fancy with your layouts. There are a couple of properties that you can change on the fly, like height, width, alpha and hidden.

With the introduction of watchOS 2, you can even animate most of these properties.

In **Interface.storyboard**, drag a **button** element beneath the group that holds both of the buttons you added in the previous section. You might have to use the document outline to sneak it in there.

One nice thing about buttons in WatchKit is that they can either use the template background and label *or* act as their own group! This means you can stuff all sorts of other elements inside them and make the entire group interactive.

In the Attributes Inspector for the button you just added, change **Content** to **Group**. While you're there, change the new group's **Layout** to **Vertical**.

Drag three **labels** into your new button group.

Now come up with a quote to add for the WWDC image, something like, "My first WWDC was awesome! Can't wait for next year!" Set this as the text of the **first two labels** — yes, the *same* text for both labels. This will make sense in a minute!

Next, change each of the labels' attributes:

- Give the **first label** a **Font** of **Footnote**.

- Also give the **second label** a **Font** of **Footnote**, set **Lines** to **0** for an unlimited number of lines and **check** the **Hidden** box.

- Lastly, change the **Text** of the **last label** to **Tap to view more...**, give it a **Font** of **System 11.0** and set **Text Color** to **Light Gray Color**.

Your document outline and storyboard will look something like this:

You're going to be using the button's tap interactions to toggle between the single and unlimited line labels to make it appear as if you're expanding and collapsing the text!

But to make this work, you're going to have to leave the storyboard and write some simple code.

In the assistant editor, open **InterfaceController.swift**. Drag and create an IBOutlet for each of the three labels that have your comment text. Name them expandedCommentLabel, collapsedCommentLabel and moreLabel, from top to bottom. You'll have to use the document outline to make an outlet for the hidden label.

While you're at it, **right-click** the **button** in the **document outline** and drag from the **action** option to InterfaceController. Name the action onMoreButton.

Open **InterfaceController.swift** in the main editor, add a variable named expanded just beneath your outlets and initialize it to false. Your class will now have the following variables and method:

```swift
@IBOutlet var expandedCommentLabel: WKInterfaceLabel!
@IBOutlet var collapsedCommentLabel: WKInterfaceLabel!
@IBOutlet var moreLabel: WKInterfaceLabel!
var expanded = false

@IBAction func onMoreButton() {}
```

Add the following code inside onMoreButton():

```swift
// 1
expanded = !expanded
```

```
// 2
collapsedCommentLabel.setHidden(expanded)
expandedCommentLabel.setHidden(!expanded)
// 3
moreLabel.setText(
  "Tap to " + (expanded ? "view less" : "view more") + "...")
// 4
if expanded {
  scroll(to: expandedCommentLabel, at: .top, animated: true)
}
```

Taking each numbered comment in turn:

1. You invert the expanded flag.

2. You hide or show the collapsed and expanded label, depending on the current state of expanded.

3. You change the label's text to reflect the expanded or collapsed state.

4. If expanding, scroll to place the label at the top of the screen.

Build and run the Watch app; scroll down to the comment, then tap the comment and see how easy it is to not only add a simple interaction, but also to get automatic layout based on content size!

Screen autorotation

Have you ever been in a situation where you were showing the time on your watch to someone infront of you? You probably had to stand beside the person and move your wrist infront of him, or twist your wrist towards them to show them an upside-down screen.

watchOS 4 introduces a new feature called autorotation, which really helps with showing your watch screen to someone standing in front of you. To enable this, all it takes is setting a single **Bool** property to true!

In **InterfaceController.swift** add the following code:

```
override func awake(withContext context: Any?) {
  WKExtension.shared().isAutorotating = true
}
```

Here you set **WKExtension**'s **isAutorotating** to true when the inside awake(withContext:). This will prevent the screen from sleeping when you put ur wrist down. When you turn your wrist outwards, the app will now rotate so that anyone in front of you can see the screen in a right-side-up fashion.

Where to go from here?

This app currently represents the layout for one screen of what could be a fully functional app. Adding a new screen with a table that lists the posts and links the user to the interface you've created during this chapter would make a very usable app.

You can also wire up the Share and Like buttons, even if only to change some fake state. You'll definitely want to make sure you're comfortable with dynamically changing your interfaces with WatchKit.

Chapter 7: Tables

By Ehab Amer

When building any type of software application, you'll almost always find yourself needing to handle a dynamic amount of data. Typically, data sets are structured into arrays, sets or dictionaries, and often tables are the best way to display these collections.

Ever since the first proto-developer created the first program, we've had to build tools to abstract the handling and display of these data sets. `UITableView` in UIKit is an example of such a tool: a dynamic view that Apple has optimized to display an infinite amount of data in an efficient manner.

When creating apps for the Apple Watch, you'll undoubtedly run into the same scenario: You've got a dynamic collection of data and you need to display it on the tiny 38 mm screen. This chapter will show you how to do just that.

Tables in WatchKit

Even if you've never built an app for iOS, as an iOS user you've experienced table views... everywhere. From Settings to Mail, `UITableView` is one of the staple views in iOS.

`UITableView` isn't available in WatchKit, but Apple has your back — in the form of `WKInterfaceTable`.

WatchKit's table class

`WKInterfaceTable` is similar to `UITableView` in that it manages the display of a collection of data, but the similarities pretty much end there.

For starters, `WKInterfaceTable` can only display a single dimension of data — no sections. This forces you to give your interfaces simple data structures.

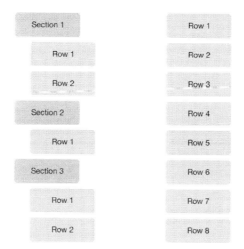

Tables in iOS   Tables in WatchKit

Just like other `WKInterfaceController` and `WKInterfaceObject` classes, `WKInterfaceTable` works perfectly with storyboards. Once you've connected a table from your storyboard to an `IBOutlet`, you simply set the number of rows to display and the row type, like this:

```
table.setNumberOfRows(10, withRowType: "IngredientRow")
```

This single line sets up a table with 10 rows. You don't need to implement any data source or delegate protocols or override any methods. That's pretty sweet.

The **row type** in the code above is an identifier that behaves just like a `UITableViewCell` reuse identifier.

Enough with the theory — let's get cracking!

Getting started

Open **Recipes.xcodeproj** and build and run the iPhone app to get a feel for your Watch app's companion. This app is a simple recipe list that lets you browse each recipe's ingredients and directions.

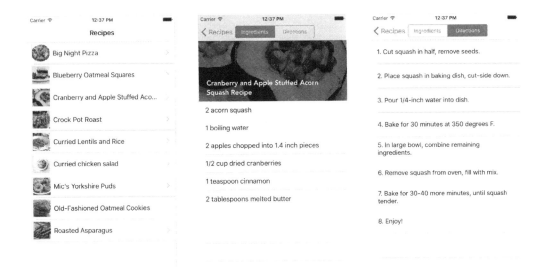

Notice how the iPhone app takes advantage of `UITableView`. There are a dynamic number of recipes, ingredients and directions — exactly what a table is meant to handle.

Open **Recipes WatchKit App\Interface.storyboard** and find the only controller in the scene. It's completely blank, waiting for you to fill it out.

First you need to display a list of all the recipes you have available. From the Object Library, drag a **table** into the controller.

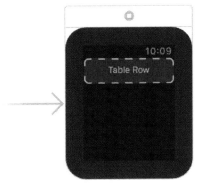

A new table gives you a placeholder row with an etched outline. You'll recognize this as almost identical to the placeholder for a `WKInterfaceGroup`, as you found in Chapter 6, "Layout". Take a look at a side-by-side comparison of the two placeholders.

Click on the **Table Row** and notice in the document outline that it *actually is* a group! Each row in a `WKInterfaceTable` gets a base group interface element.

Drag two **labels** into the placeholder table row group. The labels will align themselves horizontally, but since the text will quickly expand, a vertical layout would be more manageable.

Select the **group** of the table row and change the **Layout** to **Vertical**. The row is now cutting off a little bit of the bottom label.

There's an easy fix. Since the base element of a table row is a group, it too can automatically size itself based on its content. With a couple of clicks in Interface Builder, Xcode will size all of your table rows *automatically*. No more mucking with dynamic cell heights or doing manual calculations!

Select the **group** of the table row and set the **Size Height** to **Size To Fit Content**. This will expand your table row to fit both labels.

The topmost label will display the name of the recipe, while the bottom label will display the total number of ingredients. This will give the user a clue about how much time they'll need to spend on the recipe. It might not be the night for an elaborate meal!

Select the **top label** and change **Lines** to **0**. This will allow the label to word wrap for as many lines as it needs. Since you've already set the group to size itself relative to its content, this means all the layout and sizing will happen automatically.

Next, select the **bottom label** and change the **Font** to **Footnote** and the **Color** to **Light Gray Color**, so the label has less visual prominence:

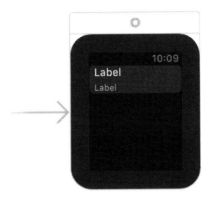

Controlling each row

Just as each cell in a UITableView is powered by a UITableViewCell subclass, WKInterfaceTable requires you to create what's called a **row controller** to represent each row.

A row controller has outlets and actions that are wired to the row in the storyboard. The WKInterfaceController that owns the table is then responsible for setting up and configuring your row controllers.

> **Note:** There is no row controller class. Each row controller only needs to inherit from NSObject to work with WKInterfaceTable rows. Remember that WatchKit interface objects are *proxy objects*, and not views themselves. Refer back to Chapter 3, "Architecture", for more information about proxy objects in WatchKit.

Right-click the **Recipes WatchKit Extension** group and select **New File....** Create a new **watchOS/WatchKit Class** that inherits from NSObject and name the file **RecipeRowController**.

Open **Recipes WatchKit App\Interface.storyboard** in the main editor and select the **Table Row Controller** from the document outline.

In the Identity Inspector, change the **Class** of the row to `RecipeRowController`. Then in the Attributes Inspector, change the **Identifier** to `RecipeRowType`.

Open **Recipes WatchKit Extension\RecipeRowController.swift** in the assistant editor.

Right-click and drag from the **top label** in the row to `RecipeRowController` and create a new outlet named `titleLabel`. Repeat this for the bottom label and name the outlet `ingredientsLabel`.

While you have **Interface.storyboard** open in the main editor, open **RecipesController.swift** in the assistant editor. **Right-click** and drag from the **table** in the storyboard to `RecipesController` to create a new outlet named `table`.

Filling the table with data

Unlike `UITableView`, `WKInterfaceTable` has no delegate or data source protocols that you have to implement. Instead, there are only two main functions you need to use to add and display data:

- **`setNumberOfRows(_:withRowType:)`** specifies the number of rows in the table as well as each row controller's **identifier**, which in this case would be the string `RecipeRowType` that you added to the row controller in your storyboard. Use this method if all the rows in the table have the same identifier.

- **`rowController(at:)`** returns a row controller at a given index. You must call this after adding rows to a table with either `setNumberOfRows(_:withRowType:)` or `insertRows(at:withRowType:)`.

Open **Recipes WatchKit Extension\RecipesController.swift** and add an instance variable so you have access to recipe data:

```
let recipeStore = RecipeStore()
```

You can find `RecipeStore` in the `Shared\Storage` group; it reads recipe data in a specific scheme from `Recipes.json` and loads it into memory. Once you've initialized it, you can access available data through the `recipes` property.

Next, implement `awake(withContext:)` for `RecipesController`:

```
override func awake(withContext context: Any?) {
  super.awake(withContext: context)
  // 1
  table.setNumberOfRows(recipeStore.recipes.count,
    withRowType: "RecipeRowType")
  // 2
  for (index, recipe) in recipeStore.recipes.enumerated() {
    // 3
```

```
    let controller =
      table.rowController(at: index) as! RecipeRowController
    // 4
    controller.titleLabel.setText(recipe.name)
    controller.ingredientsLabel.setText(
      "\(recipe.ingredients.count) ingredients")
  }
}
```

Taking this step by step:

1. Use the `count` of the recipes to set the number of rows in the table. This table only has one type of row, so you pass `RecipeRowType` for the identifier.

2. Iterate through the rows with the handy Swift `enumerated()` function, so you can get the object *and* the index in one pass.

3. Next, get a row controller for each row in the table. You can force-unwrap to `RecipeRowController`, since you're only using one type of row in the table.

4. Finally, set the title to the recipe's name, and the ingredients to a count of the total number of ingredients in the table.

Build and run the Watch app. Check out your new list of recipes, now conveniently available on your wrist!

Getting directions

You have the recipes available in a list, but the app isn't *useful* yet. What good is the name of a recipe without any directions? If you're hungry, it might be a mild form of torture. To include the directions, you need another controller to display all the steps in a recipe.

With the dynamic nature of each recipe's list of steps, a table would be an excellent choice here, just like in the iPhone app counterpart.

Open **Recipes WatchKit App\Interface.storyboard** and drag a new **interface controller** into the scene.

From the document outline, select the **RecipeRowType**, right-click and drag to your new controller. When you let go, a modal will appear. Select the **Push** option to create a segue between the two controllers.

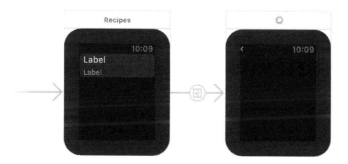

`WKInterfaceTable` rows have the ability to trigger navigation events when someone selects them. In this case, you're implementing a *push* navigation to the new controller from the selected row.

> **Note:** To learn more about different navigation types, like modals and pages, check out Chapter 8, "Navigation".

Open **RecipesController.swift** and add the following method:

```
override func contextForSegue(withIdentifier
  segueIdentifier: String, in table: WKInterfaceTable,
  rowIndex: Int) -> Any? {
  return recipeStore.recipes[rowIndex]
}
```

Overriding this `WKInterfaceController` method lets you decide what context to pass to the receiving controller, via `awake(withContext:)`, when you trigger a segue from a table row selection. This method is *incredibly* convenient, because it gives you all the information you need: the identifier of the segue and the index of the selected row.

Since you only have one row and one segue, you can safely assume this method is called only when someone taps a recipe!

Go back to **Interface.storyboard** to start setting up your new controller.

Drag a **table** into the new controller. In the Attributes Inspector, change **Prototypes** to **2**. You're going to use the first row as the "header" of the recipe and then add a row for each step in the recipe's directions.

Drag a **label** element into the **first row group**. Change this label's **Lines** to **0** so it will word wrap, as you did for the previous table; also, change the **Font** to **Headline**. This label will display the name of the recipe.

Drag another **label** into the **second row group** and change the **Lines** to **0**. You don't need to do anything else for this label, which will contain the text for one of the recipe's directions.

Select the **first row's group** and change the **Color** to **Clear Color** to help the header stand out from each of the steps.

For both of the **row groups**, change the **Size Height** to **Size To Fit Content**.

Your interface should now look like this:

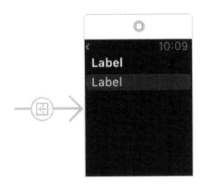

Using multiple rows

As you did in the previous section, you need to make row controller classes for each row, so that you can connect interface element outlets and relate a class to a specific identifier.

Right-click **Recipes WatchKit Extension** and select **New File...**. Create a new **watchOS/ WatchKit Class** that subclasses NSObject, and name it **RecipeHeaderController**.

Do this again to create a class named **RecipeStepController**.

Back in **Interface.storyboard**, select the **first row controller**. Change its **Class** to RecipeHeaderController and its **Identifier** to RecipeHeader. Also, since you can't tap these rows, **uncheck** the **Selectable** option.

Repeat this process for the **second row controller** using the class RecipeStepController and the identifier RecipeStep.

Open **RecipeHeaderController.swift** in the assistant editor. Create an outlet from the label in the row and name it `titleLabel`.

Next, open **RecipeStepController.swift** in the assistant editor, create an outlet for that row's label and name it `stepLabel`.

You need a class for your new controller, so right-click **Recipes WatchKit Extension** and select **New File...**. Create a new **watchOS/WatchKit Class** that inherits from `WKInterfaceController` and name it **RecipeDetailController**.

Back in **Interface.storyboard**, change the **Class** of your new controller to `RecipeDetailController`. Make sure that the **Module** is set to **Recipes_WatchKit_Extension** and *not* to the main app.

Finally, select the **table** in the new controller and, with **RecipeDetailController.swift** open in the assistant editor, create an outlet named `table`.

Just to recap, you should now have:

- `RecipeDetailController`, created with a `WKInterfaceTable` outlet and set to the new controller's class;

- `RecipeHeaderController`, created with one `WKInterfaceLabel` outlet and connected to the first row in the table;

- `RecipeStepController`, created with one `WKInterfaceLabel` outlet and connected to the second row in the table.

Good work setting everything up! Now let's get cooking.

Open **RecipeDetailController.swift** and replace `awake(withContext:)` with the following code:

```
override func awake(withContext context: Any?) {
  super.awake(withContext: context)
  // 1
  if let recipe = context as? Recipe {
    // 2
    let rowTypes: [String] = ["RecipeHeader"]
    table.setRowTypes(rowTypes)
    // 3
    for i in 0..<table.numberOfRows {
      // 4
      let row = table.rowController(at: i)
      if let header = row as? RecipeHeaderController {
        header.titleLabel.setText(recipe.name)
      }
    }
  }
}
```

1. You make sure that whatever context is being passed exists and is of type `Recipe`.

2. Next, you create an array of the row controller identifiers and set it on the `WKInterfaceTable`. You have to use `setRowTypes(_:)` when dealing with multiple row controller types. For now, you simply set up the header row controller. The number of rows in the table will directly correlate with the length of the array passed in this method.

3. Next, you iterate the rows in the table by using the convenience `numberOfRows` property on the table.

4. Finally, you get the row controller at each index, and if the controller is of type `RecipeHeaderController`, you set up the `titleLabel` with the recipe's name.

Build and run, and select a recipe to view your one cell!

Go back to **RecipeDetailController.swift** and update the `if`-statement inside `awake(withContext:)` to the following:

```swift
if let recipe = context as? Recipe {
  // 1
  let rowTypes: [String] =
    ["RecipeHeader"] + recipe.steps.map({ _ in "RecipeStep" })
  table.setRowTypes(rowTypes)
  for i in 0..<table.numberOfRows {
    let row = table.rowController(at: i)
    if let header = row as? RecipeHeaderController {
      header.titleLabel.setText(recipe.name)
    // 2
    } else if let step = row as? RecipeStepController {
      step.stepLabel.setText("\(i). " + recipe.steps[i - 1])
    }
  }
}
```

1. Swift makes dealing with arrays incredibly simple. Here you create an array of `"RecipeStep"` identifiers for each `step` in the recipe. You also append the mapped array of identifiers to the header identifier array, giving you a list of strings. The first string is for the header and the rest are for the steps.

2. You add an `else-if` statement to check if the row controller is of type `RecipeStepController`. If it is, you set the text of the step label to the step number and the step text. Remember, because you added a header, you need to subtract 1 from the index to map the row index back to your data.

Build and run the watch app. Now you'll see the name of the recipe as well as all the cooking instructions.

Creating multiple sections

`UITableView` has a data source that has methods to return the number of sections, as well as the number of rows in each section — not to mention all of the convenient APIs in `UITableViewDelegate` that let you construct and configure section and row views.

`WKInterfaceTable` is conspicuously absent of any such APIs. All of the `WKInterfaceTable` methods expect a *single-dimensional* list of data—in other words, just an array. You can't use nested data types.

To work within this limitation, you somehow need to convert any *multi-dimensional* data structures into a flat structure.

You're going to simulate headers in a WatchKit table using the two different row prototypes you created in the previous section.

The following image demonstrates how you can use the differently styled prototype rows to give the *appearance* of section headers:

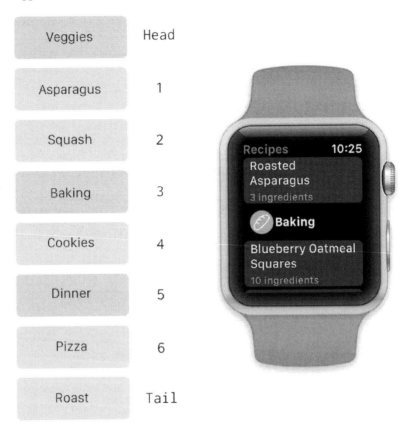

There are three methods that add data to a table:

- **setNumberOfRows(_:withRowType:)** adds rows that all have the same row controller identifier. This won't help you create sections, since you can only have a single row type!

- **setRowTypes(_:)** lets you pass in an array of varying row controller identifiers as strings. The identifiers need to match the ones configured in your storyboard, but they can be completely different from one another.

- **insertRowsAtIndexes(_:withRowType:)** inserts a single row type for the provided NSIndexSet. But, there's no limit to the number of times you can call this method. So in theory, you could iterate your sections and insert as you see fit!

Before you can go adding new rows, you first need the interface all set up. Open **Interface.storyboard** and select the **table** of your first WKInterfaceController, the one titled "Recipes". Open the **Attributes Inspector** and set **Prototypes** to 2.

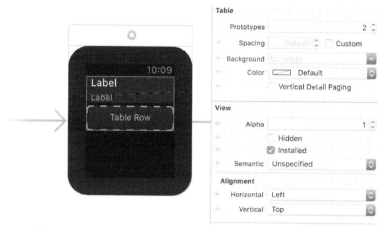

Add an **image** and **label**. Make the following property changes:

- The image's **image** property to **veggies**
- The image and label's **vertical alignment** to **center**
- The label's **font** to **headline**
- The group's **color** to **clear color**

Your interface builder should look like this:

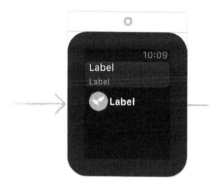

Right-click the **Recipes WatchKit Extension** group and select **New File...**. Create a new **WatchKit Class** named **HeaderRowController** that subclasses **NSObject**.

Go back to **Interface.storyboard** and select the **row controller** prototype that you just added. In the identity inspector, change the **class** to your new HeaderRowController class. Then in the Attributes Inspector, change the **identifier** to **HeaderRowType** and uncheck **selectable**.

Open **HeaderRowController.swift** in the assistant editor. Right-click and drag to create IBOutlets for the **image** and **label** that you just added. Name them **image** and **label**, respectively. Your HeaderRowController should just look like this:

```
class HeaderRowController: NSObject {
  @IBOutlet var image: WKInterfaceImage!
  @IBOutlet var label: WKInterfaceLabel!
}
```

Now that your new row controller is ready to go, its time to add them to the table and map your data!

You're going to use insertRows(at:withRowType:) to simplify adding and configuring your sections, but since you're going to do this for *each type string*, you'll want to abstract some of that work.

Open **RecipesController.swift** and add this new method:

```
func add(withType type: String, recipes: [Recipe]) {
  // 1
  let rows = table.numberOfRows

  // 2
  table.insertRows(at: NSIndexSet(index: rows) as IndexSet,
withRowType: "HeaderRowType")

  // 3
  let itemRows = NSIndexSet(indexesIn: NSRange(location: rows +
1, length: recipes.count))
  table.insertRows(at: itemRows as IndexSet, withRowType:
"RecipeRowType")
}
```

1. You will call this function multiple times, so each time you need the current number of rows in the table before adding new ones.

2. Insert a HeaderRowType row. This is your section header row controller that you just created.

3. Insert RecipeRowType row controllers after the section header.

Calling insertRows(at:withRowType:) will only insert the row controllers, it doesn't actually *configure* them. This is the same as when you called setRowTypes(_) earlier: the correct row counts will be there, they just aren't set up.

At the end of your new add(withType:recipes:) method, add the following code:

```
for i in rows..<table.numberOfRows {
  // 1
```

```
    let controller = table.rowController(at: i)

    // 2
    if let controller = controller as? HeaderRowController {
      controller.image.setImageNamed(type.lowercased())
      controller.label.setText(type)
    // 3
    } else if let controller = controller as? RecipeRowController
  {
      let recipe = recipes[i - rows - 1]
      controller.titleLabel.setText(recipe.name)
      controller.ingredientsLabel.setText("\
  (recipe.ingredients.count) ingredients")
    }
  }
```

1. Iterate over the rows that you just added and fetch a row controller for each index.

2. If the row controller is a `HeaderRowController` just use the `type` parameter and setup the `label` and `image`.

3. If the row controller is a `RecipeRowController`, grab the `Recipe` from the array parameter (subtracting 1 because of the header) and setup the row controller like you did before.

An awesome abstraction is only as good as the way you use it.

Next, add a new instance variable:

```
var map = [String: [Recipe]]()
```

Replace the implementation of `awake(withContext:)` with the following:

```
override func awake(withContext context: Any?) {
  super.awake(withContext: context)

  // 1
  for recipe in recipeStore.recipes {
    var arr = map[recipe.type] ?? [Recipe]()
    arr.append(recipe)
    map[recipe.type] = arr
  }

  // 2
  for (type, recipes) in map {
    add(withType: type, recipes: recipes)
  }
}
```

1. Create a `Dictionary` mapping the recipe type `String` to an array of the recipes. This lets you collect and organize the recipes to their category.

2. Add each section with the `type` and `recipes` from the `Dictionary` you just created.

Lastly, replace the the implementation of `contextForSegue(withIdentifier:in:rowIndex:)` with the following:

```
override func contextForSegue(withIdentifier segueIdentifier:
String,
  in table: WKInterfaceTable, rowIndex: Int) -> Any? {
  var originalIndex = rowIndex
  for (_, recipes) in map {
    originalIndex -= 1
    if originalIndex < recipes.count {
      return recipes[originalIndex]
    }
    originalIndex -= recipes.count
  }
  return nil
}
```

> **Note:** There is plenty of room for improvement here for a better user experience. For instance, how would you go about sorting the types and recipes within each section?

Build and run the watch app. You should see all of the same recipes, now sorted into different sections with headers. It's time to go make yourself lunch!

Where to go from here?

What you've seen here is just the beginning of what you can do with tables. For instance, because row controllers each have their own sizable groups, you can get creative by adding lots of interface elements with as much dynamic content as you like.

`WKInterfaceTable` is designed to be simple, but you can definitely bend it to your will.

Chapter 8: Navigation

By Ehab Amer

To build anything more than a single-screen app for the Apple Watch, you're going to need some means of navigating around the Watch app itself.

You're likely used to the many ways of navigating in iOS: navigation controllers, modal presentations, tab controllers, page controllers and so forth. On top of the built-in means of navigation, you can also take matters into your own hands and build custom `UIView` and `UIViewController` containers.

Navigation in WatchKit uses familiar concepts and takes the following forms:

- **Hierarchical**: Similar to `UINavigationController`.

- **Page-based**: Similar to `UIPageViewController`.

- **Modal**: Any type of presentation or dismissal transition.

- **Menus**: A system modal menu with option buttons.

In WatchKit, unlike in UIKit, you are strictly limited to these navigation methods. There is no custom navigation. In fact, you can't even mix and match hierarchical navigation and page-based navigation.

Well, not *strictly*. You can use modals with either type — that is, you can modally present one type from the other. All you need to do is pick a base navigation type for your app and then decide whether mixing with modals is appropriate.

In this chapter, you'll first take a closer look at each of the different forms of navigation in WatchKit. After that, you'll dive into implementing a mixed navigation hierarchy in an app designed to help you navigate a color palette!

Getting around in WatchKit

Since the navigation systems in WatchKit are so limited, it's worth taking a moment to familiarize yourself with each type of navigation before turning to an app.

Hierarchical navigation

Hierarchical navigation will be one of the concepts most familiar to developers coming from iOS. In UIKit, `UINavigationController` manages pushing and popping child controllers and their animations.

WatchKit has a very similar system:

- You can push instances of `WKInterfaceController` onto the navigation stack.

- Swipe gestures and back buttons are built-in.

- You can use storyboards to set up the navigation, or you can do it in code.

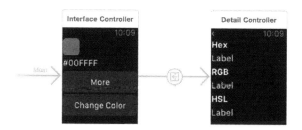

Instead of having a master navigation controller, WatchKit handles all of the navigation for you. You can simply Control-drag from a button to a controller, or simply call `pushController(withName:context:)` in your code.

Chapter 3, "Architecture", briefly touched on an important concept, and it's worth repeating here. When using a hierarchical navigation system, WatchKit gives you an optional `context` parameter that you can pass between controllers as you navigate.

You'll most commonly use the `context` parameter when you're pushing from a master controller to a detail controller in the navigation stack. Instead of intercepting "stringly" typed segues or adding lots of custom methods and properties, you can simply pass context objects between controllers.

UIKit has a great architecture for creating views, laying out their subviews and separating the concerns between controllers and views. However, communication between controllers has always been difficult. Using context-passing in WatchKit will keep your app's architecture clean and expressive.

> **Note**: You'll get your hands on context objects later in this chapter as well as throughout the rest of the book!

Page-based navigation

This is the second main form of navigation in WatchKit. A page-based navigation structure is essentially a group of `WKInterfaceController` instances strung together laterally, between which you can swipe. Each page should contain a unique chunk of information and perform a unique function. In UIKit, this would be most similar to a `UIPageViewController`, which manages several instances of `UIViewController`, as seen in the Weather app.

When building a page-based WatchKit app, you aren't able to pass a context object between the different controllers in the group, nor are you able to use a hierarchical navigation within its pages, *ever*. It's one or the other.

Note: You *can* get a mix of page-based navigation and hierarchical navigation by presenting either one modally from the other.

Apple presented an example of a page-based Watch app at the Apple Watch announcement — a timepiece app that has pages containing different representations of time, like digital, analog and solar.

To wire up a page-based interface, you simply have to connect each `WKInterfaceController` in Interface Builder, defining it as the next page. You'll have an initial controller — the one shown first — and a list of other controllers between which you can swipe back and forth.

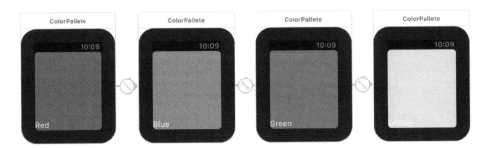

You do have limited control of a page-based app's hierarchy in code. There are three methods you can call:

- `becomeCurrentPage()`: Call this from within an instance of `WKInterfaceController` to animate that controller into view.

- `reloadRootControllers(withNamesAndContexts:)`: You can use this method to dynamically load different controllers into your interface. This can be useful for enabling or disabling certain controllers, based on data availability or user settings.

- `reloadRootPageControllers(withNames:contexts:orientation:pageIndex:)`: Similar to the method above, but allows you to choose vertical or horizontal paging and set the current page.

Modal navigation

The last possible means of getting around in WatchKit is by modal navigation. This is a familiar concept to anyone who's built iOS and Mac apps: think full screen pop-ups.

When you present a `WKInterfaceController` modally, it animates into view from the bottom of the screen, taking up the entire interface.

Controllers presented modally have a built-in cancel button for getting back to the underlying controller. You can change the title of this button to something such as "Done" or "Finished", depending on the context of your modal.

You can display a `WKInterfaceController` modally by either wiring it up in Interface Builder or calling one of the following methods in code:

- **`presentController(withName:context:)`**: This method displays a single `WKInterfaceController` modally. Note that you can pass a context object just as you can in hierarchical navigation.

- **`presentController(withNamesAndContexts:)`**: This method lets you display several instances of `WKInterfaceController` modally using page-based navigation, as previously discussed.

  In the event that your modal has multiple pages, use this method to provide easy access. This is an example of how you can combine multiple types of navigation.

- **`dismissController()`**: Use this method to dismiss the modal interface controller.

You should reserve modal navigation for context-specific interfaces, option selection or quick actions, all of which allow you to interrupt the current workflow for a specific purpose.

Menus

When you force touch on a watch interface configured with menu items, it displays the context menu with all of its items. Each menu item has a title that's displayed as text in the interface and an image that's displayed as a vibrant image over a blurred background.

You create menus by adding them to `WKInterfaceControllers` in your storyboard. Simply configure the items with a title and image (custom or default) and connect an `IBAction` to execute when the user taps on the option, and you're done!

Getting started

Open the **ColorPicker.xcodeproj** starter project included with this chapter. You'll see several groups, including:

- **ColorPicker**: This group has basic functionality to run the app on an iOS device. You won't be adding anything here, but instead making the Watch app more functional than this version.

- **ColorPicker WatchKit App**: This group contains the storyboard and resources you'll need to navigate throughout the app.

- **ColorPicker WatchKit Extension**: This group contains all the classes and code required to run the Watch app.

- **ColorPickerKit**: This is simply a single shared file that the iOS app and extension use to share models and logic. `ColorManager` is a singleton that knows about the colors available to your app along with the state of the selected color.

Build and run the Watch app and check out the screen.

Right now, the app isn't very functional — neither of the buttons do anything! This app is intended to serve as a color picker, where users can select from a palette and view details about the chosen color, like its red, green and blue (RGB) values, or its hue, saturation and light (HSL) values. The standard hex color format should also be visible.

You can tell just by looking at the buttons that this app is, at its root, going to have a hierarchical navigation structure. Each button will either push to a child controller or present a modal.

You'll be making this app fully functional by wiring up these buttons to navigation controllers to access the color palette, change colors and view a color's details. By the end, you'll have had a taste of all three forms of navigation in WatchKit.

A modally-presented, paged-based palette

Open **ColorPicker/WatchKit App/Interface.storyboard** and drag in a new **Interface Controller**. Go to the Attributes Inspector and change your new controller's **Identifier** to **ColorPalette**.

Drag in a new **group** element onto this controller and set its **Width** and **Height** size attributes to **Relative to Container**. Change the group's **background color** to **red** so you can confirm it's sized correctly.

While you're setting up interface elements, add a **label** as a child element to the group you just added. Change the label's **Vertical Position** to **Bottom**.

Your storyboard will now look something like this:

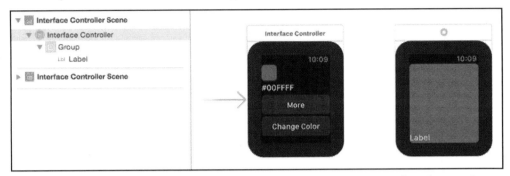

This controller will act as a template for a series of color swatches. You'll end up with a paged group of controllers that each has a background color of a swatch you can select, along with the hex value of the color.

Before you can start using the controller, you need a new class. Create one by selecting **ColorPicker WatchKit Extension** and selecting **File\New\File...**. Add a **watchOS/ WatchKit Class** named **ColorController**, and make sure it's subclassing WKInterfaceController.

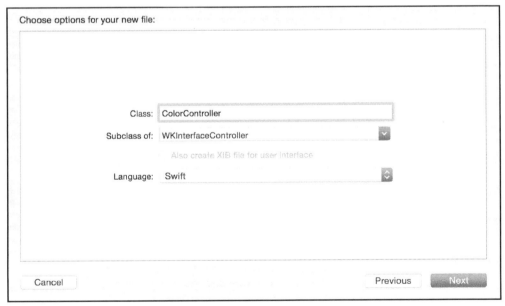

Open **ColorController.swift** and make sure that the file imports WatchKit. Sometimes Xcode will decide to import Cocoa in Watch app projects.

Open **Interface.storyboard** in the main editor and **ColorController.swift** in the assistant editor. In the storyboard, change the class of the new controller you created above to `ColorController`.

Drag an `IBOutlet` from both the **group** and **label** that you added previously and name them `backgroundGroup` and `label`, respectively.

Also, in **ColorController.swift**, add a variable to capture the current controller's color value, initialized so it's not optional:

```
var activeColor = UIColor.white
```

Remember from the previous section that you can pass a `context` object to a presented or pushed controller in WatchKit. This object is of type `Any`, so you can really make it whatever you want.

With **ColorController.swift** still open, add the following method:

```
func update(color: UIColor) {
  activeColor = color
  backgroundGroup.setBackgroundColor(color)
  label.setText("#" + color.hexString)
}
```

This method updates the controller's views and selected color state.

Replace the `awake(withContext:)` definition with the following:

```
override func awake(withContext context: Any?) {
  super.awake(withContext: context)
  if let color = context as? UIColor {
    update(color: color)
  }
}
```

This code checks that the `context` object that it receives is a `UIColor`, and if so, updates the controller.

> **Note:** `hexString`, an extension of `UIColor` in `ColorManager.swift`, simply converts the RGB values of the color to a hexadecimal representation.

Presenting the modal

Having a modal controller is great, but it's not of much value if your app doesn't present it!

Open **ColorPicker WatchKit App/Interface.storyboard** in the main editor and **InterfaceController.swift** in the assistant editor. **Right-click** the **Change Color button** and drag from the **selector** to your `InterfaceController` class. Create an `IBAction` named `changeColors`.

Update `changeColors()` to have the following implementation:

```
@IBAction func changeColors() {
  let colors = ColorManager.defaultManager.availableColors
  let namesAndContexts: [(name: String, context: AnyObject)] =
    colors.map { c in ("ColorPalette", c) }
  presentController(withNamesAndContexts: namesAndContexts)
}
```

This method takes the array of available colors from the `ColorManager` singleton and maps it to an array of (String : AnyObject) tuples. The `name` represents the identifiers you previously gave the `ColorController` in your storyboard, and the `context` is the color that will be sent to that controller when it is presented. Then, you call `presentController(withNamesAndContexts:)`, which modally presents a series of paged controllers.

Build and run the Watch app. Tap the Change Colors button. You'll now have a modal presentation of a paged list of color controllers; try swiping left and right through the controllers.

Isn't it amazing how, with very little setup, you have both a modal and a paged navigation in one?

Notice how the title of the color controller is "Cancel". That's a little harsh, isn't it? The idea is to present a list of colors and *select* one, not cancel.

To change the title of the modal return button, open **Interface.storyboard** and select the **ColorPalette** controller. Change the **Title** attribute to **Done**.

Build and run again, and check the title of the modal return button. It should look a little more user-friendly:

Maintaining color selection

You've probably noticed that when you tap the "Done" button, nothing really changes with the root controller. You're still stuck on whatever color and text the storyboard is configured with.

To change that, open **ColorController.swift** and add the following code:

```
func updateSelectedColor() {
    ColorManager.defaultManager.selectedColor = activeColor
}
```

This method updates the state of the `ColorManager` singleton used in other parts of the app. Then call `updateSelectedColor()` in this overridden method:

```
override func didAppear() {
    super.didAppear()
    updateSelectedColor()
}
```

`didAppear()` is called as soon as the controller displays on the Watch's screen. As you swipe between pages, you move from one controller to another, and `didAppear()` is called each time. Thus, you can assume that when this method is called, it is presenting the "selected" color.

All you have to do is update the value of the `ColorManager` singleton, which is what you do above.

That will update your app's state, but what about getting the root controller to update its user interface?

Open **InterfaceController.swift** and add the following implementation of `willActivate()`:

```
override func willActivate() {
  super.willActivate()
  let color = ColorManager.defaultManager.selectedColor
  colorGroup.setBackgroundColor(color)
  label.setText("#" + color.hexString)
}
```

Since this method is called *just before* the controller is displayed, it's a good place to update your interface before the color controllers are dismissed.

> **Note:** `willActivate()` is a good double-whammy, in that it's called on first run of your controller as well as any other time that the controller is about to be presented. This will feel familiar to anyone who's worked with `viewWillAppear(_:)` in `UIViewController`; it's a great opportunity to update your interface's state before you show it to the user.

Build and run the Watch app. Change to another color and dismiss. You'll be able to cycle through colors and see your UI update.

Pushing a child controller

You've saved the most common and familiar type of navigation for last: hierarchical navigation, with its typical *push and pop* style of interface.

Open **ColorPicker WatchKit App/Interface.storyboard** and add a new interface controller. Drag and drop **6** new **labels** into the controller. Change the **Font** of the **first**, **third**, and **fifth** labels to **Headline**. Also change the text of the same three labels to **Hex**, **RGB** and **HSL**, respectively.

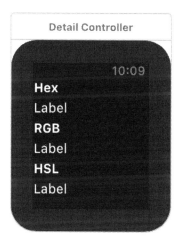

Add a new file to **ColorPicker WatchKit Extension**. Make it a **watchOS/WatchKit Class** named **DetailController**, which subclasses `WKInterfaceController`.

Open **Interface.storyboard** and change your new controller's **class** to `DetailController`.

Open **DetailController.swift** in the assistant editor and create an `IBOutlet` for the second, fourth and sixth labels:

- Name the second label `hexLabel`
- Name the fourth label `rgbLabel`
- Name the sixth label `hslLabel`

```
class DetailController: WKInterfaceController {

    @IBOutlet var hexLabel: WKInterfaceLabel!
    @IBOutlet var rgbLabel: WKInterfaceLabel!
    @IBOutlet var hslLabel: WKInterfaceLabel!

    override func awakeWithContext(context: AnyObject?) {
        super.awakeWithContext(context)
        // Configure interface objects here.
    }
```

Open **DetailController.swift** in the main editor and replace `willActivate()` with the following:

```
override func willActivate() {
    super.willActivate()
    let color = ColorManager.defaultManager.selectedColor
    hexLabel.setText("#" + color.hexString)
    rgbLabel.setText(color.rgbString)
    hslLabel.setText(color.hslString)
}
```

This code takes the currently selected color from the `ColorManager` singleton and configures the interface elements according to its values.

Now that you have your new controller, there's only one tiny step required to display it. Open **Interface.storyboard**, **right-click** and **drag** from the **More** button to your new detail controller. Let go, and then select the **push** option from the pop-up.

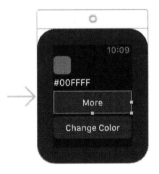 

Build and run, select a different color and then tap the **More** button. You'll see hex, RGB and HSL values for the currently selected color. It's as simple as that!

Using menus

Having a simple selection of colors is nice, but your users probably want to customize things a little. Context menus are the perfect way to present the user with options that are less-frequently used but still helpful.

Back in **Interface.storyboard**, find the red, modal interface controller. Drag a **menu** object from the object library and drop it onto the red controller.

If you expand the interface controller in the Document Outline you'll see that the menu comes with a single item. Select the **Menu Item** and open the **Attributes Inspector**. Change the **Title** to **Darker** and the **Image** to **darken**.

Find the **Menu Item** object in the object library. Drag another item into the **Document Outline**. Change its **Title** attribute to **Lighten** and **Image** to **lighten**.

> **Note:** There aren't any actual UI elements in interface builder when working with menus. You'll have to build and run before seeing any menu changes take effect.

Open **ColorController.swift** in the **Assistant Editor**. **Right-click** from the **first menu item** and create an IBAction named onDarken(). Repeat this for the second menu item with an IBAction named onLighten(). Update both methods to look like the following:

```
@IBAction func onDarken() {
  update(color: activeColor.darkerColor())
  updateSelectedColor()
}
```

```
@IBAction func onLighten() {
    update(color: activeColor.lighterColor())
    updateSelectedColor()
}
```

Each of these methods updates the view state of the controller as well as the selected color on the `ColorManager` singleton with a new, modified color object.

Build and run, tap **Change Color**, force-touch on a color to bring up the menu, and try tapping on the items. You should see the color update immediately.

Where to go from here?

Take a moment to reflect on your app's final navigational structure: beginning with an initial controller, you can either push a new controller or modally launch a series of page-based controllers. In other words, you were able to use all three navigation methods in one app by leveraging modals!

Remember that at root, your app needs to stick to either hierarchical or page-based navigation. And just because there are multiple and complex ways to navigate throughout a Watch app doesn't mean you should take every opportunity to use them all. The best apps for the Apple Watch have extremely limited navigation. Design your apps to be used for seconds, not minutes, which means very shallow navigation hierarchies.

Keep reading to learn more about how to get around in your apps!

Chapter 9: Digital Crown and Gesture Recognizers

By Ben Morrow

If you wear your Apple Watch daily, you're probably familiar with the Digital Crown: you spin this hardware knob to scroll a Watch interface. watchOS offers native `WKInterfacePicker`s that respond to scrolling the Digital Crown. You can also tap into the raw spin data for whatever you can dream up — for instance, to control the altitude of a drone! :]

Simlarly, the native interface objects respond to touch gestures, but you can also directly listen for taps, long presses, pans and swipes on the screen. The only gesture that doesn't carry over from iOS is multi-finger taps. However, the watch screen is so tiny that you won't miss it. Gestures are great for creating custom, interactive user experiences.

In this chapter, you'll work with an app named Campus. Campus shows you a graph of the number of employees at an office throughout the day. Security staff use the app to monitor how many employees are on the campus at any given time. It also empowers them to spot any irregularities in the badge-in procedures. You'll add both Digital Crown interaction and gesture interaction to the app so that the interface responds in remarkable ways.

Getting started

Open up the project, **Campus.xcodeproj**, located in the starter directory from this chapter's files.

Build and run the **Campus WatchKit App** scheme and you'll see a beautiful graph of today's census data from the badge scanners at the office.

You're going to implement three different modes of interaction:

- **Move**: Scrub backward and forward in time
- **Zoom**: Change how many data points show on screen
- **Inspect**: Highlight a particular data point and reveal its details

Preparing the app for interaction

In the project navigator, open **InterfaceController.swift** from the **Campus WatchKit Extension** group.

Representing modes of interaction is a perfect time to use an enumeration. Add the following global definition above the `class InterfaceController` declaration, right below the `import` statements:

```swift
enum InteractionMode: String {
  case move, zoom, inspect
}
```

An enumeration is a state machine. By using one, you will ensure that your app interacts in only one of those ways at any given time.

Add this code to your `InterfaceController` class below the `graphImage` property:

```swift
var interactionMode: InteractionMode!
```

Setting this as an implicitly unwrapped optional promises that you will set its value before it's used. In this example, you will set its value during the initial loading of the app.

Add the following code to `awake(withContext:)` just before the closing curly brace:

```
interactionMode = .move
```

When the app launches, your app will be ready for interaction with the *Move* mode. It will become clear later in the chapter why you're setting the default value during runtime rather than setting the default value directly on the property definition.

Listening to the Digital Crown

You'll soon compose code that will change the points on the graph. Looking ahead, you will want to give the user the option to interact either by moving their finger across the screen or by spinning the Digital Crown. You'll implement the Digital Crown interactions first and then later, you'll implement the touch gestures.

To listen for changes to the Digital Crown, you make your interface controller conform to the `WKCrownDelegate` protocol.

The best way to keep your code clean when conforming to a protocol is to add an extension to your class. That way, all the related code stays together and doesn't muddy up the definition of the class.

Add the following extension below the end of **InterfaceController.swift**:

```
extension InterfaceController: WKCrownDelegate {
  func crownDidRotate(_ crownSequencer: WKCrownSequencer?,
                       rotationalDelta: Double) {
  }

  func crownDidBecomeIdle(_ crownSequencer: WKCrownSequencer?) {
  }
}
```

Here's how these methods work:

• `crownDidRotate(_:rotationalDelta:)` gets called continuously as the user spins the Digital Crown. The `rotationalDelta` parameter passes you the change between one call and the next. One full rotation of the crown would be a delta of `1.0`. You will want to keep track of the accumulated change over time so that your interface stays in line with the total spin the crown experiences.

- crownDidBecomeIdle(_:) gets called after the user stops spinning the Digital Crown.

Next, add this code inside awake(withContext:):

```
crownSequencer.delegate = self
```

crownSequencer is a built-in property of WKInterfaceController. When you set the delegate to self, you're telling the compiler that you implement the required methods from the WKCrownDelegate protocol.

Next, inside willActivate() add this code:

```
crownSequencer.focus()
```

That code ensures that every time the user sees your interface, the crown is ready to report its changes.

Now that you have the basic setup for listening for crown updates, it's time to implement the empty protocol methods you added earlier. For that, you'll need a way to track the crown's delta.

Add the following property below the other properties in InterfaceController:

```
var accumulatedDigitalCrownDelta = 0.0
```

crownDidRotate(_:rotationalDelta:) is called over and over while the crown rotates. Every time a call happens, you want to increment accumulatedDigitalCrownDelta. Add this implementation to crownDidRotate(_:rotationalDelta:):

```
accumulatedDigitalCrownDelta += rotationalDelta
```

Now that you're accumulating the crown data, you'll want to make the interface react to the data you're gathering. You don't want to react every time crownDidRotate(_:rotationalDelta:) triggers, because the interface can't update as quickly as watchOS observes changes to the crown. You need to space out your interface update calls so that they have time to execute without overlapping. When an interface update call happens before the previous one completes, you'll see inconsistent behavior in the display of the interface.

To fix that, you will provide a threshold to accumulate the data up to a certain point and then you'll update the interface.

Add this code to `crownDidRotate(_:rotationalDelta:)`:

```
// 1
let threshold = 0.05
// 2
guard abs(accumulatedDigitalCrownDelta) > threshold else {
  return
}
// 3
handleInteraction(accumulatedDigitalCrownDelta)
```

Here's what's happening in this code:

1. You establish the threshold for how quickly you want to react to the Digital Crown spinning. I've found through trial and error that a value of `0.05` will allow just enough time for the interface updates to complete successfully while still feeling like seamless experience to the user.

2. Unless the threshold has been breached, do nothing. You use the absolute value function, `abs(_:)`, because `accumulatedDigitalCrownDelta` can be positive or negative depending on which direction the user spins the crown. watchOS will always report the logical interface direction to you regardless of the orientation of the device on the user's wrist. Up is positive, down is negative. By taking the absolute value, you monitor the threshold breach in either direction.

3. When the threshold has been breached, you perform the interface update using a method that you'll implement shortly.

You'll also want to update the interface when the user stops spinning the crown. Add the following code to `crownDidBecomeIdle(_:)`:

```
handleInteraction(accumulatedDigitalCrownDelta)
```

That code provides the last update the interface will get until the user starts spinning the crown again. In both methods, you call `handleInteraction(_:)` — but you haven't yet implemented it.

Add this code to complete the empty implementation of `handleInteraction(_:)` at the bottom of `InterfaceController`:

```
// 1
accumulatedDigitalCrownDelta = 0
// 2
switch interactionMode! {
case .move:
  break
case .zoom:
  break
```

```
  case .inspect:
    break
  }
  // 3
  generateImage()
```

Here's what this code does:

1. Since the threshold was breached, you'll need to reset the accumulatedDigitalCrownDelta so that is ready to start gathering deltas again.

2. Depending on the currently selected interaction mode, you'll adjust the interface in a distinctive manner.

3. You'll generate a new graph image with the adjustments made due to the interaction. watchOS can't handle drawing directly into an interface, so generateImage() creates an image of the graph and sets a WKInterfaceImage.

You've laid the foundation to listen to the Digital Crown rotational data. Sadly, nothing will happen in the simulator until you use that data to change the interface. In the next section, you'll make the graph move in response to the Digital Crown spinning.

Adding the Move interaction

preparedData() returns the last day's worth of census data from the full dataset of censuses. You're going to change preparedData() so that it can retrieve a different subset of the censuses dataset.

Add this property to InterfaceController:

```
  var offset = 0.0
```

offset will accumulate the amount you move backward in time. Each full integer difference represents one full day. So an offset of 0.5 would move backward in time by half a day.

Next you'll utilize the value of offset to adjust the data you use to draw the graph. Replace the implementation of preparedData() with this code:

```
  // 1
  let dataCountOffset = Int(round(Double(measurementsPerDay) *
  offset))
  // 2
  let minRange = censuses.count - measurementsPerDay -
  dataCountOffset
  let maxRange = censuses.count - dataCountOffset
  // 3
  var data = [Census]()
```

```
  for x in minRange..<maxRange {
    if x < censuses.count && x >= 0 {
      data.append(censuses[x])
    }
  }
  return data
```

Here's what's different from the previous implementation:

1. You multiply the value of the global variable `measurementsPerDay` and the value of `offset`. This will give you the number of records to shift the subset of the data you retrieve from the `censuses` dataset.

2. `minRange` and `maxRange` are both adjusted by the same number of records. The difference between `minRange` and `maxRange` is still only `measurementsPerDay`. That way, a full day's worth of census records will be shown on the graph, regardless of the value of `offset`.

3. The `data` is prepared by iterating from the `minRange` through the `maxRange` and picking out the corresponding record from the full `censuses` dataset. However, because the Digital Crown can spin infinitely, you wouldn't want to get into a situation where you are attempting to access data out of bounds in the `censuses` array. So you only keep data points within the allowed indices in the array. This effectively adjusts the zoom of the graph and only displays data points that fall within the range bounds.

You've got the data handling in place so now you need to write the code to translate the Digtal Crown movement into the data movement.

Inside `handleInteraction(_:)`, replace the implementation of the `.move` case in the `switch` statement (right now, simply: `break`) with the following:

```
// 1
var newOffset = offset + delta
// 2
let maxOffset: Double = Double(daysOfRecord) - 1
let minOffset: Double = 0
// 3
if newOffset > maxOffset {
  newOffset = maxOffset
} else if newOffset < minOffset {
  newOffset = minOffset
}
// 4
offset = newOffset
```

Here's what's happening in this code:

1. You're going to change the offset by the amount passed in as the delta from the Digital Crown spin. However, again, you have to protect yourself from the offset exceeding the range of the dataset.

2. You define the limits for the acceptable newOffset.

3. You set the newOffset to the maxOffset or the minOffset respecting the direction in which it exceeds the bounds.

4. Finally, you update the instance property of the InterfaceController with the acceptable offset value.

Now you're ready to see the interaction. Build and run the app. In the simulator, position your mouse on the virtual Digital Crown on the right side of the simulator window. You can use two-finger scrolling on the trackpad to simulate spinning the Digital Crown. If you scroll on the watch interface, you'll see the graph update.

Very, very cool — it's like a whole new world has opened up! Now the user can explore backward into time. They're not limited to just today's data.

Since you've got the *Move* interaction in place, you can now set about implementing the other two interactions, *Zoom* and *Inspect*.

Adding the Zoom interaction

The *Zoom* interaction is similar to the *Move* interaction. You'll need a way to accumulate zoom as the crown spins.

Add this property to the top of the InterfaceController implementation:

```
var zoom = 1.0
```

The zoom property stores a decimal percentage — the percentage of one day's worth of data that the graph will display.

You'll need to account for the value of zoom in preparedData(). Replace the implementation of preparedData() with this code:

```
func preparedData() -> [Census] {
  // 1
  let dataCount = Int(round(Double(measurementsPerDay) * zoom))
  let dataCountOffset = Int(round(Double(measurementsPerDay) *
self.offset))
  // 2
  let minRange = censuses.count - dataCount - dataCountOffset
  let maxRange = censuses.count - dataCountOffset

  var data = [Census]()
  for x in minRange..<maxRange {
    if x < censuses.count && x >= 0 {
      data.append(censuses[x])
    }
  }
  return data
}
```

Here's what's different:

1. By multiplying measurementsPerDay and zoom, you calculate the number of data points to display on the graph.

2. Instead of subtracting measurementsPerDay to get the start of the range, you subtract your new dataCount. Now the graph has the capability to display data points from less than one full day or more than one full day.

You're getting closer to testing *Zoom* mode. Next, you'll need to update the value of the zoom property when the Digital Crown spins.

Inside handleInteraction(_:), replace the implementation of the .zoom case in the switch statement:

```
// 1
var newZoom = zoom + delta
// 2
let maxZoom = 3.0
let minZoom = 0.1
// 3
if newZoom > maxZoom {
  newZoom = maxZoom
} else if newZoom < minZoom {
  newZoom = minZoom
}
zoom = newZoom
```

Here's what's happening in this code:

1. You increment the accumulated value of `zoom`.

2. You establish some reasonable maximum and minimum values for value of `zoom`.

3. If the new value exceeds that range, you change the new value to the maximum or minimum values respectively.

Before you can see the graph in action, you'll need to activate *Zoom* mode. Change the value of the default `interactionMode` in `awake(withContext:)`:

```
interactionMode = .zoom
```

Build and run the app. Try zooming the graph by scrolling the Digital Crown.

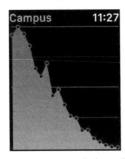 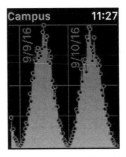

You can explore focusing in on much less than one day's worth of data, or zooming out to get an overview of many days.

Adding the Inspect interaction

The last remaining interaction to implement is *Inspect* mode. With *Inspect*, you won't be changing the data points on the graph, so there's no need to modify `preparedData()` like you did for the other two interactions. Woo hoo!

Instead, you'll focus on property modifications. Add this code to the top of `InterfaceController` next to the other properties:

```
var highlightedPointIndex: Int?
```

Inspect mode lets the user get details about a particular point on the graph. To show which point has been selected, you'll highlight it on the interface. During *Move* mode and *Zoom* mode, `highlightedPointIndex` will remain `nil` so that no point gets highlighted. However, once the user switches to *Inspect* mode, you want to highlight one point.

Add the following `didSet` action to the `interactionMode` property:

```
var interactionMode: InteractionMode! {
  didSet {
    switch interactionMode! {
    case .move, .zoom:
      self.setTitle(
        "[\(interactionMode.rawValue.capitalized) mode]")
      highlightedPointIndex = nil
    case .inspect:
      highlightedPointIndex = preparedData().count / 2
    }
    generateImage()
  }
}
```

Whenever the `interactionMode` property receives a change, `didSet` will run.
Depending on the mode, you will change the `title` of the interface and update the
value of the `highlightedPointIndex`. As a reasonable default value, the
`highlightedPointIndex` gets set to halfway through the graph data.

You have set the title of the interface controller for *Move* and *Zoom* mode, but you have
not yet set the title for *Inspect* mode. Add the following `didSet` action to the
`highlightedPointIndex` property:

```
var highlightedPointIndex: Int? {
  didSet {
    if highlightedPointIndex != nil {
      self.setTitle(stringFromHighlightedIndex())
    }
  }
}
```

You set the title here in the `didSet` of `highlightedPointIndex` rather than in `didSet`
of the `interactionMode` property. The `title` for *Inspect* mode needs to change each
time the `highlightedPointIndex` changes. The other modes change the `title` just
once when the user activates the mode.

The implementation of `didSet` calls `stringFromHighlightedIndex()`. This method
will format the properties of a particular point on the graph in a nice, concise way to use
as the title for the interface. `stringFromHighlightedIndex()` doesn't have a full
implementation yet, but you'll fix that now.

Locate the definition of `stringFromHighlightedIndex()` and replace its
implementation with this code:

```
// 1
let data = preparedData()
```

```
let census = data[highlightedPointIndex!]
// 2
let dateFormatter = DateFormatter()
dateFormatter.timeStyle = .short
let dateString = dateFormatter.string(from: census.timestamp)
// 3
let numberFormatter = NumberFormatter()
numberFormatter.numberStyle = .decimal
let numberString = numberFormatter.string(from: NSNumber(value:
census.attendance))!
return "\(dateString): \(numberString)"
```

Here's how this code works:

1. You retrieve the census for the particular data point to which highlightedPointIndex refers.

2. You use a DateFormatter to get just the time from the full Date value, like this: 10:15 AM (for the US region).

3. You use a NumberFormatter because the thousands separator will make the attendance value readable, like this: 3,000 (for the US region).

Both DateFormatter and NumberFormatter automatically adjust their output depending on the language and region settings of the Apple Watch device. Your app is already a little bit internationalized. :]

To see all this in the simulator, change the assignment of interactionMode inside awake(withContext:):

```
interactionMode = .inspect
```

Now you can see why you needed to change the value in awake(withContext:) rather than setting the default value when the property is defined. didSet only runs after the class has finished initializing. In the interface lifecycle, awake(withContext:) runs after initialization.

You have one more change to make before you can preview the app in the simulator. In the implementation of generateImage(), replace the assignment of image with this code:

```
let image = self.graphGenerator.image(self.contentFrame.size,
with: data, highlight: self.highlightedPointIndex, demarcations:
demarcations)
```

The only thing that changed is that you're now passing the highlight parameter. That tells the GraphGenerator which point to draw differently. You have to use self. because this assignment exists inside a closure. By using self. you're making it clear to the compiler that you want to keep a reference to `InterfaceController` while this code executes in the background.

Now you can see it in action. Build and run the app.

Looking good! The title tells you the details of the highlighted point. I know you're itching to scroll the highlighted point across all the data points. You can't yet because you haven't implemented that code. You'll do that now.

Inside `handleInteraction(_:)` replace the implementation of the `.inspect` case in the `switch` statement:

```
// 1
let direction = delta > 0 ? 1 : -1
// 2
var newIndex = highlightedPointIndex! + direction
// 3
let count = preparedData().count
if newIndex >= count {
  newIndex = count - 1
} else if newIndex < 0 {
  newIndex = 0
}
highlightedPointIndex! = newIndex
```

Here's what's happening in this code:

1. Instead of worrying about the fractional delta, you'll only ever increment the `highlightedPointIndex` by 1 each time this code is executed. The important thing is figuring out if you need to add a positive 1 or a negative 1 to the current value of `highlightedPointIndex`.

2. Recall that you set the value of `highlightedPointIndex` as soon as the mode changed and this code only ever runs while *Inspect* mode is active. You can be confident `highlightedPointIndex` has a value and you are safe to force unwrap it.

3. Similar to the code for the other two cases in the `switch` statement, you ensure your index never gets out of bounds.

Build and run the app. Scroll the Digital Crown and see the highlight move.

The friendly formatted title updates as you change the inspected point. You're becoming a watch wizard!

You've made the watch perform multitudes of magical visuals.

Now that you've got the Digital Crown locked down, you will tackle gestures next.

Gestures

You've got all three interaction modes implemented in code. However, before the app is ready for release, you need to devise a way to switch between the different modes on the fly. You'll accomplish this with a force touch menu.

Adding a force touch menu

In the starter project, the menu has been prepared for you with Interface Builder. Using the project navigator, open **Interface.storyboard** from the **Campus WatchKit App** group. Expand the **Menu** in the document outline by clicking the disclosure triangle.

Open the assistant editor:

Ensure that the counterpart opens **InterfaceController.swift**. Control-drag from each menu item to the end of `InterfaceController` making a method with the naming scheme: `modeMenuItemPressed()`. This way, you'll end up with four methods, one for each menu item.

```
@IBAction func zoomMenuItemPressed() {
}
@IBAction func moveMenuItemPressed() {
}
@IBAction func inspectMenuItemPressed() {
}
@IBAction func resetMenuItemPressed() {
}
```

Then fill out the implementation for each method, like this:

```
@IBAction func zoomMenuItemPressed() {
  interactionMode = .zoom
}
@IBAction func moveMenuItemPressed() {
  interactionMode = .move
}
@IBAction func inspectMenuItemPressed() {
  interactionMode = .inspect
}
@IBAction func resetMenuItemPressed() {
  reset()
}
```

When each button action runs, the value of the `interactionMode` property changes. The Reset Plot button calls `reset()` which doesn't yet have a definition. You'll fix that now.

Switch back to the standard editor:

Open **InterfaceController.swift** from the project navigator.

Add this code just above those new `@IBAction` methods:

```
func reset() {
  offset = 0
  zoom = 1
  generateImage()
}
```

`offset` and `zoom` get set back to their original values and then the graph redraws. The code has the effect of moving the graph back to today and zooming to show one full day.

Build and run the app. In the simulator menu bar, navigate to **Hardware\Touch Pressure\Deep Press**. Simulate a force touch by clicking on the interface.

You'll see the menu appear:

In the simulator menu bar, navigate to **Hardware\Touch Pressure\Shallow Press**. Click on the **Move** button. The menu will disappear and the the app will have *Move* mode activated:

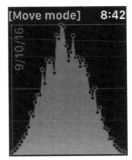

Try scrolling on your trackpad to move the data. Awesome! Now you can switch among all the different modes. You can even reset the graph back to the default perspective if you get lost in the weeds.

Adding a tap gesture recognizer

The force touch menu is great — it lets you explicitly select which mode you want. For daily use though, the security professionals that use the app would appreciate a faster user experience. A double tap on the watch screen will change the interaction mode immediately.

Earlier in the book, you learned that all `WKInterfaceObjects` are proxy objects. The WatchKit Extension target that holds all your code is sandboxed from your WatchKit App target which holds your storyboard and graphics. Due to this architecture, you can't create objects in code and add them to the interface in code like you might on iOS. Instead, you must add objects in Interface Builder during design time. That's OK though, because adding gesture recognizers in Interface Builder is a fine way to accomplish the goal.

In the project navigator, select **Interface.storyboard** to open Interface Builder.

In the Object Library, search for "**tap**":

Drag the **Tap Gesture Recognizer** object onto the **Image** placeholder.

> **Note:** Here's another difference from iOS: In watchOS, you can't use a gesture recognizer on an entire interface. You must attach a gesture recognizer to a specific object in the interface. Usually, you'll want to choose an object that will fill the screen. In this case, the Graph Image object fits the bill.

In the document outline, expand the **Graph Image** by clicking on the disclosure triangle. Select the **Tap Gesture Recognizer** child object. In the Attributes Inspector, change the **Taps** to **2**:

The tap gesture recognizer will now listen for a double tap rather than a single tap.

With the recognizer in place, you need to wire up an action for it to call when it sees a double tap. Open the assistant editor:

Control-drag from the **Tap Gesture Recognizer** in the document outline to the end of `InterfaceController`, just below the `@IBAction` methods from your menu items. In

the pop-up dialog, change the **Connection** to **Action** and name it
tapGestureRecognized:

Click **Connect**. Since you successfully wired up the action, now you'll fill in its
implementation details.

Switch back to the standard editor. Select **InterfaceController.swift** from the project
navigator.

When the double tap is recognized, you want to immediately switch to the next
`interactionMode`. However, the `interactionMode` enumeration doesn't have a built-
in way to cycle between modes. You'll have to define one yourself.

Locate the definition of `InteractionMode` at the very top of the swift file. Add the
following code to the enumeration:

```
mutating func next() {
    switch self {
    case .move:
      self = .zoom
    case .zoom:
      self = .inspect
    case .inspect:
      self = .move
    }
}
```

No matter which current value an instance has, `next()` will change the value. Since
enumerations are value types, the compiler needs to know when a method will change
the value of an instance. Methods defined as `mutating` will only be available to variable
instances, not constants.

Next, add this code to the implementation of `tapGestureRecognized(_:)`:

```
interactionMode.next()
```

Build and run the app. Double tap on the graph, and watch the title change as you cycle
through the different interaction modes:

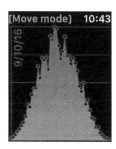 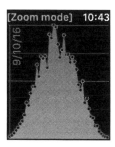 

Navigate back into Xcode. Since you implemented fancy ways to switch interaction modes, you can change the default interaction mode for the app back to Move.

Inside awake(withContext:), replace the assignment of interactionMode:

```
interactionMode = .move
```

Adding a pan gesture recognizer

At this point, the app is looking great! You've got all the interaction handled well with the Digital Crown, but your users would love to drag their fingers across the screen to interact with the graph.

Follow the same steps you used to add the tap gesture recognizer:

1. Open **Interface.storyboard**.

2. Search for "**pan**" in the Object Library.

3. Drag the **Pan Gesture Recognizer** onto the **Image** placeholder.

4. Open the assistant editor.

5. Control-drag from the **Pan Gesture Recognizer** in the document outline to the bottom of the InterfaceController implementation in **InterfaceController.swift**.

6. Change the **Connection** type to **Action**. Name the method **panGestureRecognized**. Click **Connect**.

7. Open the standard editor and select **InterfaceController.swift** from the project navigator.

That was quite a flurry of instruction, but you're on top of it like a ninja at a parkour party!

Now you're ready to implement the pan gesture recognizer.

The pan gesture recognizer triggers its action continuously as the user drags their finger. You'll use a stored property to track the distance change between each call.

Add this code to the top `InterfaceController` with the other properties:

```
var previousPanPoint: CGPoint?
```

`previousPanPoint` will remain `nil` until `panGestureRecognized(_:)` sets the value. Add this code to the body of the implementation of `panGestureRecognized(_:)`:

```
// 1
guard let panGesture = sender as? WKPanGestureRecognizer else {
  return
}
// 2
switch panGesture.state {
// 3
case .began:
  previousPanPoint = panGesture.locationInObject()
// 4
case .changed:
  guard let previousPanPoint = previousPanPoint else {
    return
  }
  let currentPanPoint = panGesture.locationInObject()
  let deltaX = currentPanPoint.x - previousPanPoint.x
  // 5
  let percentageChange = deltaX / self.contentFrame.size.width
  handleInteraction(Double(percentageChange))
  self.previousPanPoint = currentPanPoint
// 6
default:
  previousPanPoint = nil
  break
}
```

Here's what's happening:

1. The `sender` parameter of the method is an `AnyObject`. To access its properties, you have to unwrap the value as a `WKPanGestureRecognizer`.

2. Gesture recognizers have a lot of different `states` during their lifecycle. For now, you only care about `.began` and `.changed`. All the other states are handled by the `default` case of the `switch` statement.

3. When the pan gesture is first recognized, the only thing you need to do is save the location of the user's finger.

4. Each time the pan gesture reports an update, you calculate the distance the finger has moved. You only keep the x-axis distance because you designed the graph to only support horizontal movement.

5. You use the distance traveled as a percentage of the total screen width to send to `handleInteraction(_:)`. Think of it this way, a finger dragging across the whole screen would make the the percentage 1.0. That would move the data backward on the graph by one full day. Similarly, one full Digital Crown rotation will move the data backward on the graph by a full day.

6. The `default` case handles all the other `states` of the gesture. Both `.cancelled` and `.ended` occur when the user stops dragging their finger. `previousPanPoint` gets reset to `nil` since you won't need it for calculations until the next pan gesture.

Build and run the app. Click and drag in the simulator to see the pan gesture recognizer in action. The graph will move accordingly.

Since you used good app architecture practices, the pan gesture supports all the interaction modes. Switch to *Zoom* and *Inspect* and try dragging on the screen.

Where to go from here?

Congratulations on successfully utilizing the Digital Crown and gestures in your app! It's impressive how powerful the experience becomes when you use the data for custom drawing.

One improvement you could make is a slightly better *Inspect* mode. Right now, if you drag your finger across the entire width of the screen, the highlighted point doesn't keep up. You could fix this by modifying the implementation of the `.inspect` case in `handleInteraction(_:)`.

You could also improve the rendering speed. If you run this app on a device, you'll notice that the interface updates slowly. There are two approaches you might take:

1. You could reduce `measurementsPerDay`. That would reduce the number of points displayed on the screen and as a consequence, reduce the rendering time for each frame.

2. If you're really ambitious, you could translate the drawing code into SpriteKit. SpriteKit renders frames of animation efficiently using the GPU acceleration. The current CoreGraphics implementation requires you to render a bitmap image and set a WKInterfaceImage for each frame. SpriteKit would skirt this step.

In the next chapter, you'll work with a different kind of image generation: You'll learn how to use the Snapshot API to create custom screenshots to display in the Dock.

Chapter 10: Snapshot API

By Ben Morrow

watchOS 4 boasts a redesigned vertically scrolling Dock. Knowing how people interact with the Dock will go a long way to helping you best use Snapshot API.

In this chapter, you'll build **UHL**, the official app for the Underwater Hockey League. You may not have heard of this sport before, and you're not alone. Underwater hockey has a cult following. Two teams maneuver a puck across the bottom of a swimming pool. Many fans cheered for joy when they found out they could wear their Apple Watch during games, since watches are now water-resistant to a depth of 50 meters.

You're probably feeling the urge to dive in, so let's get to it. CANNONBALL!

Getting started

Open **UHL.xcodeproj** from the starter folder. Build and run the **UHL WatchKit App** scheme.

With the UHL app, you follow your favorite team and see their season schedule and record. For the sake of simplicity, the pre-selected team will be Octopi. :] Tap on each of the buttons to explore the app and check out the different interfaces.

The best way to learn about the Snapshot API is first to talk about the Dock.

The Dock

Pressing the Side button on the Apple Watch brings up the Dock. The Dock builds on the foundations that were laid by glances in the very first version of watchOS. Over the years, glances have been transitioned and massaged into the Dock. Apple designed the glances feature to be a browsable collection of timely and contextually relevant moments from people's favorite apps. The Dock serves essentially the same need.

The Dock provides a paged interface of miniaturized app cards. Each app contains a snapshot of its interface:

People use the Dock to keep all their favorite and recently used apps on hand. New in watchOS 4 is the ability to pick your poison:

The default setting is Recents. Your most recent apps will continuously change based on your usage.

If you select Favorites, you can fill up to 10 slots:

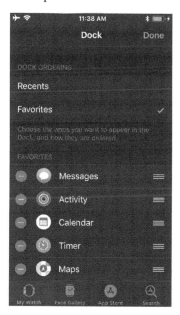

In addition, watchOS will append the most recently used app to the end of the collection. A **Keep in Dock** button appears when you focus on the recent app for a second. You can add apps to the Watch with the Keep in Dock button. When you're ready to remove a Favorite, you can swipe left and a Remove button will appear:

There is also one special card in the Dock: **Now Playing**. It has no app accessible from the Home screen, but you use it like an app in the Dock:

The Dock provides many facets in one elegant interface:

- An app launcher

- A multitasking switcher

- A glance for current status

- A speed booster (apps in it launch immediately)

- An organizer (no need to hunt the Home screen)

You can flip your way through the pages of the Dock in two ways:

- Digital Crown - *Pro*: quickly navigate to the end. *Con*: No way to select an app without tapping your finger. You might intuit that you could press the Digital Crown to select an app, but that will take you to the Home screen.

- Swipe the screen - *Pro*: your finger will be on the screen, so it's easy to select the app you want to launch. *Con*: Slower, because you page through app cards one at a time.

Apps in the Dock offer a screenshot, called a *snapshot*, so people can glance at the current status. That's pretty similar to old glances feature, but what's different is: watchOS keeps apps in the Dock in memory. That's how apps launch immediately when you tap on one. In fact, if you settle on an app for a second, the app will wake up and show a live view of the interface.

One good example for this is the Timer app. Try this out for yourself if you have an Apple Watch on hand:

1. Open the Timer app from the Home screen.

2. Start a timer.

3. Press the Digital Crown to go back to the Home screen.

4. Press the Side button to invoke the Dock.

5. Page through the apps to find the Recent slot which contains the Timer app.

6. Watch the timer in its tiny card view count down.

When you left the app, the system created a snapshot. When you first see the app in the Dock, you see that snapshot. Then when you settle for a moment on the app, you see a live view as if you had opened the app.

All the apps in the Dock are in a suspended state, ready to launch quickly at any time. They also wake up in the background to periodically fetch new data and update their snapshot.

Snapshot API

You'll use the Snapshot API exclusively for apps in the Dock. By default, when the Dock appears, the user sees what each app looked like in its last state. You can see how that could be useful... sometimes. Other times, the last interface the user saw when they exited the app will be stale, and no longer relevant. You, the developer, are responsible for making sure the snapshot is up to date with current information.

Snapshot tips

Optimizing for miniaturization

Snapshots get scaled down from the app's full-size dimensions. You'll want to avoid text and graphics becoming illegible at this small size. For that reason, the font weights for status bars and much of the text in Apple's built-in apps have been increased from Regular to Medium. At smaller sizes, bolder fonts are more legible. For really important information you should consider using larger sized type. To accomplish that, you may have to remove objects from your interface, or use abbreviations instead of full words.

Customizing your interface

The good news is, you're not limited to displaying a standard interface from your app in the snapshot. You can build an interface to use specifically for Dock snapshots. Alternatively, you can emphasize interface objects by making them bigger, bolder, or highlighted before you capture the snapshot. However, don't make the snapshot look radically different from your app. That would make your app less recognizable and harder to find. A good way to think about it is:

- Focus on important information

- Hide objects that aren't as relevant when viewed at a glance in the Dock

- Exaggerate the size of certain objects for legibility

Just don't make the interface look completely different.

Displaying progress and status

Progress screens and success screens are great use cases for modified snapshots. You definitely would want to provide these details in coordination with a complication on the clock face. However, not everyone will have your complication installed on their current clock face. Instead, they will check status in the Dock.

Imagine a pizza ordering app that communicates with an internet server and has a multi-step, long-running process. The user would want to see success snapshots for each step of the process. The caution here is that you want to avoid showing things like alerts, errors, or confirmation dialogs in your snapshot. When seen out of context, these screens will be easily misinterpreted or make no sense at all.

Remember that a snapshot is both the launch image and preview image for your app. If the app experiences a situation that needs interaction from the user, instead of updating the snapshot, you could dispatch a local notification. That way you can keep the brand positive and recognizable in the Dock.

Swapping screens

Depending on the situation, you will want to programmatically dismiss the interface you use for your snapshot after a period of time. The thing to watch out for here is, people don't like it when apps change in unpredictable ways and when app state isn't saved. It can be confusing and disorienting. So if you choose to show users a different interface, you want to do so in a way that is logical and predictable. The hope is that people won't stop to realize what's going on. However, if they do notice something awry, they should be able to make an accurate guess about why the state of the app's UI changes from time to time.

Tracking a session

Apple pulled off an analogous experience with session-based use in watchOS. If people raise their wrist inside of two minutes since they last used an app, the app will pop back up. If they haven't looked back at an app for more than two minutes, the clock face will show the next time they look. That's an example of a non-noticeable change that works in a predictable way. Snapshots can provide a similar function. Around the time of an event like an airline flight or a sports game, a snapshot should show something different than when no event is temporally close.

Anticipating a timeline

Contextual factors like time of day or location can have a huge impact on what people want to see. Your objective is to proactively anticipate people's interests and needs. Put yourself in their position. Graphing events on a timeline is a very helpful technique for doing this. Plot out significant events. Then ask yourself, "how do these events impact what people would want to know?" For a sports game, you might have:

- Before the game: Location and time

- During the game: Score and last play

- After the game: Score and season record

- Every other time: Season schedule

Adjusting preferences and expectations

Every user is not the same. So consider how you could offer preferences or even better, how you could position the purpose of your app. A fair weather fan who only cares about one team is going to need a very different experience from a fanatic who wants to follow an entire league. The fair weather fan would probably expect the score of the last game to stick around in a snapshot much longer than the fanatic who keeps up-to-date constantly. In fact, those should most certainly be different apps, rather than just a bevy of preferences in a single app.

System

watchOS automatically schedules snapshots to update on your behalf in many different scenarios:

- When the Apple Watch boots up

- When a complication update occurs

- When the user exits the app

- When the user views a long look notification

- One hour after the user last interacted with the app

- At least once an hour for apps in the Dock. (The Dock takes one snapshot every six minutes rotating through each app in sequence. If the user has fewer than ten apps in the Dock, then each app will receive more frequent snapshot tasks than one per hour.)

- At optional, scheduled times, with the Background Refresh API

Refresh lifecycle

To get a feel for how snapshots work, let's go over the lifecycle of a snapshot refresh.

Scheduling

When either you or the system want a new snapshot, you call:

```
scheduleSnapshotRefresh(withPreferredDate:userInfo:
    scheduledCompletion:)
```

Starting

Your app wakes up when the system passes a `WKSnapshotBackgroundRefreshTask` into your extension delegate's `handle(_:)` method. When the extension receives this notification, your app's root interface controller also wakes up in the background and off-screen. During this process, the following methods run in this order:

1. The root interface controller's `awake(withContext:)` method

2. The root interface controller's `willActivate()` method

3. The extension delegate's `handle(_:)` method

At any point during the execution of these three methods, you can customize the appearance of your app's interface to modify the snapshot shown in the Dock.

Ending

The final step of refreshing the snapshot happens in the extension delegate's `handle(_:)` method. You finish the snapshot by calling:

```
setTaskCompleted(restoredDefaultState:
    estimatedSnapshotExpiration:userInfo:)
```

You call this on the `WKSnapshotBackgroundRefreshTask`. As soon as you call this method, the system captures an image of your app's current interface. watchOS keeps the snapshot in memory until the next refresh.

Do this, not that

You have an undisclosed, but particular, number of seconds to finish the snapshot and call the `setTaskCompleted` method. If you neglect to call the method, the system will use the entire length of available time, wasting battery power. Once the allotted time has expired, the system will suspend your extension and you will receive a crash report.

You should not make any network calls to fetch data during a snapshot update because there's not enough time. Stick to just updating the interface with the data from your current model. Updating the model should be handled by other background tasks.

You can ensure that complex data requests do *not* get called in a snapshot interface, by moving those calls into `applicationDidBecomeActive()` in your extension delegate. That method only runs when the app is in the foreground.

Each time you finish a snapshot, you have the opportunity to schedule another one. To understand how, let's walk through the parameters from the `setTaskCompleted` method:

- `restoredDefaultState` is a `Bool` that specifies whether or not your snapshot represents the first interface controller in your app. If you have transitioned to another interface, pass in `false` for this value. That way, the system will launch the app correctly later.

- `estimatedSnapshotExpiration` is the `Date` that specifies when the system should attempt to next refresh your app's snapshot. If you don't need another update anytime soon, you can pass in the new `Date.distantFuture` class property.

- `userInfo` is an optional `NSSecureCoding` object that contains a collection of custom data that will be passed into the next `WKSnapshotBackgroundRefreshTask` if you schedule one. It usually takes the form of a dictionary. You might like to include `["lastActiveDate": Date()]` to have access to how long ago the previous snapshot happened.

If you only need to update your snapshot every hour, you can use a shortcut. Instead of setting the expiration explicitly, you can call `setTaskCompletedWithSnapshot(_:)` with `true` and the system will schedule another snapshot for you in one hour.

Working with snapshots

Now that you have a better idea how snapshots work, you're ready to implement what you've learned in the UHL app!

Handling a snapshot

In Xcode, open **ExtensionDelegate.swift** by selecting it in the UHL WatchKit Extension group from the project navigator.

When you start a new WatchKit project, Xcode helpfully includes an implementation of `handle(_:)` for you:

> **Note:** You do not need to copy this code since your starter project already has it.

```swift
func handle(_ backgroundTasks: Set<WKRefreshBackgroundTask>) {
  // Sent when the system needs to launch the application in the
  // background to process tasks. Tasks arrive in a set, so loop
  // through and process each one.
  for task in backgroundTasks {
    // Use a switch statement to check the task type
    switch task {
    case let backgroundTask as
      WKApplicationRefreshBackgroundTask:
      // Be sure to complete the background task once you're
      // done.
      backgroundTask.setTaskCompletedWithSnapshot(false)
    case let snapshotTask as
      WKSnapshotRefreshBackgroundTask:
      // Snapshot tasks have a unique completion call, make sure
      // to set your expiration date
      snapshotTask.setTaskCompleted(restoredDefaultState: true,
        estimatedSnapshotExpiration: Date.distantFuture,
        userInfo: nil)
    case let connectivityTask as
      WKWatchConnectivityRefreshBackgroundTask:
      // Be sure to complete the connectivity task once you're
      // done.
      connectivityTask.setTaskCompletedWithSnapshot(false)
    case let urlSessionTask as
```

```
    WKURLSessionRefreshBackgroundTask:
    // Be sure to complete the URL session task once you're
    // done.
    urlSessionTask.setTaskCompletedWithSnapshot(false)
  default:
    // make sure to complete unhandled task types
    task.setTaskCompletedWithSnapshot(false)
  }
  }
}
```

handle(_:) contains comments throughout the code to guide your usage. The switch statement cases showcase all the background tasks available in watchOS. You're going to focus solely on the snapshotTask in this chapter.

The first thing you'll examine is when a snapshot task fires. Add this code inside the snapshotTask case at the top of the execution block:

```
print("\n handling snapshot task \n")
```

Build and run the WatchKit app. In the simulator menu bar, navigate to **Hardware\Home**. That's the equivalent of pressing the Digital Crown on the Apple Watch. You'll see the interface return to the Home screen.

Switch back to Xcode and check out the Debug area:

Now you'll be able to tell when the system takes a snapshot because you'll see the log in the Debug area.

When you exited the app by pressing the Digital Crown, the system generated a snapshot task. However, the snapshot task may not run immediately because watchOS is busy performing other tasks. In the next section, you'll learn how to force watchOS in the simulator to take a snapshot right now.

Forcing a snapshot task in the simulator

While you're testing your app, you may want to generate snapshots on command. To execute a snapshot, first ensure that the app is *not* running in the foreground of the simulator. Instead, the simulator can show the clock face, the Home screen, or another app. watchOS won't take a snapshot of an active app. However, the app should still be running in Xcode.

Once you've verified those conditions, navigate in Xcode to **Debug\Simulate UI Snapshot**. watchOS will immediately send a snapshot task to your app.

You'll see another printed statement in the Debug area in Xcode, but nothing will change on the interface in the simulator. That's exactly the behavior you would expect. Remember that snapshot tasks happen in the background, so there is no reason to bring your app to the foreground.

Viewing a snapshot

You can check what your snapshot looks like by visiting the Dock. From the simulator menu bar, navigate to **Hardware\Side Button** and the Dock will appear. The system will place UHL in the at the end of the Dock since it is the most recently used app:

Notice that the bottom of the snapshot is obscured by the next app in the Dock.

Customizing the app name

Most of the time, the display name of your WatchKit app doesn't matter. watchOS icons on the Home screen don't have a label like they do in iOS.

However, in the Dock, you do see the name of the app above the snapshot. By default Xcode assigns a WatchKit app name as "[app name] WatchKit App". When you see a name like that in the Dock, it just feels a bit redundant.

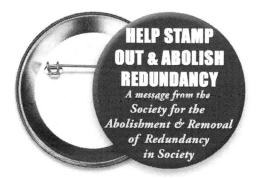

For that reason, you should change the display name.

In the project navigator, inside the **UHL WatchKit App** group, open **Info.plist**. Locate the **Bundle display name** property and change its value to **UHL**. Press Return on your keyboard to commit the change.

Build and run the app and navigate to **Hardware\Side Button** to show the Dock.

That's looking much better!

Modifying the snapshot

By default, the snapshot of your app shows whichever interface the user last viewed. However, users would love it if you would add spice to their experience. Imagine showing event information about upcoming games and scores for recently played games in the Dock. That's just what you'll do next.

In the project navigator, select **ExtensionDelegate.swift** to open it. Inside handle(_:) below the print call you added earlier, insert this code:

```
// 1
let nextMatchDate = season.upcomingMatches.first?.date
let lastMatchExpiresTimeInterval =
  season.playedMatches.last?.date.timeIntervalSince(
    Date().yesterday)
```

```
// 2
let wkExtension = WKExtension.shared()
// Always reset back to the root controller
wkExtension.rootInterfaceController?.popToRootController()
```

Here's what's happening:

1. To begin, you set up the constants you'll use to configure the modified snapshots. You retrieve the date of the next game and figure out how long ago the previous game happened.

2. No matter which interface you will eventually show, first you pop back to the initial interface. The user may have left your app from any screen. So your app in the system memory could currently be showing a detail interface multiple levels down in hierarchy. If you push another controller on top without first popping to the root controller, the user could end up with arbitrary controllers stacked. They would have to press the back button many times to get to the initial interface.

Next, you'll compose the robust logic to show the different controllers in the snapshot.

Insert this code immediately beneath the code you just added:

```
// 3
// Check if the last match was played recently
if let lastMatchExpiresTimeInterval =
lastMatchExpiresTimeInterval,
    lastMatchExpiresTimeInterval > 0 {
    let expiration =
Date().addingTimeInterval(lastMatchExpiresTimeInterval)
    // Move to record controller
    wkExtension.rootInterfaceController?.pushController(
      withName: "RecordInterfaceControllerType", context: nil)
    // 4
    snapshotTask.setTaskCompleted(restoredDefaultState: false,
      estimatedSnapshotExpiration: expiration, userInfo: nil)
    break
}
```

Here's what that code accomplishes:

3. If the last game was played less than 24 hours ago, you'll segue to the Record interface controller.

Note: The names of the interface controllers were already assigned in the starter project. To assign an identifier to interface controllers, you use the Attributes Inspector in Interface Builder:

Interface Controller

Identifier : InterfaceControllerType

4. You set the snapshot to expire 24 hours after the time the game happened. You finish the snapshot by calling `setTaskCompleted(restoredDefaultState:estimatedSnapshotExpiration: userInfo:)`, then you call `break` to exit the `switch` statement. No more code needs to execute since you already have a good snapshot.

Add this code next:

```
// 5
// Check if the next match will happen soon
if let nextMatchDate = nextMatchDate,
  nextMatchDate.timeIntervalSinceNow <
    Date().tomorrow.timeIntervalSinceNow {
    // 6
    // Move to schedule controller
    wkExtension.rootInterfaceController?.pushController(
      withName: "ScheduleInterfaceControllerType",
      context: nil)
    // 7
    // Move to schedule detail controller
    // for `context` use the index of upcoming matches, first is 0
    wkExtension.rootInterfaceController?.pushController(
      withName: "ScheduleDetailInterfaceControllerType",
      context: 0)
    // 8
    snapshotTask.setTaskCompleted(restoredDefaultState: false,
      estimatedSnapshotExpiration: nextMatchDate, userInfo: nil)
    break
}
```

Here's what's happening:

5. If you didn't make a snapshot for the last game, you check to see if the next game will happen in less than 24 hours. If so, you'll segue to show the event information.

6. Surprisingly, you push the Schedule interface controller first, and then you push the Schedule Detail interface controller. You want to push both because when the user launches the app from the snapshot, they will see the app as you've left it here. When the user taps the back button, they will expect to go back to the schedule page instead of the root interface controller.

7. The Schedule Detail interface controller uses the context passed into `awake(withContext:)` to determine which details to show. The context represents the index of the game in the set of upcoming games. The first index of 0 will always be the next game to be played. So you pass 0 for the `context` parameter.

8. You set the snapshot to expire at the time the next game begins. Then, in similar fashion as before, you call `break` to exit the `switch` statement. Again, you've finished a snapshot task.

Next, you need to account for what happens when neither the last game nor the next game are temporally on the horizon.

Add this code beneath the last addition:

```
// 9
// Check if there is any upcoming match
if let nextMatchDate = nextMatchDate {
  // Move to schedule controller
  wkExtension.rootInterfaceController?.pushController(
    withName: "ScheduleInterfaceControllerType",
    context: nil)
  // Check back 24 hours before next match
  let expiration = nextMatchDate.yesterday
  snapshotTask.setTaskCompleted(
    restoredDefaultState: false,
    estimatedSnapshotExpiration: expiration, userInfo: nil)
  break
}
// 10
// No recent matches. No need to update snapshot.
```

This is the final flourish:

9. If you haven't already created a snapshot, you'll show the Schedule interface controller and check back again for a snapshot 24 hours before the next game.

10. If there is no next game, then you'll just show the root interface controller and tell the system that the snapshot doesn't need to be refreshed anytime soon. This code finishes just above the line of code that Xcode creates for you when you create a new WatchKit app.

You've made it through the whirlwind of code!

It's time to see those snapshots in action.

Playing with snapshots

Build and run the app. Once the simulator appears, navigate to **Hardware\Home** in the menu bar to generate a snapshot. The system won't take snapshots while the app is in the foreground. You can verify that the system took a snapshot by checking for the print line in the Debug area of Xcode like you did earlier.

> **Note:** If a snapshot does not get generated immediately, you can force watchOS to take a snapshot by following the steps in the "Forcing a snapshot task in the simulator" section from this chapter.

First modified snapshot

Once you're satisfied that a snapshot did occur, swap back to the simulator. In the menu bar, navigate to **Hardware\Side Button** to show the Dock:

Depending on when the last game was played and when the next one is, you may already see a different snapshot. The image above shows the Schedule interface controller snapshot.

The starter project for this chapter comes with a magic trick so you can easily check out the other snapshots. You'll add and remove games from the season.

Second modified snapshot

Click on the **snapshot** to launch the app from the Dock. Once UHL launches, navigate to **Schedule** if you're not there already. You'll end up on the table of upcoming games:

The starter project includes a force touch menu that lets you add and delete games at will. From the simulator menu bar, navigate to **Hardware\Touch Pressure\Deep Press**. Then, click on the Watch interface to show the force touch menu:

From the simulator menu bar, navigate to **Hardware\Touch Pressure\Shallow Press**. Click on **Add Match**. A game will be added to the schedule, playing 24 hours from now.

> **Note:** You can also remove games by pressing the **Remove next match** button. Use this button when you want to test a snapshot for no upcoming games.

Follow the process of generating a snapshot:

1. In the menu bar, navigate to **Hardware\Home** to generate a snapshot.

2. If you don't see a snapshot logged in the Debug area, force one from Xcode by navigating to **Debug\Simulate UI Snapshot**.

3. In the simulator, navigate to **Hardware\Side Button** to show the Dock.

You'll see your brand new snapshot in all its glory.

Tap on the snapshot again to launch the app. You're taken directly to the game information interface. The changes you made during the snapshot task to push the controller directly affected the state of the app for the user. Be cognizant of how and when you do change the state of the app like this. It could be jarring if the user left the app on a certain screen and expected to return to that screen a few hours later.

The good news is that the snapshot matches the underlying interface — you'll want to maintain this. While you can capture a snapshot of a screen that is not the underlying interface of the app in memory, you should avoid it. That would be jarring for the user to tap on a snapshot and see a different interface. So, you've got a good compromise here:

1. You changed the interface to make it contextually relevant for the snapshot.

2. You allowed the user to jump right into that interface in the app when they launch the app from the Dock.

Third modified snapshot

You wrote code to prefer showing the score of a recently played game over of the details of an equally recent an upcoming game. You'll test that now.

The app should still be running in the simulator. Tap **Back** and **Back** again to get to the root interface controller. Tap **Record** to see the history of game scores.

Next, you'll add a game — played right now — to show the third modified snapshot.

From the simulator menu bar, navigate to **Hardware\Touch Pressure\Deep Press**. Then, click on the Watch interface to show the force touch menu.

From the simulator menu bar, navigate to **Hardware\Touch Pressure\Shallow Press**. Then, click on **Play now**. That adds game — which finished playing just now — to the record:

> **Note:** Similar to the Schedule menu, you can also remove played games from the Record by pressing the **Remove last** button on the force touch menu. Use this button when you want to test a snapshot with no recently played games.

Follow the process to generate the last snapshot:

1. In the menu bar, navigate to **Hardware\Home** to exit the app and generate a snapshot.

2. If you don't see a snapshot logged in the Debug area, force one from Xcode by navigating to **Debug\Simulate UI Snapshot**.

3. In the simulator, navigate to **Hardware\Side Button** to show the Dock.

You'll see the third modified snapshot of the game results:

Well done! The app correctly cycles between four snapshots. Thanks to the rules you added, the system knows when to expire them and generate new ones.

Note: Before you release your app to the App Store, you'll want to remove the handy debugging features from the app: the force touch menus for adding and removing games and the `print("\n handling snapshot task \n")` call.

Where to go from here?

Now you're a Dock app connoisseur, and you've gained a deep understanding of how watchOS uses snapshots. You also learned how to modify snapshots based on contextual relevance.

If you'd like to take this further, try tweaking the size or color of objects in the snapshot. Remember that the snapshot is miniaturized so you might want to make text more readable. To make changes in the root interface controller, you can call its `awake(withContext:)` from the extension delegate. That way, you can pass in a flag as the `context` to trigger the changes before the snapshot.

In this chapter, you saw how watchOS wakes up your app up in the background to take a snapshot. But you can do so much more than that in the background! In the next chapter, you'll learn how to fetch data in the background.

Chapter 11: Networking

By Scott Atkinson

In the bad old days of watchOS 1, developers had to do crazy things to make their Watch apps *appear* to get data from the Internet. Common mechanisms included:

- Having your Watch extension call `openParentApplication(_:reply:)` and making the `UIApplicationDelegate` get data from the extension and return results to the extension.

- Having the parent application get data and share it in a common file location.

- Passing small bits of data around using "Darwin Notifications" and having the main app perform requests upon receipt.

Needless to say, the process was cumbersome, and it resulted in a lot of confusing and often duplicated code.

Since watchOS 2, you can use `URLSession` to make network calls directly from your Watch extension. Most of the time, these calls will still be executed by the iPhone. But it will, at least, be transparent to you as a developer. Even better, if your Watch doesn't happen to be connected to your iPhone but you're in range of a known Wi-Fi network, the Watch will make the network request itself!

In this chapter, you'll add network requests to a watchOS 4 app that provides personalized access to human population data. Along the way, you'll experiment with some of watchOS's networking features.

Getting started

Short of some very simple utility apps like calculators, and maybe a few games, you'd be hard-pressed to find many apps that don't require networking of some sort. Whether it's downloading images, files or other assets, or making web service requests, it's inevitable that you'll need to deal with networking at some point in your iOS career.

Since the Apple Watch currently seems to be much more of a consumption device than a creation device, it's even more likely that the watchOS apps you build will require data from somewhere else.

A brief overview of URLSession

As you've probably experienced, networking can be challenging. A large range of complicated sounding protocols, layers, devices and stacks conspire to hinder you in your quest to get data from remote servers.

Luckily for you, many have created iOS and watchOS libraries to help simplify your interactions with the network. Two excellent and popular tools are **AFNetworking** (afnetworking.com) and its "Swiftified" sibling, **Alamofire** (github.com/Alamofire/Alamofire). These are great tools, and, for very large projects, are probably the way to go.

Apple also provides a set of straightforward APIs in URLSession. For simple projects, it's probably URLSessionDelegateURLSessionTaskDelegatesufficient for all of your networking needs. You won't plumb the depths of URLSession in this chapter; for that, check out Apple's *About the URL Loading System* (apple.co/1JeMx0I) and in particular, the "Using NSURLSession" section (apple.co/1DPOcHE). But let's walk through some of the basics.

The URLSession class provides functionality for asynchronously getting or sending data from a remote server using the HTTP or HTTPS protocols. It supports authentication, exchanging cookies and various other configuration options.

You can configure a session to run in the foreground or the background of an app. Generally, you'll create a session once and reuse it for multiple data requests, called "tasks". There are a number of class methods that make it easy to create a pre-configured URLSessionConfiguration instance, but once it's configured, it cannot be changed.

After you've created and configured your URLSession object, you'll need to create one of three types of tasks on that session — **data**, **download** or **upload** — using an URLRequest object. This object wraps a URL and lets you customize things, like timeout values, for the particular task you're about to execute.

Curiously, you call resume() on a task to actually kick it off.

Finally, for most tasks, the data is returned in a completion handler associated with the task. However, sometimes you'll need more advanced control — for example, if you need to react to authentication challenges or execute a task in the background. If you do need more control, then you'll need to implement one or more of the URLSession-related delegate protocols, like URLSessionDelegate or URLSessionTaskDelegatc.

Well, that was a whirlwind! Let's check out an app and add some code already!

Introducing Populace

The nice folks over at The World Population Project, <u>population.io</u>, have provided a really nice API to access their human population data. You'll be working with a cool little app called **Populace** that collects simple information from the user and then displays interesting data derived from the World Population Project, like an individual's life expectancy and rank by age in the selected country.

Open **Populace.xcodeproj** and have a look around. You'll see there's both an iOS and a watchOS app. You'll get to the code in a moment, but first select the **Populace** scheme and build and run. It will look like this:

The app presents you with a configuration screen where you can enter your birthdate, gender and country of birth. Of course, you can enter this information for any real or hypothetical person to see the corresponding age-related data.

Enter the details of your choice and tap **Done**: you'll be presented with a blank screen. Don't worry, that's OK for now.

Back in Xcode, select the **Populace WatchKit App** scheme and build and run. You'll see the welcome screen. Tap **Configure** and check out the configuration screen:

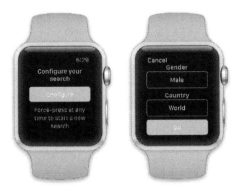

Pick your options and tap **Go**: you'll get some fascinating data!

Hold on a minute. What just happened? Well, you haven't implemented the networking features for the Watch extension. So... no data.

In Xcode, open **WebService.swift** from the **Shared/BaseClasses/Service** group and take a couple of minutes to look through the network-based code in the project. In short, this class provides basic networking for calls to a generic web service.

Find `init(rootURL:)`. You'll see it creates an `URLSession` with a default configuration, one that makes HTTP requests in the foreground of the app. This class also provides a generic method, `executeRequest<>(_:completion:)`, for making web service requests that are expected to return a response object deserialized from JSON. You can also see that it's currently empty - you're going to fix that soon.

Next, review `checkResponseForErrors(_:)`. Every `URLSessionTask` returns an `URLResponse` object when it completes. This method is responsible for looking through the response for errors.

This class forms the basis of all the network requests you'll make in Populace. You'll update or implement concrete subclasses of `WebService` to talk to specific web services like population.io.

In the next section, you'll use an existing `WebService` subclass to make your first calls directly from the watchOS extension.

Calling the web service

As you saw when you ran the iPhone version of the app, the project is not able to call population.io's web services yet. You'll add web service functionality in a bit, but for now, you'll simply call some existing, but empty, methods from the Watch extension.

Open **PopulationController.swift** from the **Populace WatchKit Extension** group and give it a quick review. This class is responsible for displaying results from web service calls in a table on the Watch.

First, you need to create a `WorldPopulationService` object. Find the `Models MARK` near the top of the file and add the following line:

```
let populationService = WorldPopulationService()
```

Population controller will use the `populationService` object throughout the lifecycle of the controller to make web service requests to get population data.

Now, scroll to `refresh(_:)`. This method is called whenever the table needs to be updated with new data from the Internet. You'll need to be sure that the user has properly configured their information, so add the following code immediately after the end of the first if-statement in `refresh(_:)`:

```
// If there is no configuration, get one first
guard let configuration = configuration else {
  changeConfiguration(sender)
  return
}
```

This `guard` statement simply checks to make sure the optional `configuration` object has been set. If it hasn't, the method ends early.

Once the user has properly entered his information, you'll call a series of web services. Immediately after the `self.interfaceStatus = .loading` line, add the following:

```
// Get Rank Data
populationService.getRankInCountry(configuration) {
  rank, error in
```

```
// 1
print("""
  Rank: \(String(describing: rank))
  Error: \(String(describing: error?.localizedDescription))
""")

// 2
// Hide the Loading Indicator
DispatchQueue.main.async {
    self.interfaceStatus = .results
}

// 3
guard let rank = rank else {
    return
}

// 4
DispatchQueue.main.async {
    self.addFactToTable(rank)
}
}
```

This code block uses the `populationService` object to make a call to `getRankInCountry(_:completion:)`. Don't worry too much about the implementation of this method; later, you'll build a very similar method yourself. For now, all you need to know is that it will get the rank within a country based on the passed-in configuration. Once the rank data web service returns, the service object calls the `completion` closure.

Here's what you do with the code you've just added:

1. You print the results of the web service call to the console for debugging.

2. You hide the loading indicator.

3. You ensure that the web service returned a valid `PopulationRank` object.

4. You add the rank data as a new cell to the `WKInterfaceTable`.

That's all you need to make your first Watch-based web service call. Select the **Populace WatchKit App** scheme and build and run. Configure your information and tap **Go**.

Now what's happened? You added a call to retrieve rank data, but still got a spinning wheel.

If you open **WorldPopulationService.swift** in the **Shared** group, you may notice that getRankInCountry() calls executeRequest(), defined in the WebService superclass, whose implementation is still missing. Maybe it's time to put some code there.

Making a network request

Open **WebService.swfit** in the in the **Shared** group. Locate the executeRequest<>(_:completion:) method, it's what you'll use to make a network request.

Probably you've already noticed that it's a generic method: its signature defines a ResponseType type, whose only constraint is to adopt the new Swift 4's Decodable protocol. This new feature is a win-win beacuse:

• it makes this method work with any response type (as long as it adopts Decodable)

• it lets Swift 4 handle the process of decoding a JSON document, and put it into an instance of the generic type

> **Note:** Decodable is a new protocol, introduced in Swift 4 along with Encodable and Codable - the latter being just a typealias for Encodable & Decodable. When a type adopts one of these protocols, the Swift compiler automatically implements the JSON serialization and/or deserialization code for you, so that you will never have to do that manually. Go to apple.co/2afu73m if you want to know more.

Add this code to the executeRequest() method:

```
print("Executing Request With Path: \(requestPath)")
if let request = requestWithURLString(requestPath) {
  // TODO
} else {
  // It was a bad URL, so just fire an error
  let error = NSError(domain:NSURLErrorDomain,
    code:NSURLErrorBadURL,
    userInfo:[ NSLocalizedDescriptionKey :
      "There was a problem creating the request URL:\n" +
      "\(requestPath)"] )
  completion(nil, error)
}
```

Here you create an `URLRequest` using the path passed to the `requestWithURLString()` method. Recall that `URLRequest` wraps an URL and can optionally add request-level options like a unique timeout value. In this case, you're not adding any additional options, so the request simply embodies the `requestPath` appended to the root URL. In the case of `WorldPopulationService`, the URL would end up looking like this:

```
http://api.population.io/1.0/population/1973/United%20States
```

In the event that `requestWithURLString(_:)` couldn't create a URL, you return a `NSURLErrorBadURL NSError` object to the caller in the `else` branch.

Now that you have a valid request, you'll create a data task related to that request. Inside the `if`-statement you just added, insert the following code:

```
// Create the task
let task = session.dataTask(with: request) {
  data, response, error in
  // TODO
}
task.resume()
```

Using the session, you create an `URLSessionDataTask` with the request you created above. An `URLSessionDataTask` represents a task that will execute an HTTP GET request. Since you don't need to do anything fancy like answer authentication requests, you use a variant of `dataTask(with:completionHandler:)` that takes a completion closure. Finally, you kick off the request by calling `resume()`.

The most important logic is still missing though. Add the following to the body of the `completionHandler` closure of `dataTask(with:completionHandler:)`:

```
// 1
if error != nil {
  completion(nil, error as NSError?)
  return
}

// 2 - Check to see if there was an HTTP Error
let cleanResponse = self.checkResponseForErrors(response)

// 3
if let errorCode = cleanResponse.errorCode {
  print("An error occurred: \(errorCode)")
  completion(nil, error as NSError?)
  return
}

// 4 - Make sure there's some data
```

```
guard let data = data else {
  print("No response data")
  completion(nil, error as NSError?)
  return
}

// 5 Deserialize the JSON data
let decoder = JSONDecoder()
let response: ResponseType

do {
  response = try decoder.decode(ResponseType.self, from: data)
} catch (let error) {
  print("Parsing Issues")
  completion(nil, error as NSError?)
  return
}

// 6 - Things went well, call the completion handler
completion(response, nil)
```

If you've built any apps that use networking, you know that much of your development and testing time is spent dealing with the myriad ways that a network request can fail. The code above is a small sample of the checks that you need to make with a network response. Let's walk through them:

1. If the data task returns a generic error, simply call the passed-in `completion` closure and exit the method.

2. Assuming there are no generic errors, take the `URLResponse response` object and attempt to further inspect it for errors. `checkResponseForErrors(_:)` takes the response and runs a few checks on it.

   First, it makes sure there is an actual response. Then, it converts the response to an `HTTPURLResponse`. You can do this because you know that you're making HTTP calls in this scenario, so the cast will work.

   Next, it checks to see if the response contained an HTTP response code of something other than 200, meaning success. Finally, it returns the findings as a tuple containing a `HTTPURLResponse` and an error code.

3. With that `cleanResponse` tuple, you check for an error code. If you find one, you again call the `completion` closure and exit.

4. If you've gotten this far, the web service successfully returned you *something*. At least, it should, so you check if there's some data, otherwise you just call the `completion` closure and return.

5. So the web service did actually return some JSON data. It's now time to deserialize that JSON into an instance of **something**, where the something is the ResponseType type, the generic type adopting the Decodable protocol.

6. Finally, it seems that you have an instance of an object and no errors! So return it to the caller.

Time to build and run again. Do the configuration, then tap on Go. Now it's much better, you can see that you've got... What? A black screen? Now what's happened?

Configuring App Transport Security

In Xcode, open the debugging console by pressing **Shift-Command-Y**. You'll see logging information that looks something like this:

```
2017-09-09 21:56:04.765405-0400 Populace WatchKit
Extension[10863:1070700] App Transport Security has blocked a
cleartext HTTP (http://) resource load since it is insecure.
Temporary exceptions can be configured via your app's Info.plist
file.

2017-09-09 21:56:04.770849-0400 Populace WatchKit
Extension[10863:1070700] Task <6F8CA42B-
ED92-4446-83B6-90C4F6A9E3C1>.<1> finished with error - code:
-1022
```

Back in iOS 9 and watchOS 2, to better protect user information, Apple increased the default level of security. By default, iOS will not allow any URLSession tasks using HTTP. Apple expects developers to use only HTTPS (TLS).

Open **WorldPopulationService.swift** from the **Shared/Population/Services** group and find this line:

```
private let baseURL = URL(string: "http://api.population.io")!
```

Notice that baseURL uses just HTTP. Luckily, Apple has provided a mechanism to opt-out of the HTTPS requirement by adding some keys to **Info.plist**. In the project navigator, expand the **Populace WatchKit Extension** group and right-click the **Info.plist** file in that group. Select **Open As/Source Code** from the menu.

Immediately above the very last <\dict> line, insert the following XML:

```
<key>NSAppTransportSecurity</key>
<dict>
    <key>NSAllowsArbitraryLoads</key>
    <true/>
</dict>
```

This key instructs the WatchKit app extension to allow the loading of non-HTTPS URLs. Build and run again, and *watch* what happens.

Congratulations: You've just completed your first network request from the Apple Watch!

> **Note:** The key you've entered is the simplest of all the App Transport Security functionalities. If you'd like to learn more about what it can do, be sure to check out WWDC 2015 Session #711 on `URLSession`: apple.co/1hBa4g8.

Making another call

Now that you know you can get data from the Internet on a watchOS app, you'll add one more method. This method will use the population service to get life expectancy values from the web service.

In Xcode, open **PopulationController.swift**, and add the following to `refresh(_:)`, immediately after the call to `getRankInCountry(_:completion:)`:

```
// Get Life Expectancy Data
populationService.getLifeExpectancy(configuration) {
  expectancy, error in

  print("""
    Expectancy: \(String(describing: expectancy))
    Error: \(String(describing: error?.localizedDescription))
    """)

  // Hide the Loading Indicator
  DispatchQueue.main.async {
    self.interfaceStatus = .results
  }
  guard let expectancy = expectancy else {
    return
  }
  DispatchQueue.main.async {
```

```
      self.addFactToTable(expectancy)
  }
}
```

This code looks familiar! You simply call `getLifeExpectancy(_:completion:)`, which returns a `LifeExpectancy` object to the `completion` closure. Like before, you check to make sure you received good data, and if so, you add the new data to the table.

Notice that in this second call, you've reused the `populationService` object. This, in turn, reuses the same `URLSession` object.

Build and run again to see how it looks. Make sure you select a gender so you can get a life expectancy:

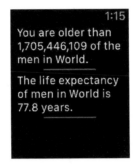

Looking good! In the next section, you'll explore `URLSession` a bit more by creating your own data task.

Getting a table of data

With all of this interesting information about ages and life expectancies around the world, wouldn't it be smart and cool to get a table of data, instead of just a single datapoint? Luckily for you, population.io provides a couple of APIs that will return multiple data points.

Before you write your networking code, first have a look at how it will eventually be used. Open **WorldPopulationService.swift** in the **Shared/Population/Services** group in Xcode and locate `getPopulationTable(_:country:completion:)`.

Here's the code for reference:

```
func getPopulationTable(_ year: Int, country: String,
  completion: @escaping (_ table:PopulationTable?,
  _ error: Error?) -> Void) {

  // 1
```

```swift
let path = "/1.0/population/\(year)/\(country)"

// 2
let encodedPath = path.addingPercentEncoding(
  withAllowedCharacters: CharacterSet.urlPathAllowed)

// 3
executeRequest(encodedPath!) {
  (response: PopulationTable?, error: Error?) -> Void in

  // 4
  // Make sure you get an array back
  guard let response = response else {
    completion(nil, error)
    return
  }

  // 5
  completion(response, error)
  }
}
```

Here's what's going on in the code above:

1. First, you create a `path` string that represents the RESTful web request to get population data. In this case, you call the "population" method and pass it the birth year and country that the user entered.

2. Because some of the data inserted into `path` may contain invalid characters, like spaces, the string is URL-encoded.

3. Next, you call `executeRequest<>(_:completion:)`, passing in the encoded string.

4. Once the request is complete, you check to make sure it returned a response. If it didn't, you call the completion handler passed to `getPopulationTable(_:country:completion:)` without a returned table.

5. If you do have a response, you know it's an instance of `PopulationTable` object, which you simply return in the completion closure.

At this point, you *could* run that app and it would go get data from the web service. However, not much would happen with the results. You still need to write the code to take the data returned and do something with it. Time to write code to do the initial error-checking and parsing of the response.

Populating the table

You're not quite at the point where you can see anything happen in the app. But you can make the web service call and log the results.

Open **PopulationController.swift** in the **Populace WatchKit Extension** group and add the following to the bottom of `refresh(_:)`:

```
populationService.getPopulationTable(configuration.dobYear,
    country: configuration.country) { table, error in
    print("""
        Table: \(String(describing: table))
        Error: \(
            String(describing: error?.localizedDescription))
    """)
}
```

Build and run the Watch extension. As before, enter your information and tap **Go**. Open the debugging console, and you'll see a couple of lines in the log that look like this:

```
Table: Optional(Populace_WatchKit_Extension.PopulationTable)
Error: nil
```

The fact that *something* is listed on the `Table:` line shows that the web service returned data and the population service created a `PopulationTable` object. Now you'll write code to do something impressive with it!

Fetching a chart

Right now, your apps look a bit bland. Why don't you spruce them up with a nice bar graph? It's a good thing you just figured out how to download a table of data from the web service.

You'll be using the Google Charts API to request a stacked bar graph image. The graph will show the male and female population by age, in 10 year increments, for the country you select. In Xcode, open **GoogleChartService.swift** in the **Shared/Chart/Services** group. This `WebService` subclass contains one public method: `getStackedBarChart(_:bottomSeries:bottomColor:topSeries:topColor:completion:)`. You're going to implement that method.

As you can see from the method signature, it takes a number of parameters:

- The size of the image to get

- An array of integer values for the bottom stack

- The fill color for the bottom data series

- An array of integer values for the top stack (Optional)

- The fill color for the top data series (Optional)

- A completion closure that returns the image or an error (Optional)

Much like the population.io web services, the Google Chart APIs use data encoding in a GET request URL to return the proper graph image.

First, construct a path by adding the following to the beginning of `getStackedBarChart(_:bottomSeries:bottomColor:topSeries:topColor:completion:)`:

```
var path = "/chart?cht=bvs&chbh=a"
path +=
  "&\(seriesMaxValueString(bottomSeries, series2: topSeries))"

path += "&\(sizeParameterString(size))"
path +=
  "&\(seriesColorParameterString(bottomColor,color2: topColor))"

path +=
  "&\(seriesParameterString(bottomSeries, series2: topSeries))"

let encodedPath = path.addingPercentEncoding(
  withAllowedCharacters: CharacterSet.urlQueryAllowed)
```

You are constructing the `path` string by using a number of utility methods that encode the size and scale of the image, the data in the chart and the colors for the chart. Once constructed, you URL-encode paURLSessionDownloadTaskth so that all characters can be properly represented.

> **Note:** In this case, you are passing `addingPercentEncoding()` the `CharacterSet.urlQueryAllowed` set. Google Charts uses query strings to encode data, so the path must be encoded with the allowed query string parameters. In `WorldPopulationService`, the methods use `CharacterSet.urlPathAllowed`, as the data is encoded in the URL's path instead.

Now that you've encoded the population data into a query string, you need to create the request and the task. Add the following to the method:

```
if let request = requestWithURLString(encodedPath!) {
  // Create the download task
  let downloadTask = session.downloadTask(with: request) {
```

```
    url, response, error in
    // TODO
  }
  downloadTask.resume()
}
```

Like before, you create an URLRequest object that represents the path you just created. Then, instead of creating a data task, you create a URLSessionDownloadTask.

Unlike data tasks, download tasks are designed to download large files or objects. These tasks are generally used for background downloads, although here you're using one in the foreground.

Notice that the parameters for the completionHandler closure include url. Download tasks don't return their results to the completionHandler — they might be huge! Instead, the URLSession returns a local file URL that tells the closure where it can find the downloaded results on disk. And as before, you'll initiate the network request by calling resume() on the downloadTask.

Once the request finishes, you need to process the results. Implement the body of the completionHandler with the following code:

```
// 1 - There was an error
if error != nil {
  completion(nil, error)
  return
}

// 2 - Check to see if there was an HTTP Error
let cleanResponse = self.checkResponseForErrors(response)
if let errorCode = cleanResponse.errorCode {
  print("An error occurred: \(errorCode)")
  completion(nil, error)
  return
}

// 3 - Check to see if a URL was returned
guard let url = url else {
  print("No Results URL")
  completion(nil, error)
  return
}

// 4 - Get the image from the local URL
guard let data = try? Data(contentsOf: url),
  let image = UIImage(data: data) else {
    print("No Image")
    completion(nil, error)
    return
}
```

```
// 5 - Everything worked out, send back the image
completion(image, error)
```

Much of this code looks similar to the executeRequest<>(_:completion:) method you implemented above. Here's the breakdown:

1. First, you check for generic errors and return early if there are any.

2. Then, exactly like before, you look at the response object to see if there are any errors there.

3. If there are no errors, you check to make sure the URL you were given is valid. If it isn't, you return early.

4. At this point, you use the URL to get an Data object from the contents of the local file. If the data exists, you attempt to convert it into a UIImage object. If either of these steps fail, you stop processing the data.

5. All the tests have passed! You have a valid image that you can return to the caller via the completion closure.

This is getting exciting, isn't it? You now have an image in memory, so all you have to do is show it!

Displaying the chart

Open **PopulationController.swift** in the **Populace WatchKit Extension** group and declare a GoogleChartService constant below the populationService declaration:

```
let chartService = GoogleChartService()
```

Scroll down to refresh(_:) and add the following to the bottom of the completion closure for your call to getPopulationTable(_:country:completion:):

```
// 1
guard let table = table else {
  // Hide the Loading Indicator
  DispatchQueue.main.async {
    self.interfaceStatus = .results
  }
  return
}

// 2 - Get the Bar Chart for the population data
self.chartService.getStackedBarChart(
  CGSize(width: 300, height: 300),
```

```
      bottomSeries: table.malePopulationByDecade,
      bottomColor: maleColor,
      topSeries: table.femalePopulationByDecade,
      topColor: femaleColor,
      completion: { image, error in

        // 3
        DispatchQueue.main.async {
          self.interfaceStatus = .results
          self.table.insertRows(
            at: IndexSet(integer: self.facts!.count),
            withRowType: "ChartRowController")
          let row = self.table.rowController(
            at: self.facts!.count) as! ChartRowController
          row.image = image
        }
  })
```

By adding this code inside the completion closure of the call to get the data table, you daisy-chain the calls together. Once you get your population table, you use that data to create a graph of it.

Walking through the specifics:

1. First, you check to make sure that you actually did get back a non nil `PopulationTable` object. If you didn't, you simply hide the loading indicator.

2. You now make the call to the method you just created. The `PopulationTable` object does much of the work of organizing the data into arrays of decades instead of single years. So you simply pass the decade data for both men and women, along with some color choices and the size of the image you wish to receive.

3. Assuming everything goes well and `GoogleChartService` returns a valid image, you now hide the loading indicator and insert a new cell into the `WKInterfaceTable`.

Build and run the Watch extension and then run a new query. If all went well, you'll see the graph appear at the bottom of the table:

Nicely done! Now you can see both how old you're getting *and* just how many young people there are in the world!

The last thing you need to do is update your iPhone app to show the graph. Open **PopulationViewController.swift** in the **Population** group and add a `GoogleChartService` instance right below the `populationService` declaration.

```
let chartService = GoogleChartService()
```

Just like in the Watch app, `refresh(_:)` makes a call to `getPopulationTable(_:country:completion:)`. In the `completion` closure, add the following:

```
guard let table = table else {
  return
}

DispatchQueue.main.async {
  let width = self.table.frame.size.width
  self.chartService.getStackedBarChart(
    CGSize(width: width, height: width),
    bottomSeries: table.malePopulationByDecade,
    bottomColor: maleColor,
    topSeries: table.femalePopulationByDecade,
    topColor: femaleColor,
    completion: { (image, error) -> Void in
      DispatchQueue.main.async {
        self.graphImage = image
        self.table.reloadSections(IndexSet(
          integer: self.kGraphSection), with: .automatic)
      }
  })
}
```

This will look very familiar. With the exception of how rows are added to the `UITableView` of the `PopulationViewController`, this code is identical to the code in the Watch extension.

That's it! Switch to the **Populace scheme**, and build and run one last time. Enter your information and tap **Done**.

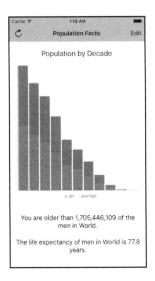

Where to go from here?

You can feel proud: Your Apple Watch can now make network calls all by itself! In this chapter, you explored a number of interesting things about URLSession:

- Designing reusable web service classes

- How to create, configure and execute an URLSessionTask

- The differences between an URLSessionDataTask and a URLSessionDownloadTask

- A couple of cool — and free! — web services

- App Transport Security

Take some time to explore the rest of the project. In particular, have a look at the init(from:) methods of the PopulationTable, PopulationRank, LifeExpectancy and PopulationData classes to see how you can customize JSON decoding.

Also, play around with your Watch to see how it behaves when it's not connected to your iPhone. If you're near a known Wi-Fi network, Populace will still work!

For more in-depth coverage of URLSession, and more generally about networking, study some of the networking tutorials on our site:

URLSession Tutorial: Getting Started: bit.ly/1h4DRxG

Cookbook: Using NSURLSession: bit.ly/1gC3hln

Chapter 12: Animation

By Jack Wu

When Apple originally released watchOS, WatchKit offered only one way to perform your own animations — by flipping through image frames like a GIF. Even with such a limited API, developers sprang into action, creating some truly impressive animations. However, deep down, we weren't satisfied; the dream of the ability to captivate users through animations lived on.

Nowadays, watchOS has a few more additional animation APIs. There are still very few compared to the APIs on iOS, but now, with some extra creativity and cleverness, you can bring just as much or even more delightfulness to your users through animations in watchOS.

This chapter will get you going by first introducing the three main ways you can perform animations in watchOS and the different effects achieved by each method. Then, you'll get your hands dirty and create some animation effects for a beautiful — but not yet animated — app named Woodpecker.

Getting started

No one really knows how long it takes to form a habit. Some say three weeks, others say three months. In reality, most people don't care how long it takes — unless it takes too long!

Woodpecker is an app that focuses on what you know for sure: habits are formed through repetition. That's all there is to it. A woodpecker doesn't say "I'll peck this wood for 3 hours"; it pecks until it finds the food. The Woodpecker app takes this and applies it to your habits.

Simply add a task, set a goal for the habit-forming repetition count, and peck away! Can't think of a task? How about "complete a raywenderlich.com tutorial"? 800 times should be enough, right? :]

Now that you're excited to work on this app, locate the starter project for Woodpecker and open **Woodpecker.xcodeproj** in Xcode.

Build and run the iPhone app. Get a feel for the app and how it works. Create a few tasks and finish them. It's very simple, and a bit delightful, if I do say so myself. :]

Now build and run the Watch app. Again, create a few tasks and finish them.

The simplicity is there, but the delightfulness? Well, you're about to add that. :]

> **Note:** You need to use Force Touch to add multiple ongoing tasks. This is a bit of a pain on the simulator if you don't have a force touch trackpad. Press **Command-Shift-2** to perform a force touch, then press **Command-Shift-1** to perform a regular touch on the menu item.

Take a moment and browse through Woodpecker's source code. Pay extra attention to the two interface controllers in the WatchKit extension — that's where you'll be adding the magic.

Animation overview

The animation APIs, like most things in WatchKit, are extremely simple yet very powerful. There are three main types of animations in WatchKit:

- Implicit animations
- Property animations
- Animated images

WatchKit performs implicit animations for you — for free.

Implicit animations

WatchKit performs most implicit animations for you when updating tables, which animate the insertion and deletion of rows whenever you use either of these two methods:

```
func insertRowsAtIndexes(_ rows: NSIndexSet,
   withRowType rowType: String)
func removeRowsAtIndexes(_ rows: NSIndexSet)
```

You can also get a nice scrolling animation in a table, for free, whenever you call the following:

```
func scrollToRow(at index: Int)
```

The best free animation — and thus, my favorite of favorites — occurs when you update a table row. Whenever you make an update to the contents of a table row that changes the height, WatchKit reloads the row for you with an implicit, free animation.

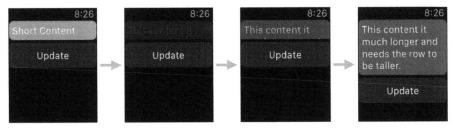

This is quite powerful, and sometimes even justifies placing an *entire* Watch interface into a single table row.

watchOS 4 also introduces a scrolling API for any interface controller, even without tables:

```
func scroll(to object: WKInterfaceObject,
   at scrollPosition: WKInterfaceScrollPosition,
   animated: Bool)
```

This works similarly to `UITableView`'s scrolling methods, and lets you scroll any interface object to either the top, center or bottom of the screen. Note the `animated` argument, guess what happens when you pass in `true`? Free animations!

Property animations

Property animations were introduced in watchOS 2 and added a single new method on `WKInterfaceController`:

```
func animate(withDuration duration: TimeInterval,
   animations: @escaping () -> Swift.Void)
```

Does this look familiar? It might, because it's identical to a method that `UIView` has in UIKit! But this is all you get in WatchKit. No completion handlers, options, springs — just the animation duration.

If you aren't very familiar with UIKit, don't worry; this method is simple to use. In the `animations` block, you perform all the changes you want to animate, and WatchKit will animate them for you. For example, if you want to animate the `alpha` of `ghost` to 1 over `0.4` seconds, you simply have to type:

```
animate(withDuration:0.4) {
    ghost.alpha = 1
}
```

| Time = 0s | Time = 0.2s | Time = ...Boo! |

That's it! As you can see, the method works beautifully with trailing closure syntax, resulting in very readable code.

Not everything is animatable, though, so disappointingly you can't just throw any change into that block and be done with animations in your Watch app.

The following properties are animatable on anything that descends from `WKInterfaceObject`:

- Alpha
- Width and height
- Horizontal and vertical alignment
- Color and background color (*not* text color)

And on `WKInterfaceGroup`:

- Content inset

It might not seem like a lot of power, but with a few tricks, this one method will cover the vast majority of your WatchKit animation needs!

Animated images

Last but definitely not least, WatchKit can display animated images. These can be thought of as flip-books: You provide several images as frames and then *flip* through them. If you do it fast enough, you get an animation.

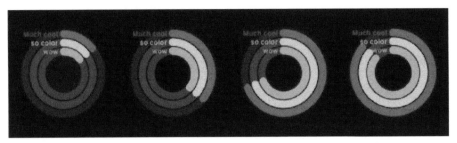

You can display animated images on interface objects that conform to the new `WKImageAnimatable` protocol. Currently, only `WKInterfaceGroup`, `WKInterfaceButton`, and `WKInterfaceImage` conform to `WKImageAnimatable`.

That's it for now; you'll learn how to use animated images later in this chapter.

With that, you know the basics of creating animations in WatchKit. In the remaining sections, you'll implement each of these animation methods in the world's best habit creation app — Woodpecker!

Animations in practice

It's time to create some animations! In this section, you'll see in action all the animation methods described earlier, starting with my favorite: free animations.

Shuffling rows

Open **TaskInterfaceController.swift**. You can see that `TasksInterfaceController` is implemented using two tables, `ongoingTable` and `completedTable`.

After the user adds a new task, the app dismisses `NewTasksInterfaceController` and calls `updateOngoingTasksIfNeeded()` on `TasksInterfaceController`. Currently this method simply reloads the entire table. That definitely sounds inefficient, since you know the only change that *can* happen is adding a new row.

Delete the `loadOngoingTasks()` call in `updateOngoingTasksIfNeeded()` and replace it with the following snippet:

```
// 1
let newRowIndex = tasks.ongoingTasks.count - 1
ongoingTable.insertRows(at: IndexSet(integer: newRowIndex),
    withRowType: OngoingTaskRowController.RowType)

// 2
let row = ongoingTable.rowController(at:newRowIndex) as!
    OngoingTaskRowController
```

```
row.populate(with: tasks.ongoingTasks.last!,
    frameWidth: contentFrame.size.width)
```

Here's a breakdown of what's happening:

1. You use `insertRows(at:withRowType:)` to add a new row to the end instead of reloading the entire table.

2. Since you added a new row, you must populate it. This is similar to when you populate the table for the first time.

This looks a lot more efficient. Build and run. When you create a new task, notice you also get an animation for the new row, *gratis*. Awesome! I'm sure you want more free animations now, and luckily there's another great place for them.

When the user completes a task, the app removes the task from `ongoingTable` and adds it to `completedTable`. Currently, you do this by simply reloading both tables after the task is completed. These two actions are also perfect candidates for free table row animations. After that, you will also scroll the screen down to the newly added row, using just one call of `scrollToRow(at:)`!

Still in **TaskInterfaceController.swift**, find `table(_:didSelectRowAt:)` and then find the two lines of code inside the `if task.isCompleted` block:

```
loadOngoingTasks()
loadCompletedTasks()
```

Replace these lines with the following snippet:

```
// 1
ongoingTable.removeRows(at: IndexSet(integer: rowIndex))

// 2
let newRowIndex = tasks.completedTasks.count - 1
completedTable.insertRows(
  at: IndexSet(integer: newRowIndex),
  withRowType: CompletedTaskRowController.RowType)

// 3
let row = completedTable.rowController(at: newRowIndex) as!
  CompletedTaskRowController
row.populate(with: task)

// 4
self.updateAddTaskButton()
self.updateCompletedLabel()

// 5
self.completedTable.scrollToRow(at: newRowIndex)
```

Here's what's going on:

1. Instead of reloading the entire table, you can take advantage of the fact that you know exactly what's changed and use `removeRows(at:)` to remove the completed row.

2. Similarly, for `completedTable`, you're always adding the new row to the end, so you can use `insertRows(at:withRowType:)` to do so.

3. Since you're adding a new row, you must configure it. Here you're grabbing the newly created row and populating it with the newly completed task.

4. You want to update the state of the add task button and completed label for the changes that just occurred. These two methods will handle that for you.

5. Scroll down to the newly added completed task, with animation.

Notice, again, that these changes are *not* animation-related. They're simply best practice. Your performance will increase, since you're not reloading entire tables and best of all, you get free animations!

Build and run. Complete a few tasks and observe the animations.

The row removal is noticeable when there's more than one ongoing task in the table after you complete one. When there's only one, the appearance of the new task button covers up the nice animation. Hmm... If only that button faded in slowly... over time... like an animation!

> **Note:** You can use **Command-T** in the Watch simulator, or **Debug -> Slow Animations** in its menu, to slow down the animation speed. This works in the iPhone simulator as well!

Fading in, changing size and more!

In Woodpecker, the Add Task button simply pops out when you complete the last ongoing task. The scrolling away helps a bit, but this is still quite jarring for users — they might think that this is a bug or that they did something wrong.

Animations to the rescue! The button should appear with an animation to reassure the user. But *how* should it appear?

The safest animation in most cases is the fade-in, which is easy to implement with property animations. Find `updateAddTaskButton()` in **TasksInterfaceController.swift** and replace its implementation with the following snippet:

```
// 1
addTaskButton.setHidden(ongoingTable.numberOfRows != 0)

if (ongoingTable.numberOfRows == 0) {
  // 2
  addTaskButton.setAlpha(0)
  // 3
  animate(withDuration:0.4) {
    self.addTaskButton.setAlpha(1)
  }
}
```

1. You use `setHidden(_:)` to show and hide the button appropriately. If the button should be shown, you want to perform an animation.

2. The button needs to be fully transparent in the beginning, before it fades in.

3. Inside the `animate(withDuration:animations:)` block, simply set the `alpha` of the button to `1` to animate the fade-in. Note how you use the trailing closure syntax here.

That's all you need! Build and run. Complete a task again and watch the Add Task button fade in. Much better!

Animations can also provide the user with important feedback. When you perform a task in Woodpecker, the progress bar is just *begging* for some action. You don't want to leave it hanging, do you?

Return to `table(_:didSelectRowAt:)` in **TasksInterfaceController.swift**. In the `else` statement after the code you previously added, wrap the call to `updateProgressWithTask(_:frameWidth:)` in an animation block, so it looks like this:

```
animate(withDuration:0.4) {
  row.updateProgress(
    with: task, frameWidth: self.contentFrame.size.width)
}
```

Could it be that easy? Build and run the Watch app. Yes, it is indeed *that* easy:

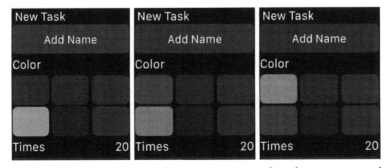

You must be getting the hang of this, so you can try the next one yourself. In **NewTaskInterfaceController.swift**, find `selectColor(_:button:)`. This is what gets called when you tap on a color button. See if you can animate the `alpha` change of the two buttons *and* the `backgroundColor` changes that occur when you choose a color.

Done already? The trick here is to use a single animation block for all the property changes.

Here's the resulting function's body:

```
selectedColor = color

animate(withDuration:0.4) {
  if let previous = self.selectedColorButton {
    previous.setAlpha(0.3)
  }
  self.selectedColorButton = button
  button.setAlpha(1)
  self.addNameGroup.setBackgroundColor(
    color.color.withAlphaComponent(0.3))
}
```

Build and run the Watch app again. Such a small change, but what an awesome effect:

Now for the last property animation! This one is going to be a bit more complicated than the previous ones.

By now, you might have noticed that if you attempt to create a task without choosing a name or a color, the app displays a little error image:

It's pretty cool, but also a bit jarring. I bet you know what it needs. :]

There's a small challenge here, because there are two stages in displaying the error. You must show it and *then* hide it later.

Without access to completion blocks like in UIKit, the best way you can chain animations together in WatchKit is to use `asyncAfter(deadline:execute:)` from Grand Central Dispatch.

Find `displayError()` in **NewTaskInterfaceController.swift** and perform your magic on it, without looking below!

I'm sure you got it right, but here's the resulting `displayError()`:

```
errorImage.setHidden(false)

animate(withDuration:0.4) {
  self.errorImage.sizeToFitHeight()
}

let delayTime = DispatchTime.now() +
  Double(Int64(1 * Double(NSEC_PER_SEC))) / Double(NSEC_PER_SEC)

DispatchQueue.main.asyncAfter(deadline: delayTime) {
  self.animate(withDuration:0.4) {
    self.errorImage.setHeight(0)
  }
}
```

Build and run. Force an error and boom — magic.

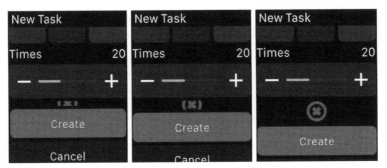

When using animations, you never want to add one *just for the effect*. Animations can serve many functional purposes in apps. Here, you've used them to draw the user's attention to changes and provide context.

That's it for now for property animations. You'll learn more cool tricks later in the book — there's so much more you can do with animators! :]

Animated images: a paradox?

That error animation was cool and all, but could it be even better? Of course it can! But first, a primer on animated images, as promised.

What *are* animated images? Does the term even make sense? Well, sort of... In WatchKit, an **animated image** is made up of a sequence of images. You can package all the images in the entire sequence into one animated image.

Yes, animated images are *just* images.

It may sound obvious, but this is quite important—it means you display an animated image just as you would a normal image, using the same APIs.

Animated images are even stored the same way, by using UIImage. UIImage has had this functionality since iOS 5, but it didn't receive much attention until WatchKit came around.

You can create an animated image in two ways:

1. You can use the `UIImage` method `animatedImage(with:duration:)` to create an animation from a sequence of images. This is also how you should cache animations on the Watch. Don't send over all the frames individually; it won't work!

2. To create an animated image from images that are already in your Watch app's bundle, you first need to number the frames by appending an integer to them, starting from 0, such as **frame0.png**, **frame1.png** and so on. You set the animated image on an instance of `WKInterfaceImage` by using `setImageNamed(_:)` and passing in the filename prefix, which in this case is **frame**.

After you've set the animated image on an interface element, you can control the animation using these methods from `WKImageAnimatable`:

- **`startAnimating()`** starts the animation with the default values set in the storyboard.

- **`startAnimatingWithImages(in:duration:repeatCount:)`** starts the animation with the specified range, duration and repeat count. A repeat count of `0` will make the animation repeat forever.

- **`stopAnimating()`** stops the animation. No surprises here!

An animated image: the error spin

Animated images are the most *powerful* in terms of what they can achieve. They are also the most *expensive* to use. They take up more disk space, more memory *and* have lower performance than all the other animation methods. Thus, you should use them conservatively.

Back to Woodpecker. If you've been poking around, perhaps you've noticed the **X-Animation** folder in the Watch app's image assets. Look in there and you'll see a series of image frames representing a rotating "x". You've probably guessed it by now: you're going to make the error spin!

Find `displayError()` in **NewTaskInterfaceController.swift** again and update the body to the following:

```
errorImage.setHidden(false)

// 1
errorImage.setImageNamed("x")

// 2
errorImage.startAnimating()
animate(withDuration:0.4) {
  self.errorImage.sizeToFitHeight()
}
```

```
let delayTime = DispatchTime.now() +
  Double(Int64(1 * Double(NSEC_PER_SEC))) / Double(NSEC_PER_SEC)

DispatchQueue.main.asyncAfter(deadline: delayTime) {
  self.animate(withDuration:0.4) {
    self.errorImage.setHeight(0)
  }
}
```

There are only three new lines here, as marked:

1. Since the images in the sequence are named **x1**, **x2** and so forth, you set the image to the WKInterfaceImage by using the common prefix x.

2. You call startAnimating() to start the animation from the beginning.

That's all you need to do! Build and run the Watch app one final time. Trigger an error again and enjoy the spinning "x". I'm sure you'll want to do that a few more times!

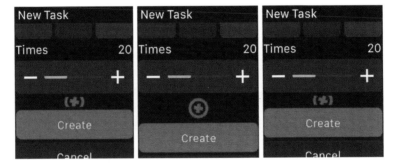

Above and beyond

Now that you have a taste of each type of animation, you can get creative! These animations can be chained, grouped and used in all sorts of ways to create delightful experiences for your users. To get you started, you will implement a few more animations in the section that are a bit more complex and exciting than the previous ones.

Sequential animations

The first appearance of a view is a great opportunity to spice up your app with animations. You can see this in watchOS in a few places; for example, when you switch to an analog watch face from the app selector.

Here, the complications fade in a tiny bit after the watch face begins animating, and finish a few moments later. It's quite a nice effect.

The color buttons in Woodpecker are a great candidate for this type of animation. The first step is to set the initial values of the buttons. Open **Interface.storyboard** and select all the color buttons.

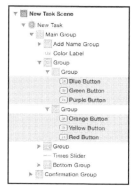

Set the **alpha** of all the buttons to **0** in the Attributes Inspector:

Note: As you will notice throughout this section, setting the initial values of interface elements in the storyboard makes it much less convenient to lay out and visualize your interface.

The alternative is to leave the values of the storyboard as-is and set up the initial values in `awake(withContext:)`.

The trade-off should be seriously considered here, since any task performed in `awake(withContext:)` needs to be completed before the interface is displayed to users. In Woodpecker, there is quite a bit of setup needed for each interface and so you will always be setting the initial values in the storyboard for the best performance.

Next, you want to add the code to animate the buttons into view. To do so, you need to take advantage of GCD's `asyncAfter(deadline:execute:)` function to start the animations one at a time, with slight delays in between.

Open **NewTaskInterfaceController.swift** and add the following function to `NewTaskInterfaceController`:

```
func animateInColorButtons() {
  // 1
  let timeStep = Int64(0.1 * Double(NSEC_PER_SEC))
  // 2
  for (i, button) in colorButtons().enumerated() {
    // 3
    let delayTime = DispatchTime.now() +
      Double(timeStep * Int64(i)) / Double(NSEC_PER_SEC)

    DispatchQueue.main.asyncAfter(deadline: delayTime) {
      // 4
      self.animate(withDuration:0.4) {
        if button === self.selectedColorButton {
          button.setAlpha(1)
        } else {
          button.setAlpha(0.3)
        }
      }
    }
  }
}
```

Here's the play-by-play of what's happening:

1. You define the delay between each animation's start time.

2. Next, you enumerate through each button, keeping track of its index.

3. For each button, the start time of the animation is `i * timeStep`. This allows the first one to start at time 0 and each subsequent one to follow suit.

4. You perform the animation as usual. :]

Note: You want to keep tabs on the *total* animation time when creating sequential animations. The times accumulate quickly and you don't want your users to be waiting for your animations to finish.

Here, the total animation time is when the last button finishes animating into view, which is 5 * 0.1 + 0.4 = 0.9 seconds, which is acceptable. A small change, such as increasing the delay between animations to 0.2, would result in a total time of 5 * 0.2 + 0.4 = 1.4 seconds, which feels a tad lengthy.

Almost done! Now you simply need to call your shiny new method. watchOS 2 introduced a new method in the WKInterfaceController lifecycle that's perfect for animations like this: didAppear(). The name speaks for itself!

Add the following code to NewTaskInterfaceController:

```
override func didAppear() {
  super.didAppear()
  animateInColorButtons()
}
```

Build and run the Watch app. Go to add a new task and watch the magic happen:

Sweet! That definitely makes me want to create more tasks. :]

Using groups in animations

Groups are key to unlocking fancy animations in watchOS and you'll likely use them a lot.

The main purpose of groups in watchOS animations can be summarized in one word: **spacing**. With groups, you can add, remove and change the spacing between two interface objects.

If you then change the height of that group, you are effectively changing the spacing between the two labels.

Sliding into view

Back to Woodpecker. Currently, when you add a new task, the new cell is already visible when you return to the tasks interface controller. It would be useful, and cool, if the cell animated to show the user that it's a new addition to the list. Hmm... using a spacer group here sounds like a great idea!

As with sequential animations, you want to set the initial state of the animation directly inside the storyboard. Open **Interface.storyboard** and find the **OngoingTaskRow** in the first scene.

Inside **Label Group**, add a new group as the first object:

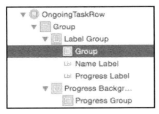

Configure the new group to have the following properties:

- Width: **Relative to Container**; **1**, **0** Adjustment

- Height: **Relative to Container**; **1**, **0** Adjustment

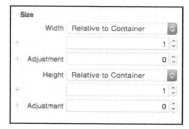

Since the labels will be sliding into view, the progress bar shouldn't be there in the beginning, either. Set the **alpha** of **Progress Background Group** to **0**.

The cell will now appear completely empty in the storyboard:

That's just how you want it! Now all you have to do to make the labels slide into view is set the width of the new spacer group to 0.

To do that, you first need an outlet connection to the new group. Open **OngoingTaskRowController.swift** in the **assistant editor**. You can do this by holding **alt** when clicking on the file.

Drag a connection from the new group into `OngoingTaskRowController` and name it `spacerGroup`:

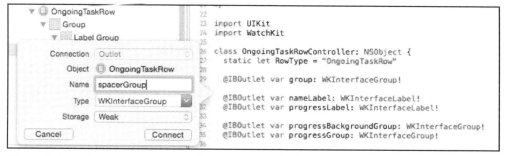

Now all the task rows are completely empty. You'll fix that next — with style!

Open **TasksInterfaceController.swift** and add the following method to
`TasksInterfaceController`:

```
func animateInTableRows() {
  animate(withDuration:0.6) {
    for i in 0..<self.ongoingTable.numberOfRows {
      let row = self.ongoingTable.rowController(at:i)
        as! OngoingTaskRowController

      row.spacerGroup.setWidth(0)
      row.progressBackgroundGroup.setAlpha(1)
    }
  }
}
```

There's nothing new here in terms of code. Inside an animation block, you iterate
through all the rows of the ongoing table and set the width of `spacerGroup` to `0` and the
alpha of `progressBackgroundGroup` to 1.

Finally, you have to call `animateInTableRows()`. Again, `didAppear()` is provided for
this exact purpose! Add the following method below `willActivate()` in
`TasksInterfaceController`:

```
override func didAppear() {
  super.didAppear()
  animateInTableRows()
}
```

Again, there's nothing much new here. But since you call this code in `didAppear()`, you
get the bonus of all the existing rows animating into view when the app launches.

Build and run the Watch app. Add a new task; now it's quite clear which row is new to
the table.

Woodpecker 11:04	Woodpecker 11:04	Woodpecker 11:04	Woodpecker 11:04
Drink Water 19	Drink Water 19	Drink Water 19	Drink Water 19
	Skip D	Skip Dessert 1C	Skip Dessert 10
Completed	Completed	Completed	Completed
Work Out 17/17	Work Out 17/17	Work Out 17/17	Work Out 17/17
Express Love 20/20	Express Love 20/20	Express Love 20/20	Express Love 20/20

As a bonus, all existing tasks animate in when the app first launches. This app just keeps
getting better and better!

Where to go from here?

You've now learned about the three main ways of creating animations and even went beyond that to put in some extra polish. Congratulations!

The next step is simple: Go polish your own apps! Find rough edges in the user experience and think about how you can smooth them out with animations. Good luck!

If you want to learn more, you can check out the following resources:

• WWDC 2015's Layout and Animation Techniques for WatchKit (apple.co/ 2bZQJnU)

• watchOS 2 Tutorial Part 3: Animation at raywenderlich.com (bit.ly/2bLY1yF)

Animations haven't changes much from watchOS 2 to watchOS 4, so most concepts and learnings carry over.

Finally, it's always great to keep the watchOS Human Interface Guidelines (apple.co/ 2buYJOh) in mind when designing animations!

Chapter 13: CloudKit

By Audrey Tam

CloudKit in watchOS: now you see it, now you don't! Then it's back!

watchOS 1 had it, because the WatchKit extension ran on the iPhone. watchOS 2 appeared soon after, moving the WatchKit extension onto the Watch, and replacing app groups and CloudKit with Watch Connectivity.

In watchOS 3, it returned — as an *alternative* to Watch Connectivity. To avoid draining its battery, the Watch communicates with iCloud via the iPhone or, if the iPhone isn't available, via a known Wi-Fi network.

At WWDC 2017, Apple showed off a completely overhauled CloudKit Dashboard! It uses the same APIs that you'll see, later in this tutorial, so you can try out parameters and debug issues, directly in the Dashboard.

Unlike Watch Connectivity, where you must add similar code to both apps, it's really easy to add CloudKit to your Watch app. Once you've done the work to implement it in the iPhone app, you simply call the same CloudKit methods in the Watch app.

> **Note:** You'll need an Apple Developer Program membership to build an app with iCloud capability. At the time of writing this chapter, you also need an Apple Watch paired with an iPhone in order to test CloudKit in watchOS 4 — the watch simulator doesn't "see" the phone simulator's iCloud login. Ideally, sign into your **Apple developer account** on the iPhone **before** you pair it with the watch. It's a lot of work to unlock a watch from an Apple ID, if you've paired it with an iPhone that's signed into a non-developer Apple ID. More about this in the section **Testing CloudKit on the Watch**.

This chapter's app is an extension of the sample app in "Core Graphics Tutorial" bit.ly/ 2boDRJi: Flo helps you keep track of how much water you drink, aiming for an average of 8 glasses per day — you could go get a drink whenever your Watch reminds you to stand up. ;]

The moment I saw it, I wanted to create a companion Watch app because it's **so much more** convenient to tap your Watch! Of course, you need to keep the two apps in sync with each other, and also with Flo on the iPad; hence, CloudKit!

Getting started

Open the **Flo starter project** in Xcode.

You'll soon change the bundle identifiers for the project's targets, but first open **FloW/ Info.plist** and in **WKCompanionAppBundleIdentifier** replace **com.raywenderlich** with a unique reverse domain of your choice:

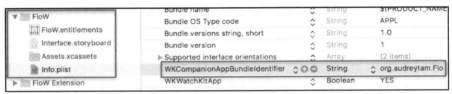

Open **FloW Extension/Info.plist** and change the value of **NSExtension.NSExtensionAttributes.WKAppBundleIdentifier** so the part before **watchkitapp** matches WKCompanionAppBundleIdentifier in FloW/Info.plist:

Now configure the **Flo** target with the same bundle identifier and select a **Team** account that's associated with an Apple Developer Program membership. This should be the Apple ID that your iPhone is signed into, and your watch is activation-locked to.

Also change the bundle identifier and Team for the **FloW** target, and for the **FloW Extension** target.

Select the **Flo** target, and scroll down in its **Capabilities** to find **Background Modes**: check that **Background fetch** and **Remote notifications** are checked.

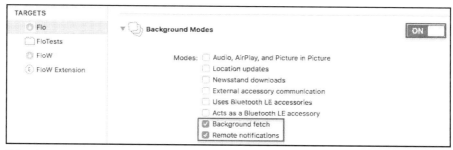

Scroll back up to set the **iCloud** capability to use your **default container**, check that **Key-value storage** and **CloudKit** are checked, then tap **CloudKit Dashboard**. This opens the Dashboard site in your web browser.

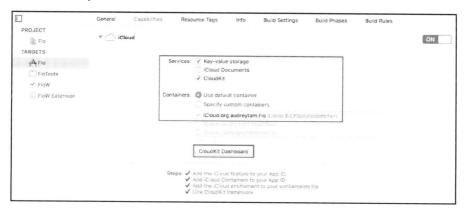

In the browser, sign into the iCloud account that matches your team account. Select your new CloudKit container from the list, and select **Development\Data\Record Types** to see that there's only the **Users** record type:

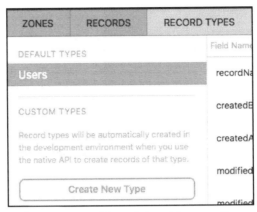

You can create new record types in Dashboard, but it's more fun to see it happen automagically when the app sends its first record. Soon, I promise!

Build and run the **Flo** scheme on the **iPhone 7 Plus** simulator. If you see an alert that you're not signed into iCloud, sign in through the simulator's Settings app — be sure it's the same iCloud account you used to sign into CloudKit Dashboard, so you can see your private database.

While you're waiting for the sign-in to finish, open a Watch simulator: **Simulator\Hardware\Device\watchOS 4.0\Apple Watch Series 2 - 42mm**. Leave it to boot up while you explore the iPhone app.

Now that you're signed into iCloud, the app has created a custom zone named **Drinks**. In Dashboard's **Zones** tab, tap **List Zones** to see it:

Back in the iPhone simulator, tap the + button:

This updates the view, but more important is what happens in Dashboard. Refresh the **Record Types** tab: saving the first record created the custom record type **DrinkEvent**!

Next, you'll query the Drinks zone's records, but first, you must make the DrinkEvent's **recordName** field queryable. Hover the cursor in the Indexes column, and click the **View Indexes** link that appears:

Now you're in the **Indexes** tab. Tap **Add Index**, then select **recordName** from the menu, leave **QUERYABLE** as **Index Type**, and tap **Save Record Type**.

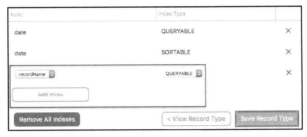

In the **Records** tab, tap **Query Records**:

There's your record!

Tap its **recordName** to view it:

Tap the **X** to close it.

> **Note:** The date display is localized to Australian format (dd/mm/yyyy).

Now create a record in Dashboard, then fetch it: still in the **Records** tab, tap **Create New Record...** to open the **Edit** popover.

Set a date (mm/dd/yyyy) and time (hh:mm:ss), then tap **Save**:

Note: Use the US date format, with the **month first**, or the date won't be what you expect, and will confuse Flo's calendar!

Tap **Query Records** again, to see the record you just created:

In the iPhone simulator, tap the **refresh button** to pull the new record from the iCloud database into the app:

> **Note:** The simulator doesn't support remote notifications. To see the app update itself from a silent notification, install the app on an iPhone where you've signed into the same iCloud account as Dashboard, then add a record in Dashboard.

Now move to the **Watch simulator**, and press its **digital crown** (the small button): FloW installed while you were exploring Flo!

> **Note:** If you don't see the **digital crown** in the watch simulator, it's because you don't have device bezels enabled. To do so, look for the **Window -> Show Device Bezels** menu item. If you don't want to enable that, you can use the **command-shift- h** shortcut instead.

Open it to see it already has the same data as Flo, courtesy of Watch Connectivity:

Tap the Watch app's + button, and both displays increment:

And there's a new record in the dashboard, too!

This magic is also courtesy of Watch Connectivity sending the Watch app's Date object to the iPhone app, which saved it to the iCloud database.

Most of this chapter walks you through how the iPhone app uses CloudKit. Then you'll add a few lines of code to the Watch app to let it send data directly to iCloud.

Note: During development, you might want to delete everything in the iCloud container and start fresh. In Dashboard, tap the container link in the top bar, then tap the red **Reset** button at the bottom of the **Development** menu:

Check the box to confirm, and do the deed.

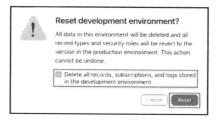

Also delete the Flo apps from the phone and watch simulators/devices.

CloudKit: an aerial view

Why CloudKit? Several reasons:

- Your app's users can keep their data synchronized across all their devices via a back-end server with generous free amounts of storage and network activity, and demonstrated scalability — just look at Apple's own iCloud-enabled apps, like Photos, Notes and Reminders. Scroll down in developer.apple.com/icloud/cloudkit/ to see the free amounts and how they scale up with the number of active users.

- Your app gets no-fuss user authentication: users don't have to create an account, which is often a major turn-off. Many iPhone owners stay signed into iCloud to take advantage of Apple's iCloud apps, so your app will usually work as soon as it's installed.

- Unique, stable user IDs allow you to build user profiles, so when your app notices a high level of engagement, it can ask the user for information, to provide better service.

- Apple is committed to using and improving CloudKit, responding to developers' requests for a web service API and server-to-server access for administrative users.

Container, databases, zones

When you create an app with iCloud capability, you get a **container** on the iCloud server. The container contains the app's databases: a **public database** accessible to all users, and a **private database** for each user's private data. Apple's News app stores articles in its public database, whereas the Notes app uses the private database.

If other users share records with you, they'll be stored in the **shared database**.

There's an image in Session 226 of WWDC 2016 (apple.co/2b0xZI3) showing the three database types:

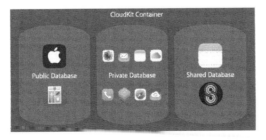

Records in a private database count against the *user's iCloud quota*, not your app's.

Each database has a **default zone** where your app can store records without specifying a **zone ID**. But your app can create **custom zones** in the private database, allowing it to use the new zone-based operations. Custom zones are also handy for sharing records with other users.

CloudKit Dashboard (apple.co/2czY1T5) provides web access to the container, where you can create record types and records, view usage data and perform other management tasks.

If you're in a hurry to port an existing database schema to iCloud, you don't have to create the record types in Dashboard before running the app. The first time your app saves a record of a type that doesn't exist, CloudKit creates it!

Operations vs convenience API

CloudKit provides a convenience API for working with single records and various operations for batch processing. `CKOperation` is a subclass of `Operation`, so you can add dependencies, specify priorities or quality of service, fetch only specific keys, or even cancel an operation.

Using operations reduces your app's network activity, helping you stay within your quota while improving your users' experience. From a coding viewpoint, operations look complicated, but they actually make it easier to perform intricate tasks like fetching all changes to a database.

For example, this project's `saveDate(_:viaWC:)` saves only one record to the database, so it calls the `CKDatabase` *convenience* method `save(_:completionHandler:)`. The corresponding *operation* `CKModifyRecordsOperation(_:recordIDsToDelete:)` can save changes to an array of records, and can also delete records.

Notice the absence of a completion handler argument. Operations have handler properties — yes, more than one!

For the modify-records operation, you define two handlers:

```
perRecordCompletionBlock: ((CKRecord?, Error?) -> Void)

modifyRecordsCompletionBlock:
  (([CKRecord]?, [CKRecordID]?, Error?) -> Void)
```

To display a progress bar for a long operation, you can also define:

```
perRecordProgressBlock: ((CKRecord, Double) -> Void)
```

After setting all the properties that you care about, you add the operation to the database's operations queue.

To fetch changes from the database, this project creates a `CKFetchDatabaseChangesOperation(_:)` — an operation of breathtaking complexity. More about that soon.

Getting notifications of changes to a database

To keep your devices in sync, you subscribe to changes in a database by creating a `CKDatabaseSubscription` object, specifying the record type and setting up its `notificationInfo` object. Apple recommends **silent** notifications. Your app doesn't have to ask the user for permission for silent notifications, since the notifications won't ping or request the user's attention.

> The WWDC speaker on this topic pointed out that users often say "no" automatically in response to permission requests; in that case, your app has to **pull** changes, which isn't as good for keeping devices in sync.

Saving a subscription

To create a silent notification, set only this property:

```
notificationInfo.shouldSendContentAvailable = true
```

The convenience method `save(_:completionHandler:)` can save a single subscription. If you're interested in more than one record type, use a `CKModifySubscriptionsOperation`. This project uses an operation to show you what it looks like.

The record type you subscribe to must exist in the container, or the subscription will fail. To take advantage of the auto-creation of record types, this project saves the subscription in the save-record completion-handler.

Registering for and receiving remote notifications

You register for remote notifications in the usual way, invoking `registerForRemoteNotifications()`, and obtaining the token via the `application(_:didRegisterForRemoteNotificationsWithDeviceToken:)` delegate method.

> **Note:** The simulator doesn't support remote notifications, so this triggers
> `application(_:didFailToRegisterForRemoteNotificationsWithError:)`

Then you listen for remote notifications with
`application( _:didReceiveRemoteNotification:fetchCompletionHandler:)`
— all this does is call the method that creates the scary fetch operation.

So take a deep breath, and here we go ...

Fetching and handling changes to a database

The motivation for using `CKFetchDatabaseChangesOperation(_:)` is the fine print disclaimer that "pushes can be coalesced": if the server sends several notifications, your app is only guaranteed to receive at least one.

Fetching all changes used to require a lot of messy code, checking notification objects and marking them read, then fetching records in batches. And you had to keep track of the `more` flag, and keep sending fetch requests.

Can't you just hear the complaints from Apple's own iCloud apps engineers? So the CloudKit engineers devised a more convenient way to fetch all changes, caching server change tokens to keep devices in sync.

Figuring out how it works felt like opening a Matryoshka doll (bit.ly/2bXdhDQ) but I think it's worth spending a bit of time on, so fill your water glass and settle in for some exploration!

> I can figure this out.
> Yeah like this.
> Or no, this other way.
> Actually, it's like this.
> No, let me try that.

In `AppDelegate`, `didReceiveRemoteNotification` receives two parameters, a `userInfo` dictionary and a `completionHandler` callback, which you must call as soon as the notification processing is completed.

This completion handler is passed to fetchDatabaseChanges, implemented in the CloudKitCentral class. It creates a CKFetchDatabaseChangesOperation, passing previousServerChangeToken — if this argument is nil, the operation fetches everything. The operation always returns a new token, which must be saved locally.

The operation has five event handling closure properties, but fetchDatabaseChanges implements only three for this project:

- changeTokenUpdatedBlock caches intermediate tokens when the number of records requires multiple fetches; the parent operation automatically queues up the necessary fetch operations.

- fetchDatabaseChangesCompletionBlock sets the local token to newToken, then calls the callback argument — for push notifications, this is the fetchCompletionHandler argument of didReceiveRemoteNotification.

- recordZoneWithIDChanged receives the zoneID of a changed zone, and creates a CKFetchRecordZoneChangesOperation to fetch and handle all the changed records in this zone. This is the main workhorse of the operation:

```
// Block to handle zones with changed records
changesOperation.recordZoneWithIDChangedBlock = { zoneID in
  let queryOperation = CKFetchRecordZoneChangesOperation(
    recordZoneIDs: [zoneID], optionsByRecordZoneID: nil)
  queryOperation.fetchAllChanges = true  // default
  queryOperation.recordChangedBlock = { record in
    if let update = self.updateLocalData {
      update(record)
    }
  }
  self.privateDB.add(queryOperation)
  ...
}
```

This creates a CKFetchRecordZoneChangesOperation with a block to handle each fetched record. It simply calls a handler defined in ViewController.swift, which updates the local array of dates.

Setting the fetchAllChanges property to true automatically sends enough requests to fetch all the changed records. This is the default value, because Apple thinks it's what most of us want to happen.

The other two event handlers, not implemented in this project, are:

- recordZoneWithIDWasDeleted: if a subscribed zone has been deleted from the database, this handler removes it from local storage — this is a shared-record scenario, so not needed for this project.

- `recordZoneWithIDWasPurgedBlock`: invoked when a single record zone has been purged.

> **Note:** This operation's `qualityOfService` property is the default value `.utility` when it's fetching **pushed** changes — the network timeout interval is 7 days. When the app **pulls** changes, `qualityOfService` is `.userInitiated` — the default timeout interval is 1 minute.

So that was the aerial view of CloudKit. You'll see more details when you add CloudKit to the Watch app.

Watch app vs iOS app

Time for a brief word about the main differences between the two apps, then you'll get to work adding CloudKit to the Watch app.

The iPhone app maintains a local array of drink event dates. If the user is conscientious about drinking water and using the app, this array can grow quite large. You don't want, or need, to store that in the Watch app: the Watch app just needs the start date and the drink count.

watchOS 4 doesn't support `CKSubscription` classes, so whenever the iPhone app fetches database changes, it sends the drinks total to the watch app, via WatchConnectivity. This keeps the watch app up to date, without the need for separate database queries to *pull* changes.

Adding CloudKit to the Watch app

Configure the **FloW Extension** target for **iCloud** capability: check the **Key-value storage** and **CloudKit** boxes, then select **Specify custom containers** and check the box for **Flo's** iCloud container.

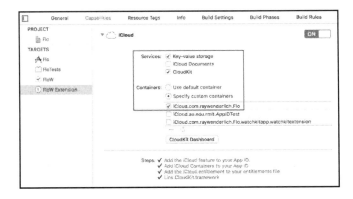

> **Note:** If Xcode complains at this point, check this target's **General** tab, to make sure you've set the same team as the Flo target.

Sharing CloudKitCentral.swift

The Watch app supports most of CloudKit, so it can use most of the code written for iOS in CloudKitCentral.swift. Select **CloudKitCentral.swift** in the project navigator — it's in the **Shared** group — and open the file inspector. Under **Target Membership**, check the box for **FloW Extension**.

Wait a bit, and you'll see 3 error flags appear in subscribeToChanges(), next to the statements that call CKNotificationInfo(), CKDatabaseSubscription(_:) and CKModifySubscriptionsOperation(_:subscriptionIDsToDelete:). The error messages tell you these methods are *unavailable*.

> **Note:** If the errors don't appear, press **command-B** to build the app — the errors will appear!

What to do? One option is to move `subscribeToChanges()` to a new extension in its own file, then don't check the FloW target. But the Watch app will definitely use `saveDate(_:viaWC:)`, which calls `subscribeToChanges()` — so no, that won't work.

Conditional compilation directives to the rescue! Hashtags to warm the hearts of C programming old-timers! Bracket `subscribeToChanges()` with `#if os(iOS)` and `#endif`, like this:

```
#if os(iOS)
// Subscription op fails if record type doesn't exist
func subscribeToChanges() {
  ...
  privateDB.add(subscribeOperation)
}
#endif
```

This gets rid of one error.

Do the same with the if-block in `saveDate(_:viaWC:)` and `fetchDatabaseChanges(_:)` that calls `subscribeToChanges()`:

```
#if os(iOS)
if !self.subscribedToPrivateChanges {
  self.subscribeToChanges()
}
#endif
```

One last task you need to do in **CloudKitCentral.swift**: in `init()`, replace the first line:

```
self.container = CKContainer.default()
```

with these two lines:

```
let containerIdentifier = "iCloud.com.raywenderlich.Flo"
self.container = CKContainer(identifier: containerIdentifier)
```

then **replace** `iCloud.com.raywenderlich.Flo` with the identifier of **your** container. This is now necessary, because the default container of the iPhone app is **not** the default container of the watch app.

Saving records to the database

You need only a few lines of code to enable the Watch app to send records directly to the iCloud database. Open **InterfaceController.swift** in the standard editor, then open **ViewController.swift** in a separate window alongside, as a guide to what goes where, and to see where the code differs.

Add ckCentral property

Add this line near the top of `InterfaceController`, just above the declaration of `floData`:

```
let ckCentral = CloudKitCentral.sharedInstance()
```

You're creating a reference to all the CloudKit code that the iPhone app uses.

Check iCloud account status

Add this line at the beginning of `awake(withContext:)`, just below the **CloudKitCentral housekeeping** comment:

```
ckCentral.checkiCloudAccountStatus()
```

You're checking whether the user's iCloud account is available. Soon you'll write the `.noAccount` case handler that prompts the user to sign in.

Define the ckCentral handlers

Still in `awake(withContext:)`, add the following code below the matching comments:

```
// 1. recordChangedBlock calls this to handle new record
ckCentral.updateLocalData = { record in
  self.floData.drinkTotal += 1
  print("updateLocalData with \(record["date"] as! Date)")
}

// 2. ckCentral calls this to cache change token locally
ckCentral.cacheLocalData = { object, key in
  UserDefaults.standard.set(object, forKey: key)
}

// 3. checkiCloudAccountStatus() calls this to show
//    sign-in alert
ckCentral.alertUserToSignIn = {
  DispatchQueue.main.async {
    let okAction =
        WKAlertAction(title: "OK", style: .default) { }
    self.presentAlert(withTitle: "Not Signed In",
      message: "Please sign into iCloud on your paired iPhone",
      preferredStyle: .alert, actions: [okAction])
  }
}
```

These handlers perform device-specific tasks:

1. `updateLocalData`

`fetchDatabaseChanges` invokes this handler when pulling changes from the iCloud database. So, for each changed record, `updateLocalData(_:)` just increments the local copy of `drinkTotal`.

Its implementation is much simpler than the iPhone app's handler counterpart, which maintains a local array of `DrinkEvent` dates, and ensures both apps are using the earliest date as `startDate`.

The iPhone app's handler keeps the Watch app's data up-to-date via Watch Connectivity, so the Watch app's handler isn't really needed. The iPhone version also handles **pushed** changes, which aren't available on the Watch.

2. `cacheLocalData`

The `fetchDatabaseChangesCompletionBlock` receives the final change token from the iCloud database, and passes it to `cacheLocalData(_:key:)`, which saves it to `UserDefaults`.

When one of the user's devices saves a record to the database, the database assigns a **token** to identify that change. The originating device is up-to-date for that new record, but the other devices must fetch it. The database sends the token to the completion block, and the app is responsible for caching it so that it can use it to create the next `CKFetchDatabaseChangesOperation`.

The originating device doesn't get the token for the change it created. If it's registered for push notifications, it doesn't even receive a notification, because the database is smart enough to avoid that.

The iPhone version of this handler also caches the `subscriptionsSaved` flag, to avoid sending another subscription request if the app relaunches. The iCloud database saves the subscriptions for each app installation, and returns an error if that app instance requests the same subscription.

The Watch app can't subscribe to notifications, so doesn't cache this flag. Actually, the iPhone app can keep it up-to-date, so it doesn't really need to pull changes or cache tokens, either.

3. `alertUserToSignIn`

The Watch uses its paired iPhone's iCloud account, so this handler displays an alert asking the user to sign into iCloud on the paired iPhone.

Call ckCentral.saveDate(_:viaWC:)

In saveData(), substitute the following lines for the NotificationCenter post:

```
if ckCentral.iCloudAccountIsAvailable {
    print("Watch saving directly to iCloud")
    ckCentral.saveDate(floData.lastDate, viaWC: false)
} else {
    // send to iPhone via Watch Connectivity
    NotificationCenter.default.post(name:
        NSNotification.Name(rawValue:
        NotificationDrinkDateOnWatch), object: nil)
}
```

You're saving a new record directly to the iCloud database if the user is signed in, and keeping the Watch Connectivity transfer as a fallback option.

Testing CloudKit on the Watch

At the time of writing this chapter, you can't test CloudKit in a watch simulator. It seems this statement from the watchOS 3 Beta Release Notes still applies:

> CloudKit usage is blocked in watchOS Simulator. Running any test will throw a "Not Authenticated" error even though you are signed in via the paired iOS Simulator.

So, you need to use your iPhone. Check that it's signed into the same iCloud account as Dashboard. Plug your iPhone into your Mac (unless you've already configured it for wireless debugging), select it in the **Flo** scheme list, then build and run. This also installs the watch app, which you can start manually.

Tap the iPhone app button: a new record should appear in Dashboard, and the watch app should increment.

Tap the watch app button: a new record should appear in Dashboard, and the iPhone app should increment. Console messages should show that the iPhone received a remote notification.

You can also look at the **Development Logs**, to see from which platform (iOS/watchOS/web) the zone modify operations originated.

> **Note:** If the watch app isn't creating new records, it's probably linked to an Apple ID different from the one you used to login to Dashboard. Even if your iPhone's

Apple Watch app shows your developer account as the watch's Apple ID, the watch still thinks it belongs to your other Apple ID.

This means it cannot access the private database of your developer account, and is merrily writing to its own private database, which you cannot see in Dashboard.

Login with your other Apple ID to www.icloud.com, or on another iOS device. Locate your watch in **Find iPhone** and erase it.

Unfortunately, Apple's only scenario for this is that you've lost your watch, and the process is somewhat garbled. My watch and iPhone kept unpairing and re-pairing, and Find iPhone never admitted that the erase had completed. But eventually, the Apple Watch app asked me to enter the password for my developer Apple ID, and all was well in the end.

Where to go from here?

In this chapter, you learned about using CloudKit operations to keep the user's data synchronized across their iOS and watchOS devices.

CloudKit can be a good alternative to Watch Connectivity, provided it doesn't increase storage or power requirements.

Cool things this chapter doesn't cover, but you might want to explore:

- Web service API and CloudKit JS

- Server-to-server communication for administrative users

- Sharing records with the sharing UI

- Long-lived operations

- Operation groups

- Logs and Telemetry

- Many-to-one reference

- Managing conflicts

These are all covered in the WWDC sessions listed below, plus the CloudKit JS sample code in CloudKit Catalog bit.ly/2bIX3n9.

WWDC sessions

- WWDC 2017 Session 226 - Build Better Apps with CloudKit Dashboard apple.co/2vo2VL6

- WWDC 2016 Session 226 - What's New with CloudKit apple.co/2b0xZI3

- WWDC 2016 Session 231 - CloudKit Best Practices apple.co/2b0xDS2

- WWDC 2015 Session 715 - CloudKit Tips and Tricks apple.co/2aWJYFy

Tutorials on our site

- Beginning CloudKit video tutorial series (subscribers only) bit.ly/2f3NIrN

- Push Notifications Tutorial: Getting Started bit.ly/2w0WlaA

- CloudKit Tutorial: Getting Started bit.ly/2ciWPmx

- CloudKit JS Tutorial bit.ly/2cCQG10

- iOS8 By Tutorials, Chapters 15 and 16 (oldie but goodie) bit.ly/2b0pjeS

Chapter 14: Notifications

By Matthew Morey

Local and remote notifications let backgrounded apps inform users about new and relevant information. Notifications have been around since iOS 3, and iOS 7 introduced silent remote notifications support, letting apps wake up in the background to perform important tasks. Actionable notifications, added in iOS 8, let users take an action on notifications without first opening the app.

In iOS 10 and watchOS 3, Apple refactored notification support and introduced the User Notifications framework. This framework supports the delivery and handling of local and remote notifications from both iPhone and Watch apps. Now notifications can be scheduled from both devices.

Existing iPhone apps that support notifications will work on the Apple Watch without any changes. watchOS uses a default system interface to show notifications.

However, with a little work, you can build beautiful, custom Watch notification interfaces. Since version 1.0, watchOS has provided two notification types: the short look and the long look notifications.

In this chapter, you'll add a custom long look notification interface to an iPhone and Watch app called Pawsome.

Pawsome is for all the cat lovers who procrastinate during the day by looking at cute cat pictures. The Pawsome app will make this easier by interrupting you throughout the day with cute cat pictures that are certain to trigger a smile.

> **Note:** If you're not familiar with the way notifications work in iOS or you find this chapter a little difficult, I recommend you read our Apple Push Notification Services tutorial: bit.ly/1fs7fok.

Getting started

Open the Pawsome starter project in Xcode and then build and run the **Pawsome** scheme. On first launch, you'll be told Pawsome wants to send you notifications; tap **Allow**.

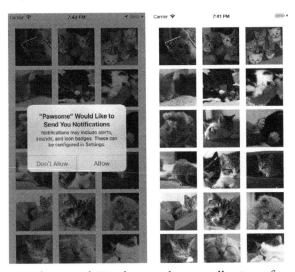

The existing Pawsome iPhone and Watch apps show a collection of cute cat pictures that you can easily browse.

Unlike the iPhone version of Pawsome, the Watch version doesn't support custom notifications just yet. Don't worry — it will soon, but first you need to know how to test notifications on the Watch.

Testing notifications with the Watch simulator

Xcode 6.2 introduced the ability to test remote notifications on the Watch simulator using a local file to mimic the JSON payload file that's sent by Apple's Push Notification Service.

To use this feature, you simply need to add a new file with the extension .apns to your project.

In Xcode, show the project navigator. **Right-click** on the **Supporting Files** group in the **PawsomeWatch Extension** group and select **New File...**. Select the **Watch OS\Other\Empty** template and click **Next**.

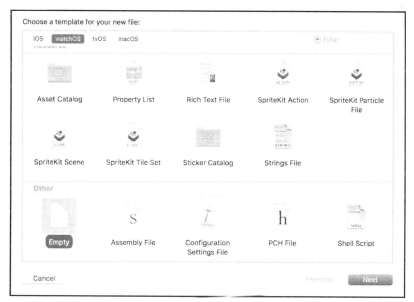

Name the file **PawsomeNotificationPayload.apns**, ensure no Targets are checked and click **Create**.

Now add the following JSON to the newly created **PawsomeNotificationPayload.apns**:

```json
{
  "aps":{
    "alert":{
      "body":"Pawsome time!"
    },
    "category":"Pawsome"
  },
  "WatchKit Simulator Actions":[
    {
      "title":"More Cats!",
      "identifier":"viewCatsAction"
```

```
        }
      ]
    }
```

If you've implemented remote notifications before, you know that the **aps** dictionary includes the notification title, body and optionally, a category. When the iPhone or iPad receives a notification and the app is in the background, the device displays a system dialog or banner showing the title and message.

Because the Watch simulator doesn't have access to the app's registered notification actions, the JSON payload includes a special key for testing, `WatchKit Simulator Actions`, which will come into play later when you implement the long look notification. The value of this key is an array of items, with each item representing a single action button that will be appended to the Watch's notification interface.

Even though the notification you're building is a local notification, you can pretend it's a remote notification for testing purposes. To the watchOS SDK, there's no fundamental difference in the UI between a local and a remote notification, as it shows both to the user in the same manner.

Now that you have a sample JSON payload for testing notifications on the Watch, you need to create a new scheme to run the notification.

To add a new scheme, you'll first duplicate the current Watch app scheme. Choose **Product\Scheme\Manage Schemes…**, select the **PawsomeWatch** scheme, click on the **gear icon** and then click **Duplicate**.

Name the scheme **Notification - PawsomeWatch** by selecting the new scheme and pressing the **Enter** key.

Next, click **Edit...** to edit the scheme. Select the **Run** option in the left-hand column of the scheme editor. In the **Info** pane, select the **Dynamic Notification** option from the **Watch Interface** drop-down. Xcode should automatically set the **Notification Payload** option to the **PawsomeNotificationPayload.apns** file.

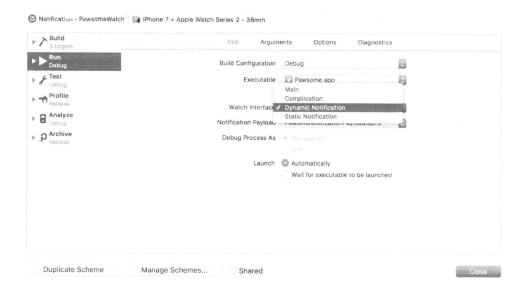

> **Note:** If your app supports more than one notification, you can add multiple APNS files and multiple schemes to make it easy to test each one. You can also select the **Static Notification** option to test the static version of a notification. Keep reading to learn more.

Close the scheme editor to return to the main Xcode interface. Build and run the new **Notification - PawsomeWatch** scheme. You'll see the short look notification on the Watch simulator for about a second, followed by the long look notification:

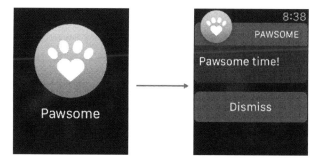

Xcode used the "Pawsome time!" string from **PawsomeNotificationPayload.apns** to populate the notification interface.

This feature in Xcode allows you to focus on the notification user interface without having to worry about servers, device tokens and the other complexities related to testing notifications.

Great job! It's not the *purrrtiest*, but you'll soon fix that.

Short looks

When the iPhone app receives a remote or local notification, iOS decides whether to display the notification on the iPhone or on the Watch. In general, the notification is shown on the device currently in use. If neither device is in use, the notification will appear on the Watch.

If the Watch receives the notification, it will notify the user via a subtle vibration. If the user chooses to view the notification, which she'll do by raising her wrist, the Watch will show an abbreviated version called a short look. If the user continues to view the notification for more than a split second, the Watch will show a more detailed version or a long look.

The short look notification is a quick summary for the user. Short looks show the app's icon and name, and the optional notification title, in a predefined layout.

The optional notification title is a very short blurb about the notification, such as "New Bill", "Reminder" or "Score Alert", and is added to the `alert` key's value. This lets the user decide whether or not to stick around for the long look interface.

The Pawsome notification you're building doesn't need a title, as the app has only one type of notification — which also happens to be the name of the app.

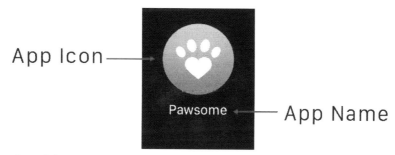

The text color of the app name is perhaps the only thing customizable about the short look notification interface. You can change it by setting the tint color in the Attributes Inspector for the notification interface controller.

Long looks

The long look is a scrolling interface that you can customize, with a default static interface or an optional dynamically-created interface. Unlike the short look interface, the long look offers significant customization.

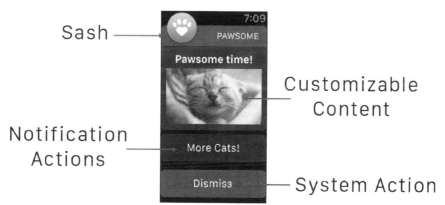

The sash is the horizontal bar at the top. It's translucent by default, but you can set it to any color and opacity value.

You can customize the content area as if it were a standard interface, but without any interactive controls such as buttons and switches.

Long look interfaces can show up to four custom notification actions. These actions need to be registered by the iPhone app. If they are, the long look interface displays them automatically, based on the notification's category.

The system-provided Dismiss button is always present at the bottom of the interface. Tapping Dismiss hides the notification without informing the iPhone app or the Watch extension.

You've just learned how to test notifications on the Watch using the special APNS file. You also now know the differences between a short look and a long look notification, and which parts of each you can customize.

In the next section, you'll learn how to create a custom long look notification by building one for Pawsome.

Creating a custom notification

Now that you've done all the prep work, you get to build the Pawsome custom long look static and dynamic notification, which will look like this when you're done:

Static notification

Open **Interface.storyboard** from the **PawsomeWatch** group and drag a **notification interface controller** from the Object Library onto the storyboard. Your storyboard will now look like this:

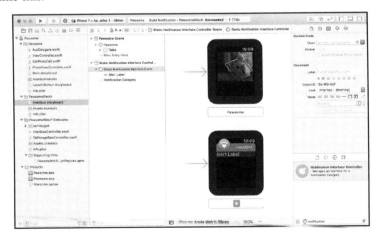

In your storyboard, notification categories are shown as arrows, or entry points, which point to a notification scene. Since apps can have multiple notification types, categories are used to differentiate one notification scene from another.

Select the **notification category** for the notification scene you just created — that's the arrow itself. Next, in the Attributes Inspector, set the notification category name to **Pawsome**, which is the same string you used earlier in **PawsomeNotificationPayload.apns**.

> **Note:** Notification categories are typically registered in the app delegate of the containing iOS app, but can also be registered in the Watch app. If you're curious, open **AppDelegate.swift** or **InterfaceController.swift** to learn how and where Pawsome configures the notification category.

Select the **Alert Label** and then show the Attributes Inspector. Change the **Lines** parameter to **0** so that the label text will automatically wrap without truncating. Set the **Font** to **Headline** and the **Horizontal** alignment to **Center**.

Next, drag an **image** from the Object Library and place it under the label. This image will show the cute cat picture.

After selecting the image, open the Attributes Inspector and set the **Image** to **cat01**. Change the **Mode** to **Aspect Fill**. Finally, set the **Horizontal** alignment to **Center**.

Your storyboard will now look like this:

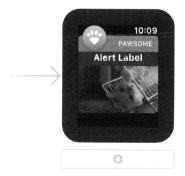

Build and run. As your joyful eyes can now see, the notification shows a cute cat picture.

Static notification interfaces such as this are important, as they provide a fallback in situations where dynamic interfaces are unavailable or fail to load.

You can only configure a static notification interface in the storyboard. That means you can't run any code to update its contents or configure its interface.

The only content dynamically updated in a static notification is the label, which is connected to a special outlet named `notificationAlertLabel`. The system automatically updates the text of this label with the alert message from either a remote or local notification or a test APNS file.

> **Note:** You might be wondering why a dynamic long look notification interface would fail to load. Imagine your dynamic interface received an image URL from the notification payload and downloaded the image for display. If the URL for the image was no longer valid or had been removed, the network request could potentially take a long time to fail.

Instead of making the user wait — or worse, not even showing the notification — watchOS will automatically fall back to using the static interface.

Now that you've completed the static long look interface, it's time to create the dynamic version.

Dynamic notification

With **Interface.storyboard** still open, select the **Pawsome** notification category (remember? the arrow pointing to the static notification scene). In the Attributes Inspector, enable **Has Dynamic Interface**.

Interface Builder will automatically create a new scene and add a segue from the static interface to the dynamic interface.

Interface.storyboard now looks like this:

Next, drag a **label** from the Object Library onto the new dynamic interface.

This label will show the notification message. After selecting the label, open the Attributes Inspector and set the **Text** to **<message>**, the **Font** to **Headline**, the **Lines** to **0**, and the **Horizontal** alignment to **Center**.

Next, drag an **image** from the Object Library and place it under the label. This image will show a random cute cat picture each time.

After selecting the image, open the Attributes Inspector and set the **Image** to **cat01**. Change the **Mode** to **Aspect Fill**. Finally, set the **Horizontal** alignment to **Center**.

> **Note:** You may be tempted to add interactive controls to the long look interface, such as buttons and switches. Don't do it; they won't work! Interactive elements aren't allowed in notification interfaces. You add buttons by setting up related notification actions when registering for notifications in the accompanying iPhone app. watchOS will always show them at the bottom of the long look interface.

Your dynamic notification scene will now look like this:

To update the label and show a random cat image each time a notification is received, you need to write some code.

With the project navigator visible, right-click on the **PawsomeWatch Extension** group and select **New File**. Select **watchOS\Source\WatchKit Class** and click **Next**.

Name the file **NotificationController**, set the **Subclass** to `WKUserNotificationInterfaceController`, and ensure you're adding the file to the **PawsomeWatch Extension** target.

Replace all the code in the new file with the following:

```swift
import WatchKit
import Foundation
import UserNotifications

// 1
class NotificationController:
  WKUserNotificationInterfaceController {

  // 2
  @IBOutlet var label: WKInterfaceLabel!
  @IBOutlet var image: WKInterfaceImage!

}
```

Here's what you're doing with this code:

1. You create the class `NotificationController`, a subclass of `WKUserNotificationInterfaceController`.

2. This class includes an outlet for the notification message label of type `WKInterfaceLabel` and an outlet for the random cat image of type `WKInterfaceImage`.

Now add the following to the end of the class:

```swift
// 1
override func didReceive(_ notification: UNNotification,
  withCompletion completionHandler:
  @escaping (WKUserNotificationInterfaceType) -> Void) {

  // 2
  let notificationBody = notification.request.content.body
  label.setText(notificationBody)

  // 3
  if let imageAttachment =
    notification.request.content.attachments.first {
    let imageURL = imageAttachment.url
    let imageData = try! Data(contentsOf: imageURL)
```

```
    let newImage = UIImage(data: imageData)
    image.setImage(newImage)
} else {
    let catImageName = String(format: "cat%02d",
        arguments: [Int.randomInt(1, max: 20)])
    image.setImageNamed(catImageName)
}

// 4
completionHandler(.custom)
}
```

Going through this code step by step:

1. First, you override didReceive(_ notification:withCompletion:), which watchOS calls when it receives a remote notification or during testing when an APNS file is selected. watchOS calls the method before displaying the notification interface, allowing you to configure the interface.

2. Next, you set the <message> label to the notification body content.

3. Then you set the cat image to the image attached to the notification. If the notification payload doesn't have an attachment, such as when testing using the APNS file, a random image is chosen from the asset catalog.

4. Finally, you call completionHandler() with the .custom parameter. If you were to call completionHandler() with the .default parameter, the app would show the static interface.

Now open **Interface.storyboard**, select the dynamic notification interface and, in the Identity Inspector, set the **Class** to **NotificationController**. Also verify that **Inherit Module From Target** is unchecked, and that the module name is set to **Pawsome**.

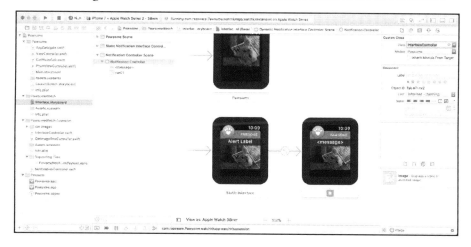

It's time to wire up the outlets for the <message> label and the cat image.

Show the assistant editor and Control-drag from the **<message>** label to the `label` outlet declared in the code.

Do the same thing for the cat image, but drag to the `image` outlet this time.

With the notification scheme selected, build and run. You'll see the following customized, dynamic long look notification:

It's *purrrfect*!

Great work! Now you know how to add custom notification interfaces to your Watch apps.

Where to go from here?

You can find the final project in the folder for this chapter.

In this chapter, you tested Watch notifications, learned about short look and long look interfaces and how they differ, and most impressively, you built a custom, dynamically updating, long look local notification for the Apple Watch.

Now you know the basics of showing custom notifications on watchOS, but there's a lot more you can do from here, including handling actions selected by users from your notifications. A great place to go to for additional information is Apple's Local and Remote Notification Programming Guide: apple.co/2afu73m.

Chapter 15: Complications

By Jack Wu

By now, you know that you should strive to make your Apple Watch apps *simple*. When you're designing for user interactions that last for mere seconds, the user experience should be uncomplicated and intuitive. Well, where's the fun in that? In this chapter, you'll go the extra mile and dare to add complications to your app.

Just kidding! Not *that* kind of complication — a *watch* complication. According to Wikipedia, a watch complication refers to any feature in a timepiece beyond the simple display of hours and minutes. That definition doesn't really work for the Apple Watch since the vast majority of features don't involve displaying hours and minutes. By that definition, the Watch is *full* of complications! :]

On the Apple Watch, complications have been slightly redefined as elements on the Watch face that display small, immediately relevant bits of information. They are by far one of the most compelling and useful features of the Apple Watch. They lie *right* on the Watch face, which makes accessing information as fast as raising your wrist.

In watchOS, complications are more important as ever and *every* Watch app should include *at least* one.

A new category of interaction

I repeat, *complications are more important as ever and every Watch app should include at least one.* That means your app.

Simply including a complication that displays no data lets the user launch your app more quickly from the home screen. On top of that, watchOS provides several benefits when the complication is active:

• watchOS keeps your app in memory and gives it extra update time, making app launches almost instant.

• Your complication can receive 50 pushes per day.

• Your complication can be featured in the Apple Watch Face Gallery on the phone.

But why stop at that, when you can populate the complication with useful data for the user?

Imagine the possibilities here. "What's the score?" *Raises wrist.* "Is it time for tea?" *Raises wrist.* "Is this class over yet?" *Raises wrist.* "Should I use the washroom?" Uh... I *guess* you could follow a schedule for that. *Raises wrist.*

As a developer, complications give you a whole new way to engage your users. The closest relative to complications on the iPhone is the Today extension, which also provides quick access to important information, but lacks the immediacy of a watchOS complication. To craft complications, you'll be using **ClockKit**, a framework introduced in watchOS 2.

As you think about implementing a complication, lots of technical questions probably come to mind: *How will the data be available so quickly? How can I update the data continuously? How can I make sure my data is displayed properly in such a small area?*

This chapter, along with Chapter 20 "Advanced Complications", will answer all these questions and more.

You'll explore the architecture of ClockKit and learn how to take advantage of complications to give users the most concisely engaging experiences.

So you'll add a complication to your app that doesn't complicate it. On the contrary, it will make your app even simpler to use! :]

Getting started

It's a well-known fact that Apple Watch users love to surf. It is *crucial* that they have up-to-the-moment access to tide conditions at their favorite surfing spot to catch the big breakers.

Luckily for your users, Tide Watch provides exactly that. With Tide Watch, users can monitor tide conditions on their phones, their Watches, and once you're done, right on their Watch faces!

It's all in your hands now, so locate the starter project for **TideWatch** and open **TideWatch.xcodeproj** in Xcode.

Build and run the iPhone app and then the Watch app. Play around with both to get a sense of the data they display — and how they display it. The data is pulled live from the Center for Operational Oceanographic Products and Services (CO-OPS) API for tide predictions.

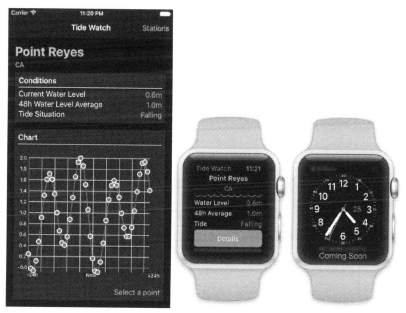

Take a few moments to browse the source code, paying extra attention to how the data is retrieved and modeled in **TideConditions.swift** and the other data models. That's the same data you'll display in the complication.

You don't want to keep the eager surfers waiting too long, though — it's time to complicate!

Adding a complication

In Xcode, open the project settings of the **TideWatch WatchKit App Extension** target. On the **General** tab, you'll see the **Complications Configuration** section:

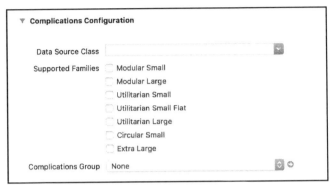

There are three fields here:

- **Data Source Class** will refer to a class that implements CLKComplicationDataSource to provide all the data.

- **Supported Families** is where you choose which Watch face families you'll support.

- The **Complications Group** stores the images for your complications within the assets file of your WatchKit extension target.

Most of this probably doesn't make sense yet, but it will soon. You'll fill in these fields one by one, beginning with the families.

Complication families

Most types of Watch faces can display complications: Modular, Utilitarian and Circular can all do this.

Look closely at the images below, and you can see the seven different **complication families**, grouped by the type of Watch face on which they appear:

- `ModularSmall`
- `ModularLarge`
- `UtilitarianSmall`
- `UtilitarianSmallFlat`
- `UtilitarianLarge`
- `CircularSmall`
- `ExtraLarge`

You can choose to support any number of these families, but it's best to support at least one from each Watch face. It's easy to add support for more families, so for your first foray into complications you'll add support for **Utilitarian Small** and **Utilitarian Large** to Tide Watch. Select both of these options from the list of supported families:

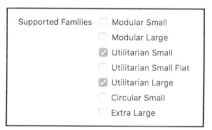

Creating the data source

The data source will provide the system with everything it needs to display a complication. The data source itself is simply an `NSObject` that conforms to `CLKComplicationDataSource`.

The main job of the data source is to package your complication's data into templates that the system can display. The system will request data from the data source to update the complication throughout its life cycle.

The data source needs to respond *as fast as possible*. It shouldn't perform any expensive network fetches or computations — the app should have already handled those. The data source should only be responsible for packaging that data for the system.

To begin, within the **TideWatch WatchKit App Extension** file group, create a new **WatchKit Class** named **ComplicationController** as a subclass of `NSObject`:

Click **Next** and add the class to the **TideWatch WatchKit App Extension** target.

Go back to the project settings and set $(PRODUCT_MODULE_NAME).ComplicationController as the **Data Source Class**:

Open the newly created **ComplicationController.swift** and replace its contents with the following:

```
import ClockKit

class ComplicationController: NSObject,
  CLKComplicationDataSource {

}
```

Here you import ClockKit and declare your new class as conforming to
CLKComplicationDataSource. The compiler will complain that you don't conform to
CLKComplicationDataSource. To fix this, add the following method stubs to
ComplicationController:

```
// MARK: Register
func getLocalizableSampleTemplate(for complication:
  CLKComplication, withHandler handler:
  @escaping (CLKComplicationTemplate?) -> Swift.Void) {
    handler(nil)
}

// MARK: Provide Data
func getCurrentTimelineEntry(for complication:
  CLKComplication, withHandler handler: @escaping
  (CLKComplicationTimelineEntry?) -> Swift.Void) {
    handler(nil)
}

// MARK: Time Travel
func getSupportedTimeTravelDirections(for complication:
  CLKComplication, withHandler handler: @escaping
  (CLKComplicationTimeTravelDirections) -> Swift.Void) {
    handler([])
}
```

Here's what you've added:

- **getLocalizableSampleTemplate(for:withHandler:)** provides the sample
  template that reflects what this complication will look like. This will return a sample
  to let the user know what they should expect.

- **getCurrentTimelineEntry(for:withHandler:)** provides the current template to
  display. You'll take a deeper look at this shortly.

- **getSupportedTimeTravelDirections(for:withHandler:)** enables an incredibly
  useful feature called **Time Travel** for your complication. You won't explore Time
  Travel until Chapter 20, "Advanced Complications", so here you return a simple [] to
  signal that you don't currently support any of the time travel directions.

Note how the data source methods don't return anything. Instead, they use the handler
function passed in by the caller to return the data.

That's all you need to do to create a complication! At this point, it's not a *very good*
complication, but it's good enough to add to the home screen and enable all the benefits
of having a complication.

Build and run the Watch app target. Go to a **Utility** watch face once the app loads and
perform a **deep press**. Go to **Customize** and swipe left two times to go to the

complications customization screen. On the large complication at the bottom, scroll until you find your brand new complication for Tide Watch:

Not bad for only a few minutes of work! If your goal is to add a blank complication like this, you're almost done. For all complications, you will want to add a **complication bundle** in order for the Watch app on the phone to display it in the Faces Gallery.

Including a complication bundle

If your Watch app has a complication, it should include a complication bundle. Luckily, the process is quite simple.

In the **Apple Watch Simulator**, make sure Tide Watch is running in the foreground. Go to **File\Save Complication Bundle** and save it to your disk as **TideWatch.ckcomplication**:

Find where you saved the bundle (which is simply a folder) on the disk, and drag the entire folder into Xcode to add it to **TideWatch**. Make sure the target is the main app and **Create Folder References** is checked.

That's it! Build and run the **Phone app**. Once it's finished launching, open the **Watch app** on the phone. Choose the Utility watch face and scroll down to see the complications. You should now see Tide Watch's new complication in the list!

Even if you're only implementing the simplest complication, don't leave yet! There's one more thing you can do that requires little to no effort but offers a lot of benefits.

Launching from a complication

If your complication serves as a simple "launcher", it would be nice to know when the user launches your Watch app from the complication as opposed to somewhere else.

watchOS provides you this functionality through the Handoff API. In `ExtensionDelegate.swift`, add the following method to `ExtensionDelegate`:

```
func handleUserActivity(
  _ userInfo: [AnyHashable : Any]?) {
  if let date = userInfo?[CLKLaunchedTimelineEntryDateKey]
```

```
        as? Date {
        print("launched from complication with date:\(date)")
    }
}
```

`handleUserActivity(_:)` is the method called when using Handoff. Here, `userInfo` is populated with the special key `CLKLaunchedTimelineEntryDateKey` that provides you with the date of the timeline entry that was tapped by the user to launch your app.

Since Tide Watch isn't a simple "launcher" complication, you won't further develop this method here.

Now that you have a complication, it's time to make it better. In the upcoming sections, you'll supply some templates so your complication can display useful data to the user.

Complication templates

A complication template represents the types of data it can display and the arrangement of that data:

- The **data** is usually a combination of text and images but can sometimes be other things, such as the percentage to fill a ring.

- The **arrangement** describes how the template will display the data. Most arrangements are simple, like the text positioned next to the image, but they can also be complex, like a table layout.

Each subclass of `CLKComplicationTemplate` represents a single arrangement and uses properties to define what types of data it displays.

Glance at the documentation, and you'll notice over *20* different subclasses of `CLKComplicationTemplate` that you can use! Don't panic: you'll see that you can organize them neatly.

Complications are organized according to the family that can display them. Each complication family can display a number of different templates. You can further break down most templates by the types of data they display:

- **Only Text:** `SimpleText`, `StackText`, `Columns`, `Body`.

- **Only Images:** `SimpleImage`, `Square`.

- **Text and Image:** `LargeFlat`, `SmallFlat`, `StackImage`.

- **With Ring:** `RingImage`, `RingText`.

For small templates, Tide Watch can simply provide the current water level as text. For larger templates, Tide Watch can provide an icon, water level and tide condition. Thus, Tide Watch can provide the following templates:

1. `CLKComplicationTemplateModularLargeStandardBody`

2. `CLKComplicationTemplateModularSmallSimpleText`

3. `CLKComplicationTemplateUtilitarianLargeFlat`

4. `CLKComplicationTemplateUtilitarianSmallFlat`

5. `CLKComplicationTemplateCircularSmallSimpleText`

6. `CLKComplicationTemplateExtraLargeStackImage`

In most cases, you'll choose one template for each family, but you can also use different ones at different times if you need them. For example, if it makes sense in your app to show an image at certain times and no image at other times, you can use `SmallFlat` when you need to display the image and `SimpleText` when you don't.

Data providers

Templates don't directly accept images and strings for display. ClockKit uses **providers** to help you display your data properly at all times. Providers are extremely convenient; they allow you to specify your *intentions* and leave the actual formatting to the system. You don't have to worry about shortening your strings or formatting your dates — the system will handle it all!

For text, there are a few providers to choose from:

- **CLKSimpleTextProvider** displays any text directly.

- **CLKDateTextProvider** displays a date using the `calendarUnits` you specify.

- **CLKTimeTextProvider** displays a time either within the user's current timezone or within an optionally specified timezone.

- **CLKRelativeDateTextProvider** displays the difference between a specified date and the current date. You can choose from many display styles, such as "2hrs 26mins", "2 hours" and "2:26".

- **CLKTimeIntervalTextProvider** displays a time interval between any two dates, such as "2:35–3:20PM".

For images, there is only `CLKImageProvider`, which has five properties you can set:

- **twoPieceImageForeground** is a template image you can display on top of a background image, which you can set using `twoPieceImageBackground` property. `twoPieceImageForeground` is *always* tinted white, and used only in multicolor environments. You may specify `nil` for this property.

- **twoPieceImageBackground** is a template image tinted with `tintColor` and displayed behind the foreground image. You may specify `nil` for this property.

- **onePieceImage** must not be nil and is a template image to render if your image doesn't need two pieces. The one-piece image is always used in monochrome environments.

- **tintColor** is the color in which to render `onePieceImage` or `twoPieceImageBackground`.

- **accessibilityLabel** is a short string you can use to identify the purpose of the image for accessibility.

A template-image means that only the transparency of the image is taken into account when displaying. The color information will be ignored, and the system will tint the image for you. The image provider will always resize your images properly for display.

That's all you need to know to create a template. Now you're going to apply this knowledge to Tide Watch.

Providing a sample template

The sample template is simply a template that doesn't display any real data — it's shown when the user scrolls between complications. This is called only **once** when your app is installed and watchOS caches the result for any future uses.

Back in **ComplicationController.swift**, replace the implementation of `getLocalizableSampleTemplate(for:withHandler:)` with the following code:

```
// 1
if complication.family == .utilitarianSmall {
  // 2
  let smallFlat = CLKComplicationTemplateUtilitarianSmallFlat()
  // 3
  smallFlat.textProvider = CLKSimpleTextProvider(text: "+2.6m")
  // 4
  smallFlat.imageProvider = CLKImageProvider(
    onePieceImage: UIImage(named: "tide_high")!)
  // 5
```

```
    handler(smallFlat)
  }
```

Here's what's happening:

1. You always need to check which family is requested so you can return the correct template.

2. You create the `CLKComplicationTemplateUtilitarianSmallFlat` template using the empty initializer.

3. Next, you create a `CLKSimpleTextProvider` that provides a sample of the data and assign it to `textProvider`.

4. Then, you create a `CLKImageProvider` to provide a sample of an image and assign it to `smallFlat.imageProvider`.

5. Finally, you call the handler to return the data.

You're supporting *two* families here, so you need to check for the other one, as well. Add the following `else` statement right after the previous block:

```
else if complication.family == .utilitarianLarge {
  let largeFlat = CLKComplicationTemplateUtilitarianLargeFlat()
  largeFlat.textProvider = CLKSimpleTextProvider(
    text: "Rising, +2.6m", shortText:"+2.6m")
  largeFlat.imageProvider = CLKImageProvider(
    onePieceImage: UIImage(named: "tide_high")!)

  handler(largeFlat)
}
```

The difference here is that since you have more room to display text, you can take advantage of the ability of `CLKSimpleTextProvider` to take both long and short versions of your text and display them appropriately.

Uninstall the Watch app if already installed (remember that the sample is created only once during install time). Build and run the Watch app.

Once it's running, return to the Watch face and **deep press** on your utility watch face.

Scroll down in any of the complication slots and you'll see Tide Watch:

Don't select it, though; it doesn't display any data... yet!

> **Note**: Make sure you're on a Utilitarian Watch face — either Utility or Mickey — since Tide Watch currently only supports Utilitarian families.

Not bad for a few lines of code. To provide real data for your shiny new complication, you'll need a bit more information on top of the template. You're going to package this together into a timeline entry.

Timeline entries

You've chosen and created a few templates, and now it's time to provide real data. For this to happen, ClockKit needs to know *when* to display your templates. ClockKit uses a `CLKComplicationTimelineEntry` to represent a template for a certain time.

This class has only three properties:

1. **date**: The `NSDate` on which to show the data.

2. **complicationTemplate**: Your packaged template, which you learned how to create above.

3. **timelineAnimationGroup**: This allows you to animate between entries.

Ignore the third one for now; you'll learn all about this in Chapter 20, "Advanced Complications". That means you only need to worry about the date.

Display time

The date is the first point in time that this entry will become visible to the user. For example, a time of 3 p.m. means that the complication will start displaying this entry at exactly 3 p.m., and continue until it's time to display the next entry

The time that you should specify is greatly contextual to your data. Generally, your data is going to be useful for a certain period of time — but that doesn't necessarily mean you should provide the start time of that period as the date for the entry.

If you're displaying events in a calendar, you want the complication to show the upcoming event before it happens, not the one that just ended. To do so, you provide the end time of the *previous* event as the date for the current event. For example:

Here, at 12 p.m., the user should see "Afternoon Tea at 3PM" and not "Morning Tea at 10AM" since that's already happened. To achieve this, you should use 11 a.m. as the date for the "Afternoon Tea" entry.

On the other hand, if you're displaying up-to-date information as you are in Tide Watch, you want to display the latest data. In the case of Tide Watch, the user wants to see what the tide conditions are at that moment, and so you need to set date to the beginning of the time period when that tide condition is valid.

In summary, the date you select should be the answer to the question, "When should the user first see this entry?", which could well be different from the answer to, "When does this entry begin?"

Providing a timeline entry

Now that you know what's going into your timeline entry, you can build one — which is the last step in creating your complication for Tide Watch.

To make it easier to package data into templates, add a few helper methods to Tide Watch's data models. Open **WaterLevel.swift** and add the following two methods to WaterLevel:

```swift
var shortTextForComplication: String {
  return String(format: "%.1fm", height)
}
```

```
  var longTextForComplication: String {
    return String(format: "%@, %.1fm", situation.rawValue, height)
  }
```

You'll use these methods along with `CLKTextProvider` to display the data.

Open **ComplicationController.swift** again — it's time to implement `getCurrentTimelineEntry(for:withHandler:)`. Replace the contents of the method with the following:

```
  let conditions = TideConditions.loadConditions()
  guard let waterLevel = conditions.currentWaterLevel else {
    // No data is cached yet
    handler(nil)
    return
  }
```

First, you load the data from the cache. Here, you check if the data exists and simply exit if it doesn't. Remember that the data source's job is to return existing data as quickly as possible and it shouldn't attempt to fetch data over the network.

After you've confirmed the data exists, you want to determine which tide image to show. Add the following code to the end of `getCurrentTimelineEntry(for:withHandler:)`:

```
  let tideImageName: String
  switch waterLevel.situation {
    case .High: tideImageName = "tide_high"
    case .Low: tideImageName = "tide_low"
    case .Rising: tideImageName = "tide_rising"
    case .Falling: tideImageName = "tide_falling"
    default: tideImageName = "tide_high"
  }
```

Here you simply do a `switch` on the tide situation to determine which image to use.

You've got all the information, so you can create the templates. Continue in `getCurrentTimelineEntry(for:withHandler:)` and add the following snippet to the bottom:

```
  // 1
  if complication.family == .utilitarianSmall {
    let smallFlat = CLKComplicationTemplateUtilitarianSmallFlat()
    smallFlat.textProvider = CLKSimpleTextProvider(
      text: waterLevel.shortTextForComplication)
    smallFlat.imageProvider = CLKImageProvider(
      onePieceImage: UIImage(named: tideImageName)!)

  // 2
```

```
    handler(CLKComplicationTimelineEntry(
      date: waterLevel.date, complicationTemplate: smallFlat))
  }
```

This is similar to the way you created the placeholder:

1. First, you check the family and create the template. You create the providers using the data you have and package it all up.

2. Here you create a `CLKComplicationTimelineEntry`, which includes the date along with the template.

Don't forget the other family. Add the following `else` statement right below the end of the previous `if` statement:

```
else {
  let largeFlat = CLKComplicationTemplateUtilitarianLargeFlat()
  largeFlat.textProvider = CLKSimpleTextProvider(
    text: waterLevel.longTextForComplication,
    shortText:waterLevel.shortTextForComplication)
  largeFlat.imageProvider = CLKImageProvider(
    onePieceImage: UIImage(named: tideImageName)!)

  handler(CLKComplicationTimelineEntry(
    date: waterLevel.date, complicationTemplate: largeFlat))
}
```

Once again, you can take advantage of the extra space by using the longer version of the text while keeping the shorter version as a backup.

That's it! Build and run the Watch app. Remember to let it finish loading the data that your complication will display. Activate your complication and observe your app instantly populate your data directly on the Watch face!

Where to go from here?

If this is your first complication, congratulations! Not only have you made strides toward building a legacy of happy and efficient surfer communities, you've also acquired the knowledge you need to add the convenience of complications to your Watch apps.

Before you move on, play around with Tide Watch's complications. Try out the different templates and even add all the missing families, if you can.

The power of complications doesn't end here. Head over to Chapter 20, "Advanced Complications", to learn all about time travel and how to keep your data always up to date.

Chapter 16: Watch Connectivity

By Matthew Morey

The magic of the Apple Watch experience comes from seamless interactions between Watch and iPhone apps. This was difficult to achieve in the past; the first version of watchOS limited developers to simple file or key-value pair sharing. However, since watchOS 2 you have at your disposal a more robust communication framework called **Watch Connectivity**.

Watch Connectivity lets an iPhone app and its counterpart Watch app transfer data and files back and forth. If both apps are active, communication happens in real-time; otherwise, communication happens in the background so data can be available as soon as the receiving app launches.

In this chapter, you'll implement data transfers between the iPhone and Watch versions of **CinemaTime**, an app for patrons of a fictional cinema. It lets customers view movie show times and buy tickets right from their iPhones and Watches.

Getting started

Open the CinemaTime starter project in Xcode then build and run the **CinemaTimeWatch** scheme. Tap **Purchase Ticket** and explore the app to see what you have to work with:

Build and run the **CinemaTime** scheme and explore the iPhone app as well:

The two apps are pretty similar; they both show the movie schedule for a cinema and let you purchase tickets.

Buy a movie ticket in either app, then view the list of purchased movie tickets in the other app. Do you see the issue?

Movie tickets purchased in one app don't show as purchased in the other app. It's clear the apps aren't transferring ticket purchase data between them. Imagine if a customer bought a movie ticket in the iPhone app. If she then tried to use the Watch app to get into the cinema, she'd be turned away, as the Watch wouldn't have the ticket!

Customers have a reasonable expectation that data should be accessible from both versions of an app — regardless of which app created the data.

In the rest of this chapter, you'll use the Watch Connectivity framework to sync the customer's purchased movie tickets between the iPhone and Watch versions of the app.

Setting up Watch Connectivity

Before you can transfer data between apps, you must first set up and activate a connectivity session. You should do this early in the app's lifecycle so any pending transfers can happen right away.

If the app launches in the background, a view controller's `viewDidLoad()` won't get called, and any connectivity-related code located in that method won't run. You'll want your session to be set up and activated outside of any view controller.

For CinemaTime, you'll add the setup and activation code to the iPhone's app delegate and the Watch's extension delegate in `application(_:didFinishLaunchingWithOptions:)` and `applicationDidFinishLaunching()`, respectively. These methods are always executed — even when the app launches in the background.

You'll use the `WCSession` class and `WCSessionDelegate` protocol as shown below to configure and activate connectivity sessions in both apps:

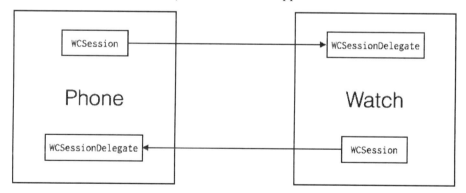

iPhone connectivity setup

Open **AppDelegate.swift** and update the `import` section to include the Watch Connectivity framework.

```
import WatchConnectivity
```

The app delegate needs to conform to the `WCSessionDelegate` protocol to receive communication from the Watch. Update the class extension at the bottom of the file to include the `WCSessionDelegate` protocol:

```
extension AppDelegate: WCSessionDelegate {
```

Now add the required asynchronous session activation functions to the extension:

```
// 1
func sessionDidBecomeInactive(_ session: WCSession) {
  print("WC Session did become inactive")
}

// 2
func sessionDidDeactivate(_ session: WCSession) {
  print("WC Session did deactivate")
  WCSession.default.activate()
}

// 3
func session(_ session: WCSession, activationDidCompleteWith
    activationState: WCSessionActivationState, error: Error?) {
  if let error = error {
    print("WC Session activation failed with error: " +
      "\(error.localizedDescription)")
    return
  }
  print("WC Session activated with state: " +
    "\(activationState.rawValue)")
}
```

These functions are required to support a user with multiple watches connected to the iPhone. Here's how this works:

1. The session calls this method when it detects that the user has switched to a different Apple Watch, and the previous session is now inactive. The session sits in this state for a small amount of time so it can deal with any data that's already been transferred but not processed. CinemaTime doesn't need to do anything when this is called, but other apps could use this callback to clean up local data stores.

2. The session calls this method when there is no more pending data to deliver to the app and the previous session can be formally closed. The iPhone app must call `activate` to connect to the new Watch to the new session.

3. `session(_:activationDidCompleteWith:error:)` is called when the activation of a session finishes. This callback gives an app the opportunity to know if the session

activation was successful. CinemaTime doesn't need to do anything when this is called.

Before you can send or receive data via the Watch Connectivity framework, you must configure the session and assign a delegate.

Locate `setupWatchConnectivity()`, which is called in `application(_:didFinishLaunchingWithOptions:)`. Setting up the Watch Connectivity framework at app launch ensures any pending communication is taken care of right away.

Add the following code to the method:

```
func setupWatchConnectivity() {
  // 1
  if WCSession.isSupported() {
    // 2
    let session = WCSession.default
    // 3
    session.delegate = self
    // 4
    session.activate()
  }
}
```

Here's what you're doing with this code:

1. You check if the current device supports Watch Connectivity. This method returns `true` for all iPhones that support pairing with an Apple Watch running watchOS 2 or higher.

2. Next, you set `session` to the singleton session object `default` for the current device.

3. Then you set the session delegate to `self`. You must set the `delegate` property *before* activating the session.

4. Finally, you signify that the app is ready to send and receive communication by calling `activate()`.

Calls to any `WCSession` communication methods must happen after the `WCSession` object has an assigned delegate and is active.

There is only ever one session object per app — `WCSession.default` — and only a single object can conform to the `WCSessionDelegate` protocol. These limitations mean that most of your connectivity-related code will need to exist in a single class. For simplicity, all the connectivity code in the CinemaTime iPhone app lives in the app delegate.

> **Note:** In general, avoid lumping too many things in a central location like the app delegate. Instead, try to separate functionality by areas of concern. Because the amount of connectivity code you're writing is minimal, I've chosen to place this code in the app delegate, as it's easier to understand. If your connectivity code gets more complex than what you're writing for CinemaTime, you should consider moving it into a separate class.

You've finished setting up a connectivity session in the iPhone app, so now you need to add identical code to the Watch version. Prepare yourself — a lot of this will sound familiar!

Watch connectivity setup

Open **ExtensionDelegate.swift** and add the following import to include the Watch Connectivity framework:

```
import WatchConnectivity
```

Update the class extension at the bottom of the file to include the `WCSessionDelegate` protocol:

```
extension ExtensionDelegate: WCSessionDelegate {
```

Now add the required asynchronous session activation functions to the extension:

```
func session(_ session: WCSession, activationDidCompleteWith
  activationState: WCSessionActivationState, error: Error?) {
  if let error = error {
    print("WC Session activation failed with error: " +
      "\(error.localizedDescription)")
    return
  }
  print("WC Session activated with state: " +
    "\(activationState.rawValue)")
}
```

Locate `setupWatchConnectivity()`. Yup, you guessed it. `setupWatchConnectivity()` is called in `applicationDidFinishLaunching()` to ensure any pending communication happens right away. Now replace it with the following code:

```
func setupWatchConnectivity() {
  if WCSession.isSupported() {
    let session   = WCSession.default
```

```
    session.delegate = self
    session.activate()
  }
}
```

Are you experiencing déjà vu?

You should be, as the code to configure and establish a Watch Connectivity session is identical for both apps! :]

Build and run the **CinemaTimeWatch** scheme; this will launch the Watch app in the Watch simulator. Next, build and run the **CinemaTime** scheme to launch the iPhone app.

Both apps look and behave exactly as they did before because all you've done is set up and activated the connectivity session.

Next, you'll send movie tickets data back and forth between the iPhone and Watch apps.

Device-to-device communication

There are two types of device-to-device communication in Watch Connectivity: interactive messaging and background transfers.

Interactive messaging

Interactive messaging is best used in situations where you need to transfer information immediately. For example, if a Watch app needs to trigger the iPhone app to check the user's current location, the interactive messaging API can transfer the request from the Watch to the iPhone.

When both apps are active, establishing a session allows immediate communication via interactive messaging. The `WCSession` methods `sendMessage(_:replyHandler:errorHandler:)` and `sendMessageData(_:replyHandler:errorHandler:)` send information.

The `WCSessionDelegate` methods `session(_:didReceiveMessage:)` and `session(_:didReceiveMessageData:)` receive information sent from the other side.

Before you implement interactive messaging in your app, consider how likely it is for your iPhone app and Watch app to be active at the same time. Given the short lifespan of Watch apps, and the likelihood that they're used while the user's phone is tucked away in her pocket, your apps probably have little opportunity to make use of interactive messaging. That's definitely the case for Cinema Time.

> **Note:** To learn more about interactive messaging, see Chapter 19, "Advanced Watch Connectivity" and Apple's Watch Connectivity Framework Reference: apple.co/1JlPcnH.

Background transfers

If only one of the apps is active, it can still send data to its counterpart app using one of the background transfer methods.

Background transfers let iOS and watchOS choose a good time to transfer data between apps, based on such things as the battery use and how much other data is still waiting to be transferred. This has the benefit of reducing battery usage while still guaranteeing the data transfers in a timely manner.

There are three types of background transfers: user info, file, and application context.

User info transfers

User info transfers send dictionaries of data to the counterpart app in a first-in, first-out order. Once a data transfer is started, it's handled by the Watch Connectivity framework. The transfer will happen regardless of the state of the app that initiated it. The `WCSession` method `transferUserInfo(_:)` sends the dictionaries, and the counterpart app receives the dictionaries via the `WCSessionDelegate` method `session(_:didReceiveUserInfo:)`.

For example, a Watch game that needs to transfer the user's progress to its counterpart iPhone app would require a user info transfer. Using `transferUserInfo(_:)`, the iPhone app would receive notice of each completed level from the Watch app.

File transfers

File transfers send a local file and an optional dictionary to the counterpart app. Like user info transfers, file transfers let you queue up files in the background for sending. The `WCSession` method `transferFile(_:metadata:)` initiates a file transfer. The counterpart app receives the files via the `WCSessionDelegate` method `session(_:didReceiveFile:)`.

Think of a social app that lets you tag photos as favorites. When you tag an images on the iPhone, this could trigger a file transfer to the Watch via `transferFile(_:metadata:)`.

> **Note:** To learn more about user info transfers check out Chapter 19, "Advanced Watch Connectivity". Once you finish the current chapter, I encourage you to work through Chapter 19 to gain a really good understanding of the Watch Connectivity framework.

Application context transfers

The application context transfer is the most appropriate transfer method for the CinemaTime apps. These are like user info transfers, in that both let you transfer a dictionary containing data from one app to another. What makes them different is that only the *most recent* dictionary of data, called a **context**, transfers over. That means, if one app starts multiple transfers, the framework discards everything but the most recent one, and the counterpart app will only receive the last dictionary sent.

The `WCSession` method `updateApplicationContext(_:)` sends the context, and the `WCSessionDelegate` method `session(_:didReceiveApplicationContext:)` receives it in the counterpart app.

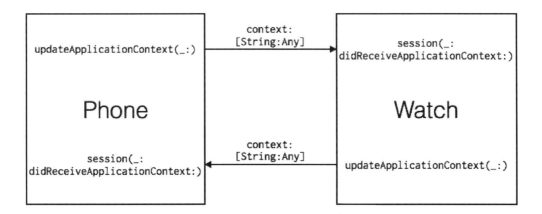

> **Note**: Although `updateApplicationContext(_:)` accepts a dictionary of type `[String : Any]` this doesn't mean you can send just anything. The dictionary can only accept property list types such as arrays, dictionaries, and strings. See the Property List Programming Guide (apple.co/1PZEPXD) for a complete list of supported types.

A cheap gas-finding iOS app could track the user's location on the iPhone, package up a list of the cheapest gas stations nearby and use an application context transfer to send that data to the Watch app via `updateApplicationContext(_:)`.

First, you'll implement an application context transfer to send purchased movie tickets from the iPhone to the Watch. Once that's done, you'll use a similar approach to transfer tickets purchased on the Watch to the iPhone.

iPhone-to-Watch communication

Find `sendPurchasedMoviesToWatch(_:)` in **AppDelegate.swift**. This function is called when the user purchases a movie ticket in the iPhone app, which fires off the `NotificationPurchasedMovieOnPhone` notification.

Replace the `TODO` in `sendPurchasedMoviesToWatch(_:)` with the following:

```
func sendPurchasedMoviesToWatch(_ notification: Notification) {
  // 1
  if WCSession.isSupported() {
    // 2
    if let movies =
      TicketOffice.sharedInstance.purchasedMovieTicketIDs() {
        // 3
```

```
    let session = WCSession.default
    if session.isWatchAppInstalled {
      // 4
      do {
        let dictionary = ["movies": movies]
        try session.updateApplicationContext(dictionary)
      } catch {
        print("ERROR: \(error)")
      }
    }
  }
 }
}
```

Taking the code step by step:

1. First you check if the current device supports Watch Connectivity.

2. Next, you call `purchasedMovieTicketIDs()` on the `TicketOffice` singleton class
   to set the `movies` constant to an array of strings that represent all movie tickets
   purchased on the iPhone.

3. You set the constant `session` to the default connectivity session, and verify
   installation of the counterpart Watch app. If the user hasn't installed the Watch app,
   there's no point in trying to communicate with it.

4. Finally, you call `updateApplicationContext(_:)` on the active session to transfer
   a dictionary with the `movies` key set to the already-created `movies` array.

Now that the iPhone app is transferring purchased movie tickets, you'll set up the Watch
app to receive them.

Open **ExtensionDelegate.swift** and add the following to the end of the class:

```
// 1
func session(_ session: WCSession, didReceiveApplicationContext
  applicationContext:[String:Any]) {
  // 2
  if let movies = applicationContext["movies"] as? [String] {
    // 3
    TicketOffice.sharedInstance.purchaseTicketsForMovies(movies)
    // 4
    DispatchQueue.main.async {
      WKInterfaceController.reloadRootPageControllers(
        withNames: ["PurchasedMovieTickets"],
        contexts: nil,
        orientation: WKPageOrientation.vertical,
        pageIndex: 0)
    }
  }
}
```

Here's what you're doing:

1. Your code implements the optional `WCSessionDelegate` protocol method `session(_:didReceiveApplicationContext:)`. The active connectivity session calls this method when it receives context data from the counterpart iPhone app.

2. Next, you set `movies` to the String array from the `applicationContext` dictionary that represents the movie tickets purchased on the iPhone.

3. Next, you call `purchaseTicketsForMovies(_:)` on the `TicketOffice` singleton class with the `movies` array to update the list of purchased movies in the Watch app.

4. Finally, you reload the root interface controller on the main queue to display the purchased movie tickets. The delegate callback takes place on a background queue, so the reload must happen on the main queue to trigger UI updates.

Build and run the **CinemaTime** scheme to launch the iPhone app, and buy a movie. Next, stop the iPhone app, and build and run the **CinemaTimeWatch** scheme. Voilà! The movie you purchased on the iPhone app appears on the Watch app.

> **Note:** Notice that if you have both the iPhone app and the Watch app running at the same time, this use case will still work. While interactive messaging is the most immediate way to transfer data between two running apps, background transfers will work as well.

You've just added the ability to transfer purchased movie tickets from the iPhone to the Watch. Guess what you're going to do next. :]

Watch-to-iPhone communication

Yep, you need to perform a similar transfer between the Watch and the counterpart iPhone app.

Open **ExtensionDelegate.swift** and find `sendPurchasedMoviesToPhone(_:)`. When the user buys a ticket on the Watch, the `NotificationPurchasedMovieOnWatch` notification fires and the extension delegate calls `sendPurchasedMoviesToPhone(_:)`.

Replace the `TODO` in `sendPurchasedMoviesToPhone(_:)` with the following code:

```
func sendPurchasedMoviesToPhone(_ notification:Notification) {
  // 1
  if WCSession.isSupported() {
    // 2
    if let movies =
      TicketOffice.sharedInstance.purchasedMovieTicketIDs() {
      // 3
      do {
        let dictionary = ["movies": movies]
        try WCSession.default
          .updateApplicationContext(dictionary)
      } catch {
        print("ERROR: \(error)")
      }
    }
  }
}
```

Although this code is similar to what you just added in the iPhone-to-Watch communication section, there are some minor differences:

1. You check if the current device supports Watch Connectivity. On the Watch, this will always return `true`. Even so, it doesn't hurt to be careful in case this API behavior changes in future versions of watchOS.

2. Next, you call `purchasedMovieTicketIDs()` on the `TicketOffice` singleton class to set `movies` to the String array of all purchased movie tickets.

3. Finally, you call `updateApplicationContext(_:)` on the active session to transfer a dictionary to the iPhone with the `movies` key set to the already-created `movies` array.

The Watch app code is slightly different than that of the iPhone app: you don't need to check that the iPhone app is installed because the only way the Watch app can exist is if the counterpart iPhone app is already installed.

Now that the Watch is sending purchased movie tickets, you'll set up the iPhone to receive them.

Open **AppDelegate.swift** and add the following code to the `AppDelegate` extension:

```
// 1
func session(_ session: WCSession, didReceiveApplicationContext
  applicationContext:[String:Any]) {
  // 2
  if let movies = applicationContext["movies"] as? [String] {
    // 3
    TicketOffice.sharedInstance.purchaseTicketsForMovies(movies)
    //4
    DispatchQueue.main.async {
      let notificationCenter = NotificationCenter.default
      notificationCenter.post(name: NSNotification.Name(
        rawValue: NotificationPurchasedMovieOnWatch),
        object: nil)
    }
  }
}
```

Here's what you're doing with this code:

1. The app delegate implements the optional `WCSessionDelegate` protocol method `session(_:didReceiveApplicationContext:)`. The active connectivity session uses this method to receive context data from the counterpart Watch app.

2. Next, you set `movies` to the String array from the `applicationContext` dictionary that represents the movie tickets purchased on the Watch.

3. Next, you call `purchaseTicketsForMovies(_:)` with the `movies` array on the `TicketOffice` singleton class. Calling this method updates the list of purchased movies in the iPhone app.

4. Finally, you post the notification `NotificationPurchasedMovieOnWatch` on the main queue signifying there are new purchases. The view controllers listening for this notification now know to update their views to show the newly purchased movie

tickets. You use the main queue to post the notification, because the delegate callback happens on a background queue, and all UI updates need to happen on the main queue.

If you've made it this far, déjà vu must not faze you. If you've made it this far, déjà vu must not faze you. Oh, wait!

Conquering déjà vu...
Conquering déjà vu...
Conquering déjà vu...
Conquering déjà vu...
Conquering déjà vu...

...aaaaaahhh forget it!

Build and run both apps, but this time, buy a movie ticket on the Watch app. After you purchase the ticket, the iPhone app will refresh and show the purchased ticket.

Congratulations! CinemaTime customers can now buy and view movie tickets from either app — without worrying about where they made the purchase.

Where to go from here?

You can find the final project in the folder for this chapter.

In this chapter, you set up the Watch Connectivity framework, learned about the different ways to transfer data between counterpart iPhone and Watch apps, and finally, successfully implemented the application context transfer method.

Application context transfers provide a simple yet powerful way to share data between apps. However, they're not the only transfer in town. Chapter 19, "Advanced Watch Connectivity", will teach you all about more advanced Watch–iPhone communication protocols.

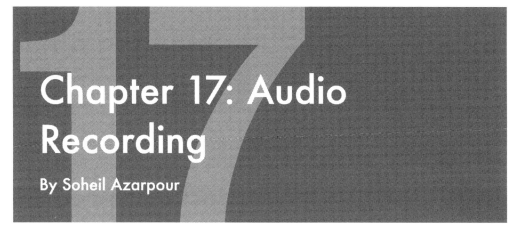

Chapter 17: Audio Recording

By Soheil Azarpour

In watchOS 2, Apple introduced a new API to play and record multimedia files on the Apple Watch. In watchOS 4, Apple has greatly improved the multimedia API and created great opportunities to build innovative apps and enhance the user experience.

In this chapter, you'll learn about watchOS 4's audio recording and playback APIs and how to use them in your apps. You'll add audio recording to a memo app so that users can record and review their thoughts and experiences right from their wrists. Let's get started!

Getting started

The starter project you'll use in this chapter is called **TurboMemo**. Open **TurboMemo.xcodeproj** in Xcode and make sure the **TurboMemo** scheme for iPhone is selected. Build and run in the iPhone simulator, and you'll see the following screen:

Users can record audio diaries by simply tapping the plus (+) button. The app sorts the entries by date, and users can play back an entry by tapping it.

Try adding some entries to create some initial data.

Now, stop the app and change the scheme to **TurboMemoWatch**. Build and run in the Watch Simulator, and you'll see the following screen:

The Watch app syncs with the iPhone app to display the same entries, but it doesn't do anything else yet. You're about to change that.

> **Note:** TurboMemo uses Watch Connectivity, which is covered in depth in Chapter 16 and Chapter 19.

Audio playback

There are two ways you can play an audio file in watchOS. You can either use the built-in media player, or build your own. You'll start with the built-in media player as it's simpler and more straightforward. In the next section, you'll build your own media player.

The easiest way to play a media file is to present the built-in media player controller using the `presentMediaPlayerController(with:options:completion:)` method of `WKInterfaceController`. All you have to do is to pass in a file URL that corresponds to the index of the row selected by the user in `WKInterfaceTable`.

Open **TurboMemoWatchExtension/InterfaceController.swift**, find the implementation of `table(_:, didSelectRowAt:)` and update it as follows:

```
// 1
let memo = memos[rowIndex]
// 2
presentMediaPlayerController(
  with: memo.url,
  options: nil,
  completion: {_,_,_ in })
```

Going through this step-by-step:

1. You get the selected memo by passing the selected row index to the array of memos.

2. You present a media player controller by calling `presentMediaPlayerController(with:options:completion:)` and passing in the URL of the selected memo. You can optionally pass in a dictionary of playback options. Since you don't want any particular customization at this point, you pass `nil`. In the completion block, you can check playback results based on your specific needs. Because the API requires a non-nil completion block, you simply provide an empty block.

That's it! Build and run the app. Tap on a row in the table and you can now listen to the memos!

> **Note:** To learn more about playback options and playing video files, check out Chapter 21: Handoff Video Playback.

Building an audio player

The media player controller in watchOS is great for playing short media files but it comes with limitations: As soon as the user dismisses the player, playback stops. This can be a problem if the user is listening to a long audio memo, and you want to continue playing the file even when the user closes the media player.

The built-in media interface can't be customized either. So if you want more control over the playback and appearance of the media player, you need to build your own.

You'll use `WKAudioFilePlayer` to play long audio files. `WKAudioFilePlayer` gives you more control over playback and the rate of playback. However, you're responsible for providing an interface and building your own UI.

> **Note:** Apps can play audio content using `WKAudioFilePlayer` only through a connected Bluetooth headphone or speaker on a real device. You won't be able to hear the audio using `WKAudioFilePlayer` either in watchOS simulator or via Apple Watch speaker. Therefore, to follow along with this section, you'll need an Apple Watch that's paired with Bluetooth headphones.

The starter project includes `AudioPlayerInterfaceController`. You'll use `AudioPlayerInterfaceController` as a basis for your custom audio player. But before you go there, while you're still in `InterfaceController`, you can rewire the code to call the `AudioPlayerInterfaceController` instead.

Once again, find the implementation of `table(_:didSelectRowAtIndex:)` in **InterfaceController.swift**, and update it as follows:

```
override func table(
  _ table: WKInterfaceTable,
  didSelectRowAt rowIndex: Int) {

    let memo = memos[rowIndex]
    presentController(
      withName: "AudioPlayerInterfaceController",
      context: memo)
}
```

Make sure you place the existing code entirely. Here, instead of using the built-in media player, you call your soon-to-be-made custom media player. If you build and run at this point, and select a memo entry from the table, you'll see the new media player that does ... nothing! Time to fix that.

Open **AudioPlayerInterfaceController** scene in **TurboMemoWatch/ Interface.storyboard**. `AudioPlayerInterfaceController` provides a basic UI for audio playback.

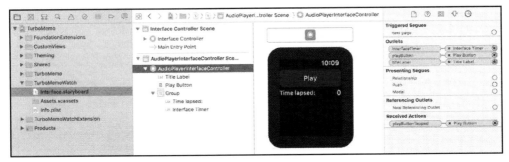

This has has:

- `titleLabel` which is blank by default

- `playButton` that's hooked up to `playButtonTapped()`.

- a static label that says `Time lapsed:`.

- `interfaceTimer` that is set to `0` by default.

Now, open **AudioPlayerInterfaceController.swift** and add the following properties at the beginning of `AudioPlayerInterfaceController`:

```
// 1
private var player: WKAudioFilePlayer!
// 2
private var asset: WKAudioFileAsset!
// 3
private var statusObserver: NSKeyValueObservation?
// 4
private var timer: Timer!
```

Taking this line-by-line:

1. `player` is an instance of `WKAudioFilePlayer`. You'll use it to play back an audio file.

2. `asset` is a representation of the voice memo. You'll use this to create a new `WKAudioFilePlayerItem` to play the audio file.

3. `statusObserver` is your key-value observer for the player's `status`. You'll need to observer the `status` of the `player` and start playing only if the audio file is ready to play.

4. `timer` that you use to update the UI. You kick off the timer at the same time you start playing. You do this because currently there's no other way to know when you're finished playing the audio file. You'll have to maintain your own timer with the same duration as your audio file.

You'll see all these in action in a moment.

Now, add the implementation of `awakeWithContext(_:)` to
`AudioPlayerInterfaceController` as follows:

```
override func awake(withContext context: Any?) {
  super.awake(withContext: context)
  // 1
  let memo = context as! VoiceMemo
  // 2
  asset = WKAudioFileAsset(url: memo.url)
  // 3
  titleLabel.setText(memo.filename)
  // 4
  playButton.setEnabled(false)
}
```

Again, taking this line-by-line:

1. After calling `super` as ordinary, you know for sure the `context` that's being passed
    to the controller is a `VoiceMemo`. This is Design by Contract!

2. Create a `WKAudioFileAsset` object with the voice memo and store it in `asset`.
    You'll reuse the asset to replay the same memo when user taps on the play button.

3. Set the `titleLabel` with the filename of the memo.

4. Disable the `playButton` until the file is ready to be played.

You prepared the interface to playback an audio file, but you haven't done anything to
actually play it. You'll kick off the playback in `didAppear()` so that playback starts when
the interface is fully presented to the user.

Speaking of `didAppear()`, add the following to `AudioPlayerInterfaceController`:

```
override func didAppear() {
  super.didAppear()
  prepareToPlay()
}
```

Here, you simply call a convenient method, `prepareToPlay()`. So let's add that next:

```
private func prepareToPlay() {
  // 1
  let playerItem = WKAudioFilePlayerItem(asset: asset)
  // 2
  player = WKAudioFilePlayer(playerItem: playerItem)
  // 3
  statusObserver = player.observe(
    \.status,
    changeHandler: { [weak self] (player, change) in
      // 4
      guard
```

```
          player.status == .readyToPlay,
          let duration = self?.asset.duration
          else { return }
      // 5
      let date = Date(timeIntervalSinceNow: duration)
      self?.interfaceTimer.setDate(date)
      // 6
      self?.playButton.setEnabled(false)
      // 7
      player.play()
      self?.interfaceTimer.start()
      // 8
      self?.timer = Timer.scheduledTimer(
        withTimeInterval: duration,
        repeats: false, block: { _ in

        self?.playButton.setEnabled(true)
      })
   })
  }
```

There's a lot going on here:

1. Create a `WKAudioFilePlayerItem` object from the `asset` you set earlier in `awake(withContext:)`. You have to do this each time you want to play a media file, since `WKAudioFilePlayerItem` can't be reused.

2. Initialize the `player` with the `WKAudioFilePlayerItem` you just created. You'll have to do this even if you're playing the same file again.

3. The `player` may not be ready to play the audio file immediately. You need to observe the `status` of the `WKAudioFilePlayer` object, and whenever it's set to `.readyToPlay`, you can start the playback. You use the new Swift 4 key-value observation (KVO) API to listen to changes in `player.status`.

4. In the observer block, you check for the player's `status` and if it's `.readyToPlay`, you safely unwrap `duration` of the `asset` and continue. Otherwise, you simply ignore the change notification.

5. Once the item is ready to play, you create a `Date` object with the duration of the memo, and update `interfaceTimer` to show the lapsed time.

6. Disable the `playButton` while you're playing the file.

7. Start playing by calling `player.play()`, and at the same time, start the countdown in the interface.

8. Kick off an internal timer to re-enable the `playButton` after the playback is finished so the user can start it again if they wish.

That was a big chunk of code, but as you see, it's mostly about maintaining the state of the WKAudioFilePlayer and keeping the interface in sync.

> **Note**: Unfortunately, at the time of writing this tutorial, currentTime of WKAudioFilePlayerItem is not KVO-complaint so you can't add an observer. Ideally, you would want to observe currentTime instead of maintaining a separate timer on your own.

Before you build and run, there's one more thing to add!

When the timer is up and playButton is enabled, the user should be able to tap on **Play** to restart playing the same file. To implement this, find the implementation of playButtonTapped() in **AudioPlayerInterfaceController.swift** and update it as follows:

```
@IBAction func playButtonTapped() {
  prepareToPlay()
}
```

It's that simple! Merely call the convenient method, prepareToPlay(), to restart the playback.

Next, build and run, and select a voice memo from the list. The app will present your custom interface. The interface will automatically start playing the audio file, and once it's stopped, the **Play** button will be re-enabled and you can play it again.

If you have more than one item to play, such as in a playlist, you'll want to use WKAudioFileQueuePlayer instead of WKAudioFilePlayer and queue your items. The system will play queued items back-to-back and provide a seamless transition between files.

Background audio playback

In watchOS, very much like in iOS, you can specify that your app should use background audio. This lets the system prepare to take over and continue playing the audio file if a user dismisses your media player.

To declare support for background audio, you'll update the Info.plist for the Watch app. Open **TurboMemoWatch\Info.plist**, select the **Information Property List** entry and tap the + button:

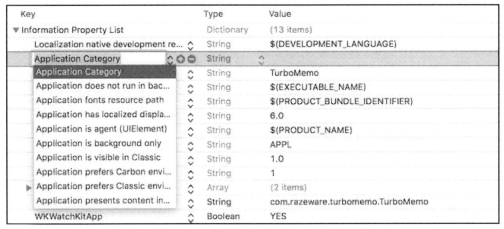

Change the value of the new key to UIBackgroundModes. Make sure its type is Array and then expand the key and add a new value named audio. Xcode will most likely change the values to more readable versions:

Key	Type	Value
▼ Information Property List	Dictionary	(13 items)
Required background modes	Array	(1 item)
Item 0	String	App plays audio or streams audio/video using AirPlay
Localization native development re...	String	$(DEVELOPMENT_LANGUAGE)
Bundle display name	String	TurboMemo
Executable file	String	$(EXECUTABLE_NAME)
Bundle identifier	String	$(PRODUCT_BUNDLE_IDENTIFIER)
InfoDictionary version	String	6.0
Bundle name	String	$(PRODUCT_NAME)
Bundle OS Type code	String	APPL
Bundle versions string, short	String	1.0
Bundle version	String	1
▶ Supported interface orientations	Array	(2 items)
WKCompanionAppBundleIdentifier	String	com.razeware.turbomemo.TurboMemo
WKWatchKitApp	Boolean	YES

Adding this key lets the Watch app continue running for the purpose of playing audio. If the key is not present, playback ends when the user stops interacting with your app.

Recording audio

One of the most exciting features of watchOS is its access to the microphone. Being able to add a voice memo to Turbo Memo on the Apple Watch is definitely something users will appreciate — so let's do it!

When you start recording, it's the Watch app that does the recording and has access to the microphone. Prior to watchOS 4, the WatchKit extension had to provide a shared container using App Groups to which both could read and write, allowing the Watch app to write the audio and the WatchKit extension to grab it.

Even though the WatchKit extension code was bundled and copied to the Apple Watch along with the Watch app itself, from the system's standpoint, they were still two separate processes that were sandboxed within their own containers. In other words, the Watch app and the WatchKit extension didn't share the same sandbox!

New in watchOS 4, thanks to Unified Process Runtime, both the Watch app and the WatchKit extension run in the same process so they both have access to the same sandbox.

> **Note:** The good news is that if you're dropping support for watchOS versions prior to watchOS 4, you can simplify your code by removing the code related to communication between App Groups and your app's container. The bad news is that if you want to have a backward-compatible watchOS app, you need to enable App Groups. To learn more about App Groups, check out the "Sharing Data with Your Containing App" section of Apple's *App Extension Programming Guide*: apple.co/1I5YBtZ

The starter project includes a menu item called **+ Voice** that's accessible in the app's main interface by force-touching the screen:

In code, it's hooked up to addVoiceMemoMenuItemTapped() in
InterfaceController.swift, and currently does ... (surprise) nothing.

It's time to tune up this code and do some recording.

Open **InterfaceController.swift**, find the empty implementation of
addVoiceMemoMenuItemTapped() and update it as follows:

```
// 1
let outputURL = MemoFileNameHelper.newOutputURL()
// 2
let preset = WKAudioRecorderPreset.narrowBandSpeech
// 3
let options: [String : Any] =
  [WKAudioRecorderControllerOptionsMaximumDurationKey: 30]
// 4
presentAudioRecorderController(
  withOutputURL: outputURL,
  preset: preset,
  options: options) {
    [weak self] (didSave: Bool, error: Error?) in

    // 5
    guard didSave else { return }
    self?.processRecordedAudio(at: outputURL)
}
```

This is the action method you'll call when a user wants to add a new voice memo. Here's
what you're doing:

1. Create a new URL by calling MemoFileNameHelper.newOutputURL() which is a
    convenient helper module. All it does is that it generates a unique file name based on
    the current date and time, appends .m4a as the file extension to it, and creates a URL
    based on user's documentDirectory on the current device — it's a shared code
    between the iPhone and the Watch app. This is basically where you'll save the audio
    file.

2. Configure presets for the recorder. See below for more information on the presets
    you can use.

3. Create an options dictionary to specify the maximum duration of the recording
    session. Here, it's 30 seconds.

4. Present the system-provided audio recording controller.

5. In the completion block, if the audio file is successfully saved, you pass it on to a
    helper method, processRecordedAudio(at:) which will then broadcast it to the
    iPhone app and update your data source for the interface table.

When you present an audio recording controller, there are a number of things you can specify. First, the `preset` you select determines the sample and bit rates at which the audio will record:

- **NarrowBandSpeech**: As its name implies, this is a good preset for voice memos and voice messages. It has a sample rate of 8 kHz, and it records at a bit rate of 24 kbps with an AAC codec and 128 kbps with an LPCM codec.

- **WideBandSpeech**: This preset has a higher sample rate of 16 kHz, and it records at a bit rate of 32 kbps with an AAC codec and 256 kbps with an LPCM codec.

- **HighQualityAudio**: This preset has the highest sample rate at 44.1 kHz, and it records at a bit rate of 96 kbps with an AAC codec and 705.6 kbps with an LPCM codec.

You can also specify various recording options:

- **WKAudioRecorderControllerOptionsMaximumDurationKey**: You can set the maximum duration of recorded audio clips by passing in a `TimeInterval` value in seconds. There's no maximum recording time if you don't set a value for this key.

- **WKAudioRecorderControllerOptionsAlwaysShowActionTitleKey**: You can use this key to pass either `true` or `false` to modify the behavior for showing the action button. If you specify `false`, the audio recorder controller shows the button only after the user has recorded some audio. By default, the action button is always visible.

- **WKAudioRecorderControllerOptionsActionTitleKey**: You can use this key to pass in a `String` to customize the display title of the button that the user taps to accept a recording. By default, the button's title is **Save**.

- **WKAudioRecorderControllerOptionsAutorecordKey**: By passing a Boolean value for this key, you can change the automatic recording behavior of the audio recorder controller. If you set it to `true`, once the controller is presented, it automatically starts recording; otherwise, the user has to tap on the record button to start recording. The default value is `true`.

That's it! Build and run. Bring up the contextual menu using the force touch gesture and tap on the **+ Voice** button. The app will present you with an audio recording controller. Tap the **Save** button, and you'll have recorded your first voice memo on an Apple Watch, using your own code!

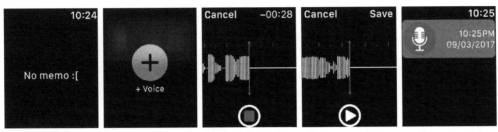

If you try recording on a real device, the very first time you present the system-provided audio recording controller, watchOS will ask for the user's permission.

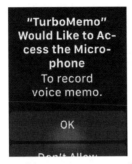

Very much like in iOS, the user should grant access to the microphone on the Watch. However, unlike iOS, you don't explicitly ask for user's permission as there's no API for that. Instead, the watchOS uses the `NSMicrophoneUsageDescription` key in the iPhone's app to present the appropriate UI and ask the user for their permission. If user doesn't grant access, the audio recorder will still work, but it will only record silence!

> **Note:** At the time of writing this tutorial, the watchOS simulator doesn't present the dialog asking for the user's permission. The iPhone simulator, on the other hand, does present the permission dialog.

Where to go from here?

The audio recording and playback API of watchOS 4 makes it possible to deliver a smooth multimedia experience on the Apple Watch even when the paired iPhone isn't in proximity. This is a technology with endless possibilities.

If you're curious to learn more, be sure to check out these resources:

- App Programming Guide for watchOS, "Audio and Video" section: http://apple.co/2xSQFA9

- WWDC 2017 - What's New in watchOS: http://apple.co/2f8Kn83

- WWDC 2017 - What's New in Audio: http://apple.co/2wNeh9a

- WWDC 2015 - Introducing WatchKit for watchOS 2: http://apple.co/29FDaMZ

Chapter 18: Interactive Animation with SpriteKit and SceneKit

By Ben Morrow

SpriteKit and SceneKit are the 2D and 3D game development frameworks for Apple platforms. They're available across all your favorite platforms: macOS, iOS, tvOS, and... watchOS!

Although people generally think of them as game development frameworks, you can use them to design interactivity with lively animation into any kind of app.

In this chapter, you'll expand a game app in a variety of ways and learn how to apply SpriteKit and SceneKit in your Watch apps. SpriteKit and SceneKit are complex topics, which would require a book each. This chapter won't teach you the detailed mechanics you'd use for the next hit game in the App Store. Instead, you will learn:

- The theory behind SpriteKit and SceneKit
- Migrating from iOS: API differences and how you share code across targets
- Using gestures and the accelerometer in games
- Animating a ring chart
- Creating an animated scene in a notification
- Combining SceneKit and SpriteKit in one interface

By the end of the chapter, you'll have the know-how to create interactive animations of your own.

Getting started

You'll build upon an iOS game named Escape. The player's objective is to roll towards the light emanating from the single opening in the wall; if the player runs into the wall, the game ends. Each opening leads to the next level.

> **Note:** As of the time of writing, SpriteKit and SceneKit do not run well in the simulator. In order to complete the chapter, you'll need a newer physical Apple Watch device. The original "Series 0" watch is not supported.

Open **Escape.xcodeproj** from this chapter's **starter** directory. The Watch app hasn't been made yet, but the game is fully functional on iPhone and iPad. Before you can run the app, you'll need to update the project settings.

In the project navigator, select your project, **Escape**. In the project and targets list, locate the Target section. Go through each target - the iOS app, the WatchKit Extension, and the WatchKit App - and:

1. Change the **Bundle Identifier**, replacing "razeware" with your domain name. For example, I would use : `com.benmorrow` instead of `com.razeware`.

2. Add your developer account name in the **Team** drop-down.

Next, expand the **Escape WatchKit App** group in the project navigator and open **Info.plist**. Update the value of `WKCompanionAppBundleIdentifier` with the same root domain name.

Finally, expand **Escape WatchKit Extension** group and open **Info.plist**. Navigate through **NSExtension \ NSExtensionAttributes** by clicking their disclosure triangles. Update the value of `WKAppBundleIdentifier` with the same root domain name.

Build and run the iOS app **Escape** scheme for your physical device:

If everything works, you'll see the game load up on your iPhone or iPad. You can verify the refresh rate by looking at the numbers in the bottom right of the screen.

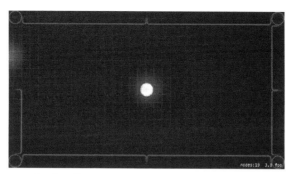

Ideally, you want to see 60 fps (frames per second) on iOS devices. The app will utilize the graphics hardware and run at a much higher frame rate than on the simulator. The app uses the accelerometer, so the ball rolls realistically across the floor as you tilt the device.

There are five levels in the game. See if you can beat it!

Introducing SpriteKit and SceneKit

When you start using SpriteKit or SceneKit, it may take your brain some time to adjust to the different coordinate systems.

Coordinate Systems

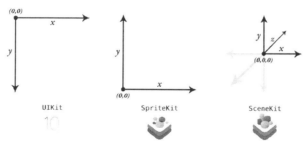

In UIKit, the origin of the screen is in the top left. Imagine how the user interface of the Mail app flows down the screen.

In SpriteKit, the y-axis is flipped, and the origin of the screen is in the bottom left. Imagine a platformer game like Mario where the character jumps up to increase his y-position.

In SceneKit, the default camera points directly at the origin in the middle of the screen. To grasp this, imagine you're flying in a helicopter, and you can travel any direction in three dimensions.

The framework authors considered the potential use cases when they designed the default viewport for each coordinate system. In both UIKit and SpriteKit negative x- and y-values will position an element off the screen.

Speaking of elements, in UIKit, the base element is a *view*. In SpriteKit and SceneKit the base element is a *node*.

Nodes

Views in UIKit have their origin at the top left — the same as the viewport. In this example, the dot shows the origin of the search field:

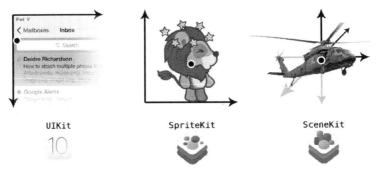

By contrast, in SpriteKit and SceneKit the origin of a node is at its center. This makes it easy to position nodes without having to account for their height, width, and depth. In the example shown above, you would position the lion by his center rather than his feet. Keep in mind that in a game, the position of a character constantly changes. Movements are relative to the previous position. Also, the lion won't fall through the floor thanks to the collision detection in the physics engine.

Scenes

Scenes in SpriteKit and SceneKit are a lot like the scene you see in a storyboard for an interface controller. Just like a storyboard, you can use a visual file format to configure a SpriteKit or SceneKit scene.

For SpriteKit and SceneKit scenes those files are .sks and .scn, respectively. Scenes contain every node you display on the screen. In the image above, you see a SpriteKit scene on the left and a SceneKit scene on the right.

Actions

Think of actions as prepared animations for nodes. The animations won't run until you make a call such as `node.run(action)`. Actions describe how a node will change over a duration of time. You can configure actions visually in the timeline of a .sks file. In the image above, you see *fade* and *scale* actions. Two other common actions are *move* and *rotate*.

Although you can configure scenes and actions in visual files, you can also create nodes and run actions directly from code. In Escape, you'll work exclusively in code.

Physics

SpriteKit and SceneKit both offer a physics engine that you control at your will. Here are some things you can deploy:

- **Gravity**: Set the strength and direction of gravity in the scene.
- **Light**: Set the color and falloff of lights. Falloff controls how far light travels before fading away.
- **Collisions**: Prevent nodes from passing through each other.

A node is merely a shape that you see on the screen. You choose whether you want the node to interact with the physics engine or not. Gravity, light, and collisions all only optionally affect each node. In Escape, gravity only affects the ball, not the wall bumpers. Light only shines off the floor, not the wall bumpers.

You can also choose to set a node's physics body to be different in size or shape than its visual appearance. In Escape, the ball's physics body is set to be slightly smaller than its actual shape. That forgiving gameplay means a collision happens only when you definitely expect it to happen.

In SpriteKit and SceneKit, *collision* means that two nodes will bounce off of each other. If you turn on collision behavior between two nodes, they are not allowed to overlap. In Escape, the ball and the wall bumpers exhibit collision behavior.

Contact occurs when two nodes' physics bodies touch. You can subscribe to contact notifications by giving SpriteKit and SceneKit the selector of a method to call when contact occurs. Nodes don't need to have collision behavior turned on to make use of the contact notification. In Escape, you handle contact between the ball and the `exitFence` even though the ball doesn't bounce off the `exitFence` in a collision. When the ball contacts the `exitFence`, the game proceeds to the next level.

Conversely, you can also choose to receive a notification for the contact between nodes that *do* exhibit collision behavior, like the ball and the wall bumper. When the ball first contacts a wall bumper you run a move action. The wall bumper moves slightly inward to the center of the floor which has the effect of pushing the ball thanks to the always-on collision behavior.

Particle systems

Both SpriteKit and SceneKit include particle generators. You can create a wide variety of rendered effects in 2D and 3D. Particles work well for fuzzy, chaotic natural phenomena like rain and fire. A particle system efficiently draws hundreds of nodes in real-time and efficiently manages memory as nodes fall outside the screen. You can choose to influence particle systems with physical forces. Later in this chapter, you'll work with a confetti particle system that responds to gravity and air turbulence.

That overview should give you an idea how you can use physics interactions and properties to make your game feel real. At your leisure, you can read through the full code in GameScene.swift and try changing values to see how they affect the gameplay. In the rest of the chapter, you'll focus in on watch-specific tricks for SpriteKit and SceneKit.

Migrating from iOS

Some of you may have built games with SpriteKit and SceneKit previously for iOS, macOS, or tvOS. For you, let's go over the differences you'll experience when building a game for watchOS.

Graphics rendering

The Apple Watch works differently than iPhone and iPad. The current GPU in the S2 chip cannot run the Metal framework like the A10 chip in the iPhone. Instead, watchOS renders SpriteKit and SceneKit graphics with OpenGL.

Due to the different architectures, there are a few features from iOS that are not available on watchOS. Here are some notable ones, along with respective workarounds:

- **Physically-based environment rendering for materials, lighting, and HDR camera effects introduced in iOS 10** (`SCNLightingModelPhysicallyBased`, `SCNScene lightingEnvironment`, `SCNCamera wantsHDR`): Instead, you can use the standard lighting and materials.

- **Audio** (`SCNAudioSource`, `SCNAudioPlayer`, `SKAudioNode`, `AVFoundation`): Instead, you can use `playSoundFileNamed(_:waitForCompletion:)` on SpriteKit and `playAudio(_:waitForCompletion:)` on SceneKit.

- **Custom Metal or OpenGL shader programs** (`SCNProgram`, `SCNTechnique`): Instead, you can customize SceneKit rendering with `SCNShadable` shader modifiers.

- **Core Image filters for node rendering** (`CIFilter`): Instead, again you can customize SceneKit rendering with `SCNShadable` shader modifiers. For SpriteKit, you can use `SKShader` and built-in `SKTransition` effects to customize node rendering.

- **Video playback** (`SKVideoNode`): Instead, you can use `WKInterfaceMovie`.

There are a few other minor differences between UIKit and WatchKit that you'll see as you work your way through the chapter. That said, the limitations are rare. Most of the features you will need in SpriteKit and SceneKit are available for apps you build for the Watch.

Adding a WatchKit App to the project

To save time, the starter project contains an empty new *Game app\SpriteKit* Watch target.

> **Note:** The only difference between a Game App target and a normal WatchKit App target is that Xcode preconfigures a SpriteKit or SceneKit scene in the storyboard.

The Shared group in the project navigator contains files that both the iOS app and the Watch app will share. The first thing you'll change in the project is to move the game code there.

Sharing code

From the **Escape WatchKit Extension** group in the project navigator, select **GameScene.swift**. Holding Command on your keyboard, also select **GameScene.sks**. Press **Delete** on your keyboard and click **Move to Trash**. Xcode creates both of these files when it generates a Watch SpriteKit Game App target. You'll share the code from the iOS app so you won't need watch-specific GameScene.swift file. You also won't need the visual scene .sks file since you'll create all the nodes with code.

Select **GameScene.swift** from the Escape group in the project navigator. Drag it into the **Shared** group.

Xcode 9 automatically adds the Watch target for you when you move the file to the shared group--but it doesn't actually recognize the new target. For a workaround, select **GameScene.swift** in its new location. Open the **File Inspector** in the right sidebar. In the Target Membership box uncheck **Escape WatchKit Extension** and then check it again. Now both the iOS app and the WatchKit extension can see the file.

Expand the **Bundled Extensions** group and expand both folders inside of it as well. The Bundled Extensions group includes libraries that will help you build the app quickly. The largest of these is SKTUtils, an open source project published by the raywenderlich.com team. You can check it out on GitHub at bit.ly/2dcyDyz.

There's only one file inside that's not shared with the WatchKit Extension, SKTAudio.swift. Its code refers to `AVFoundation` which is not available in watchOS.

Collapse the **Bundled Extensions** group to tidy up your project navigator. Lookin' good!

Using the shared code

Open **InterfaceController.swift** from the Escape WatchKit Extension group in the project navigator.

Add this code right underneath the definition of `skInterface`:

```
var scene: GameScene!
```

With that code, you declare `scene` as a property so that you can refer to it in methods you'll add later.

Replace the implementation of `awake(withContext:)` with this code:

```
super.awake(withContext: context)
scene = GameScene(size: contentFrame.size)
skInterface.presentScene(scene)
skInterface.preferredFramesPerSecond = 30
```

The default implementation provided by Xcode loads the scene from a .sks file. Instead, you instantiate `GameScene` from code. The shared GameScene.swift file contains all the gameplay details.

Now your WatchKit app will run the same code as the iOS app! You're making great progress.

However, inconveniently, the shared code in `GameScene` has a few calls that watchOS can't run. You'll fix those next.

Cleaning up the shared code

Open **GameScene.swift** inside the Shared group. The first fix is a snap! Near the top of the file, there's the definition of a function with this signature: `override func didMove(to view: SKView)`. watchOS doesn't use views; it uses interfaces. So you won't be able to listen for the scene to move to a view because there is no view. Instead, replace that signature with this one:

```
override func sceneDidLoad() {
```

Both watchOS and iOS trigger `sceneDidLoad()` at a similar time in the scene lifecycle to when iOS calls `didMove(to:)`. You've successfully made your first substitution.

Implementing gesture recognizers

To save time, the starter project contains tap, pan, and long press gesture recognizers hooked up in the storyboards for both the iOS app and the Watch app.

> **Note:** You can use pan and long press gestures in the simulator to control gravity instead of the accelerometer on physical devices. At the time of this writing, you won't be able to try the game in the simulator. But the game includes touch gestures that allow you to play in the simulator in the future. For the WatchKit Extension, you'll simply need to uncomment the code in `gestureRecognized(_:)`.

The tap gesture controls restarting the game. You'll implement the `@IBAction` method for the Watch app.

Open **InterfaceController.swift** from the Escape WatchKit Extension group in the project navigator.

For `tapRecognized(_:)` add this code to its implementation:

```
scene.handleTap()
```

That was easy enough. You're calling a method from `GameScene`.

Transforming the accelerometer data

Notably, a game scene in watchOS *does* have access to `CoreMotion`. So you get to keep the accelerometer code in `GameScene` from the original iOS source. That's a win!

However, if you try to run the app on a physical watch device right now, you'd notice that the ball doesn't roll how you would expect.

The reason is that the iOS app is set to always run in the *Landscape Right* orientation. The landscape orientation provides a nice experience on an iPhone or an iPad. However, the Apple Watch can only run in portrait mode while strapped on your wrist.

You'll need to adjust the data from the accelerometer to account for the different orientations of the devices.

Open **GameScene.swift** from the Shared group in the project navigator. Scroll down to the end of the class and you'll see `update(_:)`.

For every frame shown on screen, SpriteKit calls `update(_:)`. You can see the clever trick the code uses to change functionality between the simulator and physical devices:

```
#if (arch(i386) || arch(x86_64)) // Simulator: touch gestures
  // ...
#else // Device: accelerometer
  // ...
#endif
```

The `#if-else` compiler directive checks the processor architecture running your Swift code. If the processor architecture matches a macOS device then the simulator must be running and the game uses touch events to update the gravity in the physics engine. Otherwise, you can assume that an ARM processor is running the code on an iPhone, iPad, or Apple Watch. In that case, the game uses the accelerometer to update the gravity vector.

Since you need to update the accelerometer code, replace the implementation inside the `#else` block with this code:

```
if let accelerometerData = motionManager.accelerometerData {
  var dx: Double, dy: Double
  // 1
  let multiplier = pow((Double(min(size.height,
                                    size.width)) / 136), 2)
  let accelerationX = accelerometerData.acceleration.x
  let accelerationY = accelerometerData.acceleration.y
  if size.height > size.width {
    // 2
    dx = accelerationX * multiplier
    dy = accelerationY * multiplier
```

```
    } else {
        // 3
        dx = accelerationY * -multiplier
        dy = accelerationX * multiplier
    }
    physicsWorld.gravity = CGVector(dx: dx, dy: dy)
}
```

This code not only accounts for the change in orientation, but it also adjusts the accelerometer data so the ball rolls at a different speed for each device class. Here's what's happening step-by-step:

1. You create a multiplier for the accelerometer data. `pow(someNumber, 2)` squares the value of `someNumber`. The graph of a squared function curves up exponentially if you can recall back to the school days of graphing calculators. The squared function exhibits an increasing rate of change. In this case, for the x-value inside the squared function, you use the minimum between the two values of height and width. You then divide that minimum value by 136.

Note: The 38 mm Apple Watch has a horizontal resolution of 136 points. Therefore you use the 38 mm Apple Watch as your baseline. That device will have a ball speed of 1 and as the device screen size increases, the ball speed will grow larger and larger. Faster acceleration on larger devices will move the ball across more pixels. Additionally, a user has finer control with two hands, so again a high ball speed makes sense on a large device.

2. If the screen height is greater than the width, the device is in portrait orientation. That means you can pass the accelerometer data directly into the `gravity` vector property of the `physicsWorld`.

3. Otherwise, you assume the screen is in the landscape orientation. You pass y-component from the accelerometer into the x-component of the gravity and vice versa for the other axis. You also add a negative sign to the multiplier to account for the *Landscape Right* orientation as opposed to the *Landscape Left* orientation.

The best way to find out if you're interpreting the accelerometer data correctly is to try the app on a device. I settled on these values by running the app and seeing how the code performed.

If you have a physical Apple Watch device, you can try the game now. Connect your iPhone to your computer with the USB cable. Wait for Xcode to index the device. Then, build and run the [**your iPhone**] + [**your Watch**] scheme.

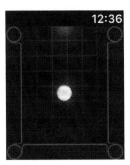

If the app launches correctly, you'll be able to play the game by tilting your wrist!

Your game looks great and works well on any size screen for iPhone, iPad and Apple Watch. Next, I'll teach you a couple more ways you can use SpriteKit in watchOS to add some extra oomph.

Animating a ring chart

The Activity app is one of the prominent features of the Apple Watch. Imagine if the Activity app's rings could animate to their current value with a bounce effect or change color depending on how recently you moved. Those animations would be both magical and useful. However, before SpriteKit, you would have to use a sequence of images to create those animations. Now that you can use SpriteKit, your animations can become more rich and detailed.

Still working in **GameScene.swift**, scroll down to the bottom of the file, and look for the comment heading, "Celebration animations".

You're going to build a ring chart to show the player how far they made it in the game.

Replace the implementation of runCelebration() with this code:

```
// 1
gameOver = true
// 2
```

```
ring = SKRingNode(center: CGPoint(x: frame.midX,
                              y: frame.size.height / 5 * 3),
                 diameter: frame.midY)
ring.color = SKColor.white
// 3
ring.name = "ring"
// 4
addChild(ring)
```

Here's what's happening in that code:

1. You flag gameOver to stop the physics simulation.

2. You create an instance of SKRingNode and assign it to a property of the scene. SKRingNode performs the bulk of the calculations and drawing of the ring so that you can focus on the animations you'll add to it. The initializer accepts two parameters. You set the ring's center point to an x-value of half of the width and y-value of 3/5 of the height of the scene. You also set the ring's diameter to half the height of the scene.

3. You set the ring's name to "ring". For this game, you won't need the name of the ring node. However, it's a good idea to get into the habit of setting a name for every node you create in SpriteKit because the name can be useful during debugging.

4. You add the ring into the scene. Nodes won't display on the screen until you call addChild(node).

Next, you'll add some animations to the ring during the celebration sequence.

Add this code to the end of runCelebration() immediately after the code you just added:

```
// 1
let blinkAction = SKAction.sequence(
  [SKAction.fadeOut(withDuration: 0.1),
   SKAction.fadeIn(withDuration: 0.1)])
let quadBlinkAction = SKAction.repeat(blinkAction, count: 4)
// 2
let arcEnd = CGFloat(level) / CGFloat(levelsToWin + 1)
let ringValueEffect = SKTRingValueEffect(for: ring,
                                         to: arcEnd,
                                         withDuration: 4)
ringValueEffect.timingFunction = SKTTimingFunctionBounceEaseOut
let ringValueEffectAction =
  SKAction.actionWithEffect(ringValueEffect)
// 3
let red = UIColor(red: 237 / 255.0,
                  green: 30 / 255.0,
                  blue: 95 / 255.0,
                  alpha: 1)
```

```
let blue = UIColor(red: 36 / 255.0,
                   green: 160 / 255.0,
                   blue: 255 / 255.0,
                   alpha: 1)
let finalColor = lerp(start: red, end: blue, t: arcEnd)
let ringColorEffect = SKTRingColorEffect(for: ring,
                                         from: red,
                                         to: finalColor,
                                         withDuration: 4)
ringColorEffect.timingFunction = SKTTimingFunctionBounceEaseOut
let ringColorEffectAction =
  SKAction.actionWithEffect(ringColorEffect)
// 4
let valueAndColorGroup =
  SKAction.group([ringValueEffectAction, ringColorEffectAction])
```

Here's what's happening with those actions:

1. The first animation you prepare is blinkAction. The ring will fade in and then fade out. You then prepare another animation that repeats blinkAction four times.

2. The ringValueEffect will fill the value of the ring. You set the timing function to bounce-out which will only bounce the end of the animation. SKTUtils includes a whole suite of timing functions. You can play around with different timing functions once you get this animation up and running. You then create an SKAction out of the bounce SKTEffect to prepare the animation to run later.

3. You establish a couple of colors for the 0% and 100% statuses of the animation. Then you use a linear interpolation function, lerp(start:end:t:), to calculate a color in between the 0% and 100% colors. In linear interpolation, you pass the percentage of the transition you desire to the t parameter. The function calculates the final color for the animation based on the how far the player made it in the game. You then create an SKTRingColorEffect to animate between the start and end values of the color. Again you use a bounce-out timing function for extra style and create an action from the effect so you can run the animation later.

4. You package up the value fill animation and the color change animation into a group so that they will run together.

You've built some solid ring animations. Now you'll prepare the final flourishes of the celebration sequence.

Add this code immediately below the last lines you added:

```
// 1
let showClosingMessage = SKAction.run {
  if self.level > self.levelsToWin {
    self.closingMessage = SKSpriteNode(
```

```
        imageNamed: "congratulations")
  } else {
    self.closingMessage = SKSpriteNode(imageNamed: "try_again")
  }
  // 2
  self.closingMessage.position = CGPoint(
    x: self.frame.midX, y: self.frame.size.height / 5)
  self.closingMessage.name = "closingMessage"
  self.addChild(self.closingMessage)
}
// 3
let fadeColorEffect = SKTRingColorEffect(for: ring,
                                          to: SKColor.white,
                                          withDuration: 12)
fadeColorEffect.timingFunction = SKTTimingFunctionBounceEaseOut
let fadeColorEffectAction =
  SKAction.actionWithEffect(fadeColorEffect)
// 4
let sequence = SKAction.sequence([quadBlinkAction,
                                  valueAndColorGroup,
                                  showClosingMessage,
                                  fadeColorEffectAction])
// 5
ring.run(sequence)
```

1. You will display the "Congratulations" or "Try again" image depending on whether the user beats the game or not. You package this code up into a special SKAction that runs a closure. You can use the run type of SKAction anytime you want to execute arbitrary code during an animation sequence. In this case, you're going to run all the actions on ring. Since the closingMessage is a different node entirely, you use SKAction.run(_:) to execute the block of code.

2. You set the position of the closingMessage to an x-value of half the width of the scene and a y-value of one-fifth of the height of the screen. Remember that the origin of a scene is the bottom left, so the closingMessage will display near the bottom of the screen.

3. You add another color change action that will desaturate the ring color after value fill completes. During the value fill, the ring will animate from red to blue. Then after the bounce stops, the ring will animate to white to evoke the feeling that the ring settles down.

4. You package up all the actions into a sequence. The sequence runs actions one after another as they complete. So first the ring will blink four times. Then the ring will fill its value and change its color at the same time. Then the closing message will display, and finally, the ring will change colors again to settle on white.

5. You run the entire sequence of animations on the ring.

There's one more thing to do before you can see the ring in action. You need to remove the ring when the player starts a new game.

Locate the next method, `removeCelebration()`, in the file. Add this code to the top of the implementation right after the opening curly brace:

```
ring.removeFromParent()
```

`removeFromParent()` will delete the node from the scene so that the ring won't get in the way of the gameplay when the player starts a new game.

Build and run the **Escape WatchKit App** scheme. See how far you can make it in the game. Pay special attention to the celebration sequence when the game ends.

Phenomenal work! The animated ring adds extra punch to the celebration sequence.

SceneKit

So far you've worked strictly in SpriteKit. If you'd like to import real 3D models into your scene, then you'll want to use SceneKit. You'll create a SceneKit scene in the next section.

Adding animation to a WatchKit notification

Imagine when you put the game into the App Store you use a freemium business model. All players receive 25 rolls per day for free. You offer an "unlimited rolls" in-app purchase for the true fans.

Since you want to turn the casual players into true fans, you keep them engaged and addicted by dispatching a notification to announce the arrival of their daily rolls.

The Watch app target from the starter project included a notification scene in the storyboard. To check it out, open **Interface.storyboard** from the Escape WatchKit App group in the project navigator.

The notification scene resides below the interface controller scene. Scroll down to find it. A notification scene includes both a static interface on the left and a dynamic interface on the right. The static interface only shows what you configure in Interface Builder. So to display a SceneKit scene, you'll need to use the dynamic interface.

Search the Object Library for a **SceneKit Scene**. Drag it onto the dynamic interface, the **Notification Controller** in the Notification Controller Scene. With the SceneKit scene object selected, open the Attributes Inspector and change the **Height** to **Fixed** and set its value to **80**.

Your Notification Controller Scene should look like this:

Next, you'll hook up an outlet for the SceneKit scene. Reveal the assistant editor. Control-drag from the **SceneKit Scene** to the top of the **NotificationController** class. Name the outlet **scnInterface**.

Working in the **NotificationController.swift** file, locate `init()`. Beneath the `super.init()` line, add this code:

```
let confettiScene = ConfettiScene()
scnInterface.scene = confettiScene
scnInterface.preferredFramesPerSecond = 30
```

In that code, you instantiate `ConfettiScene`, a class included in the starter project. `ConfettiScene` is a SceneKit scene which has a particle system that generates small, colorful planes. You'll get to see the code for `ConfettiScene` soon, but first you'll finish one more thing in this file.

Uncomment the built-in method at the end of the class by removing `/*` and `*/` from the beginning and end of of the method. You'll end up with this code:

```
override func didReceive(_ notification: UNNotification,
```

```
    withCompletion completionHandler:
      @escaping (WKUserNotificationInterfaceType) -> Swift.Void) {
    completionHandler(.custom)
  }
```

watchOS calls `didReceive(_:withCompletion:)` when a notification needs to be presented. You must implement this method to use a dynamic notification interface as you learned in Chapter 14.

Now you're ready to dive into the SceneKit code. Open **ConfettiScene.swift** from the Escape WatchKit Extension group in the project navigator. Switch back to the standard editor so you can see the file fill the middle pane of Xcode.

You'll see code like this:

```
// 1
class ConfettiScene: SCNScene {
  override init() {
    super.init()
    // 2 - Create the particle system
    // [...]
    // 3 - Create the turbulence field
    // [...]
  }
}
```

> **Note**: You don't need to copy this code because it will already be in the file.

Here's what's happening:

1. `ConfettiScene` inherits support for 3D graphics from `SCNScene`.

2. You set 28 different properties on the particle system. That's how you can create wildly different effects from rain to fire to confetti. The confetti will travel downwards because `isAffectedByGravity` is set to `true`.

3. You create air turbulence which acts as a varying wind to gently blow the confetti around.

You'll need to add a camera because the scene won't display correctly at the moment. Adding a camera will cause the scene to render according to the camera's perspective.

Add this code to the end of `init()`, just below the turbulence code:

```
let cameraNode = SCNNode()
cameraNode.camera = SCNCamera()
cameraNode.position = SCNVector3(x: 0, y: 0, z: 1.5)
```

```
rootNode.addChildNode(cameraNode)
```

With that code, you create a camera and add it to the scene. If you remember from the coordinates lesson at the beginning of the chapter, setting the x- and y-components of `position` to the origin and setting a positive z-component will position the camera straight-on like your eyes looking at the screen of your phone.

`rootNode` is a special property of an `SCNScene` to which you add all the child nodes in your scene. That's slightly different than how you treated a SpriteKit scene where you could add nodes directly to the scene.

Build and run the **Escape WatchKit App (Notification)** scheme. The simulator will launch to the clock face and then you'll see your notification pop up.

You've just *seen* your first official SceneKit *scene* on the Apple Watch! :]

SceneKit is a massive framework that can do so much more than generate particles. It's chock-full of other 3D objects and effects. Now that you've tasted the sweet 3D nectar, you can explore SceneKit more on your own.

Next, you'll add a SpriteKit scene overlay on top of your SceneKit scene.

Combining SpriteKit and SceneKit

Open **NotificationController.swift** from the Escape WatchKit Extension from the project navigator.

Add this code to the end of the implementation for `init()` just above the closing curly brace:

```
// 1
```

```
let width: CGFloat = contentFrame.width - 16
let height: CGFloat = 80 // set in Interface Builder
// 2
let followPathScene =
  FollowPathScene(size: CGSize(width: width, height: height))
// 3
scnInterface.overlaySKScene = followPathScene
```

Here's what's going on in that code:

1. You didn't have to set the size for the SceneKit scene because the camera provides the perspective for the scene. SpriteKit scenes work differently and require you to set their size upon initialization. You want to size the SpriteKit scene appropriately for the notification. You calculate the width based on the width of the `contentFrame`. Then, you take into account the 8-point padding that notifications have on each side around their content.

2. You create an instance of `FollowPathScene` with the calculated size.

3. You overlay the SpriteKit `followPathScene` on top of the SceneKit interface.

With that code in place, you're ready to build out the implementation of `followPathScene` and create a spectacular Watch app notification.

Creating a SpriteKit animation scene

Every time the user receives a notification, you will show her a different visual to keep things exciting. The notification will show the ball following a random path across the screen. Then a text message will animate in to announce the 25 rolls.

Open **FollowPathScene.swift** from the Escape WatchKit Extension in the project navigator.

Add this code for the implementation of `FollowPathScene`:

```
var player: SKSpriteNode!
var playerPath = SKShapeNode()
var message: SKLabelNode!

override func sceneDidLoad() {
  playerPath.lineWidth = 4
  playerPath.strokeColor = UIColor(red: 33 / 255.0,
                                   green: 235 / 255.0,
                                   blue: 235 / 255.0,
                                   alpha: 0.2)
  addChild(playerPath)

  player = SKSpriteNode(imageNamed: "orb")
  addChild(player)
```

```
    let singleLineMessage = SKLabelNode()
    singleLineMessage.fontSize = min(size.width, size.height) / 3
    singleLineMessage.verticalAlignmentMode = .center
    singleLineMessage.text = "Your 25\ndaily rolls\nare here!"
    message = singleLineMessage.multilined()
    message.position = CGPoint(x: frame.midX, y: frame.midY)
    message.zPosition = 1001
    message.alpha = 0
    addChild(message)

    play()
}

func play() {
}
```

With that code, you configure the size and color of the sprites: the path, the ball, and the text message. SpriteKit does *not* include support for multiline text, so you perform a little extra work to display the text in three lines. After configuring each sprite, you add it to the scene. You'll see how the sprites look on the scene soon, but first you'll add the code to draw the random path.

Add this code for the implementation of `play()`:

```
// 1
let numPoints = 6
// 2
var randomPoints: [CGPoint] = (-2...(numPoints + 2)).map {
  column -> CGPoint in
  let x = frame.width / CGFloat(numPoints) * CGFloat(column)
  // 3
  let minY = player.size.height / 4 * 3
  let maxY = frame.height - player.size.height / 4 * 3
  let y = (frame.height * CGFloat.random()).clamped(minY, maxY)
  return CGPoint(x: x, y: y)
}
// 4
let swapQuantity = numPoints / 2
let midindex = randomPoints.count / 2
let swapRange =
  (midindex - swapQuantity / 2)...(midindex + swapQuantity / 2)

randomPoints[swapRange] =
  ArraySlice(randomPoints[swapRange].reversed())
// 5
guard let path = UIBezierPath(
  catmullRomInterpolatedPoints: randomPoints,
  closed: false,
  alpha: 0.5) else {
  return
}
```

```
// 6
playerPath.path = path.cgPath
```

Here's what's happening with that code:

1. You set the number of points that will make up the path for the ball to follow.

2. You add two extra points to the beginning and end of the path. The algorithm you'll use to find a smooth path between the points requires one extra point at the beginning and one extra point at the end to act as handles for the path.

   Then, you add another extra point on the beginning and the end so that the ball will move off the screen entirely instead of stopping at the edge.

3. You constrain the height of the path to ensure the ball never crosses the top and bottom edges of the frame.

4. You horizontally flip the middle points to achieve a squiggle in the path.

5. The path generation algorithm creates a smooth curve to connect the points.

6. You assign the path to a shape node which will draw it on the screen immediately.

Build and run the **Escape WatchKit App (Notification)** scheme. Exit the first notification if it is still visible by scrolling down and tapping **Dismiss**. Wait for a second, and the new notification will pop up.

Brilliant work so far. The random path goes across from left to right, and the ball sits still in the lower left corner. Next, you'll make the ball follow the path.

Add this code to the bottom of `play()` just before the closing curly brace:

```
let traverseDuration = 3.0
let traverse = SKAction.follow(path.cgPath,
                               asOffset: false,
                               orientToPath: false,
                               duration: traverseDuration)
let traverseForwardsAndBackwards = SKAction.run {
  let sequence = SKAction.sequence([traverse,
```

```
                                        traverse.reversed()])
    self.player.run(sequence)
}
let waitForTraverse =
  SKAction.wait(forDuration: traverseDuration)
let fadeOutPathAndBall = SKAction.run {
  self.playerPath.run(
    SKAction.fadeOut(withDuration: traverseDuration))
  self.player.run(SKAction.fadeOut(
    withDuration: traverseDuration))
}
let waitForHalfTraverse =
  SKAction.wait(forDuration: traverseDuration / 2)
let revealMessage = SKAction.run {
  let scaleEffect = SKTScaleEffect(
    node: self.message,
    duration: traverseDuration / 3,
    startScale: CGPoint(x: 0.01, y: 0.01),
    endScale: CGPoint(x: 1, y: 1))
  scaleEffect.timingFunction = SKTTimingFunctionBounceEaseOut
  let scaleEffectAction = SKAction.actionWithEffect(scaleEffect)
  let fadeIn =
    SKAction.fadeIn(withDuration: traverseDuration / 3)
  let group =
    SKAction.group([fadeIn, scaleEffectAction])
  self.message.run(group)
}
let sequence = SKAction.sequence([traverseForwardsAndBackwards,
                                  waitForTraverse,
                                  fadeOutPathAndBall,
                                  waitForHalfTraverse,
                                  revealMessage])
run(sequence)
```

You've seen code like this before, when you implemented runCelebration(). The code constructs SKActions and then runs them in a sequence.

There's really only one tricky thing worth noting. Normally a sequence will not run the next animation until the previous one finishes. However, in this case, the SKActions run blocks of code, rather than a standard move animation or rotation animation. You've architected it this way because you want to chain together animations that run on different nodes. run-type SKActions complete immediately, so you build in delays to wait for the completion of each step before proceeding to the next animation in the sequence. By architecting the code like that, you can run the sequence on the scene itself rather than a particular node.

Build and run the notification scheme. Exit the old notification if it is still visible by scrolling down and tapping **Dismiss**. Wait for a second, and the new notification will pop up. You'll see the ball follow the path and a message spring onto the scene pronouncing the 25 daily rolls.

Well done! You've built a SpriteKit game for the Watch with awesome animations as well as a SceneKit notification to boot! Take what you learned in this chapter and find places you can inject SpriteKit and SceneKit animations into your apps.

Where to go from here?

You could add many effects to Escape to make it even cooler and practice your SpriteKit skills:

- Add a warp effect to the floor to create the illusion of gravity as the ball distorts space

- Play sound as the ball rolls around

There are a couple of videos from WWDC 2016 that will help you fully explore the possibilities:

- What's New in SpriteKit: apple.co/2cKa11s

- Game Technologies for Apple Watch: apple.co/2deaeNA

Apple released a full 3D game built in SceneKit for the Watch. Check out the WatchPuzzle sample app: apple.co/2cnb2cG

> **Note**: In case WatchPuzzle won't build due to errors, use **Edit\Convert\To Current Swift Syntax...** to update the code.

If you have a strong desire to build games you can also check out our other two books which go into detail about game mechanics and physics:

- 2D Apple Games by Tutorials: bit.ly/2dpZtaA

- 3D Apple Games by Tutorials: bit.ly/2dpG9pV

Now that you've built a game that a user can play on her iPhone and her Watch, imagine if you synced player statistics between the devices. You'll learn how to keep the iPhone and the Apple Watch in sync with the same data in the next chapter, "Advanced Watch Connectivity".

Chapter 19: Advanced Watch Connectivity

By Matthew Morey

In Chapter 16, "Watch Connectivity", you set up the Watch Connectivity framework, learned about the different ways to transfer data between iPhone and Watch apps, and successfully implemented the application context transfer method, all while working on an app for movie theater patrons called CinemaTime. By the end of Chapter 16, users could purchase a movie ticket from either the iPhone or Watch CinemaTime app and see their purchase on the other app.

In this chapter, you'll employ the **user info** mode to transfer movie rating data between the CinemaTime apps. User info transfers are like the application context transfers you implemented in Chapter 16, in that both allow you to transfer a dictionary of data. The difference is that all dictionaries are transferred over, not just the most recent one.

You'll also use **interactive messaging** to transfer movie ticket QR codes from the iPhone to the Watch. Interactive messaging is best used in situations that need information transferred immediately.

> **Note:** If you're not familiar with the basics of the Watch Connectivity framework, make sure you work through Chapter 16 before continuing with this chapter. This chapter's starter project is a continuation of the final project from that chapter. You can use either your final project from that chapter, or the starter project for this chapter.

Getting started

Open the CinemaTime starter project in Xcode and then build and run the **CinemaTimeWatch** scheme. Tap on **Purchase Ticket** and explore the app.

The existing CinemaTime apps show the movie schedule for a cinema. Customers can buy movie tickets and rate movies from within either app.

Build and run the **CinemaTime** scheme and explore the iPhone app.

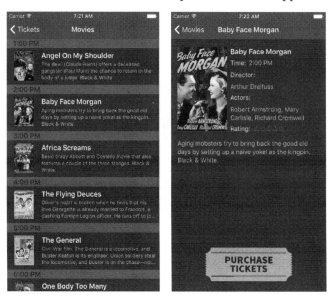

If you haven't already, rate a movie in either app and then view the same movie in the counterpart app. Do you see the issue?

Movie ratings in one app don't show up in the other app — the apps aren't sharing the rating data. If a user rates a movie in the iPhone app, and then later tries to view the same rating on the Watch, she might think she never rated the movie in the first place!

You better rate
my movies!

Or else...

In the iPhone app, buy a movie ticket and view the purchased ticket, represented by a QR code, that now appears instead of the Purchase Ticket button.

Now view the same purchased movie in the Watch app. Although purchased movies from one app appear in the counterpart app, the QR code does not.

Don't worry — you're a development superstar and can solve both problems with the Watch Connectivity framework.

User info transfers

User info transfers send dictionaries of data to the counterpart app in first-in, first-out order. Once a data transfer begins, it will continue, even if the sending app is no longer running. The WCSession method transferUserInfo(_:) sends the data, and the counterpart app receives the dictionary via the session(_:didReceiveUserInfo:) method declared by the WCSessionDelegate protocol.

transferUserInfo(_:) returns a WCSessionUserInfoTransfer object that stores information about in-progress data transfers. The class provides a transferring property that indicates whether the transfer has completed. The cancel() method can be used to stop the transfer, so long as the transferring property is still true.

The WCSessionDelegate protocol includes the optional session(_:didFinish:error:) method. When the WCSession object that initiated a transfer completes — or cancels — the transfer, it calls session(_:didFinish:error:). This method can be used to notify the sender that their work is complete.

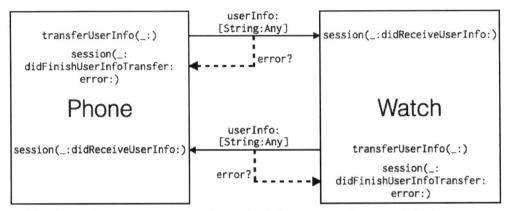

Unlike the application context transfer method discussed in Chapter 16, "Watch Connectivity", WCSession guarantees that all user info transfers are received in the order they are sent. Subsequent transfers do not overwrite previous ones like in an application context transfer.

A Watch game that needs to transfer the user's progress to the counterpart iPhone app would require a user info transfer. Using transferUserInfo(_:), the iPhone app would receive notice of each completed level from the Watch app.

Now you'll give user info transfers a try by writing code to send movie ratings from the iPhone to the Watch. After that, you'll tackle it the other way around.

Transferring from the iPhone to the Watch

In Xcode, open **MovieDetailViewController.swift** and find sendRatingToWatch(_:). The iPhone app calls this method whenever the user taps on the rating stars and then selects a rating from the action sheet.

Implement the method with the following code:

```
// 1
if WCSession.isSupported() {
  // 2
  let session = WCSession.default
  if session.isWatchAppInstalled {
    // 3
    let userInfo = ["movie_id":movie.id, "rating":rating]
    session.transferUserInfo(userInfo)
  }
}
```

Going through this code step-by-step:

1. First you check if the current device supports Watch connectivity.

2. You then set `session` to the default connectivity session, and check to verify installation of the Watch app. There's no need to communicate if nothing is listening!

3. Finally, you call `transferUserInfo(_:)` on the active session to transfer a dictionary that contains the `movieID` and `rating` properties.

> **Note:** Before calling any Watch Connectivity framework methods, including `transferUserInfo(_:)`, you must first set up and activate a connectivity session. The starter project for this chapter already does this for you. If you'd like a refresher, please go back to Chapter 16, "Watch Connectivity", for the details.

Now that the iPhone app is sending movie ratings, you'll set up the Watch app to receive them. `WCSessions` that receive user info transfers call the optional `WCSessionDelegate` `session(_:didReceiveUserInfo:)` protocol method when they receive data.

Open **ExtensionDelegate.swift** and add the following to the end of the extension:

```
func session(_ session: WCSession,
  didReceiveUserInfo userInfo: [String : Any] = [:]) {
  if let movieID = userInfo["movie_id"] as? String,
    let rating = userInfo["rating"] as? String {
    TicketOffice.sharedInstance.rateMovie(movieID,
      rating: rating)
  }
}
```

The `userInfo` dictionary will contain the data sent from the iPhone app. You set the `movieID` and `rating` constants from that dictionary. Then you call `rateMovie(_:rating:)`, from the `TicketOffice` singleton class, passing `movieID` and `rating`. Calling this method updates the rating for the movie in the Watch app.

Build and run the **CinemaTime** scheme to launch the iPhone app then rate a movie. Next, build and run the **CinemaTimeWatch** scheme and view the same movie you rated in the iPhone app. The apps will both have the rating. Nice work!

> **Note:** If you have both the iPhone and Watch apps running at the same time, this use case will still work. While interactive messaging is the most immediate way to transfer data between two running apps, background transfers will work equally well.

You've just added the ability to transfer movie ratings from the iPhone to the Watch. Guess what you're going to do next? :]

Transferring from the Watch to the iPhone

Open **MovieRatingController.swift** and locate sendRatingToPhone(:_). When the user rates a movie on the Watch, the app calls sendRatingToPhone(_:). Replace the TODO with this code:

```
if WCSession.isSupported() {
  let userInfo = ["movie_id":movie.id, "rating":rating]
  WCSession.default.transferUserInfo(userInfo)
}
```

This code looks like what you added in the previous section, but there are some minor differences. Although, on the Watch, `WCSession.isSupported()` will always return `true`, it doesn't hurt to be careful and check. You never know if this behavior will change in future versions of watchOS. After that, you call `transferUserInfo(_:)` on the active session to transfer to the iPhone a dictionary containing information about the rating.

This code is slightly simpler than the iPhone app because it checks to verify the installation of the Watch app. On the Watch, you don't need to check for iPhone app installation, because the only way the Watch app can exist is if there's also an installed iPhone app.

Now that the Watch is sending movie ratings, you'll set up the iPhone to receive them.

Open **AppDelegate.swift** and add the following code to the `AppDelegate` extension:

```
// 1
func session(_ session: WCSession,
  didReceiveUserInfo userInfo: [String : Any] = [:]) {
  // 2
  if let movieID = userInfo["movie_id"] as? String,
    let rating = userInfo["rating"] as? String {
    // 3
    TicketOffice.sharedInstance.rateMovie(movieID,
                                rating: rating)
  }
}
```

Here's what you're doing with this code:

1. You implement the `WCSessionDelegate` `session(_:didReceiveUserInfo:)` protocol method. The active connectivity session uses this method to receive a dictionary of data from the counterpart Watch app.

2. Next, you set the `movieID` and `rating` constants using the `userInfo` dictionary.

3. Finally, you call `rateMovie(_:rating:)`, from the `TicketOffice` singleton class, with the `movieID` and the `rating`. Calling this method updates the rating for the movie in the iPhone app.

Build and run both apps, but this time, rate a movie in the Watch app, and then view the same movie on the iPhone app to see the new rating.

Voilà! CinemaTime customers can now rate movies from within either app and their ratings will sync across both. You're quickly becoming an A-list celebrity.

Everyone's a critic!

Now that you've solved the first problem, you'll work on the issue of the missing QR codes.

Interactive messaging

When both apps are active, establishing a session allows immediate communication between them via interactive messaging.

The `WCSession` methods `sendMessage(_:replyHandler:errorHandler:)` and `sendMessageData(_:replyHandler:errorHandler:)` send data, while the `WCSessionDelegate` methods `session(_:didReceiveMessage:)` and `session(_:didReceiveMessageData:)` receive sent data. Additionally, the delegate methods also each have a counterpart method that takes a `replyHandler` closure. This is used if the sender wishes to receive a reply to the message it sends.

The following diagram shows the basic flow of sending a message and receiving a reply from the Watch to the iPhone:

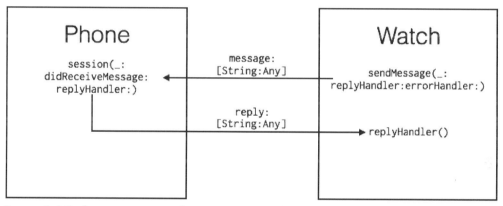

In watchOS, the counterpart iPhone app is considered active, or reachable, when a matching session is enabled and the iPhone is within range of communication. The iPhone app doesn't have to be in the foreground to be reachable.

In iOS, the Watch app is considered reachable when the paired Watch is in range and the Watch app is running in the foreground. If the Watch app isn't running or is in the background, then it's not reachable.

That means the app doesn't have to be running on the iPhone in order to be reachable, but the app *must* be running on the watch and in the foreground to be reachable.

Interactive messaging in best for situations where you need information transferred immediately. For example, if your Watch app needs to trigger its companion iPhone app to do something, such as track the user's location, the interactive messaging API can communicate the request from the Watch to the iPhone.

In this section, you'll use interactive messaging to send movie ticket QR codes from the iPhone to the Watch.

> **Note:** You could also use the background file transfer method of communication to send the movie ticket QR codes to the Watch app. For CinemaTime, I've chosen to use interactive messaging because the transfer happens immediately, which means the customer sees no delay when trying to view a ticket code in the Watch app.

Messaging from the iPhone to the Watch

Right now, only the iPhone app generates a movie ticket QR code, because to do so requires the Core Image framework, which isn't available in watchOS.

The only way to show the QR code in the Watch app is to generate it in the iPhone app and then transfer the PNG version of it over to the Watch for display. When the user views the details of a purchased movie on the Watch, the app will send a message to the iPhone requesting a particular movie's QR code. The iPhone will respond with data representing a PNG of that code.

First, you'll make the request. Find `requestTicketForPurchasedMovie(:_)` in **MovieDetailInterfaceController.swift**. Replace the `TODO` with this code:

```
// 1
if WCSession.isSupported() {
  // 2
  let session = WCSession.default
  if session.isReachable {
    // 3
    let message = ["movie_id": movie.id]
    session.sendMessage(message,
      replyHandler: { (reply: [String : Any]) -> Void in
        // 4
        if let movieID = reply["movie_id"] as? String,
          let movieTicket = reply["movie_ticket"] as? Data,
          movieID == self.movie.id {
            // 5
            self.saveMovieTicketAndUpdateDisplay(movieTicket)
          }
      }, errorHandler: { (error: Error) in
        print("ERROR: \(error.localizedDescription)")
      }
    )
  } else { // reachable
    self.showReachabilityError()
  }
}
```

Taking each numbered section in turn:

1. First, you check if the current device supports Watch connectivity.

2. Next, you get the default session and check if the iPhone app is available for communication. If the iPhone app isn't reachable, you show the user an error by calling showReachabilityError().

3. You send the message "request" dictionary to the iPhone app by calling sendMessage(_:replyHandler:errorHandler:).

4. By providing a closure for replyHandler, you are signaling that you want the receiver to reply with a dictionary of data as well. When the receiver does reply — by calling the closure — you set movieID and movie_ticket using the reply dictionary. You also verify that you received the data for the correct movie by checking if the movie_id key in the dictionary matches the current movie's ID.

5. Finally, you save the movie ticket as a PNG file and update the display by calling the method saveMovieTicketAndUpdateDisplay(_:).

> **Note:** If the data to send is better expressed as a sequence of bytes rather than a dictionary, instead of calling sendMessage(_:replyHandler:errorHandler:), you can call sendMessageData(_:replyHandler:errorHandler:), which takes a Data object instead of a dictionary.

Now that the Watch app is sending a request for the movie ticket and reacting to replies, you'll set up the iPhone app to receive and reply to the request.

Open **AppDelegate.swift** and add the following to the end of the extension:

```swift
// 1
func session(_ session: WCSession,
  didReceiveMessage message: [String : Any],
  replyHandler: @escaping ([String : Any]) -> Void) {
  // 2
  if let movieID = message["movie_id"] as? String {
    // 3
    if let movieTicket = QRCode(movieID) {
      // 4
      let reply: [String:Any] = ["movie_id":movieID,
                  "movie_ticket":movieTicket.PNGData]
      replyHandler(reply)
    }
  }
}
```

Here's what you're doing:

1. Your code implements the optional `WCSessionDelegate` protocol method `session(_:didReceiveMessage:replyHandler:)`. The active connectivity session uses this method to receive interactive messages from the counterpart Watch app. You are using the version that takes a `replyHandler` because you passed a closure when you called `sendMessage(_:replyHandler:errorHandler:)`, which means that the Watch app expects to receive a response.

2. Next, you get the `movie_id` value from the passed-in `message` dictionary.

3. Then you create a `movieTicket` `QRCode` by passing `movieID` to the `QRCode` initialization method.

4. Finally, you execute `replyHandler(_:)` to transfer back to the Watch a dictionary containing the movie ID and the PNG version of the movie ticket's `QRCode`.

Build and run the **CinemaTimeWatch** scheme to launch the Watch app and then buy and view a movie on the Watch. Scroll to the bottom of the movie details view to see the movie ticket QR code.

Congratulations movie star — you've made it! CinemaTime customers can now buy and view movie tickets from either app.

You were
born to be
a star!

Where to go from here?

If you followed both Chapter 16 and this chapter all the way through, you've turned two independent apps that don't share data into apps that are always in sync. You'll find the final project in the folder for this chapter.

To learn more about communication methods between the Watch and iPhone, check out Apple's Watch Connectivity Framework Reference: apple.co/1JlPcnH.

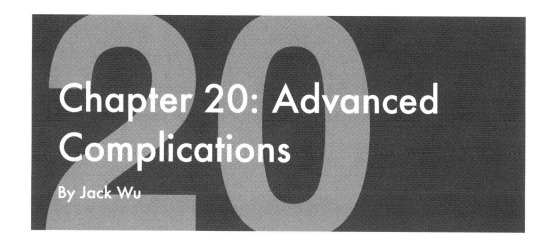

Chapter 20: Advanced Complications

By Jack Wu

In Chapter 15, "Complications", you built an Apple Watch complication that displays currently relevant information, much like a complication on a traditional watch. But the Apple Watch is definitely *way* more than a traditional watch!

In this chapter, you'll continue to explore the fun, innovative features of complications in WatchOS. Complications will become quite a bit more *complicated* in this chapter, but you will get to implement one of the coolest features of all time: Time Travel.

No longer will the information on the Watch face be relevant only to the current time. At the user's whim, the complication will rewind to show historically relevant information, and even fast-forward to show information about the future.

Want to let your users check the score of an ongoing game, and then immediately check both the score of the last game and the date and time of the next? All with a mere lift of the wrist? That's the power of Time Travel.

Above: an accurate photo of me when I learned about Time Travel!

You're probably now asking yourself two important questions: "How do I keep my complication data up to date?" and, "How do I keep potentially sensitive complication data private?" You need to know the answers to these questions to complete your complication. Keep reading to discover them.

Getting started

This chapter will build on the Tide Watch app from Chapter 15. Make sure you use **the new starter project** included with this chapter, as quite a few changes have been made for you.

Open **TideWatch.xcodeproj** in Xcode and take a swim through the code. There are two changes you should pay attention to:

1. The code now uses Watch Connectivity to sync the data between the iPhone and the Watch. The implementation is very similar to that of Chapter 16, "Watch Connectivity".

2. `ComplicationController` has been slightly refactored and sports some new methods, but most of the code should look familiar.

It's time to dive in!

Traveling through time

Time Travel doesn't defy the laws of physics, but it does defy the one-dimensional conventions associated with traditional timepieces to provide a similar experience: scrolling forward or backward through time-specific information using the digital crown. And it's completely open to you as a developer to define the relevant context.

You can transport your users to past or future weather conditions, stock prices, calendar events... and perhaps most excitingly, tide conditions for surfing!

How Time Travel works

At its core, you make Time Travel possible simply by providing a *list* of timeline entries, instead of just one. The system can then display the timeline entry that corresponds to the time the user selected using the digital crown.

> **Note:** Recall from Chapter 15, "Complications" that a timeline entry specifies the appearance of a complication via its template and when to display it.

ClockKit lets you specify whether your app will travel backward or forward in time, or both. Some apps will only need to travel in one direction.

For example, you might come under the suspicions of your financial regulatory agency if your stock market app could travel forward in time.

Tide Watch already loads 48 hours of data, making it the perfect candidate for Time Travel in both directions.

Providing the data

To get started, open **ComplicationController.swift** and find `getSupportedTimeTravelDirections(for:withHandler:)`. In Chapter 15, you returned [] to the handler to disable Time Travel. You can now replace that with:

```
handler([.forward, .backward])
```

This tells the system that your complication can travel both forward and backward in time. You could omit either one if you only wanted to support one direction.

For each direction your complication supports, the system calls two datasource methods to retrieve the past or future data. These methods are declared in the `CLKComplicationDataSource` protocol, which your `ComplicationController` class adopts.

The first method asks for the start or end date of your timeline. Add the following method to `ComplicationController`:

```
func getTimelineStartDate(
  for complication: CLKComplication,
  withHandler handler: @escaping (Date?) -> Swift.Void) {
  let tideConditions = TideConditions.loadConditions()
  guard let waterLevel = tideConditions.waterLevels.first else {
    // No data is cached yet
    handler(nil)
    return
  }
  handler(waterLevel.date)
}
```

Not too much is going on here. You check if you have any data and simply return the date of the earliest data point. If the user travels to a time earlier than this date, the system will dim out your complication to indicate there's no more relevant data.

You need a similar method for the end date, so implement the following in ComplicationController:

```
func getTimelineEndDate(
  for complication: CLKComplication,
  withHandler handler: @escaping (Date?) -> Swift.Void) {
  let tideConditions = TideConditions.loadConditions()
  guard let waterLevel = tideConditions.waterLevels.last else {
    // No data is cached yet
    handler(nil)
    return
  }
  handler(waterLevel.date)
}
```

The only difference here is that you return to the handler the date of the last available water level, instead of the first.

Now that the system knows the bounds of your data, it calls two more delegate methods to retrieve the data. To provide data from the past, add the following method to ComplicationController:

```
func getTimelineEntries(
  for complication: CLKComplication, before date: Date,
  limit: Int, withHandler handler: @escaping
  ([CLKComplicationTimelineEntry]?) -> Swift.Void) {

  let tideConditions = TideConditions.loadConditions()

  // 1
  var waterLevels = tideConditions.waterLevels.filter {
    $0.date.compare(date) == .orderedAscending
  }
```

```
  // 2
  if waterLevels.count > limit {
    // Remove from the front
    let numberToRemove = waterLevels.count - limit
    waterLevels.removeSubrange(0..<numberToRemove)
  }

  // 3
  let entries = waterLevels.flatMap { waterLevel in
    timelineEntryFor(waterLevel, family: complication.family)
  }

  handler(entries)
}
```

The method asks for the data before a certain date, up to a certain limit.

1. After loading all the data, you filter out the water levels that come after `date`.

2. If the number of remaining data points exceeds the limit, you remove data from the beginning of the array. This way, you keep the most recent data.

3. For each water level, you create a `CLKComplicationTimelineEntry` using the helper method and finally, pass it to the handler.

Now for the much more exciting data, the *future* data. Implement the following, extremely similar method in `ComplicationController`:

```
func getTimelineEntries(
  for complication: CLKComplication, after date: Date,
  limit: Int, withHandler handler: @escaping
  ([CLKComplicationTimelineEntry]?) -> Swift.Void) {

  let tideConditions = TideConditions.loadConditions()

  var waterLevels = tideConditions.waterLevels.filter {
    $0.date.compare(date) == .orderedDescending
  }

  if waterLevels.count > limit {
    // Remove from the back
    waterLevels.removeSubrange(limit..<waterLevels.count)
  }

  let entries = waterLevels.flatMap { waterLevel in
    return timelineEntryFor(waterLevel,
      family: complication.family)
  }

  handler(entries)
}
```

This time, you filter out earlier dates instead of later ones. You also remove any data points that exceed the limit from the end of the array, keeping the nearest values. You finish up by passing the future entries to the handler.

That's all it takes for your app to support Time Travel. Currently, the complication still completely relies on the Watch app to download and store the data it displays, but you're going to fix that very soon.

Build and run the Watch app and let it load some data. Switch to a Utilitarian clock face and activate the Tide Watch complication. Turn the digital crown and watch as your complication bubbles to life!

> **Note:** In the simulator, you can use the scroll wheel on your mouse, or simply move your finger if you're using a Magic Mouse, to simulate the digital crown.

This is unquestionably a better way to display tide conditions for Tide Watch—it provides more information without sacrificing usability at all.

Animating through time

ClockKit provides a simple animation you can use to emphasize certain transitions when traveling through time. You can choose from three animation behaviors:

1. **None** is the default value of no animation, which is your app's current behavior.

2. **Always** animates the change every time.

3. **Grouped** lets you use animation groups to specify which transitions to animate. Here, timeline entries are divided into groups, identified by a string. Animations will only occur when the displayed timeline entry changes between groups.

Tide Watch will use the most interesting of the three: grouped animations. The app already has a natural way to split the complication displays into groups: each tide condition, such as Rising or Falling, will be its own group. This way, the complication will animate whenever the tide condition changes.

To get started, add the following `CLKComplicationDataSource` protocol method to `ComplicationController` to use grouped animations:

```
func getTimelineAnimationBehavior(
  for complication: CLKComplication,
  withHandler handler: @escaping
  (CLKComplicationTimelineAnimationBehavior) -> Swift.Void) {
  handler(.grouped)
}
```

This method returns the type of animation behavior directly to the handler.

Next, you can use the `timelineAnimationGroup` property of `CLKComplicationTimelineEntry` to specify the animation group for each entry. An animation will occur whenever the group changes.

Find the helper method `timelineEntryFor(_:family:)` in `ComplicationController` and locate the two calls to the initializer of `CLKComplicationTimelineEntry`. Add the optional argument `timelineAnimationGroup` and pass in `waterLevel.situation.rawValue` to each of them:

```
if family == .utilitarianSmall {
  let smallFlat = //...
  //...
  return CLKComplicationTimelineEntry(
    date: waterLevel.date, complicationTemplate: smallFlat,
    timelineAnimationGroup: waterLevel.situation.rawValue)
} else if family == .utilitarianLarge {
  let largeFlat = //...
  //...
  return CLKComplicationTimelineEntry(
    date: waterLevel.date, complicationTemplate: largeFlat,
    timelineAnimationGroup: waterLevel.situation.rawValue)
}
```

Recall that animation groups are specified by a string. Here you use `waterLevel.situation.rawValue` to identify the animation group so the animation group changes only when the situation changes, which triggers an animation.

That's all there is to do, so build and run. Reload your complication and surf through time. The animations add a bit of sparkle to the transitions, and make it even easier for users to tell when the tide conditions change.

Keeping your data current

Your complication looks great and with its nifty animations, it feels complete. This is the perfect time to make improvements on the data-loading side.

Right now, Tide Watch's complication displays whatever it has in the cache. The system only updates the cache when the user opens the iPhone app or Watch app, which means the complication's data will be completely out of date if the user doesn't use the app for a day. Even when the user opens the app, the complication doesn't know there's new data to display, since it relies solely on the cache.

It would be nice if you could reload the complication's when the user chooses a new location, or when either the iPhone or Watch app retrieve fresh data.

Furthermore, Tide Watch's "future data" is a prediction, which means the data can become more accurate over time. So it would also be nice if you could update the complication's data from time to time, even if the user hasn't done anything.

ClockKit provides this functionality through a few APIs that let you extend or invalidate your data, as well as a few others that let you specify when your app should "wake up" to fetch and supply more data to the complication. You can also update your complications through special push notifications to your app. In this section, you'll take advantage of these features to keep Tide Watch as up-to-date as possible.

It's already time for another update?

Budgeting your time

Before you begin, notice that there's a slight conflict of interest between the system and complications. You want your complication to provide the most up-to-date data possible, but the system also needs to worry about power consumption and giving all complications a chance to update.

The system manages this by allocating **time budgets** to each complication. Your complication can take time to update as long as it stays within its budget. Once time exceeds the budget, the system won't let the complication update its data *at all* until the system replenishes your complication's budget.

Scheduled updates

You can schedule the time of your complication's next update the same way you schedule background refresh tasks. This is very useful for any app that displays time-relevant information, such as weather, stocks or tide conditions.

Because the system is enforcing a time budget, you want to provide as much data as you can manage during each update, and request updates as infrequently as possible.

If you already have data, you request that the next update take place at the time of the last known water level, ensuring the complication never runs out of data. If you don't yet have any data, you pass in the current time to request an immediate update.

The system will call this method upon activation of your complication, and again after every update, so you'll always have an update scheduled.

Next, you need a method to update the data. A scheduled update doesn't necessarily mean you'll have new data to display. When you *do* have new data, you might want to invalidate all the existing data or only add new data to the timeline. You can communicate these intentions to ClockKit with the following:

- To invalidate the existing data, call `reloadTimeline(for:)` on `CLKComplicationServer`.

- To add new data, call `extendTimeline(for:)`, also on `CLKComplicationServer`.

- If you don't have any new data, you simply don't call either of those methods. The system will still allow you to schedule the next update.

This new method will thus call `extendTimeline(for:)` to add new data to the end of the timeline in the case of a scheduled update. It also needs to handle the case where the user changes the measurement station, which requires a call to `reloadTimeline(for:)` to invalidate all the current data for the previous station.

Still in `ComplicationController`, implement a new helper method as follows:

```
func reloadOrExtendData() {
  // 1
  let server = CLKComplicationServer.sharedInstance()
  guard let complications = server.activeComplications,
    complications.count > 0 else { return }

  // 2
  let tideConditions = TideConditions.loadConditions()
  let displayedStation = loadDisplayedStation()

  // 3
  if let id = displayedStation?.id,
    id == tideConditions.station.id {
    // 4
    // Check if there is new data
    if tideConditions.waterLevels.last?.date.compare(
      server.latestTimeTravelDate) == .orderedDescending {
      // 5
      for complication in complications  {
        server.extendTimeline(for: complication)
      }
    }
  } else {
    // 6
    for complication in complications  {
      server.reloadTimeline(for: complication)
    }
  }
  // 7
  saveDisplayedStation(tideConditions.station)
}
```

This is quite a bit of code, so let's go through it step by step:

1. The shared instance of `CLKComplicationServer` provides you with all your active complications. You can safely return if none are active.

2. You load the cached data as well as the currently displayed station.

3. Then, you check if the station has changed.

4. If the station hasn't changed, you check if there's any new data loaded. If there's no new data, you don't have to do anything.

5. If there is new data, you call `extendTimeline(for:)` on the complication server, once for each active complication.

6. If the station has changed or hasn't even been loaded yet, you can call `reloadTimeline(for:)` on the server, once for each active complication.

7. Finally, you save the station as the currently displayed station.

This method will update the complication with the current data stored within the shared instance `TideConditions`. This information might not be completely current, so you'll want to update this data before calling `reloadOrExtendData()`. Since complication updates are handled in the `ExtensionDelegate`, add the following two helper methods inside `ExtensionDelegate`:

```swift
func updateComplicationDisplay() {
  let complicationsController = ComplicationController()
  complicationsController.reloadOrExtendData()
}

func reloadComplicationData(backgroundTask:
WKApplicationRefreshBackgroundTask) {
  let tideConditions = TideConditions.loadConditions()
  let yesterday = Date(timeIntervalSinceNow: -24 * 60 * 60)
  let tomorrow = Date(timeIntervalSinceNow: 24 * 60 * 60)
  tideConditions.loadWaterLevels(
  from: yesterday, to: tomorrow) { success in
    if success {
      TideConditions.saveConditions(tideConditions)
      self.updateComplicationDisplay()
      WKExtension.shared().scheduleBackgroundRefresh(
        withPreferredDate: tomorrow, userInfo: nil) { _ in }
    } else {
      WKExtension.shared().scheduleBackgroundRefresh(
        withPreferredDate: Date(), userInfo: nil) { _ in }
    }
    backgroundTask.setTaskCompletedWithSnapshot(false)
  }
}
```

`reloadComplicationData(backgroundTask:)` will be called from the background task handler and so takes the background task as an argument. It first loads fresh data for the current station, saves it, and then calls `updateComplicationDisplay`, which then calls the helper method you just created, `reloadOrExtendData()` on `ComplicationController`.

After the data is loaded, `reloadComplicationData(backgroundTask:)` then schedules the next update, depending on the status of loading water levels. Lastly, you

need to complete the background task by calling
`backgroundTask.setTaskCompletedWithSnapshot(_:)`.

When the time comes for an update, the system will start a background task, calling
`handle(_:)` on `ExtensionDelegate`. WatchKit creates a default `handle(_:)`
implementation for you already so all you need to do is reload the complication data
when it's time to refresh. Inside `handle(_:)`, add a call to your helper method by
replacing the body of the first switch case for
`WKApplicationRefreshBackgroundTask`:

```
case let backgroundTask as WKApplicationRefreshBackgroundTask:
// Be sure to complete the background task once you're done.
reloadComplicationData(backgroundTask: backgroundTask)
```

This call the same helper method you just created, `reloadComplicationData()`, in a
fashion very similar to how the Watch app or iPhone app loads new data. Since this is
handled like any other background task, it will update whenever your app requests for an
update! You can have great control over when these updates, as you learned in Chapter
10, "Snapshot API".

It's a bit tricky to see this functionality in action. You can modify the call of
`scheduleBackgroundRefresh()` to specify an update date in the very near future.
Remember, though, that the system has total control and can't guarantee the exact time
of your update. If you schedule the update for a few seconds into the future, keep a
breakpoint around and go make some tea; with any luck, your update will have started
by the time you get back.

Updating from the Watch app

Whenever a user opens the Tide Watch app and loads new data, you can directly inform
the system to refresh the complication using the same `CLKComplicationServer`
methods.

This will let you reduce the amount of your complication's time budget consumed by
network requests.

In Tide Watch, you should update the complication's timeline whenever your app
retrieves new tidal data. Conveniently, Tide Watch calls `conditionsUpdated(_:)` in
`ExtensionDelegate` each time new data arrives in order to send the new data to the
iPhone.

You can take advantage of this and refresh the complication at the same time. Add the
call to `updateComplicationDisplay()` near the end of `conditionsUpdated(_:)`,
inside the `DispatchQueue.main.async` closure:

```
func conditionsUpdated(_ tideConditions:TideConditions) {
  TideConditions.saveConditions(tideConditions)
  DispatchQueue.main.async {
    let notificationCenter = NotificationCenter.default
    notificationCenter.post(
      name: Notification.Name(
        rawValue: PhoneUpdatedDataNotification),
      object: tideConditions)
    self.updateComplicationDisplay()
  }
}
```

The Watch app will now refresh the complication whenever it retrieves new data.

Updating from the iPhone app

You'll also want to refresh the complication whenever the user changes the measurement station on the iPhone app.

As you saw in Chapter 16, Watch Connectivity handles all the communication between the iPhone and the Watch. Watch Connectivity includes a special method precisely for when a complication needs updating: `transferCurrentComplicationUserInfo(_:)`.

To implement this functionality, you can again hook into the existing Watch Connectivity code. Open **AppDelegate.swift** in the **TideWatch** group and find the private method `sendUpdatedDataToWatch(_:)`.

Replace the inner `if` statement with the following snippet:

```
if session.isWatchAppInstalled,
  let conditions =
    notification.userInfo?["conditions"] as? TideConditions,
  let isNewStation = (notification.userInfo?["newStation"] as?
    NSNumber)?.boolValue {
  do {
    let data =
      NSKeyedArchiver.archivedData(withRootObject: conditions)
    let dictionary = ["data": data]
    // Transfer complications info
    if isNewStation {
      session.transferCurrentComplicationUserInfo(dictionary)
    } else {
      try session.updateApplicationContext(dictionary)
    }
  } catch {
    print("ERROR: \(error)")
  }
}
```

There's only a small change here at the comment: If the user switches stations, you call `transferCurrentComplicationUserInfo(_:)` to directly refresh the complication instead of updating the application context. By refreshing the complication, you're still updating the Watch app.

The Watch extension's `ExtensionDelegate` now requires a new method to receive this data. Open **ExtensionDelegate.swift** and implement the following method:

```
func session(_ session: WCSession,
  didReceiveUserInfo userInfo: [String : Any]) {
  if let data = userInfo["data"] as? Data {
    if let tideConditions =
      NSKeyedUnarchiver.unarchiveObject(with: data) as?
      TideConditions {
      conditionsUpdated(tideConditions)
    }
  }
}
```

After retrieving the data, you call the helper method `conditionsUpdated(_:)`, which in turn updates the Watch app as well as the complication.

Updating from a server

The final way to send updates to a complication is via push notifications sent directly from your server. iOS 9 introduced a new type of push notification — designed especially for complications — that is delivered only if your complication is active.

The iPhone receives the push notification, so Watch Connectivity is required to send the payload to the Watch. Time spent processing the information from the push notification *on the iPhone* also counts towards your complication's budget.

Since you don't own the Tide Watch server, you won't need to implement this type of update in Tide Watch. However, this is an important way to refresh your complications, so here are the steps you would take:

1. First, create a delegate class that conforms to `PKPushRegistryDelegate`.

2. Next, create a `PKPushRegistry` and set its delegate to the delegate class.

3. Set `desiredPushTypes` of the push registry to `PKPushTypeComplication`.

4. The system will call `pushRegistry(_:didUpdatePushCredentials:forType:)` on the delegate to provide you with a push token.

5. Upload the push token to your server just like a regular push notification.

6. When the iPhone receives a push notification, the system will call `pushRegistry(_:didReceiveIncomingPushWithPayload:forType:)`.

7. You can then parse the payload and send it to the Watch using
    `transferCurrentComplicationUserInfo(_:)`.

The advantage of this special push notification over regular push notifications is that it doesn't require permission from the user. However, with this extra freedom comes extra responsibility, and the system will stop delivering your notifications if you exceed the daily push limit.

Now you know all the ways you can keep your complications up to date!

Privacy in complications

The finish line is coming right up! There's one last method in `CLKComplicationDataSource` that `ComplicationController` doesn't implement.

Complications can sometimes display extremely private information. Tide Watch is not one of these cases, but many complications, such as calendars and fitness apps, may display information that the user wouldn't want others to see.

ClockKit provides a way to indicate that the information your complication displays is private. The result is that the system will hide your complication's data if the Watch is locked.

Open **ComplicationController.swift** and implement the following method:

```
func getPrivacyBehavior(
  for complication: CLKComplication,
  withHandler handler: @escaping
  (CLKComplicationPrivacyBehavior) -> Swift.Void) {
  handler(.showOnLockScreen)
}
```

There are two self-explanatory options here, `.showOnLockScreen` and `.hideOnLockScreen`. To see the effect, change the value to `.HideOnLockScreen` and then build and run. Reload the complication and go to the lock screen. The Watch will no longer display the data, similar to the activity rings.

> **Note:** The simulator doesn't display the lock screen, so you'll need a device to see this effect.

Treating users' data seriously is exactly the behavior users expect — and deserve — and with a device as personal as the Apple Watch, privacy has never been more important.

Where to go from here?

Congratulations — you've covered every single method in `CLKComplicationDataSource`!

With all of this new knowledge, you may have developed your own ideas for complications. The next step is to turn them into reality.

Complications are truly one of the most exciting features to come to any computing device in recent years. I can't wait to see all the exciting ways you find to make use of them!

Chapter 21: Handoff Video Playback

By Soheil Azarpour

The content of this book has changed quite a bit since its first edition. In this chapter, you are going to explore two very interesting components of watchOS — video playback and Handoff — and combine them together to make an awesome app.

In the first section of this chapter, you'll learn about playing multimedia files and build a custom interface. In the second section, you'll use Handoff to create continuity between the Apple Watch and a paired iPhone for your multimedia app.

It's time to make some magic!

Getting started

It's a well-known fact that laughter decreases your stress and increases your immune cells, and adding cute puppies to the mix only makes it better. The starter project you'll use in this chapter is **Cute Puppies**; it shows user a handful of funny moments starring cute puppies, to make users laugh and decrease their stress!

Open the starter **Cute Puppies.xcodeproj** project in Xcode and make sure the **Cute Puppies** scheme for iPhone is selected. Build and run using the iPhone simulator, and you'll see the following screen:

Whoever said you can't buy happiness forgot little puppies.

Buy a pup and your money will buy love unflinching.

Play around to get a sense of the app. The list of video clips uses a tile layout, and there's a poster image for each video clip with a humorous quote. When user taps on a tile, the video clip starts playing in a full screen presentation. Watch a couple of these clips — they're entertaining!

Now stop the app and change the scheme to **Cute Puppies Watch**. Build and run using the Watch Simulator.

When you run the Watch app for the first time, it shows a loading message as it's waiting for poster images to arrive from the iPhone using Watch Connectivity framework. The Watch app also displays a list of video clips.

Tapping on any of the clips *doesn't* play the video. You're about to change that.

> **Note:** Watch Connectivity is covered in depth in Chapter 16 and Chapter 19.

Playing video

It would be satisfying if your users could play the video clips on the Watch instead of simply looking at a list of them. The simplest way to play a media file is to present a built-in media player controller using the `presentMediaPlayerController(with:options:completion:)` on `WKInterfaceController`. All you have to do is to pass in a file URL that corresponds to the index of the row user selects from the `WKInterfaceTable`.

Open **Cute Puppies Watch Extension/InterfaceController.swift** and add the following to the end of `InterfaceController`:

```swift
override func table(
  _ table: WKInterfaceTable,
  didSelectRowAt rowIndex: Int) {
    // 1
    let clipURL = clipProvider.clips[rowIndex]
    // 2
    presentMediaPlayerController(
      with: clipURL,
      options: nil,
      completion: {_, _, _ in })
}
```

Going through this step-by-step:

1. You get the URL that corresponds to the selected row. You do this using `clipProvider`, an instance of helper class `VideoClipProvider`, which contains the data model.

2. You present a media player controller by calling `presentMediaPlayerController(with:options:completion:)` and passing in the URL of the video clip. You can optionally pass in a dictionary of playback options. Since you don't want any particular customization at this point, you pass `nil`. In the completion block, you can check playback results based on your specific needs. Because the API requires a non-nil completion block, you simply provide an empty block.

> **Note:** You can also pass a remote content URL to the media player. The media player will display a loading indicator and then display the media file.

That's it! Build and run the app. Tap on a row in the table and you'll see a full screen video clip.

One simple API works for both audio and video playback! How handy is that? But there's more you can do.

Playback options

You can customize the behavior of the media player — to some extent. Here are the options you can specify:

*   **WKMediaPlayerControllerOptionsAutoplayKey**: specifies a media file should automatically start playing when it is displayed. The value of this key is a `NSNumber` representation of a Boolean and `true` by default.

- **WKMediaPlayerControllerOptionsStartTimeKey** specifies the point in time from which the media file will begin to play. This is particularly useful when you want to resume playback when the user returns to the app.

  You could alternatively offer the user shortcuts to jump to certain timestamps in a clip. The value for this key is a **NSNumber** representation of **TimeInterval**.

- **WKMediaPlayerControllerOptionsVideoGravityKey** specifies how the video stretches to fit its container. The value should be a member of the **WKVideoGravity** enumeration. The value for this key is also a **NSNumber** representation of one of **WKVideoGravity** constants.

- **WKMediaPlayerControllerOptionsLoopsKey** determines whether the content should loop. The value for this key should be a **NSNumber** representation of a Boolean.

To specify these options, you simply wrap them in a dictionary and pass them to **presentMediaPlayerController(with:options:completion:)**.

Supported formats

The Watch can play many common audio and video types, but due to the Watch's limited processor and memory Apple recommends the following formats:

- **Audio:** 32 kbps bit rate, AAC Stereo

- **Video:** H.264 high profile, 160 kbps bit rate, 30 FPS frame rate

- **Video:** full screen, 208x260 pixel resolution

- **Video:** 16:9 aspect ratio, 320x180 pixel resolution

Using the recommended formats gives your user the best experience possible on the limited real estate of the Watch.

Making custom interface

While showing a video clip using the full screen media player is very convenient, sometimes you want more control over the content. Luckily, watchOS gives you two options, **WKInterfaceMovie** and **WKInterfaceInlineMovie**.

- **WKInterfaceMovie** takes a URL for a media file and displays a playback icon over a preview image, which can be customized via the **posterImage** property. When the user taps the icon, **WKInterfaceMovie** will automatically play the associated movie. It's a great option if you want a consistent feel and look alongside other multimedia system apps on watchOS.

- `WKInterfaceInlineMovie` object is very similar to `WKInterfaceMovie`, but it gives you more flexibility to create your own custom interfaces. Since both `WKInterfaceMovie` and `WKInterfaceInlineMovie` have very similar API, you'll pick `WKInterfaceInlineMovie` to make a custom interface.

Add WKInterfaceInlineMovie

Open **Cute Puppies Watch/Interface.storyboard**, drag a new **Interface Controller** from the Object Library and drop it next to **Cute Puppies! Scene**:

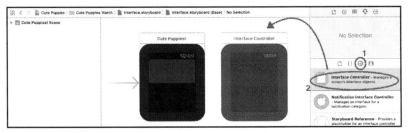

Find and drag an **Inline Movie** and a **Label** from the Object Library into the new controller.

Select the inline movie element you just added and open the Attributes Inspector. Change the **Height** property to **Relative to Container** with a **multiplier** of **0.7**, and the **Alignment** property to center horizontally.

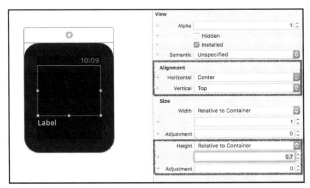

You also need to update the **Lines** property of the text label to **0** so that long texts display properly.

While you're still in there, expand **Cute Puppies! Scene** in the Document Outline, and Control-drag from **VideoRowController** to the new interface controller to make a **Push** segue.

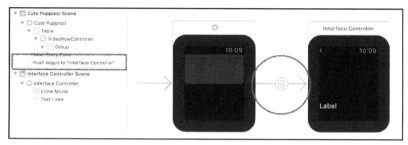

To make this work, you're going to have to leave the storyboard and write some code! It's okay — there isn't *that* much code.

In the Xcode navigation pane, right click on **Cute Puppies Watch Extension** and select **New File\watchOS\WatchKit Class** from the menu. Name it **PlayerInterfaceController**, make it a subclass of **WKInterfaceController** and ensure your new file is added to the **Cute Puppies Watch Extension** target.

Go back to **Interface.storyboard**, and change the class of the interface controller you recently added to `PlayerInterfaceController` from the Identity Inspector.

In the assistant editor, open **PlayerInterfaceController.swift**. Control-drag and create an `IBOutlet` for the inline movie and another one for the label. Name them `inlineMovie` and `textLabel`. Your class will now have the following properties:

```
@IBOutlet var inlineMovie: WKInterfaceInlineMovie!
@IBOutlet var textLabel: WKInterfaceLabel!
```

Next, add a property below the two outlets:

```
private var clipIndex: Int?
```

You use it to keep track of the index of the clip that's being played.

Replace awake(withContext:) with this code:

```swift
override func awake(withContext context: Any?) {
  super.awake(withContext: context)
  // 1
  let index = context as! Int
  // 2
  let provider = VideoClipProvider()
  let clipURL = provider.clips[index]
  let quote = provider.quotes[index]
  // 3
  clipIndex = index
  inlineMovie.setMovieURL(clipURL)
  textLabel.setText(quote)
  setTitle(clipURL.lastPathComponent)
  // 4
  if let data =
    PosterImageProvider().imageDataForClip(withURL: clipURL) {

    let image = WKImage(imageData: data)
    inlineMovie.setPosterImage(image)
  }
}
```

Taking each numbered comment in turn:

1. You expect the context that's being passed into awake(withContext:) to be the index of a video clip.

2. Using the VideoClipProvider utility class, you get the URL and the humorous quote based on the index that was passed in.

3. You save the clip index, update the inline movie by setting the video clip URL and the text label by setting the quote. You also update the title of the interface controller with the name of the video clip.

4. If the image data is available, you also update the poster image property of WKInterfaceInlineMovie using the PosterImageProvider utility class. The poster image appears when the video is paused.

Finally, open **Cute Puppies Watch Extension/InterfaceController.swift**. Delete table(_:didSelectRowAt:) that you added earlier. Then add the following to the end of InterfaceController:

```swift
override func contextForSegue(
  withIdentifier segueIdentifier: String,
  in table: WKInterfaceTable,
  rowIndex: Int) -> Any? {
  return rowIndex
}
```

Build and run the Watch app; now when you tap on a movie clip, it pushes your custom video player interface controller onto the navigation stack, where you display both the movie and the humorous quote in one screen:

When you add an inline movie in Interface Builder, you can specify whether it should loop or auto-play directly from the storyboard. You can also change the video gravity that specifies how the video should stretch to fit its container.

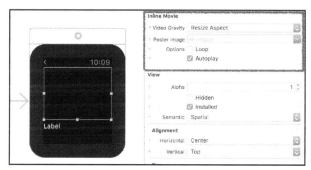

For your inline movie, make sure AutoPlay is set to on in storyboard. These properties are also available in code.

Finishing touches

It would be nice to let user pause and play the video. Open **Cute Puppies Watch/Interface.storyboard**, drag a **Tap Gesture Recognizer** from the Object Library and drop it on **Inline Movie**.

In the assistant editor, open **PlayerInterfaceController.swift**. Add a new property to PlayerInterfaceController as shown below:

```
private var isPlaying: Bool = true
```

You need to keep track of the state of player. Since the inline movie player's **Autoplay** property is set to true in the storyboard, you set the initial value of isPlaying to true.

Control-drag from the tap gesture recognizer and create an IBAction. Name it onTap, and update its implementation as follows:

```
@IBAction func onTap(_ sender: AnyObject) {
  if isPlaying {
    inlineMovie.pause()
    isPlaying = false
  } else {
    inlineMovie.play()
    isPlaying = true
  }
}
```

Here, you simply check the state. If it's playing, you pause it. If it's already paused, you play it.

Build and run the Watch app; now when you drill down to the player interface, you can pause and play with a single tap!

Handoff

In this section, you'll add Handoff to Cute Puppies app for a magical user experience! Handoff is a continuity feature that facilitates the seamless transfer of tasks between two devices. When it comes to the Apple Watch, you are limited to a subset of content or functionality from your main app. There is no better mechanism than Handoff to let the user see your full content without interruption. For example, Handoff lets you start watching a cute puppy chasing his tail on your watch, and then continue watching that video on your phone.

> **Note:** Handoff does not work on the iOS simulator. Therefore, to follow along with this section, you'll need an Apple Watch that's paired with an iPhone.

Handoff functionality depends on few things:

1. **An iCloud account:** You must be logged in to the same iCloud account for each device you wish to use Handoff.

2. **Bluetooth LE 4.0:** Handoff broadcasts activities via Bluetooth LE signals, so both the broadcasting and receiving devices must have Bluetooth LE 4.0 support.

3. **iCloud paired:** Devices should have been already paired through iCloud.

In the context of the Apple Watch, both the Watch and the iPhone that supports Apple Watch have Bluetooth LE 4.0, and they are paired. So you're good to go!

Setting your team

In Handoff you always have two apps: a sending app and a receiving app. For Handoff to work, both the sending and receiving apps must be signed by the same Team ID. From your app's standpoint, unless streaming, Handoff is a one-time data exchange event during which the sending device delivers a package of data to the receiving device.

Select the **Cute Puppies** target from your project settings, and in the **General** tab, switch the **Team** to your team:

Similarly, update the **Team** for the **Cute Puppies Watch** and **Cute Puppies Watch Extension** targets.

Build and run the app on your iOS device as well as on the Watch to make sure it runs without issue.

Configuring activity types

Handoff is based on the concept of a user activity. You'll learn more about user activity in a bit. When you create a user activity, you must specify an activity type for it. An activity type is simply a unique string, usually in reverse DNS notation, like `com.razeware.cutepuppies.home`.

The activity type won't be shown to the user, but, as a best practice, make sure you choose a meaningful activity type that clearly indicates its intention.

Each app that's capable of receiving a user activity must declare the activity types it will accept. This is much like declaring the URL schemes your app supports.

To configure the activity types, expand the **Cute Puppies** group in the project navigator and find and open **Info.plist**. Click the + button that appears next to **Information Property List** to add a new item to its dictionary, like so:

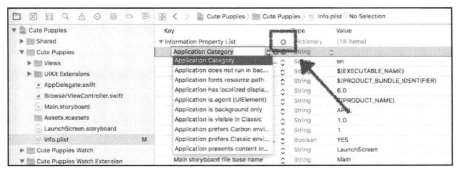

Enter NSUserActivityTypes for the key name and make it an Array type. Add two items under NSUserActivityTypes — Item 0 and Item 1 — and set their types to String. Enter com.razeware.cutepuppies.home for Item 0, and com.razeware.cutepuppies.clip for Item 1.

When you're done, your new entry will look like this:

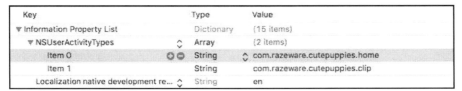

Here you add two different activity types because you're going to implement two distinct behaviors, and each should have its own unique identifier:

• Hand off the top level screen where all clips are displayed.

• Hand off a specific video clip where you'll start playing that specific video clip.

These are arbitrary activity types unique to your app. Since you'll refer to them in code from multiple places in the app, it's good practice to add them as constants in a separate file. So:

1. Right-click on the **Shared** group in the project navigator and from the menu.

2. Select **New File\iOS\Source\Swift File**.

3. Name it **HandoffHelper.swift** .

4. Ensure that both **Cute Puppies** and **Cute Puppies Watch Extension** targets are selected.

5. Click the **Create** button.

Open **HandoffHelper.swift** and add the following to the end of the file:

```
// 1
struct Handoff {
  // 2
  enum Activity: String {
    case viewHome = "com.razeware.cutepuppies.home"
    case playClip = "com.razeware.cutepuppies.clip"

    var stringValue: String {
      return self.rawValue
    }
  }
  // 3
  static let activityValueKey = "activityValue"
}
```

Here's what you're doing with the above code:

1. You'll use some constants with Handoff and refer to them from multiple places in the app. It's good practice to modularize those constants in a well-defined structure.

2. You add an `enum` that represents the registered user activity types from the app's Info.plist. For each registered user activity type, you add a distinct `enum` value.

3. Some activity types may have an associated value. For example, if a user is watching a clip, you also want to specify which clip it is. You'll see this in action in a little bit.

Before moving on to performing a simple Handoff, let's take a look at the essential user activity dictionary.

User activities

Handoff is based on the concept of **user activities**: stand-alone units of information that you can hand off without any dependencies on other information. Consider the task of writing an email. To continue the email on another device, the activity must include the recipient, subject, message body, any attachments and possibly even the insertion point of the cursor at the time the email is handed off.

Handoff uses `NSUserActivity` objects to package information to transfer. The user activity that you pass from the Watch app contains a `userInfo` dictionary where you store information about the current state of the app. When user continues an activity on the iPhone, that contextual information is passed to the app delegate of the iPhone app, which you can then use to configure the receiving app appropriately.

Keys and values in the dictionary may only be classes compatible with the plist format: NSArray, NSData, NSDate, NSDictionary, NSNull, NSNumber, NSSet, NSString or NSURL. Under the hood, Handoff uses the plist format to exchange data with different devices.

When passing instances of NSURL, you shouldn't pass local file URLs, as the receiver won't be able to translate and map the URL properly. Instead, send a relative path and reconstruct the URL manually on the receiving side. Likewise, don't use platform-specific values like the content offset of a scroll view. Instead, send a landmark that makes sense in the context of your data model, like an index to an array.

A quick end-to-end Handoff

It's time to implement a simple end-to-end Handoff that takes the user from the home screen of the Watch app to the home screen of the iPhone app. Open **InterfaceController.swift** and add the following to the end of willActivate():

```
let userInfo: [AnyHashable: Any] = [
  Handoff.activityValueKey: ""
]
updateUserActivity(Handoff.Activity.viewHome.stringValue,
  userInfo: userInfo,
  webpageURL: nil)
```

Here's what's going on:

WKInterfaceController has a method updateUserActivity(_:userInfo:webpageURL:) that updates and begins to broadcast a NSUserActivity. You can call this method at any time during the execution of the interface controller's code. The system stores the userInfo dictionary and will transfer it to the target device when appropriate.

However, if the device suspends execution of your code, you need to start broadcasting again, so you need to put your Handoff code somewhere it will trigger when the app returns to the foreground. This typically makes willActivate() a good place to start broadcasting Handoff.

You wrap the state of the app in the userInfo dictionary. When the user is viewing the top-level video clips, you broadcast a user activity with the Handoff.Activity.viewHome type. Since there's no specific associate value, you pass an empty string for activityValueKey in the userInfo dictionary.

> **Note:** Although `userInfo` dictionary is optional and you can pass `nil`, as a best practice you usually want to pass something meaningful. At the end of the chapter, you'll add an important versioning value to the dictionary.

You pass in `nil` for `webpageURL`, as this handoff won't navigate to data in your app that could also be shown in Safari. You can learn more about native app-to-web browser handoff and vice versa in Apple's **Handoff Programming Guide**: apple.co/1uIWL00

At this point, you have the minimum you need to start broadcasting, so you can move on to receiving.

On the receiving side, when user swipes up on your app icon on the lock screen, the operating system launches your app then starts downloading the Handoff payload in the background. As transfer of data happens, you'll get callbacks in your iPhone app delegate, which you'll see next.

Open **AppDelegate.swift** and add the following code:

```
// 1
func application(_ application: UIApplication,
  continue userActivity: NSUserActivity,
  restorationHandler: @escaping ([Any]?) -> Void) -> Bool {
  // 2
  print("Received: \(userActivity.userInfo ?? [:])")
  appRootViewController.restoreUserActivityState(userActivity)
  // 3
  return true
}
```

Here's what's going on:

1. You implement `application(_ application:, continue userActivity:, restorationHandler:)`. This method in `UIApplicationDelegate` is called when everything goes well and a user activity is successfully transferred.

2. You log a message to the console and forward the user activity to the app's root view controller. `restoreUserActivityState(_:)` is the designated method for Handoff state restoration. It's declared at the `UIResponder` level, so many common UIKit classes like `UIViewController` inherit it. You'll learn more about state restoration later in this chapter.

3. You return `true` to indicate you handled the user activity. If you return `false`, you leave it to the OS to handle Handoff, which usually does nothing except launching your app! :]

That's it for a quick, simple, end-to-end Handoff. Time to try it out! There's a little coordination required to get this working on two devices, so follow along carefully:

1. Install and run the app on your iPhone.

2. Make sure the app gets installed on the paired Apple Watch. You may need to open the Watch app on the iPhone and manually flick the switch.

3. Make sure you're debugging the app in Xcode so you can see your `print()` output.

4. Put the iPhone to sleep by pressing the power button.

5. On the Watch, launch the app, and on the iPhone, press the Home button to light up the screen. In a couple of seconds, you'll see the Cute Puppies app icon appear in the bottom-left corner of the screen. From there, you'll be able to launch the app and see the log message in Xcode's console:

```
Received: [AnyHashable("activityValue"): ]
```

> **Note:** If you don't see the app icon on the lock screen, make sure the Watch screen stays on for a while. You may also put the palm of your hand on the Watch screen to put it to sleep, then tap on the Watch screen again to wake it up. This triggers `willActivate()` and forces the OS to restart broadcasting. Also, check the device console to see if there are any error messages from Handoff.

Alerting the user and handling errors

Even though the app seems to work well, there are a few things you need to implement to ensure everything is handled properly.

When the user swipes up on the app icon to indicate she wants to continue a user activity, the OS launches the corresponding app, then calls `application(_:willContinueUserActivityWithType:)`. This is where you can get prepared for an incoming Handoff. Open **AppDelegate.swift** and add the following method:

```swift
func application(_ application: UIApplication,
    willContinueUserActivityWithType
    userActivityType: String) -> Bool {
      return true
}
```

At this point, your app hasn't yet downloaded the NSUserActivity instance and its userInfo payload, but the OS tells you in advance what type of activity is coming your way. If you want to alert your user that the activity is on its way and you need to do some preparations, this is the place to do it.

It's also conceivable that the Handoff activity will fail at some point. Add the following method to **AppDelegate.swift** to handle failures:

```swift
func application(_ application: UIApplication,
  didFailToContinueUserActivityWithType
  userActivityType: String,
  error: Error) {

  print("Handoff Error: \(error.localizedDescription)")

  let error = error as NSError
  guard error.code != NSUserCancelledError else {
    return
  }

  let message = """
    The connection to your other device
    may have been interrupted. Please try again.
    """

  let title = "Handoff Error"

  let alertController = UIAlertController(
    dismissOnlyAlertWithTitle: title, message: message)
    as UIViewController

  appRootViewController.present(
    alertController, animated: true, completion: nil)
}
```

If you receive anything except NSUserCancelledError, then something went wrong along the way, and you won't be able to restore the activity. In this case, you display an appropriate message to the user. However, if the user explicitly canceled the Handoff action, then there's nothing else for you to do here but abort the operation.

Build and run to ensure that the handoff still works as expected. Now, if an error happens during hand off, you display an appropriate error message.

Handoff state restoration

While broadcasting from the main interface controller is handy, it's not very useful to the user. One very important place to broadcast a handoff is from `PlayerInterfaceController`.

Open **PlayerInterfaceController.swift** and override `willActivate()`:

```
override func willActivate() {
  super.willActivate()

  guard let clipIndex = clipIndex else { return }
  let userInfo: [AnyHashable: Any] = [
    Handoff.activityValueKey: clipIndex
  ]
  updateUserActivity(Handoff.Activity.playClip.stringValue,
    userInfo: userInfo,
    webpageURL: nil)
}
```

Much like the main interface controller, when the user selects a video clip in the Watch app, `willActivate()` is called. You then create and broadcast a `playClip` activity that contains the video clip index.

Build and run. Verify that everything works as expected by navigating to a video clip in the Watch app and handing it off to the iPhone app. You'll see the index of the video clip is logged to the console:

```
Received: [AnyHashable("activityValue"): 2]
```

Now it's time for state restoration. Remember how in the `AppDelegate`, you passed the `userActivity` object to app's root view controller by calling `restoreUserActivityState(_:)`? The default implementation of `restoreUserActivityState(_:)` doesn't do much for you. You need to override it and perform your own state restoration to suit.

Open **BrowserViewController.swift** and override `restoreUserActivityState(_:)`:

```swift
override func restoreUserActivityState(_ activity:
NSUserActivity) {
  // 1
  super.restoreUserActivityState(activity)
  // 2
  guard let userInfo = activity.userInfo else { return }
  switch activity.activityType {
  // 3
  case Handoff.Activity.viewHome.stringValue:
    dismissVideoPlayer(completion: nil)
  // 4
  case Handoff.Activity.playClip.stringValue:
    guard let index = userInfo[Handoff.activityValueKey] as? Int
      else { return }
    dismissVideoPlayer(completion: {
      self.playClip(at: index)
    })
  // 5
  default:
    break
  }
}
```

Here is a detailed explanation:

1. You call `super` so that it gets a chance to do anything it has to do for state restoration.

2. You safely unwrap the `userInfo` dictionary and evaluate the activity type of the handoff.

3. For a `viewHome` activity type, you dismiss the video player if there is one.

4. If it's a `playClip` activity type, you safely try to get the index of the video clip and start playing it.

5. For all other unknown activity types, you do nothing.

Build and run. Start watching a video clip on the Watch app and hand it off to the iPhone app. This time, you'll be magically taken to the same video clip on your iPhone!

Stopping the broadcast

There are times that you want to stop broadcasting for Handoff because the context has changed. Note that you can broadcast only one activity at a time. In the context of the Apple Watch, the recommended way is to leave it to the OS to stop broadcasting on the Watch. Unlike iOS, you'll manually invalidate Handoff on the Watch only when you need to do so. This is because the OS does some optimizations to ensure that Handoff broadcasts lasts a bit longer — even after the Watch screen turns off — for the convenience of the user. You usually don't want to interrupt that.

`WKInterfaceController` has a convenient method, `invalidateUserActivity()`, that you can use to stop the broadcast. You can call `invalidateUserActivity()` at any time during the execution of your code.

Versioning support

Versioning is an important best practice when working with Handoff. You might change data formats or remove values from your `userInfo` dictionary in future versions of the app. You want to make sure older versions of the app don't break if they receive a newer version of Handoff, or vice versa.

One strategy to deal with this is to add a version number to each handoff you send, and only accept handoffs from the known versions. For a basic versioning system, add a version key-value to the Handoff `userInfo` dictionary on the broadcasting side like below:

```
let userInfo: [AnyHashable: Any] = [
  "handoff-version": 1,
  // some other values.
]
```

You want to do this anywhere that you broadcast a Handoff. In Cute Puppies project that would be in both InterfaceController.swift and PlayerInterfaceController.swift.

On the receiving side in the iPhone app, when you receive an activity in `application(_ application:, continue userActivity:, restorationHandler:)` of `AppDelegate`, the first thing you want to check is the version number.

```
func application(_ application: UIApplication,
  continue userActivity: NSUserActivity,
  restorationHandler: @escaping ([Any]?) -> Void) -> Bool {
  // Guard against unknown versions.
  guard
    let userInfo = userActivity.userInfo,
    let version = userInfo["handoff-version"] as? Int,
    version == 1
  else { return false }
  // The rest of the code.
}
```

If it's a version that you know about, you perform the state restoration. Otherwise, you simply return `false`.

Where to go from here?

The audio and video API of watchOS makes it possible to deliver a smooth multimedia experience on the Apple Watch, and Handoff makes it easier to provide users with a seamless app experience across multiple devices.

If you're curious to learn more, be sure to check out these resources:

• WWDC 2014 - Adopting Handoff on iOS and OS X: apple.co/2v1sbam

• Handoff Programming Guide: apple.co/1uIWL00

Chapter 22: Core Motion

By Audrey Tam

Are you keeping your Apple Watch happy by standing and walking more often? Seeing your stats in the Activity app is great motivation to rack up those last few minutes of exercise and reach today's calorie-burn target.

But the Activity app only displays your daily stats and totals for the current week. Don't you wish you could watch your distance *add up*? Then you could set imaginary goals, like walking the distance of a marathon or three, then moving on to walk the length or breadth of your continent.

iOS 4 introduced the Core Motion framework, letting developers access an iOS device's accelerometer and gyroscope data. Later iOS versions added compass, altimeter and pedometer data, as well as detection of the user's probable activity, such as being stationary, walking, running or even driving.

watchOS 2 brought Core Motion to Apple Watch (well, *some* of Core Motion), and watchOS 3 brought a little bit more.

In this chapter, you'll use watchOS 4's **Core Motion** framework to build an app that tracks your progress towards your dream walk. Imagine you're on a long distance trek in an exotic location; the more you walk, the closer you get to your goal! **DreamWalker** tracks your progress towards ten dream walks, ranging from a 10-kilometer fun run to the 2663-mile Pacific Crest Trail.

You'll learn what *is* and *isn't* in Core Motion on watchOS 4, and uses `CMPedometer` distance data in a Watch app that calculates your progress along walks of different lengths. Ever wanted to know how many steps it would take to walk the Tour du Mont Blanc or hike the entire Pacific Coast trail? If you haven't, this app might inspire you to find out!

> **Note:** You'll need an Apple Watch paired with an iPhone in order to test Core Motion in watchOS 4.

Getting started

Open the **DreamWalker** starter project. This project uses sample pedometer data, so you can run it in the simulator. Select the **DreamWalker WatchKit App**, then build and run it. Once the Watch app runs, open the iPhone app in the simulator. The app shows progress towards each goal using the total distance recorded in the sample data. All sample data can be displayed by tapping the **History** button.

Select a walk to view an image of its location, a progress bar and information about the walk. Tap the **map** button to open **Maps** in hybrid mode to show the terrain of the walk.

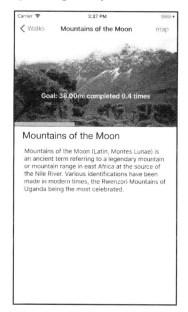

The Watch app displays a list of the ten walks, each with a progress bar indicating how much of the walk has been completed. The bars are color-coded in 25% increments. A star indicates the user has finished that walk at least once.

When the user selects a walk, the app will display information about it. The detail view shows the walk's distance and the user's progress against a background image. It also shows the number of times she's finished the walk, her total distance and total steps.

In this chapter, you'll replace the sample data with real updates from the Watch's pedometer.

Core Motion on iPhone

The Core Motion framework contains levels of abstraction ranging from raw sensor data to processed sensor data, interpreted to identify the user's current activity. Before hitting the code, take a look at the different levels of abstraction in Core Motion.

Sensors

> **Note**: At the time of writing, watchOS 4 lets you access **accelerometer** data directly, and **device motion** gives you indirect access to **gyroscope** and **magnetometer** data.

At the most fine-grained level, Apple devices might return the following data:

- **Accelerometer**: Measures the device's acceleration along the x, y and z-axes, measured in **Gs**: the standard unit of gravity. Accelerometer values include the influence of gravity; **device motion** separates gravitational forces from the acceleration imparted by the *user* as you'll see in the section below.

- **Altimeter**: Measures *changes* in the device's altitude. It works by sensing air pressure, which may not necessarily be caused by an altitude change. For instance, a pressure change caused by weather could potentially be misinterpreted. Also, if an iPhone is in a rigid waterproof case, the altimeter might not work as expected.

- **Gyroscope**: Measures the device's rotation around the x, y, and z-axes. These should be zero when the device isn't moving, but all sensors have some bias, often due to temperature changes. Device motion, see below, corrects this bias.

- **Magnetometer**: Measures the Earth's magnetic field plus bias from the device and its surroundings. Device motion, see below, removes the device's bias.

Device motion abstracts raw sensor data by encapsulating gyroscope, magnetometer and accelerometer data to provide the device's attitude — its orientation in space — and rate of rotation. It uses gyroscope data to separate raw acceleration data into `gravity` and `userAcceleration` properties. Its `rotationRate` and `magneticField` properties remove the bias from the raw gyroscope and magnetometer data.

Apple's **SwingWatch** app, which you can download at apple.co/29UjN1L, processes the Watch's device motion gravity and rotation rate to count swings as the user plays a racquet sport. Prior analysis of data determines rotation rate constants that the app uses to detect when the user swings the racquet, and to avoid double-counting on the return swing.

Processed data

Algorithms that interpret sensor data to count steps, measure distance or detect motion type rely on analyzing a lot of sample data to identify patterns and criteria. The Watch series 2 uses its GPS to fine-tune the accuracy of the steps-to-distance calculation.

- **Pedometer**: Lets you access step counts, current pace in seconds per meter, current cadence in steps per second, and estimated distance in meters. Pedometer events notify the app when users pause and resume travel. Devices with an altimeter can count the number of floors that the user walks *or* runs up or down — which means you can cheat a little by walking up escalators. :]

- **Activity**: assesses the user's current motion type: stationary, walking, running, cycling or driving — with low, medium or high confidence.

Checking availability

You should always check whether sensors and processed data are available on your app's target device before attempting to use them.

To check the availability of accelerometer, gyroscope, magnetometer and device motion, create a `CMMotionManager` object and call its `is<Sensor>Available` properties, like so:

```
let motionManager = CMMotionManager()
if motionManager.isAccelerometerAvailable {
  print("accelerometer is available")
}
```

- Use `CMAltimeter.isRelativeAltitudeAvailable()` to check for an altimeter.

- Check pedometer data availability with `CMPedometer` class methods; for example, `CMPedometer.isPaceAvailable()`.

- Use `CMMotionActivityManager.isActivityAvailable()` to check whether the device can assess motion type.

Core Motion on Apple Watch

Compared with iPhone 7, there isn't much available on the Watch:

- **Sensors**: Only the accelerometer is directly available; device motion encapsulates raw data from the gyroscope, magnetometer and accelerometer.

- **Processed data**: The pedometer provides step counting, current pace, current cadence and distance, and event tracking, but *not* floor-counting. **Activity** detects stationary, walking, running and cycling, but *not* driving. This might explain why my Watch thinks I'm exercising hard when I'm sitting on the train! :]

The good news is, the watchOS 4 documentation includes currently missing sensors and processed data, so you should check the availability of these features in every Xcode or Watch update.

Using Watch pedometer data

Open **PedometerData.swift** and add the following statement to import the Core Motion framework:

```
import CoreMotion
```

Then add the following property to the top of the `PedometerData` class, just above the **sample pedometer data** properties:

```
let pedometer = CMPedometer()
```

While you're here, initialize these **sample pedometer data** properties to zero, as shown below:

```
// sample pedometer data: set these two properties to zero
var totalSteps = 0
var totalDistance: CGFloat = 0.0
```

`CMPedometer` implements two methods to access pedometer data:

- **startUpdates(from:withHandler:)**: provides continual live updates of pedometer data from a start date to the current time. Upon calling this method, the pedometer object will start calling your handler regularly with data. When the user stops looking at the app, the app is suspended, and the delivery of updates temporarily stops. When the user looks at the app again, the pedometer object will resume updates.

- **queryPedometerData(from:to:withHandler:)**: accesses *historical data* between the specified dates. The start date may be up to seven days in the past. In the DreamWalker Watch app, you'll call this method to get the data for a complete day.

Both methods pass a `CMPedometerData` or `NSError` object to your `CMPedometerHandler`. The `CMPedometerData` object includes motion data like start and end dates, steps and distance values, current pace, average active pace and cadence.

Supplying the app with information

DreamWalker displays the total steps and distance since the app's start date, as well as steps and distance for the current day. How can you get the necessary information from `CMPedometer` using its live update and historical query methods?

The live update method provides cumulative data from a start date (the green vertical line in the diagram below) up to the current time (the purple dot) — you can't set its end date.

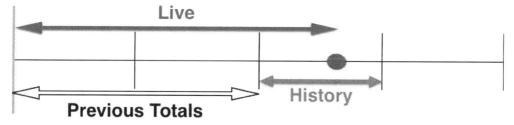

The following method call would provide the *total* steps and distance since the app's start date.

```
startUpdates(from: appStartDate)
```

The historical query lets you set both start and end dates, but you can only access data for the past seven days. The following method call would provide the *current day's* steps and distance:

```
queryPedometerData(from: startOfDay, to: now)
```

The diagram below shows a historical query getting the data for a full day, which would be useful after the next day begins:

```
queryPedometerData(from: startOfDay, to: endOfDay)
```

Here are three different options for using these methods to get both cumulative and the current day's data:

1. Get the total steps and distance from a live update, and the current day's steps and distance from a historical query. This requires two method calls to update the screen info.

2. Keep track of the total steps and distance, up to the end of the *previous* day (the **Previous Totals** arrow in the diagram above), and *subtract* these values from a live update's cumulative data to get the current day's data.

3. Keep track of the previous total steps and distance, and *add* these values to a historical query's current-day data to get the current cumulative data.

Either of the last two options would work. However, there's one more consideration: how do you trigger the method call when the user activates the app? The live update method has the advantage of resuming automatically when the user activates the app, so DreamWalker uses option 2. It gets cumulative data from a live update, then calculates the current day's data.

Choosing the start date

To allow the queries to work correctly, you'll need to set and track an `appStartDate` variable. But how should you pick this date from the past?

The live update method can retrieve all the pedometer data recorded since the day you tore open the box, strapped on your Watch, and paired it with your iPhone. But DreamWalker stores daily data, and the historical query method can only get daily data for the past seven days.

However, this would require firing off seven queries when the app first starts and sending that data to the iPhone app — a complicated and asynchronous process. There's no guarantee that processing of the seven queries would happen in the same order that you created them. And anyway, you can get daily data much more efficiently using HealthKit's `HKStatisticsCollectionQuery`. For more details on that, see the next chapter, "HealthKit".

> **Note**: Why not go straight to HealthKit? Why use Core Motion on its own? Well, Core Motion is much simpler to use, and you don't have to worry about capabilities or serious privacy issues. DreamWalker works quite well, and doesn't need the complexity of HealthKit.

If you don't care about keeping track of daily data before the day you install the app, you could set `appStartDate` to the first day you wore your Watch, and just feel good about the huge values on day 1. But you won't have the current day's data, so you won't be able to check that the app is recording the same number of steps as the Activity app.

The long and short of that is you can set `appStartDate` to be the start of the day that you first run the app on the Watch. This is already initialized in the starter app as `startOfDay`. You can check DreamWalker's values with the Activity app — the app's steps and distance values should be the same as Activity's. The app's values might be higher if Activity isn't up to date.

When the app first launches, the previous total steps and distance values are `0`, so the first day's total values will be the same as its daily values. But you'll update these previous total values *when a new day begins*. Cue the high-adrenaline music! :]

Handling pedometer data

The live update and historical query methods have handlers whose main job is to update the total and daily steps and distance values. Open **PedometerData.swift** and add the following `enum` and helper method to the `// MARK: Pedometer Data` section:

```
enum PedometerDataType { case live, history }

func updateProperties(from data: CMPedometerData,
  ofType type: PedometerDataType) {

  switch type {

  case .live:  // 1
    totalSteps = data.numberOfSteps.intValue
    steps = totalSteps - prevTotalSteps
    if let rawDistance = data.distance?.intValue,
```

```
        rawDistance > 0 {

            totalDistance = CGFloat(rawDistance) / 1000.0
            distance = totalDistance - prevTotalDistance
        }

    case .history:  // 2
        steps = data.numberOfSteps.intValue
        totalSteps = steps + prevTotalSteps
        if let rawDistance = data.distance?.intValue,
            rawDistance > 0 {

            distance = CGFloat(rawDistance) / 1000.0
            totalDistance = distance + prevTotalDistance
        }
    }
}
```

This method implements the calculations described in options 2 and 3 above.

1. You store the live update's cumulative `numberOfSteps` and `distance` data in
    `totalSteps` and `totalDistance`, with `distance` converted from meters to
    kilometers. Then you subtract the previous total values to get the current day's `steps`
    and `distance` values.

2. You store the historical query's data in the current day's `steps` and `distance`, and
    add the previous total values to get the cumulative `totalSteps` and `totalDistance`
    values.

Now find `startLiveUpdates()` in the `// MARK: Pedometer Data` section and
replace its `TODO` comment with the following lines:

```
guard CMPedometer.isStepCountingAvailable() else { return }
pedometer.startUpdates(
  from: appStartDate) { data, error in

  if let data = data {
    self.updateProperties(from: data, ofType: .live)
    self.sendData()
  }
}
```

This method checks availability of step-counting, and calls the live updates method. The
handler passes the pedometer data to `updateProperties(from:ofType:)` and then
sends the data to the iPhone app.

Similarly, implement `queryHistory(from:to:)` with the following:

```
guard CMPedometer.isStepCountingAvailable() else { return }
```

```
pedometer.queryPedometerData(
  from: start, to: end) { data, error in

  if let data = data {
    self.updateProperties(from: data, ofType: .history)
    self.sendData()
  }
}
```

Make sure that you pass `.history` as the `ofType` value.

Replacing the starter simulation code

Before you test the app, clean up the starter project's code to replace the sample pedometer data in the iPhone app. Open **WalksTableViewController.swift** and, in `viewDidLoad()`, replace the call to `loadDayData()` with the following line:

```
history.insert(DayData(), at: 0)
```

Now, delete `loadDayData()` entirely.

The iPhone app stores each day's pedometer data in its `history` array of `DayData` items — the first item is the current day's data. `loadDayData()` created a sample history array, which you don't need anymore. Instead, you create the first `history` item.

Running the apps on your devices

New in iOS 11 / watchOS 4, your app must request authorization from the user to access Motion Fitness data. In **DreamWalker/Info.plist** and in **DreamWalker WatchKit Extension/Info.plist**, add the key **Privacy - Motion Usage Description**, with value **"To show you reaching your distance goals"**.

Connect your iPhone, then select the **DreamWalker WatchKit App\iPhone + Apple Watch** devices scheme. Build and run the Watch app.

Note: Although Xcode can install onto your iPhone via wifi, it can find the paired Watch more readily when you plug your iPhone into your Mac.

While the Watch app is installing, open the iPhone app, and tap OK when this alert appears:

If you've already walked around today while wearing your Watch, the Watch app will update with non-zero values.

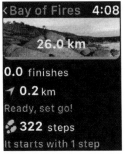

The iPhone app has also updated with non-zero values for today.

This is all you need to get live updates on the total distance the wearer has walked ... on the first day.

Starting a new day

By now, you might be feeling spooked by all this talk of *current day* and *previous totals*, because you haven't done anything to change these values. So far, the app works fine, because the first time the app launches, `appStartDate` is the same as `startOfDay`, and the previous total steps and distance values are `0`.

But what should happen at midnight?

- `startOfDay` should be reset to be the start of the new current day.

- The previous total steps and distance values should be set to the old current day's total steps and distance values.

How do you detect when a new day begins, where should you check for this, and where do you store the daily data?

after all,
tomorrow
is another
day!

Flagging dayEnded to the iPhone app

To answer the storage question, remember that the iPhone app has a `history` array where it stores each day's pedometer data. Open **WalksTableViewController.swift** and find `session(_:didReceiveUserInfo:)`. It contains the following lines:

```
if let dayEnded = userInfo["dayEnded"] as? Bool,
   dayEnded == true {

  history.insert(DayData(), atIndex: 0)
  history[0].totalSteps = history[1].totalSteps
  history[0].totalDistance = history[1].totalDistance
}
```

Aha! The iPhone app expects the Watch app to set a `dayEnded` flag when it sends the last set of data for `history`'s current day. The iPhone app then inserts a new `DayData` item at the start of the `history` array and initializes its `total` properties. The `DayData` initializer has already set the new item's `date` to today and initialized today's properties to `0`. The new `history` item is now ready to receive today's live update, so start by adding some code to `PedometerData` to set and send this `dayEnded` flag.

Open **PedometerData.swift** and find sendData(). Add a dayEnded argument:

```
func sendData(_ dayEnded: Bool) {
```

And add the corresponding item to applicationDict:

```
let applicationDict: [String : Any] = [
  "dayEnded": dayEnded,
  "steps": steps,
  "distance": distance,
  "totalSteps": totalSteps,
  "totalDistance": totalDistance
]
```

Xcode will immediately show you the two calls to sendData(_:) in
PedometerData.swift that you need to fix by adding a Bool argument. There's one in
startLiveUpdates(), in the startUpdates(from:) handler — this is the "business
as usual", not-end-of-day case, so pass false as the argument:

```
self.sendData(false)
```

The other sendData(_:) call is in queryHistory(from:to:), in the
queryPedometerData(from:to:) handler. This *is* the end-of-day case, so pass true as
the argument:

```
self.sendData(true)
```

Detecting when a new day begins

Now return to the question: how and where do you detect when a new day begins? Well,
live updates are "business as usual", except for the first time a live update's end date is
after the end of the current day. So a good place to check is in startLiveUpdates(), in
the startUpdates(from:) handler.

Find startLiveUpdates() in **PedometerData.swift**. Immediately after you check for
data via if let data = data, add the following lines:

```
// 1
if self.calendar.isDate(data.endDate,
  afterDate: self.endOfDay) {
  // 2
  self.pedometer.stopUpdates()
  // 3
  self.queryHistory(from: self.startOfDay, to: self.endOfDay)
  return
}
```

Here's what you're doing:

1. `data.endDate` is the current live update's end date. The `endOfDay` property of `PedometerData` is the start of the next day. The `calendar` object's helper method returns `true` if `data.endDate` is after `endOfDay`.

2. You stop the live updates to prevent the new day's live update data from sneaking into the iPhone app's `history` before the iPhone app has created a new item for it.

3. You get yesterday's data. `queryHistory(from:to:)` also sends the data to the iPhone app, with `dayEnded` set to `true`.

The `queryPedometerData(from:to:)` handler must also update and save the day-dependant properties and restart live updates. So find the handler in `queryHistory(from:to:)` and add the following lines below `self.sendData(true)`:

```
// update and save day-dependent properties
self.setStartAndEndOfDay()
self.prevTotalSteps = self.totalSteps
self.prevTotalDistance = self.totalDistance
self.saveData()
```

Now build and run the Watch app, walk around while wearing your Watch and take a screenshot of today's values before midnight. Check the app after midnight — the total values will be higher than your screenshot, but the Today values will be close to zero.

In the iPhone app, the history table's first item will show a new near-zero item for today.

```
5 August 2017
75 steps 0.05km

4 August 2017
7694 steps 4.70km
```

Your iPhone Activity app's history will confirm yesterday's data.

You've done it! Now get out there and *walk!*

Using the historical accelerometer

This chapter's app doesn't use the Watch's accelerometer or gyroscope directly, but some people are doing cool things with it. watchOS 2 introduced a new `CMSensorRecorder` API. This section provides a brief overview of how it works, according to the *Historical Accelerometer* segment of the WWDC 2015 "What's New in Core Motion" video #705, available here: apple.co/1KrIv4X.

> **Note:** Using accelerometer data in an app usually requires analyzing many data samples to identify significant patterns and criteria to implement as algorithms, for example, to detect the wearer falling (1.usa.gov/1JEjo9A), or to count laps in a swimming pool (bit.ly/1KpJ2Sa), or to count racquet swings (apple.co/ 29UjN1L).

`CMSensorRecorder` provides access to historical sensor data — specifically, historical *accelerometer* data. Your app can access data for up to three days, and this data is collected even when your app isn't running. When your app *is* running, it can perform custom algorithms on long streams of accelerometer data.

To begin, your app checks availability of accelerometer recordings with `CMSensorRecorder.isAccelerometerRecordingAvailable()`.

If this method returns `true`, your app creates a `CMSensorRecorder` object, which calls `recordAccelerometer(forDuration:)` to initiate the sensor recorder.

The Watch might go to sleep and your app might be suspended, but when your app is active again, it can call `accelerometerData(from:to:)` to query for sensor data. This query returns a `CMSensorDataList`, which lets you enumerate over its sequence of `CMRecordedAccelerometerData` objects. Each data object has `startDate` and `identifier` properties.

Historical accelerometer best practices

Your app might not have enough time to process large strings of sensor data, so Apple advises the following best practices:

1. Query data for the minimum duration your app needs.

2. Data is available at 50 Hz, but unless your algorithm requires a high sensor rate, sample the data at a lower frequency.

Managing limited processing time

Even using the minimum amount of data, a Watch app that processes sensor data needs to be able to cope with the limited processing time allowed by the very short activation periods that are typical for Watch apps.

1. If your app uses `CMAccelerometer` or `CMSensorRecorder` data, design it to expect data only when the app is onscreen.

2. Prepare for your task being suspended by processing the data in the block of `performExpiringActivity(withReason:using:)`.

Where to go from here?

In this chapter, you've seen how to access Apple Watch's pedometer data directly on the Watch. Getting cumulative data is pretty straightforward, but daily data requires some effort. It gets messy if you need more than a day's data when the app restarts.

Fortunately, there's another way to access historical pedometer data, and the next chapter tells you all about it! HealthKit provides access to huge amounts of data from multiple devices, and you can create a `HKStatisticsCollectionQuery` to get daily data for several days all at once, with much less date-wrangling!

This chapter's app doesn't use the pedometer's `currentCadence` and `currentPace` properties, or track pedometer events, because these are more relevant in a workout timeframe:

- **Running at a high cadence** is more efficient and can prevent injuries; the article at bit.ly/2tQYgNo describes how to find your optimal running cadence.

- **A brisk walking pace** has fitness benefits—the article at abt.cm/1eniFAK tries to answer "How Fast is Brisk Walking?".

- Workout apps should omit periods when the user isn't moving, to calculate accurate values of average cadence and pace.

You could create a Watch app that shows the wearer's current `currentCadence` and `currentPace`, or add these two properties to a workout app like the one in the next chapter.

> **Note:** The pedometer measures *current pace* in seconds per meter. The Workout app shows your *average pace* in minutes per kilometer or mile.

Chapter 23: HealthKit

By Scott Atkinson

If you're like me, you love the watchOS Workout app. It tracks your calories burned, heart rate and custom attributes for a large number of different workout types, and it stays in the foreground for the duration of your workout. A simple flick of the wrist quickly displays your stats. When you've completed your workout, the app saves all of the new data in the HealthKit database, where you can view it later via iPhone's Activity app or let other HealthKit-enabled apps consume it.

But, Workout is a bit simplistic. Wouldn't it be nice to create a more advanced app for the specialized exercises you do? Maybe you want to track HIIT bit.ly/1oVlhrP workouts, or process custom Core Motion data for very specific movement analysis. Well, watchOS makes it possible to build HealthKit-supported apps like Workout. In this chapter, you'll add HealthKit features to a Workout-style app for interval training!

The features of HealthKit are quite impressive; in this chapter, you'll focus on its fitness aspects. But Apple has designed a framework that allows developers to track and access nearly all facets of personal health. As you work through this chapter, be aware of other interesting health-related data that a user might want to track on their Watch.

> **Note:** Since you'll be jumping right into HealthKit on watchOS 4, we recommend you check out the following tutorials first if you don't already have some working knowledge of HealthKit:
>
> HealthKit Tutorial With Swift: Getting Started: bit.ly/1LPOmQu
>
> HealthKit Tutorial with Swift: Workouts: bit.ly/1OyW8gE
>
> Once you've worked through these tutorials and have a good understanding of HealthKit, you'll be ready to get to it.

Getting started

Released with iOS 8, HealthKit provides a rich system for storing and retrieving health data on a device. Its features include:

- A defined schema for categorizing health-related data, like workouts, body measurements and nutrition

- A set of units and measurement types that enable easy conversions and formatting

- A secure, shared database for storing health information

- Access-control features that allow users to grant various levels of access to apps

- A programming interface for querying, writing and deleting health data

- The Health app, where users can review all of the health data on their devices

Since then, HealthKit has shown steady improvements in tracking specific data types and introducing Apple Watch support. HealthKit's watchOS 4 functionality includes:

- The ability to create a **workout session** that places the Watch in a special mode where the app can receive sensor data and continue running in the foreground

- Access to the same programming interface as in iOS

- Seamless data synchronization between the Watch and a paired iOS device

- The ability to contribute data to the iOS Activity app

- The ability to collect workout data in the background

Well, that was a bit of a sprint through the new HealthKit features. I hope you're not too out of breath to learn more!

Introducing Groundhog

Begin by checking out the **Groundhog** starter project. It's a lot like the Apple Workout app, but it allows the user to set up an interval training workout, or one that records a repeating set of "Active" and "Rest" intervals within one session. Read more about interval training here: bit.ly/1I82m3t

Open **Groundhog.xcodeproj** and have a look around. The app contains a working version of a watch interval timer as well as a simple iOS app that allows you to see your recorded workouts. You won't see any data yet in the iOS app, as you've not yet recorded any data to HealthKit.

Choose the **Groundhog WatchKit App** scheme, and build and run. It will look like this:

Select a workout type, adjust your intervals by selecting time periods with the digital crown and tap **Go**. You'll see the timer repeat your increments over and over. Just like the movie *Groundhog Day*, it doesn't seem to end. Fear not... to stop the workout timer, force press and choose the **Stop** menu item. Finish by attempting to save the workout — it won't yet save to the HealthKit datastore. That's where you come in!

Provisioning for HealthKit

When using HealthKit, you must provision your app targets with the HealthKit entitlement.

> **Note:** To provision your app correctly and use HealthKit, you must have a valid Apple Developer account. If you don't have a valid account, the HealthKit permission requests you write in the next section will fail.

Select the **Groundhog** project from the project navigator and then select the **Groundhog** project in the editor. Select the **Build Settings** tab and scroll to the very bottom. You'll see a user-defined variable named **W4T_BUNDLE_PREFIX**. Select the existing value and enter your own. Any string will do, but generally, it's best to use your domain in reverse order.

This will change the bundle identifiers for each target in the project so that they use your own prefix, making them unique. Now you need to enable the HealthKit entitlement in each target. Still in the project editor, select the **Groundhog** target, then select the **Capabilities** tab, scroll down to HealthKit and turn **on** the capability.

Repeat the same steps for the **Groundhog WatchKit Extension** target. Finally, clean (**Shift-Command-K**) and build (**Command-B**) your targets. Your app is now properly provisioned and ready to run on your devices.

Asking for permission

Your users' health data is among the most private they may share with you. As a result, Apple has created a very fine-grained permissions system. Unlike the binary options for Location Services or access to Contacts, you need to ask your users for access to specific types of data.

Like asking for location services permissions, iOS requires the developer to explain why they want to access and write HealthKit related data. Before you can begin asking for

HeatlhKit permissions, you must edit you app's **info.plist** to add the reasons. In Xcode, in the **Groundhog** folder, Control-click on **Info.plist** and select **Open As\Source Code**. At the bottom of the file, before the closing `</dict>` tag, add the following:

```
<key>NSHealthUpdateUsageDescription</key>
<string>Groundhog saves interval workouts to your phone's
HealthKit data store.</string>
<key>NSHealthShareUsageDescription</key>
<string>Groundhog accesses health data so that saved workouts
can be accessed later.</string>
```

The two keys simply give reasons for why the app wants to save and read data.

In the **Shared\HealthKit\Services** folder, open **HealthDataService.swift**. The `HealthDataService` class provides a number of methods that your app will use to access a device's HealthKit data. Notice there are a number of `HKObjectType` constants at the top of the file; you'll use these throughout the app. Also, an internal `HKHealthStore` object has been declared. This is the main object you'll use to interact with HealthKit.

Immediately below `init()`, add the following:

```
func authorizeHealthKitAccess(
    _ completion: ((_ success:Bool, _ error:Error?) -> Void)!) {

  let typesToShare = Set([
    HKObjectType.workoutType(),
    energyType,
    cyclingDistanceType,
    runningDistanceType,
    hrType
    ])
  let typesToSave = Set([
    energyType,
    cyclingDistanceType,
    runningDistanceType,
    hrType
    ])

  healthKitStore.requestAuthorization(
    toShare: typesToShare, read: typesToSave) {
    (success, error) in
    completion(success, error)
  }
}
```

Here you create two sets of `HKObjectTypes`: a set of types that you wish to read, and a set of types that you want to write back to HealthKit. In this case, you want to read and write the same types of data. With these sets created, you call `requestAuthorization(toShare:read:completion:)` on the `healthKitStore` object.

Now you need to call this new method. Open **WorkoutTypesInterfaceController.swift**. This is the interface controller that you'll first present to the user. Locate `willActivate()` and add the following after the call to `super`:

```
let healthService:HealthDataService = HealthDataService()
healthService.authorizeHealthKitAccess { (success, error) in
  if success {
    print("HealthKit authorization received.")
  } else {
    print("HealthKit authorization denied!")
    if error != nil {
      print("\(String(describing: error))")
    }
  }
}
```

When the interface controller activates, you simply create an instance of your `HealthDataService` and make a call to its `authorizeHealthKitAccess()` method.

There's one more thing to do before you test this. In reality, it's not the Watch that requests HealthKit permissions; instead, the host iPhone app presents an interface. So you'll need to present and handle the results of the user's interactions with that UI.

Open **AppDelegate.swift** and import HealthKit:

```
import HealthKit
```

Then add the following before the closing brace of the `AppDelegate` class:

```
let healthStore = HKHealthStore()
func applicationShouldRequestHealthAuthorization(
  _ application: UIApplication) {
  healthStore.handleAuthorizationForExtension {
    (success, error) in
  }
}
```

iOS invokes this method when the watchOS 4 extension calls `requestAuthorization(toShare:read:completion:)`. Here you ask the iPhone app to handle the authorization. When the user completes the request, the completion block is fired. In your case, there's nothing to do, so you simply leave the block empty.

You're ready to go, so build and run the WatchKit app. A couple of things will happen: The Watch will show an alert telling you to open the app on your phone, and at the same time, the phone will show a similar alert.

Tap **Open "Groundhog"** on the iOS device. Groundhog will launch and present you with the "Health Access" screen. Tap **Turn All Categories On** and then **Allow**.

Note the explanations you added to **Info.plist** are displayed in the "Health Access" screen.

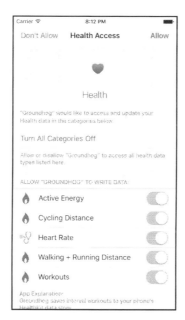

> **Note**: As of Xcode 9 Beta 6, requesting HealthKit access from the watch could fail with the following warning: `Error Domain=com.apple.healthkit Code=5 "Transaction block failed without an error.".` If it happens to you, try uninstalling the app from the iPhone, then, from Xcode, build and run again

It's possible, in fact likely, that your users will open the iOS app before launching Groundhog from their Watches, so you should probably make sure you request HealthKit access there, too. In Xcode, open **WorkoutListViewController.swift** and insert the following code at the end of `viewDidLoad()`:

```
let healthService:HealthDataService = HealthDataService()
healthService.authorizeHealthKitAccess {
  (accessGranted, error) in

  DispatchQueue.main.async {
    if accessGranted {
      self.refresh(nil)
    } else {
      print(
        "HK access denied! \n\(String(describing: error))"
      )
    }
  }
}
```

This code is pretty much the same as the code you placed in the `AppDelegate`, but in this case, you refresh the controller's `tableView` if the user grants access. Also, note that you dispatch to the main queue: `HKHealthStore` doesn't make any guarantees that it will call completion blocks on the queue that a method was called on. So you'll need to dispatch UIKit methods to the main queue, as usual.

Now you have access to HealthKit for reading and writing. Let's create some data!

Creating workout sessions

The class that really brings a watchOS fitness app to life is `HKWorkoutSession`. When HealthKit starts a session with an instance of this class, it places the Watch in workout mode. In this state, your app will stay in the foreground until the user clicks the digital crown or stops the session; at the same time, you'll be able to query for additional sensor data that the Watch generates, like distance and heart rate. You will also be able to configure your app to continue collecting workout information even when it is in the background.

HKWorkoutSession is a relatively simple object that's created with a
HKWorkoutConfiguration object. A delegate protocol provides information about the
current state of a workout session.

To implement this protocol, open **WorkoutSessionService.swift** from the **Groundhog
Watchkit Extension\Workout\Services** group and give it a quick review. This class
provides all of the functionality for managing a workout session, querying sensor data
and returning that information to a delegate. Much of it has been implemented already,
but there are important details left for you to finish.

First, locate the beginning of the class implementation. After the declaration of the
configuration constant, declare an HKWorkoutSession object:

```
let session: HKWorkoutSession
```

Now, find init?(configuration:) and add the following code after
self.configuration is set:

```
let hkWorkoutConfiguration = HKWorkoutConfiguration()

hkWorkoutConfiguration.activityType =
  configuration.exerciseType.activityType

hkWorkoutConfiguration.locationType =
  configuration.exerciseType.location
```

This creates a new HKWorkoutConfiguration object from the configuration object
that is passed in. The WorkoutConfiguration class provides a place to store an exercise
type as well as the parameters for the durations of the workout's active and rest times.

Below the code you just added, add the following:

```
do {
  session = try HKWorkoutSession(
    configuration: hkWorkoutConfiguration)
} catch {
  return nil
}
```

Here, you simply create the workout session with the configuration you just created.

Now you'll set a delegate. This is going to create a small compile error which you'll fix in
just a moment. At the bottom of the same init?(configuration:) method, add the
following:

```
session.delegate = self
```

The `WorkoutSessionService` object will act as the delegate for the `HKWorkoutSession` you just created.

You need to implement `startSession()` and `stopSession()` so that the user can start the session from the Watch's interface.

First locate the `startSession()` stub method and add the following:

```
healthService.healthKitStore.start(session)
```

Locate `stopSession()` and replace the current implementation with the following:

```
healthService.healthKitStore.end(session)
```

These two methods simply start and stop the `HKWorkoutSession`, respectively. Note that you're doing this via methods on an instance of `HKHealthStore`.

At this point, you've probably seen a pesky little error around where you assign the session's `delegate` to `self`. That's because you haven't implemented the `HKWorkoutSessionDelegate` protocol yet. So, add a new class extension to the bottom of **WorkoutSessionService.swift**:

```
extension WorkoutSessionService: HKWorkoutSessionDelegate {

}
```

Add two helper methods to the class extension to do the work of reacting to the session's changing state:

```
fileprivate func sessionStarted(_ date: Date) {
  startDate = date
  // Let the delegate know
  delegate?.workoutSessionService(
    self, didStartWorkoutAtDate: date)
}

fileprivate func sessionEnded(_ date: Date) {
  endDate = date
  // Let the delegate know
  self.delegate?.workoutSessionService(
    self, didStopWorkoutAtDate: date)
}
```

So far, these are simple methods; they record the start and end dates of the workout and then let the `WorkoutSessionService`'s delegate know that the session's state changed.

Now implement the `HKWorkoutSessionDelegate` protocol's two methods:

```
func workoutSession(_ workoutSession: HKWorkoutSession,
  didChangeTo toState: HKWorkoutSessionState,
  from fromState: HKWorkoutSessionState, date: Date) {

  DispatchQueue.main.async {
    switch toState {

    case .running:
      self.sessionStarted(date)
    case .ended:
      self.sessionEnded(date)
    case .paused:
      break
    default:
      print("Something weird happened. Not a valid state")
    }
  }
}

func workoutSession(_ workoutSession: HKWorkoutSession,
  didFailWithError error: Error) {
  sessionEnded(Date())
}
```

When the workout session's state changes, you simply call the appropriate helper method you just created. In the event of an error, you treat it as if the session has ended by calling `sessionEnded()` This app does not implement a "Pause" feature, so for now, this state will be ignored.

That's all you need to do to create an `HKWorkoutSession`! Open **ActiveWorkoutInterfaceController.swift** and check out `awake(withContext:)`. Notice that the `NSTimer` is set to call the `start()` method after a short countdown. If you scroll down to its implementation, you'll see where a `WorkoutSessionService` instance is created and started.

Build and run the Watch app to see what happens. Once the app starts, choose a workout type, adjust your time intervals and get sweating! Maybe some wind sprints?

Notice that now, the app doesn't go to the background. When you look at your Watch, Groundhog appears! Click the digital crown to return to the watch face. Notice the little green running man at the top of the screen? This indicates that the watch is running an `HKWorkoutSession`. Tap the icon to return to Groundhog. **Force press** to stop and save the workout.

Wait... did you implement a way to save the workout? Nope, not yet. But now you will.

Saving a workout

Open **HealthDataService_Watch.swift** from the **Groundhog Watchkit Extension** group and have a look around. The first thing you'll notice is that this is an extension of the `HealthDataService` class.

If you look at the File Inspector, you'll see that the file is a member of only the "Groundhog Watchkit Extension" target. Since `HKWorkoutSession` is a member of HealthKit in watchOS 4 but not in iOS, you'll add functionality to save it only on the Watch side.

Add the following code inside the extension:

```swift
func saveWorkout(_ workoutService: WorkoutSessionService,
  completion: @escaping (Bool, Error?) -> Void) {

  // 1
  guard let start = workoutService.startDate,
    let end = workoutService.endDate else {return}

  // 2
  var metadata =
    workoutService.configuration.dictionaryRepresentation()
  metadata[HKMetadataKeyIndoorWorkout] =
    workoutService.configuration
      .exerciseType.location == .indoor

  // 3
  let workout = HKWorkout(
    activityType: workoutService.configuration
      .exerciseType.activityType,
    start: start,
    end: end,
    duration: end.timeIntervalSince(start),
    totalEnergyBurned: workoutService.energyBurned,
    totalDistance: workoutService.distance,
    device: HKDevice.local(),
    metadata: metadata)
```

```
  // 4
  healthKitStore.save(workout) { (success, error) in
    // 5
    completion(success, error)
  }
}
```

That looks like a lot! But it's actually pretty straightforward:

1. First, you check to make sure that the app has recorded both a start and end date. If not, you bail out, as `saveWorkout()` was called prematurely.

2. Next, you create a small dictionary of metadata that you'll store in the HealthKit database. This data records the interval time configuration so you can reconstitute the intervals later.

3. You create an `HKWorkout` object with data from the `WorkoutSessionService` and its `configuration`.

4. You use the `HKHealthStore` object to save the workout.

5. Finally, you call the method's completion handler.

Before you can save a workout, make sure you call `save(_:withCompletion:)`. Open **WorkoutSessionService.swift** and locate `saveSession()`. Add the following implementation to the method:

```
healthService.saveWorkout(self) { (success, error) in
  if success {
    self.delegate?.workoutSessionServiceDidSave(self)
  }
}
```

You call this method, which simply saves the workout, when the user taps "Save" after stopping a workout. `saveWorkout(_:completion)` is the method you've just added to the `HealthDataService` extension, which internally invokes `save(_:withCompletion:)`.

If everything goes well, then the `WorkoutSessionService`'s delegate gets notified that the workout was saved.

Build and run the Watch extension. Run through a workout and then stop and save it.

At this point, through the magic of HealthKit, your data will be saved both to a small, local data store on the Watch and also to the main data store on the paired iOS device.

Open **Groundhog** on the iOS device. Pull down to refresh the main workout list; your saved workout should appear. Cool, right? Now open the **Health** app on the iOS device. Select the **Health Data** tab and navigate to **Activity\Workouts\Show All Data**.

Select one of the workouts to view detailed data about it.

> **Note**: Apple doesn't indicate in its documentation when exactly HealthKit data is synchronized from the Watch to the iOS device. In my experience, data can take a couple of minutes to appear, so if you experience a delay, keep trying: it will show up eventually.

Displaying data while working out

Now that you're saving basic workout data, it's time to get something a bit more interesting from the Watch: heart rate and other information. In this section, you'll create an "anchored query" that runs through the duration of the workout session and returns heart rate data as it's discovered.

An anchored object query

To receive continually updating data during an `HKWorkoutSession`, you must create an `HKAnchoredObjectQuery`. An anchored query is similar to a standard `HKQuery`, with a couple of notable exceptions:

• An anchored query returns a cursor, or anchor, to the last data returned by the query. You use that anchor to get only new data created since the last anchor.

- An anchored query contains an `updateHandler` property accepting a closure which, when set, indicates that the query should continue to run until it's explicitly stopped.

These two features are exactly what you need to get continuous streams of heart rate, energy and distance data. Open **WorkoutSessionService_Queries.swift** from the **Groundhog Watchkit Extension** group. This is a class extension of `WorkoutSessionService`. You'll see a couple of methods already written that you'll use in a bit — but first, you'll create a new query to get heart rate data.

First, implement `newHRSamples(_:)` to record the samples returned by the query:

```
private func newHRSamples(_ samples: [HKSample]?) {
  // Abort if the data isn't right
  guard let samples = samples as? [HKQuantitySample],
    samples.count > 0 else {
    return
  }
  DispatchQueue.main.async {
    self.hrData += samples
    if let hr = samples.last?.quantity {
      self.heartRate = hr
      self.delegate?.workoutSessionService(
        self, didUpdateHeartrate: hr.doubleValue(for: hrUnit))
    }
  }
}
```

This method first checks to see if the samples are the right type and that there's at least one of them. Then it updates the workout session's heart rate with the latest value, adds all the samples to an internal array and finally, informs the delegate that there's new heart rate data.

Add the following code at the top of the extension:

```
internal func heartRateQuery(withStartDate start: Date)
  -> HKQuery {
  // 1
  let predicate = genericSamplePredicate(withStartDate: start)

  // 2
  let query:HKAnchoredObjectQuery = HKAnchoredObjectQuery(
    type: hrType,
    predicate: predicate,
    anchor: hrAnchorValue,
    limit: Int(HKObjectQueryNoLimit)) {
    (query, sampleObjects, deletedObjects, newAnchor, error) in

    // 3
    self.hrAnchorValue = newAnchor
    self.newHRSamples(sampleObjects)
```

```
    }

    // 4
    query.updateHandler = {
      (query, samples, deleteObjects, newAnchor, error) in

      self.hrAnchorValue = newAnchor
      self.newHRSamples(samples)
    }

    // 5
    return query
  }
```

Did that elevate your heart rate a bit? It's straightforward, though. Here's the breakdown:

1. Using two of the `HKQuery` helper methods, you create a predicate to get all data since the workout session began on the current device.

2. Next, you create an `HKAnchoredObjectQuery` instance indicating you'd like to get heart rate samples using the predicate you just created, anchored to the anchor point you're tracking.

3. Upon the initial response from the query, you record a new anchor value and add the new heart rate samples to the data set. More on that in a moment.

4. Also, you create an `updateHandler` to indicate you want the query to run until you tell it to stop. The handler will treat the new samples just like in the initial response.

5. You return the query object to the caller.

Now that you can create a query, you'll put it to use. Open **WorkoutSessionService.swift** from the **Groundhog Watchkit Extension** group and locate `sessionStarted(_:)`. At the top of the method, create three new queries and append them to an array of queries:

```
// Create and Start Queries
queries.append(distanceQuery(withStartDate: date))
queries.append(heartRateQuery(withStartDate: date))
queries.append(energyQuery(withStartDate: date))
```

Loop through the array to start each one in turn:

```
for query in queries {
  healthService.healthKitStore.execute(query)
}
```

Don't worry, you didn't miss creating `distanceQuery` and `energyQuery`. These methods are very similar to `heartRateQuery`, which you created above, so they were provided for you in the sample code.

They're structurally very similar but they query for different pieces of data: energy and distance.

Build and run the Watch app. Start a new workout and get to work. After a few seconds, you'll see your heart rate appear on the Watch!

Background Data Processing

watchOS 4 adds a number of different background processing modes. By simply adding an entry to the Extension's **Info.plist** you can enable background workout data processing.

In the **Groundhog WatchKit Extension** folder, control-click on **Info.plist** and select **Open As\Source Code**. At the bottom of the file, before the closing `</dict>` tag, add the following:

```
<key>WKBackgroundModes</key>
<array>
  <string>workout-processing</string>
</array>
```

Build and run again. Start a workout; while it's running, move the app to the background using the digital crown. Wait a bit, and then bring Groundhog back to the foreground. It's tough to tell, but your workout data was saved, even while the app was running in the background!

Saving the sample data

If you saved that last workout and checked it out in the Health app, you may have noticed that you haven't yet saved any detailed data. Previously, when you implemented `saveWorkout(_:completion:)`, you simply saved the workout, which didn't include any detailed data.

You have to explicitly save that data, so open **HealthDataService_Watch.swift** from the **Groundhog Watchkit Extension** and locate `saveWorkout(_:completion:)`.

After you create your workout object, add the following code:

```
// Collect the sampled data
var samples: [HKQuantitySample] = [HKQuantitySample]()
samples += workoutService.hrData
samples += workoutService.distanceData
samples += workoutService.energyData
```

Do you recall in your implementation of `newHRSamples(samples:)` that you appended those samples to the `hrData` array? Here's why! In the code above, you concatenate all of the heart rate, distance and energy samples into one array. All of the samples are of the same type, `HKQuantitySample`, so you can do this in a type-safe manner with Swift.

Finally, replace the completion handler for the call to `healthKitStore.saveObject()` with the following:

```
guard success && samples.count > 0 else {
   completion(success, error)
   return
}

self.healthKitStore.add(samples, to: workout) {
   (success, error) in
   completion(success, error)
}
```

If there are no samples, or the initial save wasn't successful, you simply call the passed-in completion handler. However, if there are samples to be saved, you can add them to the current workout by calling `add(_:to:completion:)` on the `HKHealthStore`. It will immediately save the data and call a completion handler when it's done.

Build and run the Watch app one last time, perform another workout and save it.

You must really be exhausted by now! Open Groundhog on your iOS device and check out all the interval data you just saved. How well did you do?

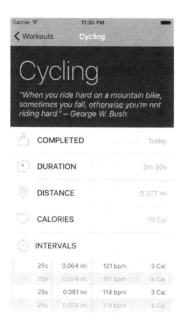

Handling pause or resume

Added in watchOS 3 is a gesture that will pause or resume a workout running in the watchOS Workout app, regardless of whether the app is currently on-screen. New for watchOS 4 is the ability to capture that gesture in your own workout app. Simply by pressing the side button and the digital crown at the same time, a `pauseOrResumeRequest` event is generated. Based on the current state of the `HKWorkoutSession` you can choose how to handle the request. You'll add simple support for the `pauseOrResumeRequest` now.

Open **WorkoutSessionService.swift** from the **Groundhog Watchkit Extension\Workout\Services** group and scroll to the extension that implements the `HKWorkoutSessionDelegate` protocol. Add the following code after the `workoutSession(_:didFailWithError:)` method:

```swift
func workoutSession(_ workoutSession: HKWorkoutSession,
                    didGenerate event: HKWorkoutEvent) {
  switch event.type {
  case .pauseOrResumeRequest:

    switch workoutSession.state {
    case .running: self.stopSession()
    case .notStarted: self.startSession()
    default: break
```

```
        }

        break
    default:
        break
    }
}
```

The `workoutSession(_:didGenerate:)` delegate method is called when the workout session needs to report an event like a lap was completed, or that the user stopped moving. In this method, you look only for events with the type `pauseOrResumeRequest`. You then check the state of the `HKWorkoutSession`. Since Groundhog does not implement a "pause" feature, you simply stop the session if it is running, or start the session if it is not running.

Build and run on your watch. Start up a workout like usual. While the timer is running, press both the digital crown and the side button. You will be asked if you want to save the workout... just like if you had force pressed on the display. Nice, now restart the timer and get back to that workout!

Where to go from here?

Congrats! You've just made a watchOS 4 workout app! In this chapter, you've seen a number of exciting techniques for using the Health functions of the Apple Watch:

- How to ask for permissions to save and access HealthKit data from the Watch

- How to create a workout session and get health data while the session is running

- How to save a workout to the HealthKit data store and add your own metadata

Take some time to explore the rest of Groundhog — the project contains a lot more HealthKit functionality. Pay particular attention to the various `Formatter` instances in **Constants.swift**. You'll see a couple of health-related formatters that will definitely make your life easier. You can see them in action in **IntervalCell.swift**.

Maybe you could use Core Motion information in your own health-related app, such as a jumping jack counter or measuring the speed of a tennis swing. If you haven't already, check out, Chapter 22, "Core Motion" for details about how to integrate step counts and other motion-related data. Also check out the chapters in background processing. Maybe you'll want to update Groundhog's snapshot using the new `WKSnapshotRefreshBackgroundTask`.

Finally, take a moment to explore `HealthKitUI` to implement your own activity rings right inside Groundhog!

Chapter 24: Core Location

By Soheil Azarpour

Core Location is one of the most eagerly awaited features that came to the Apple Watch in watchOS 2! This framework lets you determine the current position of the device — and you can even query the user's location when the iPhone isn't in the vicinity of the Watch.

In this chapter, you'll learn how to make best use of location services on the Watch, both as a standalone device and in coordination with a paired iPhone.

The starter project you'll use in this chapter is called **Meetup Finder**. With Meetup Finder for Apple Watch, users can find iOS-related meetups in their areas with just a twist of the wrist, along with details such as the meetup location and the next upcoming event. It couldn't get any easier than that!

But the app isn't quite there yet: It doesn't know about the user's current location. Your job is to add Core Location to the Watch app. By the end of this chapter, the app will look like this:

Meetup Finder uses the popular meetup.com API to find meetups near you. Most of the code to interact with the API is already in the starter project; the next section will walk you through signing up for API access.

> **Note:** Already a member of Meetup.com? You can skip right to "Getting your API key" below.

Getting started

Download the starter project for this chapter and open it up in Xcode.

Before you dive into the code, you need to sign up with Meetup.com as a developer so you can get your own private token to access its API.

Open your favorite browser and go to meetup.com.

Click **Sign up** and you'll be presented with the sign up page. Either choose a social registration, or click on **Or sign up with email** to go to a form where you can enter your name, email address and password. Click **Continue** when done, and make sure you enter a valid email address, because you'll need to verify your registration:

You'll be informed that a validation email has been sent to your email address. Wait for that email to arrive, then open it and follow the instructions to verify and enable your Meetup account.

Once you're verified, go to meetup.com again and log in:

Getting your API key

After you're logged in, go to secure.meetup.com/meetup_api/key in your browser, where you can find your private API key:

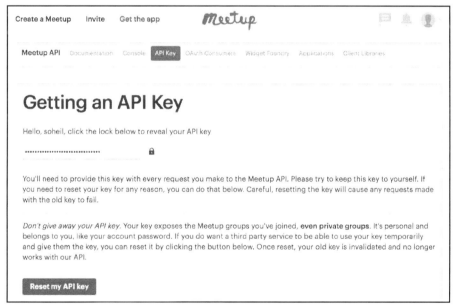

Click the **Lock** icon to reveal the key, and copy it to the clipboard.

To verify that you've done everything right and your token works, load bit.ly/1Mcmb04 in your browser. Make sure you replace **YOUR_API_TOKEN** in the address bar with your real API token. If something goes wrong, you'll get a response that says, You are not authorized to make that request.

Getting locations

With your API token in hand, you're ready to get some meetups in your vicinity using your current location. Open the **Meetup Finder** starter project in Xcode and open **MeetupRequestFactory.swift**. Replace **YOUR_API_TOKEN** with your new token:

```
private let APIKey = "YOUR_API_TOKEN"
```

Similar to iOS, a watchOS app must also provide a good reason why it requires access to the user's location and ask the user for authorization. There are two types of location authorizations:

- **When in use**, where the location is only accessible while the app is in the foreground.

- **Always**, where the location is accessible at any time, as long as the device is running.

You provide a reason for each authorization type by setting NSLocationWhenInUseUsageDescription, NSLocationAlwaysAndWhenInUseUsageDescription or both in the app's Info.plist.

Meetup Finder already has both keys set in the Info.plist of the iPhone app. You'll need to update the Info.plist for the Watch extension with NSLocationWhenInUseUsageDescription as Meetup Finder will only query user's location when user is in the app.

Expand the **Meetup Finder Watch Extension** group in the project navigator and find and open **Info.plist**. Click the + button that appears next to **Information Property List** to add a new item to its dictionary, like so:

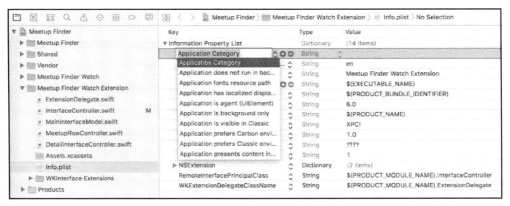

Enter NSLocationWhenInUseUsageDescription for the key name and make it a String type. Enter "Meetup Finder uses your location to find meetup groups in your vicinity." in the value field. When you're done, your new entry will look like this:

Requesting user authorization

Open **InterfaceController.swift** and add the following `import` statement:

```
import CoreLocation
```

You've linked against the `CoreLocation` framework, so you can begin to use it. Add the following variable to `InterfaceController`:

```
private let locationManager = CLLocationManager()
```

`CLLocationManager` is the main class responsible for location delivery.

You must ask the user's permission for either type of location authorization and check the current authorization status before requesting location updates. If you're familiar with Core Location on iOS, you know it's possible to subscribe to ongoing location updates from Core Location. New in watchOS, you can also ask for either a one-time location update via an API called `requestLocation()`, or subscribe to continuous change notifications by calling `startUpdatingLocation()`.

In Meetup Finder, you want to request the location every time the app launches. Add the following to the end of `willActivate()`:

```
let authorizationStatus =
  CLLocationManager.authorizationStatus()

handleLocationServicesAuthorizationStatus(
  status: authorizationStatus)
```

Here, you check the location services authorization status of your app via `authorizationStatus()`, a class method on `CLLocationManager`, and then pass its value to `handleLocationServicesAuthorizationStatus(_:)`, a helper method

you'll implement next. Find the implementation
`handleLocationServicesAuthorizationStatus(_:)` in `InterfaceController`
and update it as follows:

```
func handleLocationServicesAuthorizationStatus(
  status: CLAuthorizationStatus) {
  switch status {
  case .notDetermined:
    handleLocationServicesStateNotDetermined()
  case .restricted, .denied:
    handleLocationServicesStateUnavailable()
  case .authorizedAlways, .authorizedWhenInUse:
    handleLocationServicesStateAvailable()
  }
}
```

In the code above, you evaluate all possible values of the authorization status and call
appropriate helpers for each case:

- **.notDetermined**: You get this state when the user hasn't yet made a choice with
  regard to your app. This is usually the case when the user first installs the app and
  hasn't run it yet. You'll handle this case in
  `handleLocationServicesStateNotDetermined()`.

- **.restricted** and **.denied**: You get either of these states when the user has explicitly
  denied location access to your app, or location services are unavailable due to other
  circumstances. Either way, you'll treat this case in a generic way in
  `handleLocationServicesStateUnavailable()`.

- **.authorizedAlways** or **.authorizedWhenInUse**: Both of these cases mean the user
  has granted your app access to location services. Since `.authorizedAlways`
  and `.authorizedWhenInUse` are mutually exclusive, and you can only have one type
  of authorization at a time, you consider each case a happy path and handle it in
  `handleLocationServicesStateAvailable()`.

It's time to implement these helper methods. First, for the "not determined" case, find
the implementation of `handleLocationServicesStateNotDetermined()` in
`InterfaceController` and update it as follows:

```
func handleLocationServicesStateNotDetermined() {
  updateVisibilityOfInterfaceGroups()
  messageLabel.setText(pendingAccessMessage)
  locationManager.requestWhenInUseAuthorization()
}
```

In `handleLocationServicesStateNotDetermined()`, you update the visibility of
some interface elements, and then you display an appropriate message to the user and

instruct her to make a decision. At the end, you ask the `CLLocationManager` instance to request authorization for `authorizedWhenInUse` status by calling `requestWhenInUseAuthorization()`.

Depending on what type of authorization the app asks for by calling either `requestWhenInUseAuthorization()` or `requestAlwaysAuthorization()`, the system displays the request, along with an appropriate reason for access, in a system prompt to the user.

The system prompt in iOS is an alert view and you have to open the iPhone app in order to see it. In watchOS, the system will show the prompt to the user, but they don't have the option to accept or reject it and they have to open the iOS app for that purpose.

To see this in action, select the **Meetup Finder Watch** scheme and then build and run. You'll be presented with the following:

In the iPhone app, you'll see the system alert view while the Watch displays an appropriate message.

However, you will notice that, even if the app is not currently running, the alert is displayed anyway.

Next, you'll handle unauthorized access. From within Xcode, stop running the app. In the iPhone simulator, deny location access to the app by tapping **Don't Allow**. If you're prompted by iOS to go to the Settings, simply tap on **Cancel**.

Still in **InterfaceController.swift**, define `handleLocationServicesStateUnavailable()` as follows:

```
func handleLocationServicesStateUnavailable() {
  interfaceModel.state = MainInterfaceState.notAuthorized
  updateVisibilityOfInterfaceGroups()
  messageLabel.setText(locationAccessUnauthorizedMessage)
}
```

Here, you update the state of your interface model by setting it to `MainInterfaceState.notAuthorized`, update the visibility of the UI and display a message telling the user that location services aren't available.

Now build and run the Meetup Finder Watch scheme; you'll see the following:

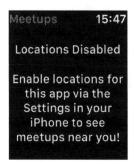

Since a user can authorize location services at any time, you need to make sure you get notified about changes in authorization status. The `CLLocationManager` will notify its delegate about these changes, so you'll need to comply with the `CLLocationManagerDelegate` protocol and implement `locationManager(_:didChangeAuthorization:)`.

Open **InterfaceController.swift** and add the following line to the end of `awake(withContext:)`:

```
locationManager.delegate = self
```

Xcode gives you an error. Now that you've indicated you want to be the delegate of `CLLocationManager`, you need to comply with the `CLLocationManagerDelegate` protocol.

Add the following extension to the end of **InterfaceController.swift**:

```
extension InterfaceController: CLLocationManagerDelegate {
  func locationManager(
    _ manager: CLLocationManager,
    didChangeAuthorization status: CLAuthorizationStatus) {

    handleLocationServicesAuthorizationStatus(status: status)
  }

  func locationManager(
    _ manager: CLLocationManager,
    didUpdateLocations locations: [CLLocation]) {

    // More to come ...
  }

  func locationManager(
    _ manager: CLLocationManager,
    didFailWithError error: Error) {

    // More to come ...
  }
}
```

Here you implement `locationManager(_:didChangeAuthorization:)` and call into the helper method you've already implemented to handle any changes in the authorization status while your app is running. To prevent a runtime exception, you also add placeholders for `locationManager(_:didUpdateLocations:)` and `locationManager(_:didFailWithError:)`.

Using the location

You've handled the error conditions, so now it's time to work with the user's location once she grants the app access. Still in **InterfaceController.swift**, find and update implementation of the following method:

```
func handleLocationServicesStateAvailable() {
  updateVisibilityOfInterfaceGroups()
  showLoadingMessageIfApplicable()
  locationManager.requestLocation()
}
```

Once again, you update the visibility of some UI elements, display a loading message and request a one-time location update from the `CLLocationManager` instance.

Now build and run the Meetup Finder Watch scheme. First the app will present you with a message that location services are disabled. In the iPhone simulator, open the **Settings** app, go to **Privacy\Location Services\Meetup Finder** and change the authorization to **While Using the App**. Once you make that change, you'll see the Watch screen update:

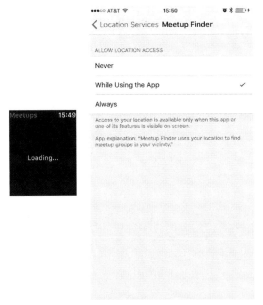

That's excellent, but where are the locations? Stop the simulator and go back to Xcode. In **InterfaceController.swift**, find the implementation of `locationManager(manager:didUpdateLocations:)` and update its implementation as follows:

```
func locationManager(
    _ manager: CLLocationManager,
    didUpdateLocations locations: [CLLocation]) {

    print("Did update locations: \(locations)")
    guard let mostRecentLocation = locations.last else { return }
    queryMeetupsFor(mostRecentLocation)
}
```

`CLLocationManager` calls this delegate method when Core Location generates location events. Since you called `requestLocation()` earlier, you'll get only one callback here. The array of `locations` always contains at least one `CLLocation` object. The objects in the array are organized by the order in which they occurred. So if you get more than one `CLLocation` at a time, the most recent location update will be at the end of the array.

Once you get the most recent location, you pass it to a helper method, `queryMeetupsFor(location:)`, to query the backend for meetups. Afterward, the UI will update automatically.

Build and run; this time, depending on the speed of your Internet connection, you'll briefly see the loading message, and then the interface will update to show meetup groups:

> Note: If the Watch simulator continues to show "Loading…" and doesn't get a location fix, stop the simulator. Select the **Meetup Finder** scheme, and build and run in the iPhone simulator once. Then, build and run the Meetup Finder Watch scheme in the Watch simulator again.

Handling location errors

Before you move on to the next section, there's another delegate method in `CLLocationManagerDelegate` that you should implement to cover all possible cases: `locationManager(manager:didFailWithError:)`.

Update its placeholder implementation as follows:

```
func locationManager(
  _ manager: CLLocationManager,
  didFailWithError error: Error) {

  print("CL failed: \(error)")
  interfaceModel.state = .error
  updateVisibilityOfInterfaceGroups()
  messageLabel.setText("Failed to get a valid location.")
}
```

Here you log the error to the console, update the state of the interface model and display an error message to the user. There isn't a great way for you to force an error to see this code in action, but you can feel good knowing you built in decent error handling for your users. :]

Limiting location queries

Just like any other backend service, the Meetup API has safety measures to prevent excessive requests. If you exceed your allotted number of requests, Meetup will temporarily deny your requests. That won't lead to a good experience for your users. To avoid such a problem, you'll update the app so it only queries the backend when a user's location has changed enough to grant a new update.

Open **InterfaceController.swift** and find the implementation of `isLocationChangedSignificantly(_:)`. This helper method takes a `CLLocation` input and returns a Boolean to indicate whether it's a significant change. Update its implementation as follows:

```
func isLocationChangedSignificantly(
  _ updatedLocation: CLLocation) -> Bool {

  guard let lastQueriedLocation = lastQueriedLocation
    else { return true }
  let distance =
    lastQueriedLocation.distance(from: updatedLocation)
  return distance >
    CLLocationDistance(MeetupSignificantDistanceChange)
}
```

Here, you use a convenience method on `CLLocation` to get the distance from the input `CLLocation` and the last queried location you have stored in a property on `InterfaceController`. The distance is in meters. If the distance is more than `MeetupSignificantDistanceChange`, you flag it as a significant change by returning `true`.

`MeetupSignificantDistanceChange` is calculated based on the app's business logic. Since the app queries the backend for meetups within a radius of 50 miles from the current location, if the new location is less than 20 miles away from the previous location, the code considers the results of the previous query to be still valid. `MeetupSignificantDistanceChange` is the result of converting 20 miles to meters; that's 20 * 1609.34.

Next, add the following `if` statement to the end of `willActivate()` in **InterfaceController.swift**:

```
if let lastQueriedLocation = lastQueriedLocation {
  queryMeetupsFor(lastQueriedLocation)
}
```

If you have a valid location from the last time you queried the API, you dispatch a request to load content for that location. You query the Meetup API at the same time as you try to get a location fix from `CLLocationManager`.

When `locationManager(_:didUpdateLocations:)` returns the result of the location update, you dispatch another request if the new location is significantly different from the previous one. This way, you won't have to wait for `CLLocationManager` to complete before loading the content. You'll have already loaded the content using the last valid location.

> **Note:** If the iPhone isn't reachable and the Watch has to get a location fix on its own, the best accuracy level you can get from `CLLocationManager` is `kCLLocationAccuracyHundredMeters`.

Build and run in the Watch simulator. First, the app will present you with meetup groups near the current location. Now, from the Watch simulator menu, select **Hardware\Lock** to lock the Watch screen and then select **Debug\Location\Apple**. Again, from the menu select **Hardware\Lock** to unlock the Watch. This triggers `willActivate()`. Verify that the app has updated the meetups based on the new location.

Your app can now discover local meetups. This would be a great time to take a break and contemplate new social networking options!

Coordination

Even though the Watch app can now query location updates and display appropriate content, it's still functioning in conjunction with its iPhone app. It's a good idea to leverage this partnership and make the Watch app faster, more efficient and more responsive to location changes.

The app already leverages the Watch Connectivity framework to communicate the last location update from the iPhone app to the Watch app. Location updates come via a `session(_:didReceiveApplicationContext:)` callback of `WCSessionDelegate`. When the Watch app isn't running, Watch Connectivity caches any updates and will deliver the most recent one on the next launch.

> **Note**: Watch Connectivity is covered in depth in Chapter 16, "Watch Connectivity" and Chapter 19, "Advanced Watch Connectivity".

Next, you'll update the Watch app so that it uses the cached location. Open **InterfaceController.swift** and find and update the implementation of `session(_:didReceiveApplicationContext:)` as follows:

```swift
func session(
  _ session: WCSession,
  didReceiveApplicationContext
  applicationContext: [String:Any]) {

  guard let data = applicationContext["lastQueriedLocation"] as?
    Data else { return }

  guard let location =
    NSKeyedUnarchiver.unarchiveObject(with: data) as?
    CLLocation else { return }

  queryMeetupsFor(location)
}
```

Here, you try to get location data from the context dictionary, turn it into a `CLLocation` and query meetups for that location by calling `queryMeetupsFor(location:)`.

It's time to see the coordination in action. If you change your iPhone location access authorization to "Always", it will turn on continuous updates.

In the iPhone simulator, open the **Settings** app, go to **Privacy\Location Services\Meetup Finder** and change the authorization to **Always**.

There's a little coordination required to get this working on two simulators, so follow along carefully:

1. Select the **Meetup Finder** scheme for the iPhone, and build and run the iPhone app in the iPhone simulator. To verify that everything is working as expected, check out the console log for the iPhone app. You'll see that the app is logging locations at approximately 1-second intervals. You'll also see a message in the console that says `"New query to meetups ignored because current location hasn't changed significantly."`

2. Still running the iPhone app in the simulator, open the Watch app in the Watch simulator. Verify that you see similar results in the Watch app.

3. While both apps are running, select **Debug > Location > Apple** from the iPhone simulator menu. After a moment, both the iPhone and the Watch app will update their contents for the new location.

Background location updates

Since continuous location updates aren't available in watchOS, it's not surprising that background location updates aren't available either. Another area where you can benefit from the coordination between the iPhone app and the Watch app is when the iOS app received continuous location updates.

In previous versions of iOS, you simply had to turn on Background Modes for your iPhone app target and select the entry for location updates:

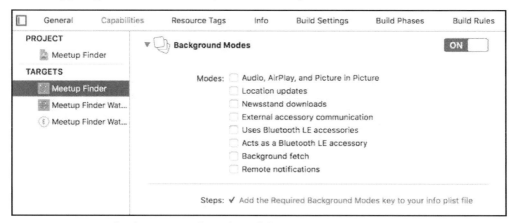

Since iOS 9, you also have to set the value of the `allowsBackgroundLocationUpdates` property on your `CLLocationManager` instance to `true`. You must set this property for each `CLLocationManager` instance.

To make sure Meetup Finder continues receiving location updates in the background, open **MeetupsViewController.swift**, find the implementation of `viewDidLoad()` and add the following line after you set the delegate of `locationManager`:

```
locationManager.allowsBackgroundLocationUpdates = true
```

Build and run to give it a try. Again, there's a little coordination required to get this working on two simulators:

1. Select the **Meetup Finder** scheme for the iPhone, and build and run the iPhone app in an iPhone simulator.

2. Still running the iPhone app in the simulator, open the Watch app in the Watch simulator. Verify the Watch app loads its content successfully and that it matches the content of the iPhone app.

3. From the iPhone simulator menu, select **Hardware\Home** to put the iPhone app in the background. You can verify that the iPhone has entered the background by checking the console log for an `Application entered background.` message.

4. Simulate a location change by selecting **Debug\Location\Custom Location** from the iPhone simulator menu. Enter **51.50998000** for **Latitude** and **-0.13370000** for **Longitude**. Verify that the Watch app updates with new meetups for the new location after a few seconds.

Optimizations

The app is in great shape, but there's a small problem: It continues to receive a significant number of background updates. The chance that the user has moved to a significantly new location is quite low, and the present way the app queries for location updates will quickly drain the user's battery.

To optimize the app for better power management, open **MeetupsViewController.swift**, find the implementation of `queryMeetupsFor(location:)` and add the following to the end of the function:

```
locationManager.allowDeferredLocationUpdates(
    untilTraveled: MeetupSignificantDistanceChange,
    timeout: MeetupSignificantDistanceChangeTimeout)
```

Here you update the private helper method that queries Meetup based on a given `CLLocation`. This method runs the query only if the new location is significantly different from the previous location, so it makes sense to tell `locationManager` that you're happy with the current location fix until the user's location changes significantly.

`allowDeferredLocationUpdatesUntilTraveled(_:timeout:)` is an old API that's been around for a long time, but it probably hasn't gotten as much attention as it deserves. In the context of the Apple Watch and its limited resources, you should optimize your code as much as you can to deliver a good user experience.

Using this API, you tell the GPS hardware to store new locations internally until the specified distance or timeout conditions are met.

When either criteria is met, the location manager calls `locationManager(_:didFinishDeferredUpdatesWithError:)` to end deferred locations and delivers the cached locations via `locationManager(_:didUpdateLocations:)`. If your app is in the foreground, the location manager won't defer the delivery of events.

There are a number of things to keep in mind about `allowDeferredLocationUpdates(untilTraveled:timeout:)`:

1. The location manager allows deferred updates only when GPS hardware is available on the device and the desired accuracy is set to `kCLLocationAccuracyBest` or `kCLLocationAccuracyBestForNavigation`. Otherwise, you'll get a `kCLErrorDeferredFailed` error. If you set the accuracy to an unsupported value, you'll get a `kCLErrorDeferredAccuracyTooLow` error.

2. You must set the `distanceFilter` property of the location manager to `kCLDistanceFilterNone` or you'll get a `kCLErrorDeferredDistanceFiltered` error.

3. Call `allowDeferredLocationUpdates(untilTraveled:timeout:)` after you've received your first batch of location updates. You call this once you're happy with your current updates and want to defer future updates until the distance or time criteria are met.

4. Don't call `allowDeferredLocationUpdates(untilTraveled:timeout:)` more often than necessary. Each subsequent call cancels the previous deferral. You should keep track of whether updates are currently deferred and call it again only when you want to change the deferral criteria.

5. The system delivers deferred updates only when it enters a low-power state. Deferred updates don't occur during debugging, because Xcode prevents your app from sleeping and so prevents the system from entering that low-power state.

Now that you've created a fantastic Meetup Finder app, get out there and meet up with your fellow iOS devs!

Where to go from here?

Core Location is a powerful technology that has many practical and far-reaching applications. In this chapter, you learned about the framework and its limitations in WatchKit Extensions and watchOS 3. You implemented authorization handling, requested locations and leveraged the Watch Connectivity framework to coordinate your iPhone and Watch apps to communicate continuous and background updates.

If you're thinking of improving the user experience by expanding coordination between the iPhone and Watch apps, head over to Chapter 16, "Watch Connectivity", to learn all about it. If you're still curious about Core Location, here are some resources that you can check out:

- Location and Maps Programming Guide apple.co/1DhsyJS
- WWDC16 Session 716 - Core Location Best Practices apple.co/2aBmH8x
- WWDC15 Session 714 - What's new in Core Location apple.co/1EcdPD7.

Chapter 25: Core Bluetooth

By Audrey Tam

Core Bluetooth has been around since 2011 on macOS and iOS, since 2016 on tvOS, and now it's available on watchOS, with an Apple Watch Series 2.

What's Core Bluetooth? It's Apple's framework for communicating with devices that support Bluetooth 4.0 low-energy, often abbreviated as **BLE**. And it opened up standard communication protocols to read and/or write from external devices.

Back in 2011, there weren't many BLE devices, but now? Well, this is from the Bluetooth site (bit.ly/2j1DqpU):

"More than 31,000 Bluetooth member companies introducing over 17,000 thousand new products per year and shipping more than 3.4 billion units each year."

BLE is everywhere: in health monitors, home appliances, fitness equipment, Arduino and toys. In July 2017, Apple announced its collaboration with hearing-aid implant manufacturer Cochlear, to create the first "Made for iPhone" implant. (bit.ly/2vZahUU)

> **Note:** Cochlear is an Australian company, and the app was built here in Australia! (bit.ly/2uztOHX)

But you don't have to acquire a specific gadget to work through this chapter: the sample project uses an iPhone as the BLE device. In the app you'll build, the iOS device provides a two-part service: it transfers text to the Watch, or the Watch can open Maps at the user's location on the iOS device. The first part is a Swift translation of Apple's BLE_Transfer sample app. It's a very useful example, because it shows how to send 20-byte chunks of data. I added the Maps part to show you how to send a control instruction to the BLE device, and I thought it's something you'd want to do from the Watch Maps app: open Maps on a larger display so you can find what you need more easily!

Getting started

> **Note:** The simulator does not support Core Bluetooth. To run the starter app, you need two iOS 11 devices. To run the finished app, you need an Apple Watch Series 2 and an iOS 11 device.

Open the starter app. Build and run on two iOS devices. Go into **Settings** to trust the developer, then build and run again.

Select **Peripheral Mode** on one device, and **Central Mode** on the other. Tap the peripheral's **Advertising** switch to start advertising.

`PeripheralViewController` has a `textView`, prepopulated with some text. When the central manager subscribes to `textCharacteristic`, the peripheral sends this text in 20-byte chunks to the central, where it appears in a `textView`:

Modify the peripheral's text, and tap **Done**. The peripheral sends the updated value to the central:

> **Note:** I deleted "sample" from the first sentence.

When the central has discovered `mapCharacteristic`, `CentralViewController` bar button's title changes to **Map Me**. Tap this bar button, allow the app to use your location, then tap **Map Me** again: the peripheral device opens the **Maps** app, at your location.

Stop the app on both devices. It's time to learn about Core Bluetooth, and look at some code!

> **Note:** You can tap **TextMeMapMe** to go back to the peripheral view, but sometimes, Maps keeps re-opening.

What is Core Bluetooth?

Lets's start with some vocabulary.

A Generic Attributes (GATT) profile describes how to bundle, present and transfer data using Bluetooth Low Energy. It describes a use case, roles and general behaviors. A device's GATT database can describe a hierarchy of services, characteristics and attributes.

The classic server/client roles are the central app and the peripheral or accessory. In the starter app, either iOS device can be central or peripheral. When you build the Watch app, it can only be the central device:

A peripheral offers **services**. For example, Blood Pressure monitor is a pre-defined GATT service (bit.ly/2lfpqwB). In the starter app, the service is TextOrMap.

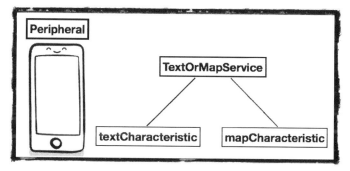

A service has **characteristics**. The Blood Pressure service has pre-defined GATT characteristics (bit.ly/2vOhGqa): Blood Pressure Feature, which blood pressure monitor features this sensor supports, and Blood Pressure Measurement. A characteristic has a value, properties to indicate operations the characteristic supports, and security permissions.

A central app can read or write a service's characteristics, such as reading the user's heart rate from a heart-rate monitor, or writing the user's preferred temperature to a room heater/cooler. In the starter app, the `TextOrMap` service has two characteristics: the peripheral sends updates of the `textCharacteristic` value to the central; when the central writes the `mapCharacteristic` value, the peripheral opens the **Maps** app at the user's location.

Services and characteristics have **UUIDs**: universally unique identifiers. There are predefined UUIDs for standard peripheral devices, like heart monitors or home appliances. You can use the command line utility `uuidgen` to create custom UUID strings, then use these to initialize `CBUUID` objects.

The **Maximum Transmission Unit** (MTU) is 27 bytes, but really 20 bytes, because each packet uses 7 bytes as it travels through three protocol layers. You can improve throughput using write without response, if the characteristic allows this, because you don't have to wait for the peripheral's response. If your central app and peripheral are running on iPhone 7, the new iPad Pro, or Apple Watch Series 2, you get the **Extended Data Length** of 251 bytes! I'm testing the sample app on an iPhone SE, so I'm stuck with 20-byte chunks.

Overview

The most interesting classes in the Core Bluetooth framework are `CBCentralManager` and `CBPeripheralManager`. Each has methods and a comprehensive delegate protocol, to monitor activity between central and peripheral devices. There's also a peripheral delegate protocol. Everything comes together in an intricate dance!

Think about what the devices need to do:

• Central devices need to scan for and connect to peripherals. Peripherals need to advertise their services.

• Once connected, the central device needs to discover the peripheral's services and characteristics, using peripheral delegate methods. Often at this point, an app might present a list of these for the user to select from.

• If the central app is interested in a characteristic, it can subscribe to notifications of updates to the characteristic's value, or send a read/write request to the peripheral. The peripheral then responds by sending data to the central device, or doing something with the write request's value. The central app receives updated data from another peripheral delegate method, and usually uses this to update its UI.

• Eventually, the central device might disable a notification, triggering delegate methods of the peripheral and the peripheral manager. Or the central device disconnects the peripheral, which triggers a central manager delegate method, usually used to clean up.

Now look at what each participant does.

Central manager

A central manager's main jobs are:

• If Bluetooth LE is available and turned on, the central manager scans for peripherals.

• If a peripheral's signal is in range, it connects to the peripheral. It also discovers services and characteristics, which it may display to the user to select from, subscribes to characteristics, or requests to read or write a characteristic's value.

Central Manager Methods & Properties:

• Initialize with delegate, queue and optional options.

• Connect to a peripheral, with options,

• Retrieve known peripherals (array of UUIDs) or connected peripherals (array of service UUIDs).

• Scan for peripherals with services and options, or stop scanning.

- Properties: `delegate`, `isScanning`

Peripheral Manager

A peripheral manager's main jobs are to manage and advertise the services in the GATT database of the peripheral device. You would implement this for an Apple device acting as a peripheral. Non-Apple accessories have their own manager APIs. Most of the sample BLE apps you can find online use non-Apple accessories like Arduino.

If Bluetooth LE is available and turned on, the peripheral manager sets up characteristics and services. And it can respond when a central device subscribes to a characteristic, requests to read or write a characteristic value, or unsubscribes from a characteristic.

Peripheral Manager Methods & Properties:

- Initialize with delegate, queue and optional options.

- Start or stop advertising peripheral manager data.

- `updateValue(_:for:onSubscribedCentrals:)`

- `respond(_:withResult:)`

- Add or remove services.

- `setDesiredConnectionLatency(_:for:)`

- Properties: `delegate`, `isAdvertising`

Central manager delegate protocol

Methods in this protocol indicate availability of the central manager, and monitor discovering and connecting to peripherals. Follow along in the `CBCentralManagerDelegate` extension of **CentralViewController.swift**, as you work through this list:

- `centralManagerDidUpdateState(_:)` is the only required method. If the central is `poweredOn` — Bluetooth LE is available and turned on — you should start scanning for peripherals. You can also handle the cases `poweredOff`, `resetting`, `unauthorized`, `unknown` and `unsupported`, but you must not issue commands to the central manager when it isn't powered on.

- When the central manager discovers a peripheral, `centralManager(_:didDiscover:advertisementData:rssi:)` should save a local copy of the peripheral. Check the received signal strength indicator (RSSI) to see if the peripheral's signal is strong enough: -22dB is good, but two iOS devices placed right next to each other produce a much lower RSSI, often below -35dB.

If the peripheral's RSSI is acceptable, try to connect to it with the central manager's `connect(_:options:)` method.

- If the connection attempt fails, you can check the error in the delegate method `centralManager(_:didFailToConnect:error:)`. If the error is something transient, you can call `connect(_:options:)` again.

- When the connection attempt succeeds, implement `centralManager(_:didConnect:)` to stop scanning, reset characteristic values, set the peripheral's `delegate` property, then call the peripheral's `discoverServices(_:)` method. The argument is an array of service UUIDs that your app is interested in. After this, it's up to the peripheral delegate protocol to discover characteristics of the services.

- In `centralManager(_:didDisconnectPeripheral:error:)`, you can clean up, then start scanning again.

Peripheral manager delegate protocol

Methods in this protocol indicate availability of the peripheral manager, verify advertising, and monitor read, write and subcription requests from central devices. Follow along in the `CBPeripheralManagerDelegate` extension of **PeripheralViewController.swift**, as you work through this list:

- `peripheralManagerDidUpdateState(_:)` is the only required method. You handle the same cases as the corresponding `centralManagerDidUpdateState(_:)`. If the peripheral is `poweredOn`, you should create the peripheral's services, and their characteristics.

- `peripheralManagerDidStartAdvertising(_:error:)` is called when the peripheral manager starts advertising the peripheral's data.

- When the central subscribes to a characteristic, by enabling notifications, `peripheralManager(_:central:didSubscribeTo:)` should start sending the characteristic's value.

- When the central disables notifications for a characteristic, you can implement `peripheralManager(_:central:didUnsubscribeFrom:)` to stop sending updates of the characteristic's value.

- To send a characteristic's value, `sendData()` uses the peripheral manager method `updateValue(_:for:onSubscribedCentrals:)`. This method returns `false` if the transmit queue is full. When the transmit queue has space, the peripheral manager calls `peripheralManagerIsReady(toUpdateSubscribers:)`. You should implement this delegate method to resend the value.

- The central can send read or write requests, which the peripheral handles with `peripheralManager(_:didReceiveRead:)` or `peripheralManager(_:didReceiveWrite:)`. When implementing these methods, you should call the peripheral manager method `peripheral.respond(to:withResult:)` exactly once. The sample app implements only `peripheralManager(_:didReceiveWrite:)`; reading the text data is accomplished by subscribing to `textCharacteristic`.

Peripheral delegate protocol

A peripheral delegate can respond when a central device discovers its services or characteristics, or requests to read a characteristic, or when a characteristic's value is updated. It can also respond when a central device writes a characteristic's value, or disconnects a peripheral. Follow along in the `CBPeripheralDelegate` extension of **CentralViewController.swift**, as you work through this list:

- The sample app just checks the error in `peripheral(_:didDiscoverServices:)`, but some apps might present a list of `peripheral.services` for the user to select from.

- And similarly for `peripheral(_:didDiscoverCharacteristicsFor:error:)`.

- When the peripheral manager updates a value that the central subscribed to, or requested to read, implement `peripheral(_:didUpdateValueFor:error:)` to use that value in your app. The sample app collects the chunks, then displays the complete text in the view controller's text view.

- Implement `peripheral(_:didUpdateNotificationStateFor:error:)` to handle the central device enabling or disabling notifications for a characteristic. The sample app just logs the information.

- There's a runtime warning if you don't implement `peripheral(_:didModifyServices:)`, so I added this stub.

watchOS vs iOS

iOS apps can be central or peripheral, and can continue using CoreBluetooth in the background.

watchOS and tvOS both rely on Bluetooth as their main system input, so Core Bluetooth has restrictions, to ensure system activities can run. Both can be only the central device, and can use at most two peripherals at a time. Peripherals are disconnected when the app is suspended.

And the minimum interval between connections is 30ms, instead of 15ms for iOS and macOS.

Now finally, you're going to build the Watch app!

Building the Watch app

As you've done many times already, select **Xcode\File\New\Target…** and choose **watchOS\WatchKit App**:

Name the product **BT_WatchKit_App**, uncheck **Include Notification Scene**, and select **Finish**:

There are now three targets: **TextMeMapMe**, **BT_WatchKit_App** and **BT_WatchKit_App Extension**. Check that all three have the same team.

Create the interface

Open **BT_WatchKit_App/Interface.storyboard**, and drag two buttons, two labels, and a menu onto the scene. Set the background color of the buttons to different colors, and set their titles to **wait...**:

Select the two buttons, then select **Editor\Embed in\Horizontal Group**. Set each button's width to **0.5 Relative to Container**, and leave **Height Size To Fit Content**:

Set each label's **Font** to **Footnote**, and **Lines** to **0**, and set the second label's **Text** to **Transferred text appears here**:

Set the **Menu Item**'s **Title** to **Reset**, with **Image Repeat**:

Open the assistant editor, and create outlets (`textButton`, `mapButton`, `statusLabel`, `textLabel`) and actions (`textMe`, `mapMe`, `resetCentral`) in **InterfaceController.swift**.

Reduce the amount of text to send

Data transfer to the Watch is slower than to an iOS device, so open the iOS app's **Main.storyboard**, and delete the second sentence from **PeripheralViewController**'s `textView`, leaving only *Lorem ipsum dolor sit er elit lamet sample text*.

Copy-paste and edit CentralViewController code

First, select **SharedConstants.swift**, and open the file inspector to add **BT_WatchKit_App Extension** to its target membership:

Now you'll mostly copy code from **CentralViewController.swift**, paste it into **InterfaceController.swift**, and do a small amount of editing.

First, import CoreBluetooth:

```
import CoreBluetooth
```

Below the outlets, copy and paste the central manager, peripheral, characteristic and data properties, then edit `mapCharacteristic` to set the title of `mapButton`, and add a similar observer to `textCharacteristic`:

```
var centralManager: CBCentralManager!
var discoveredPeripheral: CBPeripheral?
var textCharacteristic: CBCharacteristic? {
  didSet {
    if let _ = self.textCharacteristic {
      textButton.setTitle("Text Me")
    }
  }
}
var data = Data()
var mapCharacteristic: CBCharacteristic? {
  didSet {
    if let _ = self.mapCharacteristic {
      mapButton.setTitle("Map Me")
    }
  }
}
```

This lets the user know that the Watch app has discovered the text and map characteristics, so it's now safe to read or write them.

Copy and paste the helper methods `scan()` and `cleanup()`, then copy and paste the two delegate extensions. Change the two occurrences of `extension CentralViewController` to `extension InterfaceController`:

```
// MARK: - Central Manager delegate
extension InterfaceController: CBCentralManagerDelegate {
```

and

```
// MARK: - Peripheral Delegate
extension InterfaceController: CBPeripheralDelegate {
```

In `peripheral(_:didDiscoverCharacteristicsFor:error:)`, delete the line that subscribes to `textCharacteristic`:

```
peripheral.setNotifyValue(true, for: characteristic)
```

Subscribing causes the peripheral to send the text data, so you'll move this to the **Text Me** button's action, giving the user more control over how the Watch app spends its restricted BLE allowance.

In `peripheral(_:didUpdateValueFor:error:)`, replace the `textView.text` line (where the error is) with these two lines:

```
statusLabel.setHidden(true)
textLabel.setText(String(data: data, encoding: .utf8))
```

And add this line just below the line that creates `stringFromData`:

```
statusLabel.setText("received \(stringFromData ?? "nothing")")
```

Everything happens more slowly on the Watch, so you'll use `statusLabel` to tell the user what's happening while they wait. Just before the transferred text appears, you hide `statusLabel`, to make room for the text.

Use `statusLabel` in other places: add this line to `scan()`:

```
statusLabel.setText("scanning")
```

And this line to `centralManager(_:didDiscover:advertisementData:rssi:)`:

```
statusLabel.setText("discovered peripheral")
```

And to `centralManager(_:didConnect:)`:

```
statusLabel.setText("connected to peripheral")
```

Add similar log statements to peripheral delegate methods, when services and characteristics are discovered.

Next, scroll up to `awake(withContext:)`, and copy-paste this line from `viewDidLoad()`:

```
centralManager = CBCentralManager(delegate: self, queue: nil)
```

Delete the methods `willActivate()` and `didDeactivate()`.

Now fill in the actions. Add these lines to `textMe()`:

```
guard let characteristic = textCharacteristic else { return }
discoveredPeripheral?.setNotifyValue(true, for: characteristic)
```

Tapping the **Text Me** button subscribes to `textCharacteristic`, which triggers `peripheralManager(_:central:didSubscribeTo:)` to send data.

Next, copy these lines from `mapUserLocation()` into `mapMe()`:

```
guard let characteristic = mapCharacteristic else { return }
discoveredPeripheral?.writeValue(Data(bytes: [1]), for:
characteristic, type: .withoutResponse)
```

`mapUserLocation()` and `mapMe()` do the same thing: write the value of `mapCharacteristic`, which triggers `peripheralManager(_:didReceiveWrite:)` to open the Maps app.

Before you implement `resetCentral()`, add this helper method:

```
fileprivate func resetUI() {
  statusLabel.setText("")
  statusLabel.setHidden(false)
  textLabel.setText("Transferred text appears here")
  textButton.setTitle("wait")
  mapButton.setTitle("wait")
}
```

You're just setting the label and button titles back to what they were, and unhiding `statusLabel`.

Now add these two lines to `resetCentral()`:

```
cleanup()
```

```
resetUI()
```

Build and run on your Apple Watch + iPhone. You'll probably have to do this a couple of times, to "trust this developer" on the iPhone and on the Watch. At the time of writing, instead of telling you what to do, the Watch displays this error message:

Press the digital crown to manually open the app on your Watch, and trust this developer. The app will then start, but stop it, then build and run again. Select **Peripheral** mode on the iPhone, and turn on **Advertising**.

And wait. Scanning, connection and discovery take longer when the central is a Watch instead of an iPhone. When the Watch app discovers the `TextOrMap` characteristics, it updates the button titles:

Tap **Text Me**, and wait. You'll see the text appear on the Watch, and `statusLabel` disappears:

Tap **Map Me**, and allow use of your location. Tap **Map Me** again, and the iPhone opens the Maps app at your location.

Stop the Watch app in Xcode, and close the iPhone app.

Congratulations! You've built a Watch app that uses an iPhone as a Bluetooth LE peripheral! Now you can connect all the things!

Best practices

Here are a few tips from WWDC 2017 Session 712 **What's New in Core Bluetooth** apple.co/2wE5ea4:

- Do your best to digest the *Bluetooth Accessory Design Guidelines for Apple Products* apple.co/1PjdoZh

- If possible, use pre-defined GATT services (bit.ly/2lfpqwB) and characteristics (bit.ly/2vOhGqa).

- To reduce time to connect, use the shortest advertising interval possible, and optimize for when users are trying to use the accessory — for example, when they pick it up. The Design Guidelines document, Section 3.5, lists power-efficient advertising intervals.

- To reduce time to **reconnect**, use UUID to retrieve a known peripheral, and directly connect with `central.retrievePeripherals(withIdentifiers:)`

- To speed up service discovery, use as few services and characteristics as possible, and group services by UUID size.

- To increase throughput from the central to the peripheral, use write without response when possible.

Where to go from here?

- WWDC 2017 Session 712 **What's New in Core Bluetooth** apple.co/2wE5ea4 and the **Related Videos** listed there.

- Apple documentation: Core Bluetooth Programming Guide apple.co/2vsZvpg

Chapter 26: Localization

By Ben Morrow

With the painless global distribution provided by the App Store, you can release your app in over 150 countries with only a single click. You never know where your app might take off and how that might change the fortunes of your company.

Here's a story I love:

When the Evernote app launched in 2008, it unexpectedly became very popular in Japan. Since the app was built in English, the company's leaders decided they could expand sales even faster if they optimized the interface for Japanese. The team scrambled, and with a bit of local help, they were able to offer Evernote in the new language.

Interestingly, as time went on, this move began to affect the company in larger ways. The team started traveling in Japan and noticed that some local partner companies were over 100 years old. That's when CEO Phil Libin rallied the team, saying "Let's build a company that has the long-term planning and thinking of some of these great Japanese companies, combined with the best of the Silicon Valley startup mentality. We don't just want to build a 100-year company, we want to build a 100-year startup."

Before you can run like Evernote, you first have to learn to walk. To grow your reach internationally, you'll have to make sure you've optimized the language, number formatting and layout of your app for many different regions and cultures.

In this chapter, you're going to learn how to localize your app so you can reach that larger audience, as well as learn what techniques and tools are available to aid that process.

> **Note**: As of the time of writing, there is a bug in the Watch simulator that prevents changing language and locale. In order to complete the chapter, you'll need a physical Apple Watch device (Radar #22027500). Hopefully, Apple will fix this bug in a future release.

Getting started

Launch Xcode and open the **Progress** project from the starter directory for this chapter.

You'll be making localization changes to an enterprise app for an international company with operations ranging from food production to military hardware. It has recently been involved in the political scene, but most of the time, the company flies under the radar.

One important aspect of the company's culture is to always watch the numbers. Management says this will help the company shake off a few punitive slaps on the wrist it received last year for, er, "financial shenanigans".

This app lets an employee see how close the company is to meeting its sales goals. It shows units sold and total revenue for the day, week and month. The company wants to deploy the app across divisions located in different countries.

To meet your client's expectations, you'll need to adapt the app to linguistic, regional and cultural differences, and let the text in the app change to match the user's preferences.

Internationalizing your app

Internationalization? Globalization? Localization? Translation? There are many different ways to describe the myriad of work associated with preparing your app for a more diverse group of people. In truth, there's a lot of inconsistency in how people in the industry use these different words. For the purposes of this tutorial, however, let's establish a distinction between internationalization and localization.

Internationalization is the process of making strings from storyboard or code externally editable. It also involves using formatting classes for things like dates and numbers. It's up to you, the app developer, to perform internationalization.

Localization is the process of translating those externalized strings into a given language. You'll usually hire a localization company to do this work.

Together, internationalization and localization ensure your app looks as good in Chinese or Arabic as it does in English.

Language-specific thoughts

Because languages have different average word lengths, it's crucial to set up your interface to accommodate these differences. By default, the layout engine in WatchKit lets content reflow quite easily as long as you're not setting fixed sizes. Here are some language-specific considerations to remember while you're designing an app.

The layout engine supports languages that read right-to-left, like Hebrew and Arabic. If the user selects one of these languages, the engine will automatically flip the entire interface horizontally.

As of 2015, 41% of iOS users are from either China or Japan. Neither Chinese nor Japanese uses an alphabetic script, so there are no spaces to separate words. This means your layout may look a lot terser and more compact in these languages. Consider what you'd do if the interface looked too bare with vast whitespace.

On the other end of the spectrum is German. Since it's a lengthy language compared with English, you'll always want to make sure you allow enough space in your interface to accommodate longer text. This can be especially tricky with elements like buttons, where the label can wrap to multiple lines.

Adding a language

Adding the capability for a certain language is a snap. In the project navigator, select your app's name, **Progress**. Then select the **Project** in the project and targets list. In the **Info** tab, you'll see a section for **Localizations**. Click the **+** button and choose **Spanish (es)**:

The next screen asks you which files you want to localize, showing only your storyboards and `.xib` files. Keep them all selected and click **Finish**.

At this point, Xcode has set up directories behind the scenes that contain separate storyboards for each language you selected. To see this for yourself, expand **Interface.storyboard** in the **Progress WatchKit App** group in the project navigator by clicking the disclosure triangle.

About the .strings file

Open **Interface.strings (Spanish)**. Your shiny new .strings file follows a strict but fairly simple format. First, notice the comment above each line:

```
/* Comment */
```

These comments provide a little context about where the translated text will go in the app.

Then, you'll see a key/content pair:

```
"KEY" = "CONTENT";
```

These pairs work like the key and value in a dictionary. This will be where your Spanish translations eventually reside. The Interface Builder file uses its generated names, but your .strings file later in the chapter will use more human-readable components.

> **Note:** Even though you've been writing Swift code for the entire book, don't be deceived — the strings file is not in Swift! The semicolon is required at the end of every line.

Separating text from code

Like most apps, Progress has other text that's not in your storyboard. You have literal strings in code that you insert into your UI at runtime.

As an astute observer, you may have noticed a helpful convention used in this storyboard. Any text that starts and ends with square brackets will be replaced by code at runtime.

Notice how "start date", "units sold" and "average selling price" don't have square brackets; they will *not* be replaced at runtime. Everything else with brackets will be replaced based on calculations made by the app.

For the text that will be replaced, you'll use a global function to translate literal strings in your code:

```
func NSLocalizedString(
  // 1
  key: String,
  //     2
  tableName: String,
  // 3
  bundle: NSBundle,
  // 4
  value: String,
```

```
// 5
  comment: String
) -> String
```

Here's what each parameter does:

1. This is a unique key distinguishing this string from all other strings in your code.

2. For larger, complex apps, you define a `tableName` to put different localized strings in different `.strings` files. For the purposes of this tutorial, you won't need this feature and can simply leave this parameter out.

3. The bundle parameter allows you to define a language or locale for which you want to pull a string. 99% of the time, you'll want to use the default of `NSBundle.MainBundle()`, which determines the bundle based on the user's operating system settings. Since you are happy with the default here, you can also leave this parameter out in this app.

4. The `value` is the default string, which will show up for any languages that don't have translations available. In this app, that will be the English/US string.

5. The `comment` parameter contains instructions for the person translating this string; for example, "This is the title of an alert that comes up when the user did this bad thing". This is super-important because the translator can't see the context where the app uses the string; they've only got the text.

Because you'll typically only care about the key, value and comment fields, most of your string code will look like this:

```
let localString = NSLocalizedString("FOO_KEY", value: "Foo",
  comment: "This string is shown when …")
```

Note: It's very tempting to use the default value as your key. This is a big mistake that will come back to bite you as you get deeper into localization. Consider that the same word in your language might suffice in two places — in other words, it might have two completely different meanings — but you may need two separate words for those meanings in another language.

For example, in English, the word "watch" has many meanings, including "to observe" and "wristwatch" (like an Apple Watch!). However, in Spanish you would use "observar" for "observe" and "reloj" for "wristwatch". If you had chosen to use the English "watch" as the key in `NSLocalizedString`, your keys would not be unique. You'd tear your hair out trying to find out why unexpected words had shown up in the wrong places. DON'T DO IT! Stick with using a unique key for each piece of text.

Formatting values

In addition to translating text, you'll also need to format numbers and dates correctly. There are a range of formatters available; some examples of their output are below:

NSNumberFormatter

Decimal: 3.145, Currency: $3.14, Ordinal: 3rd, Percent: 314%

NSDateFormatter

Short: 11/23/37, Medium: Nov 23, 1937, Long: November 23, 1937, Full: Tuesday, November 23, 1937 AD

NSDateComponentsFormatter

Positional: 1:10, Abbreviated: 1h 10m, Short: 1hr 10min, Full: 1 hour, 10 minutes, SpellOut: One hour, ten minutes

NSByteCountFormatter

342 KB

NSLengthFormatter

621 mi

NSEnergyFormatter

239 cal

NSMassFormatter

2,205 lb

These output examples are a small introduction to the functionality of each formatter. The full capabilities of each formatter are too lengthy to list here. Check out Apple's documentation, apple.co/2bHDhqo, for each formatter for all the juicy details.

These formatters automatically transform your numbers to use the correct punctuation for the region and the correct label for the language. Here are the differences you would see between an app running on a device in Spain, versus one running in the United States:

- **NSNumberFormatter**: "3,142" versus "3.142" and "€3,14" versus "$3.56"

- **NSDateFormatter**: "21/12/12" versus "12/21/12"

- **NSLengthFormatter**: "1,000 km" versus "621 mi"

- **NSEnergyFormatter**: "1,000 J" versus "239 cal"

- **NSMassFormatter**: "1,000 kg" versus "2,205 lb"

There are a couple of caveats to watch out for when you use these formatters in your own apps:

1. For currency, you need to account for the exchange rate before formatting.

2. Store length, energy and mass as SI units: meters, joules and kilograms. Those formatters provide convenient methods to convert from the raw SI value into the correct locale formatting.

Formatting values in the Progress app

Open **ProgressInterfaceController.swift** in the **Progress WatchKit Extension** group by selecting it in the project navigator. There are three formatters in `awake(withContext:)`: `dateFormatter`, `currencyFormatter`, and `numberFormatter`. These have properties to set their style so that they'll be ready for use in the methods that follow. I'll explain their output as you walk though code in the next section.

With the formatters in place, you're ready to internationalize the literal strings in your code.

Preparing literal strings for localization

There are several places where you can see strings baked into the code. You now know that you'll have to somehow extract those strings so that a translator can work with them.

The first bit of code that has string literals is the `switch` statement in `awake(withContext:)`. Replace it with the following:

```
switch context {
  case "week":
    dayCount = 7
    self.setTitle(NSLocalizedString("oneWeekTitle",
      value: "7-day",
      comment: "label at the top of report for past 7 days"))
  case "month":
    dayCount = 30
    self.setTitle(NSLocalizedString("oneMonthTitle",
      value: "30-day",
      comment: "label at the top of report for past 30 days"))
  default:
    self.setTitle(NSLocalizedString("oneDayTitle",
      value: "Today",
      comment: "label at the top of report for just today"))
}
```

The changes here are small. You use `NSLocalizedString()` in place of a normal `String`. Notice the unique keys and the descriptive comments for each piece of text. As

I mentioned earlier, these are both important. Using unique keys will make sure every piece of text receives a unique translation instead of reusing one from a different place in the app. Comments are important so the translator can understand where this text is in the app.

The next string literal is inside `updateDateLabel()`. This method prepares a date with the correct regional formatting and fills in the corresponding label in the interface. Replace the contents of that method with this code:

```
// 1
let formattedStartDate =
  dateFormatter.string(from: summary.startDate)
// 2
let preamble = String(
  format: NSLocalizedString("dateStartLabelFormat",
  value: "beginning %@",
  comment: "start of a date range: beginning 7/11/11"),
  formattedStartDate)
// 3
let title = dayCount > 1 ? preamble : formattedStartDate
dateLabel.setText(title)
```

Here's what's going on:

1. You use the date formatter to put the month or day first, depending on regional preference. `.ShortStyle` will give output in the format "12/31/2021".

2. You're using `NSLocalizedString` as you did before, but instead of a string literal, you have a formatted string. You arrange the text this way because in some languages, the word to explain the beginning of a date range might go after the date, such as the equivalent of "31/12/2021 started". When you have text labeling a number, you want to use this string initializer with a format so the translator can swap the terms if it's appropriate for the language. In case you're unfamiliar with the format syntax, `%@` simply means "the representation of a string will go here". You can see all the string format specifiers at apple.co/1PTDz8t. The `%@` works well with the .strings file and allows the translator to choose where the date will go in the translation string.

3. The ternary operator is an inline `if`-statement. If there's more than one day, use the preamble text; otherwise, just the date is fine.

The next method, `updateRevenueLabels()`, will fill in the current status and revenue goal labels inside the progress ring. This method has some text that needs localizing. Update its contents with the following code:

```
// 1
let totalRevenue =
  currencyFormatter.string(from:
    NSNumber(value: summary.totalRevenue))
```

```
statusLabel.setText(totalRevenue)
// 2
guard let totalGoal =
  currencyFormatter.string(from:
    NSNumber(value: summary.totalGoal)) else {
    return
}
// 3
let totalGoalText = String(
  format: NSLocalizedString("totalGoalLabel",
  value: "of %@",
  comment: "before the total amount, like: of $500"),
  totalGoal).uppercased()
goalLabel.setText(totalGoalText)
```

Here's the breakdown, step by step:

1. The number formatter for currency will use the correct currency symbol and punctuation according to the regional preference, like "€5,07". The currencyFormatter has its maximumFractionDigits set to zero so there won't be any more precision than a whole integer, like "€5".

2. The totalGoal uses the currency formatter as well. This time, you're ensuring you get a string with guard let before proceeding. The number formatter can return nil if it can't parse the value. The String(format:) initializer expects a non-nil value, so you have to make sure the totalGoal is unwrapped.

3. You use NSLocalizedString as before, with one addition. uppercased() will ensure the text is delivered in all caps, like the design in the storyboard.

The last string literal in the file is in updateUnitLabels(), which calculates the average selling price per unit. Replace its implementation with this code:

```
guard let formattedTotalUnits =
  numberFormatter.string(from:
    NSNumber(value: summary.totalUnits)) else {
    return
}
let totalUnitsText = String(
  format: NSLocalizedString("totalUnitsLabelFormat",
  value: "%@ units",
  comment: "describing the total number of units sold"),
  formattedTotalUnits)
unitsLabel.setText(totalUnitsText)
let avgSellingPrice =
  summary.totalRevenue / Double(summary.totalUnits)
let formattedAvgPrice =
  currencyFormatter.string(from:
    NSNumber(value: avgSellingPrice))
averageSellingPriceLabel.setText(formattedAvgPrice)
```

This code doesn't introduce any new concepts; you simply use the best practice with number and string formatters. The number formatter will deliver the number as a string with the correct thousands separator, depending on the region.

Congratulations — you've internationalized your app! You can't test the language in the simulator, though, because the strings haven't been translated yet. That will come next. You can, however, test that the number formatters are working correctly. To do that, you need to perform a bit of setup to run a different language and locale in the simulator.

Running a language scheme

The fastest way to test language and locale in the simulator isn't what you might expect. You could, of course, go into the simulator's Settings app and change the language of the iPhone and the Watch, but thankfully, there's a less cumbersome way — a **run scheme**.

Open the **Scheme** menu and click **Manage Schemes**:

Select **Progress WatchKit App**, and using the **Gear** menu, choose **Duplicate**:

Name the scheme **watchOS Spanish**. Select the **Run** tab from the sidebar and select the **Options** tab along the top. Change the **Application Language** to **Spanish** and the **Application Region** to **Europe\Spain**.

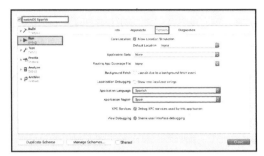

Click **Close**, and **Close** again to exit the scheme editor. You're ready to see if all of this work has been worth it! Run the new **watchOS Spanish** scheme.

Note: It's a known issue for Xcode that the language and region scheme for watchOS doesn't work in the simulator currently. As a workaround, install the app on a physical device.

You can change the language settings in the Apple Watch app for iPhone in My Watch\General\Language & Region. Change the **Watch Language** to **Español (Spanish)** and the **Region Format** to **Spain**. Once you've got this, hop back into Xcode. Make sure your iPhone is connected with the USB cable. Select the **Progress WatchKit App** scheme and choose your your [iPhone + Apple Watch] as the run device.

If you see a Code Signing error, you need to add your developer account name as the "Team" in the Xcode Project settings for each Target. In the project navigator, select your project, **Progress**. In the project and targets list, locate the Target section. Go through each target - the iOS app, the WatchKit Extension, and the WatchKit App - and add your developer account name in the **Team** drop-down.

Localizing the app

The time has come to translate the text in the app. This is a simple out-and-back-in process. You'll generate a **.xliff** (**XML Localization Interchange File Format**) file for each language.

With **Progress** selected in the project navigator, click **Editor\Export For Localization**:

Change the name to **ToTranslator** and the location to your **Downloads** folder. Ensure that **Spanish** is selected, and click **Save**:

To edit this file, you're going to use an online tool. A real translation shop would have a more robust tool that parses the XML into a user interface to make the file easier to work with.

Open your favorite browser on your Mac and navigate to bit.ly/1PySGTR.

Click **Choose File** and browse the **es.xliff** file you just generated. Click **Start Translating**.

You can see a list of all the files that need localized strings. Within each file, the strings show the `source` text as a header and have a text box for the `target` text:

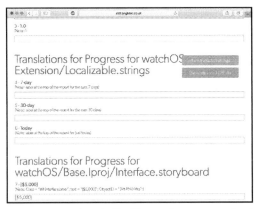

If you're curious and want to view the XML file as plaintext, it looks like this:

```
<source>7-day</source>
<target>7 días</target>
<note>label at the top of the report for the past 7 days</note>
```

It's much nicer to have a user interface to edit the values. Fill in the **target** text boxes on the web tool with these important translations:

> **Note:** This section is limited to the translations you need, so not all the fields on the form are listed here. These translations use the format: `[source]` | `[target]`

Translations for Progress WatchKit App/Base.lproj/Interface.storyboard

- date | fecha

- units sold | unidades vendidas

- average selling price | precio medio de venta

Translations for Progress WatchKit Extension/Localizable.strings

- beginning %@ | a partir %@

- Today | Hoy

- 30-day | 30 días

- 7-day | 7 días

- of %@ | de %@

- %@ units | %@ unidades

You can leave the rest of the fields alone. There is, however, one caveat: every field needs to have a value; you can't leave any blank. If you do, when you import the file into Xcode, the import wizard will crash.

So for the fields that currently have an empty text box, copy the `source` text header and paste it in the `target` text box.

These include:

Translations for Progress WatchKit App/Info.plist

- Progress WatchKit App

- `$(PRODUCT_NAME)`

Translations for Progress WatchKit Extension/Info.plist

- Progress for watchOS Extension

- `$(PRODUCT_NAME)`

Translations for Progress/Info.plist

- `$(PRODUCT_NAME)`

That was a lot of work, but it will pay off in the end! Once you're done editing the text boxes, click **Generate new XLIFF file** in the upper-right part of the screen.

Your computer will download the generated file. Hop back into Xcode. With **Progress** selected in the project navigator, click **Editor\Import Localizations**.

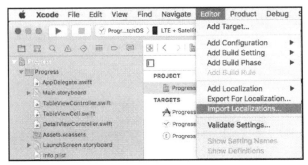

Browse to the generated file, **new.xliff**, in your **Downloads** folder. Select it and click **Open**. Xcode will run through the process of importing the localizations. If you filled out all the fields, you won't run into any errors.

Previewing the localization

The time has come to see the result of all your hard work. There are different ways to see the translated text in your app, but the fastest way is to view it directly in the storyboard.

Open **Interface.storyboard** in the **Progress WatchKit App** group by selecting it in the project navigator. Select the [**Today**] **Scene** in the storyboard:

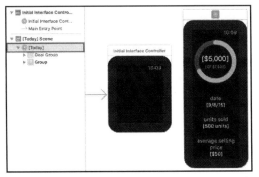

Then open the **assistant editor** and choose the **Preview** pane. In the lower-right, there's a language tool; choose **Spanish**. Scroll the interface inside the Watch down to reveal the text below the image.

Your translated strings are visible: "fecha", "unidades vendidas", and "precio medio de venta". Notice how "unidades vendidas" is cut off. You could fix that by allowing multiple lines on that label. Xcode is also drawing your attention to untranslated strings by transforming that text into all caps, as in "UNITS". You'll learn how to see this text and test the translations from the code soon enough.

But first, try a different technique. Since languages like German can be extra long, select **Double-Length Pseudolanguage** from the language tool at the lower right. Then scroll the Watch interface down again:

The preview duplicates the content inside each user interface text element, offering a quick check to see what happens when there's a lot more text. The double-length pseudolanguage is also a great way to test how your app would handle very large numbers.

In this case, some of the labels cover parts of images and others flow off the side of the screen. You'd have your work cut out for you if you wanted to prep the interface for German, but for now, let's stay focused on Spanish.

Run the app using the **Progress WatchKit App** scheme on your physical device with its language settings changed.

Jolly good show — or rather, *¡alegre buen espectáculo*!

Here's a quick check of what your efforts have yielded:

• You've translated text from literal strings in the code

• You've translated text from the storyboard

• Numbers use a period as the thousands separator

• Date components are in the correct order

• Currency uses the euro symbol

> **Note**: As of the time of writing, there is a bug in Xcode. Importing translations with XLIFF fails to generate base language strings for WatchKit apps. Curiously, the XLIFF import *does* work correctly for iPhone apps. Any time you use `NSLocalizedString(_:value:comment:)` in a WatchKit app, you will always see the translated string even if you run the app in English (Radar #22501637).
>
> In this app for example, the page title will always be in Spanish, for example, "Hoy". The fix is to add a Base language translation of the .strings file manually. By following the screenshot below, you can get English strings back into the app. Hopefully, Apple will fix this bug in a future release.

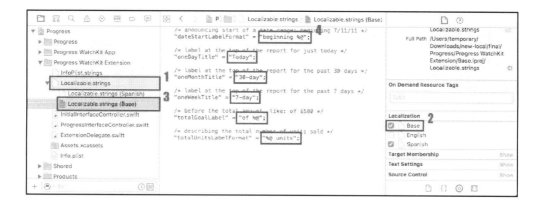

Where to go from here?

You now have a firm understanding of working with how to work with languages and locale formatting. At WWDC 2015, Apple announced that 69% of App Store revenue - more than two thirds — comes from *outside* of the United States. That's why it can be lucrative for your app to speak your customer's language.

This is a vast topic, though, so if you want to dive deeper, the "Internationalizing Your Text Code" section of **Apple Watch Programming Guide** covers some of the steps you need to take for localization: apple.co/1LBzUNV.

For localizing the words themselves, you may be able to get away with using Google's free translation service at translate.google.com, but the results are hit or miss. If you can spare a few bucks, there are several third-party vendors listed on this blog post: bit.ly/2w6mdEE. Pricing varies from vendor to vendor, but is typically less than 10 cents per word.

If you're looking to be at the top of your game, here's a couple of bonus tips:

You can use **Localizable.strings** file for image names, too. See if you can display a different image for Spanish speakers in your app by using `setImageNamed(_:)` with `NSLocalizedString(_:comment:)` for the image name.

Apple has introduced new `Unit` classes to Foundation; while you didn't need them for this app, they might be handy for your future projects. They work across languages and locales automatically, so if you can use them, you'll save a ton of boilerplate code:

- `UnitAcceleration`
- `UnitAngle`
- `UnitArea`

- UnitConcentrationMass

- UnitDispersion

- UnitDuration

- UnitElectricCharge

- UnitElectricCurrent

- UnitElectricPotentialDifference

- UnitElectricResistance

- UnitEnergy

- UnitFrequency

- UnitFuelEfficiency

- UnitLength

- UnitIlluminance

- UnitMass

- UnitPower

- UnitPressure

- UnitSpeed

- UnitTemperature

- UnitVolume

Here's a quick overview of how you'd use a `Unit` as a `Measurement` in an app. Paste this into a Swift playground to see it in action:

```
// 1
let distanceTravelled = Measurement(value: 5, unit:
  UnitLength.miles)
// 2
let distanceToGo = Measurement(value: 1, unit:
  UnitLength.kilometers)
// 3
let tripDistance = distanceTravelled + distanceToGo
// 4
if distanceTravelled > distanceToGo {
  print("On the home stretch")
}
let formatter = MeasurementFormatter()
// 5 mi (US user)
// 7.047 km (Canadian user)
let result = formatter.string(from: distanceTravelled)
```

Here's what's happening with this code:

1. The distance travelled is calculated in miles.

2. The distance to go is calculated in kilometers.

3. Even though the inputs are different units, you can add, subtract, multiply and divide them.

4. You can even compare them to each other when the inputs are different units.

5. The `MeasurementFormatter` automatically returns the correct locale and language for the user's device.

As you can see, `Units` and `Measurement` can be a joy to work with. You don't need a .strings file for these; they have the correct language automatically!

Now that your app is ready for use across the world, may your WatchKit skills take you far and wide!

Chapter 27: Accessibility

By Ben Morrow

App developers get into this business to help people do amazing things with their devices. For those users with motor, visual, hearing, or learning impairments, you can do something even more amazing: empower them to use their devices to the fullest.

iOS has an impressive array of accessibility features, including VoiceOver, Switch Control, Assistive Touch, Zoom and Guided Access. The Apple Watch is no different; it boasts many of these same features.

In this chapter, you'll discover the accessibility features available in watchOS and learn about the classes and methods available in WatchKit. Then, you'll implement many of those SDK features in a stock tracker app, making the interface more accessible to users living with visual impairments.

Getting started

The sample app for this chapter, BigMovers, shows the stocks with the biggest gains or losses for the day. Using sample stock data for some tech companies, the starter project draws each stock's graph in real time and renders it as an image. It sorts the list of stocks by those that had the highest percentage change, positive or negative. During the rest of this chapter, you'll make the app accessible for users with visual impairments by changing the interface to work with VoiceOver.

Open **BigMovers** in Xcode from the starter directory for this chapter.

Instead of using the simulator, you'll want to test the app on a real Watch.

Running on a device requires code signing. You'll need to add your developer account to the Xcode Project settings. In the project navigator, select your project, **BigMovers**. In the project and targets list, locate the Target section. Go through each target - the iOS app, the WatchKit Extension, and the WatchKit App - and add your developer account name in the **Team** drop-down:

Next, make sure your iPhone is connected with the USB cable. Select the **BigMovers WatchKit App** scheme and choose your iPhone and Watch as the run devices:

Build and run the app, and you'll see a page-based layout showing you the five-day earnings graph for different companies.

> **Note:** The app may take several minutes to install and run on a physical Watch device. Stay patient and wait until the app shows up on the Watch screen.

Assistive technology overview

Let me introduce Ava, an enthusiastic iOS and Apple Watch fan with a serious visual impairment. She'll walk you through her day and, along the way, introduce all of the accessibility features available on the Apple Watch.

Once you've learned how Ava uses these accessibility features on the Watch, you'll make BigMovers a little more accessible for a user such as Ava.

Settings on the Watch

There are several accessibility features available in the **Settings** Watch app. Open the app using a real device and navigate to **General\Accessibility** to try out these features.

VoiceOver

VoiceOver is an alternate interface for users with visual impairments. The idea behind it is simple: VoiceOver dictates whatever is under the user's finger.

For example, when Ava taps on the Clock app icon on the Home screen, VoiceOver highlights the icon with a white rectangle and reads aloud the app's name, "Clock".

Ava can use VoiceOver on the clock face, on the Home screen or inside any app. In addition to tapping, Ava can drag her finger across the screen slowly to hear interface objects read aloud, or she can swipe left and right quickly to hear items read aloud sequentially. Since a single tap on an interface item triggers the VoiceOver dictation, Ava double-taps when she wants to activate an item such as a button.

When VoiceOver is activated and the clock face is active, Taptic Time will tell Ava the time silently and discreetly using a series of distinct taps from the Taptic Engine.

Zoom

Zoom magnifies the interface so that it's easier to see. With Zoom turned on, only part of the screen is visible, so Ava uses the digital crown to scroll the viewable area horizontally. When the viewfinder reaches the end of the screen area, it hops down to the beginning of the next line like a carriage return.

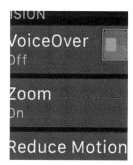

To activate Zoom, Ava uses a two-finger double-tap onscreen. To adjust the zoom level, she uses a two-finger double-tap and scrolls her fingers up and down.

Extra-large Watch face

To access the extra-large Watch face, Ava force-touches on the clock face and selects the **X-LARGE** face. Since the font is so large, it's a good fit for her limited vision.

Settings on the Watch app for iPhone

A few more small visual tweaks are available on the iPhone itself.

Open the **Watch app** and navigate to **General\Accessibility**.

Here are some of the settings you can adjust:

a   b   c

- **Bold text**: Adds weight to the in-app text (a). For Ava, this makes the text appear less blurry and more discernible.

- **Grayscale**: Replaces all colors with greyscale equivalents (b). This makes it easier for a person with color blindness to read menus, view images and distinguish between elements on the screen.

- **Reduce motion**: Removes the zoom-in animation from the clock face and Home screen, which can be nauseating to Ava.

- **Reduce transparency**: Removes blur effects (c). This helps Ava see text clearly due to the increased contrast of a simple color background.

A couple of audio settings are also useful in conjunction with a Bluetooth headset. These features benefit users with hearing impairments:

- **Mono audio**: Blends left and right audio channels into one. If a user has one ear that's more capable than the other, this setting ensures the user doesn't miss a sound on the opposite channel.

- **Left/Right Balance**: Adjusts the left and right channel balance via a slider if one of the user's ears need a higher volume than the other.

Finally, the Accessibility Shortcut setting allows Ava to triple-click the digital crown to activate her choice of VoiceOver or Zoom. This is much easier than having to drill down into Settings each time she wants to turn the feature on and off.

Turn on the **Accessibility Shortcut** for **VoiceOver**.

To see how VoiceOver works in your app, build and run the project. Triple-click the digital crown to turn on VoiceOver on your Watch device.

Try tapping on different elements, and Siri will read the accessibility label for each. Notice the following:

1. Siri will not tell you anything about the graph when you tap on it. The graph is not accessible.

2. You have to tap on each label in the bottom section individually. You can swipe left and right to focus on the next interface item, but the experience still isn't good enough. Ideally, you'd want the voice to read all the labels in that group together.

3. The labels in the bottom group are hard to tap because their tap target overlaps with the graph and the page indicator dots.

4. To scroll between pages, you have to tap on the page indicator dots, and then swipe up and down outside of the tap target.

To make the app work better with VoiceOver, you'll need to group together the adjacent labels, expand tap targets and break out the graph data points.

WatchKit Accessibility API overview

For your app to work with these accessibility features, you'll have to set a few properties on the interface items in your app.

Each interface item is a subclass of `WKInterfaceObject`. Descendants of this class have access to a number of methods that let you annotate your accessibility information and make the items accessible.

```
setIsAccessibilityElement(_:)
```

VoiceOver needs to know what is and what isn't an element. Accessibility elements are what the user swipes through and double-taps when VoiceOver is enabled. By default, the framework gives a lot of this to you: buttons, labels and switches are all accessibility elements. But sometimes you need to get away from the default, such as when you want to expose an image.

Another reason you might stray from the defaults is when you want to group a few elements to help the user to navigate quickly. An example for this would be a conversation group that contains three labels for the sender, message and date. You can do this by calling `setIsAccessibilityElement(true)` on an interface item — in this case, a group.

Ava learns what's onscreen by hearing a short description spoken aloud. It's called an accessibility label.

`setAccessibilityLabel(_:)`

VoiceOver automatically infers that the accessibility label is the text contained in standard user interface objects. This works well most of the time, but sometimes the inferred description may be misleading or nonexistent. Ava encountered an example of this earlier with the Clock icon on the Home screen. The app icons aren't associated with text, so in situations like this, you have to set the accessibility label yourself.

The Watch reads out the accessibility value after reading aloud the accessibility label:

`setAccessibilityValue(_:)`

The accessibility value is useful when the value changes on an interactive interface item. A good example of an interface object with a changing value is the picker used for the minute hand of a timer.

Sometimes, you need more of a description than just the accessibility label, so you can set an accessibility hint:

`setAccessibilityHint(_:)`

Imagine the functionality of a current location button in a Maps app. Tapping the button once moves the map to your current location. Tapping and holding — also known as long pressing — activates the compass. A hint for the current location button might be, "tap and hold to activate compass".

If an image has multiple parts, you can annotate image regions with descriptions:

`setAccessibilityImageRegions(_:)`

It's a common pattern on the Watch to put an assortment of information into an image that you then present to the user. The Weather app is a good example.

By carving up the image into different regions, you can associate particular information with each region.

You call a global function to find out when VoiceOver is running, allowing you to adjust your app for your users:

```
WKAccessibilityIsVoiceOverRunning()
```

For example, when VoiceOver is on, you might need to enlarge the tap targets for your labels. Since VoiceOver relies on the user being able to tap on the different parts of a screen, your labels might need to have greater height and width to make room for a finger tap.

Similar to VoiceOver accessibility feature, you can also check if Reduce Motion is on:

```
WKAccessibilityIsReduceMotionEnabled()
```

When the user has requested reduced motion, you should reduce animations in your app.

If you're building a custom interface component for your app, you might consider setting the combination of accessibility traits that best characterize the component:

```
setAccessibilityTraits(_:)
```

VoiceOver will treat a button differently than a label. Accessibility traits tell an assistive application how an accessibility element behaves or should be treated.

You might use the `UpdatesFrequently` trait to characterize the readout of a stopwatch. You could use the `StartsMediaSession` trait to silence VoiceOver during audio playback from your app, or during a recording session. The full list of `UIAccessibilityTraits` is below; use them to make sure your app provides the best possible user experience:

- **None**
- **Button**
- **Link**
- **Header**
- **SearchField**
- **Image**
- **Selected**
- **PlaysSound**
- **KeyboardKey**
- **StaticText**

- **SummaryElement**

- **NotEnabled**

- **UpdatesFrequently**

- **StartsMediaSession**

- **Adjustable**

- **AllowsDirectInteraction**

- **CausesPageTurn**

- **TabBar**

You don't need to add an accessibility trait for a regular old label or button, but it's good to know the full breadth of accessibility elements you have at your disposal.

Adding accessibility to your app

In the project navigator, select **PageInterfaceController.swift** and add the following code to `updateForAccessibility()`:

```
if WKAccessibilityIsVoiceOverRunning() {
  makeLayoutAccessible()
  makeGraphAccessible()
  makeGroupAccessible()
}
```

This method is called from `willActivate()`, and will run each time you show an interface to the user. If VoiceOver is turned on, you'll make several changes to the interface, represented by the three methods above. You'll write the implementation for each of those methods next.

Making the layout accessible

Remember how hard it was to tap on the stock details at the bottom of the screen? You'd like to make the graph smaller so that the labels can be a bit taller. Right now the interface elements have a height set in Interface Builder to be "Relative to Container".

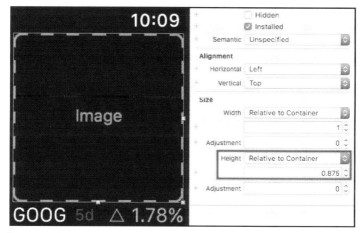

Add this implementation to `makeLayoutAccessible()`:

```
graphHeightRatio = 0.6
detailsHeightRatio = 0.4

graphImage.setHeight(graphHeightRatio * screenSize.height)
detailsGroup.setHeight(detailsHeightRatio * screenSize.height)
```

Moving from a 87.5%:12.5% ratio to a 60%:40% ratio makes the bottom details section much larger.

Build and run on the device to confirm it works. If you've got VoiceOver turned on, you'll see the tap area for the details is a lot larger:

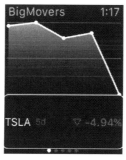

Excellent work! Now that the details group has a bit of breathing room, you can turn your attention to the graph.

Making the graph accessible

The graph is a wonderful visual, but because it's a single image there's no real way to make sense of the data for visually impaired users. Imagine if your app could read aloud the data. With image regions, it can!

Add the following code to `makeGraphAccessible()`:

```
// 1
var imageRegions: [WKAccessibilityImageRegion] = []
// 2
for index in 1..<stock.last5days.count { // skip the first day
  // 3
  let imageRegion = WKAccessibilityImageRegion()
  // 4
  imageRegion.frame = imageRegionFrameForTrailingIndex(index)
  // 5
  imageRegion.label = summaryForTrailingIndex(index)
  // 6
  imageRegions.append(imageRegion)
}
// 7
graphImage.setAccessibilityImageRegions(imageRegions)
```

There are quite a few things happening here. Going over it step-by-step:

1. First, you create an empty array of image regions so you have a spot to store each one you create.

2. You iterate through each day for the stock to find the daily change. You skip the first item, `0`, in the array, because you're looking at the change from the previous day, and the first day doesn't have a previous day before it.

3. You create a new blank image region to hold some attributes you'll add in a bit. When you're finished with this iteration of the loop, you'll add it to the array you created at the beginning.

4. You'll implement the method that calculates the size of the image in a bit.

5. Soon after that, you'll implement the method that provides the phrase for Siri to speak aloud.

6. You construct each image region out of a label, a size and a position. Once you've set those, the image region is ready to be added to the array.

7. When the `for` loop finishes, you can add the image region array to an image, and the VoiceOver feature will work as expected.

With the code in place to iterate through each day's data, you need to calculate the size of each image region.

Calculating the dimensions of an image region

Replace the implementation of `imageRegionFrameForTrailingIndex(_:)` with this code:

```
let height = screenSize.height * graphHeightRatio
let width =
  screenSize.width / CGFloat(stock.last5days.count - 1)
let x = width * (CGFloat(trailingIndex) - 1)
return CGRect(x: x, y: 0, width: width, height: height)
```

There's one fewer image region than the number of data points. This is like the space between your fingers — you have five fingers but only four spaces between them. This code calculates the dimensions and position for the image region between two data points.

Preparing a spoken description

The next nut to crack is providing the words that VoiceOver will speak aloud. Replace the code in `summaryForTrailingIndex(_:)` with this implementation:

```
// 1
let percentageDescription = percentageChangeForVoiceOver(from:
    stock.last5days[trailingIndex - 1],
  to: stock.last5days[trailingIndex])
// 2
var timeDescription = String()
switch trailingIndex {
  case 1:
    timeDescription = "3 days ago"
  case 2:
    timeDescription = "day before yesterday"
  case 3:
    timeDescription = "yesterday"
```

```
    case 4:
        timeDescription = "today"
    default:
        break
    }
    // 3
    return "\(percentageDescription) \(timeDescription)"
```

Here's what's happening in this method:

1. The stock movement change needs to make sense when spoken; it isn't enough to say "negative 5%". The conversational way to say that is "down 5%". You'll implement the method for this next.

2. Since VoiceOver will speak this summary aloud, it would also be nice to have conversational time values to go along with each data point.

3. You construct the label for the accessibility item from the percentage change from one day to the next and its "time ago" phrase.

To get the change percentage to sound conversational when spoken aloud, you need a bit of logic.

Replace the code in percentageChangeForVoiceOver(from:to:) with this implementation:

```
// 1
let numberFormatter = NumberFormatter()
numberFormatter.numberStyle = .percent
numberFormatter.minimumFractionDigits = 2
numberFormatter.maximumFractionDigits = 2
// 2
let change = (current - previous) / previous
// 3
let direction = change > 0 ? "up" : "down"
// 4
let percent = numberFormatter.string(from: NSNumber(value:
abs(change)))!
// 5
return "\(direction) \(percent)"
```

Taking each numbered comment in turn:

1. You instantiate a number formatter that will output a percentage with two decimal places.

2. You then calculate the percentage change. It can be positive or negative, depending on the way the stock moved.

3. If the change is positive, you set the label text to "up"; if the change was negative, you set the label text to "down".

4. Now that you've got the "down" phrase if the change is negative, you can remove the negative sign by using the absolute value function. The number formatter will return the percentage with the settings from step 1.

5. The complete phrase is composed of either "up" or "down" and the percentage change.

You've made it all the way though the image region code!

It takes quite a bit of code to provide a good user experience for image regions, but your users will appreciate being able to tap on the individual parts of the graph and have them read aloud.

Build and run the app on the device. With VoiceOver enabled, you can tap on the lines between data points on the graph to hear nice summaries of the daily change:

> **Note:** You might encounter a bug in watchOS. The first time the app launches, the image region is too high on the screen, overlapping the status bar. Either: 1) Use the Digital Crown to go to the Home screen and relaunch the app or 2) Swipe over to a different page within the app and the the image region will display correctly.

Making a group accessible

When you first ran the app, it took a long time to use VoiceOver to get a grip on all the content onscreen. One big problem was that you had to tap on each stock detail label independently, like the ticker symbol in this screenshot:

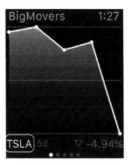

What if you could tap on the group and have the app read a summary of everything inside? With one tap, the voice could announce, "Tesla, past five days, down 4.94 percent." That's just what you'll implement in this section.

In `makeGroupAccessible()`, add the following code:

```
// 1
detailsGroup.setIsAccessibilityElement(true)
// 2
let percentage = percentageChangeForVoiceOver(
  from: stock.last5days.first!, to: stock.last5days.last!)
// 3
let label =
  "\(stock.companyName), past five days, \(percentage)"
// 4
detailsGroup.setAccessibilityLabel(label)
// 5
detailsGroup.setAccessibilityTraits(
  UIAccessibilityTraitSummaryElement)
```

Here's what's happening in this snippet:

1. First, you tell the compiler that the details group has accessibility attributes. This will override all the default accessibility attributes of the sub-items of the group, so now the labels won't have VoiceOver interactivity themselves.

2. Just as you did with the graph, you use a function to give a nice string representation of the percentage change.

3. You construct the accessibility label with the three pieces of data from each of the labels in this group.

4. You add the accessibility label to the group itself.

5. Finally, you mark the group as a `SummaryElement` by setting the accessibility trait, which lets VoiceOver know that the element provides summary information when the app starts. This is perfect for labels with current conditions, settings or state, such as the current temperature in the Weather app.

The time has come to see the finished app on your Watch! Build and run. With VoiceOver enabled, you can tap on the details at the bottom to hear the full summary for the stock during the five-day week.

Try out the trick you learned at the beginning of the chapter: navigate with VoiceOver by swiping left and right. Accessibility elements will be highlighted in sequence and you'll hear their description read aloud.

Where to go from here?

You've learned how to make your app accessible for users with visual impairments. In the process, you got acquainted with the accessibility settings and features in watchOS and WatchKit.

As a bonus, you also learned some handy tricks. Consider how the additions you made for VoiceOver might benefit the standard user experience. For example, you could make tapping on the graph show a stock's daily change even without VoiceOver enabled. Instead of using accessibility image regions on the graph, you could overlay a transparent button above each daily change and update the label appropriately when a user taps on the button.

Pervasive GPS has made it possible for all of us to journey from place to place in the world without getting lost. You have the power to give a similar freedom to your customers with visual or physical impairments, who might otherwise be shut out from what you and the Apple Watch have to offer. A Watch that speaks to you when you simply tap parts of its face might have sounded futuristic a few years ago, but the Apple Watch makes that a reality.

Not only are you capable of building wonderful experiences for your users, but with assistive technologies you can also empower them. The services you provide with assistive technology are rare and valuable, and may make a world of difference for some of your fans.

Conclusion

We hope you had a ton of fun working through this book. If you cherry-picked chapters according to your own interests and projects, then fair enough — you surely learned a lot and got your watchOS projects started off on the right foot. And if you read this entire book from cover to cover, then take a bow my friend — you're officially a watchOS ninja!

You now have a wealth of experience with watchOS and know what it takes to build rich, engaging and performant apps for the Apple Watch, using a host of exciting concepts and techniques that are unique to the platform. If you're like us, learning about all these cutting-edge technologies and concepts has you overflowing with ideas. We can't wait to see what you build!

If you have any questions or comments, please do stop by our forums at forums.raywenderlich.com.

Thank you again for purchasing this book. Your continued support is what makes the tutorials, books and other things we do at raywenderlich.com possible—we all truly appreciate it!

Best of luck with your Apple Watch adventures,

— Ehab, Ryan, Jack, Scott, Soheil, Matt, Ben, Audrey, Antonio, Eric, Chris

The *watchOS by Tutorials* team

Printed in Great Britain
by Amazon